Tradition and Innovation in Later Medieval English Manuscripts

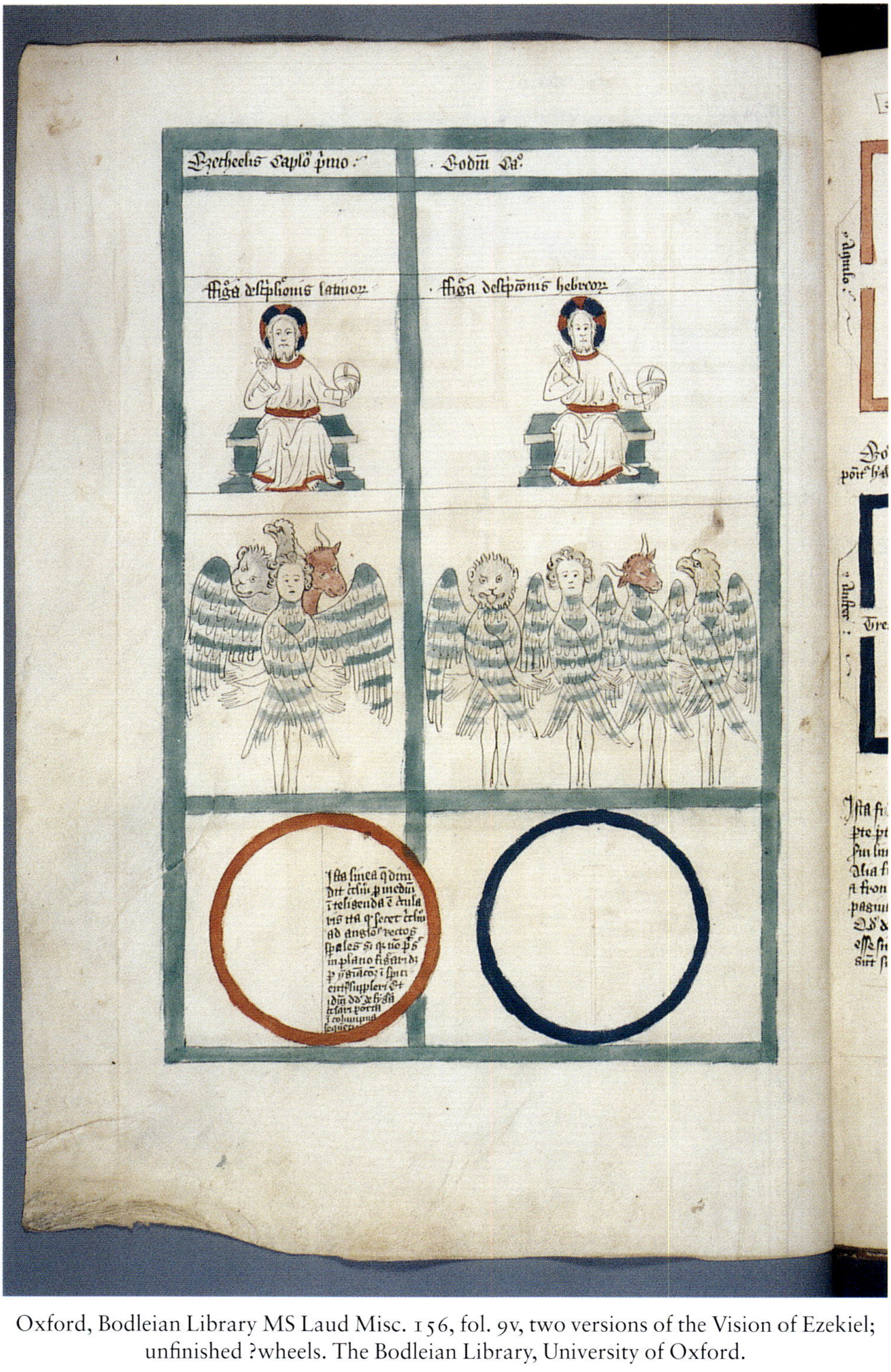

Oxford, Bodleian Library MS Laud Misc. 156, fol. 9v, two versions of the Vision of Ezekiel; unfinished ?wheels. The Bodleian Library, University of Oxford.

Tradition and Innovation in Later Medieval English Manuscripts

KATHLEEN L. SCOTT

THE BRITISH LIBRARY
2007

First published in 2007 by
The British Library
96 Euston Road
London NW1 2DB

British Library Cataloguing in Publication Data
A catalogue record for this book is
available from The British Library

ISBN 978-0-7123-4936-9

Designed by Bob Elliott
Typeset by Norman Tilley Graphics Ltd
Printed and bound in Hong Kong by
South Sea International Press

CONTENTS

'Oh, books. They get everywhere.'

Bill James, *Eton Crop*

'Want another cup of why?'

from 'The Infinite Life Poem'
by Jeremy K. Scott

PREFACE

IN October of 2000 I received, to my surprise, a letter from the Lyell Electors, inviting me to speak on 'manuscripts'. It would be difficult to say which occasioned the greater shock, the invitation or the suggested title. When I had recovered enough to accept and to begin thinking how 'manuscripts' might be reduced to five fifty-minute lectures, it occurred to me that the Lyell series would be an opportunity to give substantial attention to certain interesting English manuscripts of the later medieval period not included in my *Survey of Manuscripts Illuminated in the British Isles*, Vol. VI: *Later Gothic Manuscripts, c. 1385–1490*, edited by Jonathan Alexander (1996). The emphasis in this work was on the illustration of English manuscripts and to some extent on their decoration, especially the borderwork, as well as on grouping manuscripts through the identification of an artistic hand in more than one manuscript. Each entry in *Later Gothic Manuscripts* comprised a listing of the illustrative contents, an essay that included, where possible, a discussion of ownership, and a bibliography to about 1990.

In general, in developing the Lyell lectures, I employed a similar format: an exposition of the illustrative contents; the relationship, when relevant, of the illustration to the text, an examination of the pictorial subject matter with respect to other English miniatures containing the same pictorial subjects; and remarks on the patronage or ownership of the manuscripts and its implications for the use of the manuscript after production. The lectures were also expressly limited to studies of English manuscripts of the later period, from the early fifteenth century to, in the last lecture, the first quarter of the sixteenth century. It was, of course, not possible during the lectures to lay out a bibliography for each manuscript, beyond the occasional mention of a scholar on whom I had relied in a particular instance. In this printed version of the lectures I have been able to include much more extensive references in notes and to present, in appendices, a more complete analysis of the make up of some of the manuscripts as well as to reinstate sections of my own text omitted because of the time constraints of the lectures. Language appropriate to the immediate atmosphere of a lecture has been revised to a more formal level, and because there will have been a relatively brief time between giving the lectures in May 2004 and their publication by The British Library in 2007, only a few changes and additions have been made to my original working bibliography.

It is not surprising that in any undertaking concerning medieval manuscripts one is constantly indebted to scholars in other specialist areas regarding the Middle Ages and to librarians who give of their time in responding to enquiries. Tony Edwards read the Lyell text before publication, and I am immensely grateful to him for the care and discernment with which he examined the typescript. Malcolm Parkes was, as ever, generous with help, even long-distance from Oxford to Belchertown; I am particularly indebted for his opinion concerning the scribe '*frater* T.B.' of Bodleian Library MS Laud Misc. 156 (Chapter 1) and for direction concerning the Exeter Hospital. At his instigation Pam Robinson kindly checked for me, before the lectures, the medieval

Exeter shelfmarks in British Library Additional MS 38129 and Harley MS 3671. For his generous correspondence concerning All Souls MS 10 (Chapter 2), not to speak of his important body of work concerning French Bibles of the later Middle Ages, I am most grateful to Clive R. Sneddon; I could not have been certain of the uniqueness of the All Souls manuscript without his help. Again, with regard to this manuscript, I am also much indebted to Mary-Jo Arn for providing me with an annotated copy of Pierre Campion's book and for her kind support in my work on Charles d'Orléans. Ralph Hanna, while at first dubious that John Dygon could be associated with an illustrated manuscript of such quality, gave his imprimatur to the scribe's hand in British Library Royal MS 1.B.x (Chapter 4) and shared his work on Dygon. Ian Doyle also gave his opinion concerning Dygon's hand. Roger Wieck, of the Pierpont Morgan Library, kindly provided me with information concerning PML 43328 (ChL1816A); Andrea Clarke, Curator, Department of Manuscripts, British Library, facilitated my examination of Additional MS 21974 together with Royal MS 2.A.xix; and I owe Kate Harris, Librarian of Longleat House, for information concerning the decoration of MS 4, which contains a version of the *Abbey of the Holy Ghost* (Chapter 3). I have also to thank Richard Rouse for his thoughts concerning the continental origin of the scribe of BL Royal MS 3.D.vii. Chris de Hamel and Patricia Stirnemann both gave me helpful direction in working on medieval vernacular bibles.

I also owe thanks, which are entirely heartfelt, to the Lyell Electors for their invitation to give the lectures, and I wish especially to acknowledge former Electors, Anne Hudson and David Vaisey, whose good will I have very much appreciated over the years. It is fair to say that I would not have been able to undertake and complete the research for the Lyell lectures without the hospitality, support, and acute questioning of Linda Brownrigg, who has repeatedly and generously offered me hospitality in London. As ever, I wish to thank my family, in particular my husband David, for tolerating my absences to British libraries and for his belief in the importance of my work.

INTRODUCTION

ENGLISH fifteenth-century manuscript illustration has, with some notable exceptions, been the dull stepchild of art historical studies, shunned, and left to sit in a metaphorical corner between the exuberant book art of the fourteenth century and the appealing humanism of the sixteenth. Recently – in the last three decades or so – this apparently unlovely child has taken a few steps out of the shadows and begun to show herself as the Cinderella of the medieval book world. In the following studies of five English manuscripts, which are based on my Lyell lectures given in May 2004, I intend to bring the English book of the late period into the foreground and to show off the fine attire that actually decorates this medium. By the end of this series of studies I hope to have established for my reader some sense of the great accomplishment of English book artists of the late period, both from their knowledge of traditional illustration and from their creative adaptation of older or Continental pictorial themes. This survey of a mere five manuscripts will not provide a full grand tour of English work: just a walk between cloister and shop. And it will not conclude with a limner gazing in astonishment at a printed book.[1] I hope, in addition, to give the reader some sense of the range of English book production in the late period, of its various techniques, of its capacity for unusual page design, and, in the midst of its inevitable dependence on past designs and iconography, of its originality. I shall also explore the motives, explicit and implied, for including illustration in the fifteenth-century English book, motives that go beyond the 'pretty principle'.

The manuscripts in this study include a hitherto unrecognized modelbook in Bodleian Library MS Laud Misc. 156 (Chapter 1); an enigmatic English copy of the New Testament in French in MS 10 of All Souls College, Oxford (Chapter 2); the only surviving English copy of the *Abbey of the Holy Ghost*, with illustrations based on the text, in British Library, Stowe MS 39 (Chapter 3); a bizarrely illustrated version of Peter of Poitiers' genealogical chronicle, *Compendium historia in genealogia Christi* in British Library, Royal MS 1.B.x (Chapter 4); and a manuscript from the close of the medieval period in England, a pontifical Book of Benedictions in British Library, Additional MS 21974 (Chapter 5). All of these manuscripts contain exceptional illustrations – four are pictorially unique, and none has been studied beyond a catalogue description. Each of the manuscripts is textually and illustratively quite different from the others, and each one, given the varied illustrative programmes, acts as a kind of case-study for understanding the motive for illustration and its relationship, where possible, to the original patron or institutional owner, four of whom are identifiable. In the fifth case (All Souls MS 10) a different approach is taken, that of identifying the original *type* of ownership through the production of the text and through the iconography of its illustration.

It is a given of this study that it is critical to identify the work of an artist or border artist in as many other manuscripts of the period as possible. This kind of connection or grouping of manuscripts by artistic hand is of an importance equal to that of locating the hand of a scribe in as many manuscripts as possible. These associations can give us knowledge of the geographic range of the artist's professional presence in his society, of his status as artist as judged by the status of his patrons, as well as enabling us to make similar judgments about artists with whom he collaborated; of the possible location of a centre of artistic production; and of the preference for illustrating certain types of text in a given limner's workshop, perhaps through an on-going association with a scribe or scribal shop. A study of illustrated manuscripts can also bring in its wake interesting conclusions about the authors and types of texts that were generally considered important to illustrate.

Although the five manuscripts are discussed here roughly in chronological order, I shall in the concluding chapter detach them from this conventional presentation and consider them according to the function, form, and content of their illustrations. There is a great deal that can be said about the pictorial matter in these manuscripts, both individually and collectively, and three or four aspects of these fifteenth-century miniatures may well raise issues for the reader, which will need special attention. First and foremost, why were illustrations in books at all? Can we reconstruct a motive for the inclusion of illustration from the evidence of the illustration itself? Was the impulse the same in every manuscript? Can we tell whether the patron or the text was the ultimate force behind the illustration of a manuscript? Might there be non-textual pictorial subjects mixed in with the standard content of illustration?

Second, what can we deduce about the variety of forms in which illustrations occur in English manuscripts? Is there anything to be understood from the considerable variety in the format of miniatures? Can the variety be attributed to textual demands or to patronage?

Third, what can we learn about the nature of the pictorial subject matter and its iconography from a study of these manuscripts? Is the subject matter traditional, relatively static in inheritance and standardized, or is it prone to expand on its resources and to be creative? How malleable were miniatures with respect to their text? Do the illustrations in a given manuscript respond closely to the text? Or do they imply a concern with other outside issues? Why do some manuscripts with a narrative text show only authorial 'portraits'? What made this pictorial form take precedence over illustration of the text?

Fourth, why did English book artists of the fifteenth century stick, largely speaking, to the linear mode of painting and drawing in what must have been their certain knowledge of the deeply naturalistic styles in vogue in Italy, France, and the Low Countries?

None of the issues is necessarily simple to resolve, and they might seem to require a more substantial volume than this one, but even within the limits of these five essays it will be possible to make reasonable and, I think, convincing suggestions. Each of the five manuscripts will not speak to every issue just raised, but we shall see represented in them some of the most important factors and facets in later English medieval manuscript production.

Having remarked on the exceptional nature of the five manuscripts discussed in my Lyell lectures, I should offer some comment on the contemporary background of English book production against which these manuscripts stand out. In order not to look at these books as a series of single spotlights, I want to review the features of more ordinary manuscripts produced in England between 1400 and *c.* 1500.

On the whole, later medieval English limners were concerned to stick to the known, both in their selection of pictorial matter and in their rendering of it: by salvaging the iconography of a subject, by using stereotypical gestures, and even by transferring and reproducing groupings of figures from one pictorial subject to another.[2] The phenomenon of recycling subject matter and iconography is observable in a variety of commonly illustrated texts of the period: missals, psalters, Books of Hours, chronicles, law books, medical texts, and certain literary texts by contemporary authors such as those of Chaucer, Gower, and Lydgate. It is perhaps symptomatic of the period that even recently written texts were immediately standardized in their illustration. English limners also had a standardized approach to their work in their lack of interest in the environment of their scenes, either in interior settings or in landscape. There was, moreover, a largely common manner of drawing in a linear rather than in a modelled style[3] and in the use of colour, which was often limited to red, blue, green, and orange, with more shading and modelling likely to occur in monochrome motifs in borders and initials; occasionally, however, the handling of drapery may show modelling. Certain Continental artists worked in English shops at various times in the century, but it cannot be said that the methods of these artists were imitated or absorbed by English artists: iconography may have been taken over, yet not the manner in which it had been rendered. Penwork illustration developed considerably in the second half of the century, partly but not entirely due to the presence of foreign artists in England; there was however little, if any, interest in grisaille compared to that found on the Continent.

In the midst of this English standarization of book decoration, there were innovative artists and books; innovative with regard to the painterly mode of rendering miniatures and with regard to iconography, though less often regarding pictorial subject matter, which was, apart from patronal pictures, usually determined by the particular text and its tradition of illustration. Four such innovative manuscripts are described here (All Souls MS 10, Chapter 2; Stowe MS 39, Chapter 3; Royal MS 1.B.x, Chapter 4; and Additional MS 29714, Chapter 5.[4] The modelbook in MS Laud Misc. 156 (Chapter 1) is certainly also exceptional in its function and format, but it cannot have been unique, as it must have derived from a previous pictorial sequence, whether previously embedded in a text or not.

What the reader can expect to see, then, in the five English manuscripts of the Lyell series is a sense both of the traditional – from which it would have been unlikely that many late medieval artists could escape – and of the innovative, that which had come to English artists through a Continental model, through ideas expressed by a patron, and sometimes apparently through introduction by the artist himself.

ABBREVIATIONS

col.	colour
CUL	Cambridge, University Library
Bodl. Lib.	Bodleian Library, Oxford
BL	British Library, London
BnF	Bibliothèque nationale de France, Paris
BR	Bibliothèque Royale de Belgique, Brussels
d.	died
fol./fols	folio/s
inscr.	inscribed with; labelled
membr.	membrane
n.	note
no./nos	number/s
p./pp.	page/s
fig./figs	figure/s
Pt	Part

ABBREVIATED TITLES

Alexander and Temple	J. J. G. Alexander and E. Temple, *Illuminated Manuscripts in Oxford College Libraries, The University Archives and the Taylor Institution* (Oxford, 1985)
Bodl. Index	K. L. Scott, gen. ed., *An Index of Images in English Manuscripts from the Time of Chaucer to Henry VIII c. 1380–c. 1509: The Bodleian Library, Oxford*, I: MSS Additional-Digby, II: MSS Dodsworth-Marshall, III: MSS e Musaeo-Wood (Turnhout, 2000, 2001, 2002)
EMS	*English Manuscript Studies*
Hanna, *St. John's Catalogue*	R. Hanna, *A Descriptive Catalogue of the Western Medieval Manuscripts of St. John's College, Oxford* (Oxford and New York, 2002)
Hogg, *Carthusian Miscellany*	J. Hogg, *An Illustrated Yorkshire Carthusian Religious Miscellany*, Analecta Cartusiana 3: The Illustrations (Salzburg, 1981)
JWCI	*Journal of the Warburg and Courtauld Institutes*
Ker and Piper	*Medieval Manuscripts in Great Britain*, IV: Paisley-York (Oxford, 1992)

MLGB	N. R. Ker, *Medieval Libraries of Great Britain: A List of Surviving Books*, 2nd ed., Royal Historical Society 3 (London, 1964)
MMBL	N. R. Ker, *Medieval Manuscripts in British Libraries*, II: Abbotsford-Keele (Oxford, 1977)
Morgan, *Early Gothic Manuscripts [II]*	N. Morgan, *Early Gothic Manuscripts [II] 1250–1285*, A Survey of Manuscripts Illuminated in the British Isles, 4, gen. ed. J. J. G. Alexander (London, 1988)
ODNB	H. C. G. Matthew and B. Harrison, *Oxford Dictionary of National Biography* (Oxford, 2004)
Pächt and Alexander, 1	O. Pächt and J. J. G. Alexander, *Illuminated Manuscripts in the Bodleian Library*, 1: German, Dutch, Flemish, French and Spanish Schools (Oxford, 1966)
Pächt and Alexander, 3	O. Pächt and J. J. G. Alexander, *Illuminated Manuscripts in the Bodleian Library Oxford*, 3: British, Irish and Icelandic Schools (Oxford, 1973)
Rickert, *Carmelite Missal*	M. Rickert, *The Reconstructed Carmelite Missal: An English Manuscript of the late XIV century in the British Museum* (London, 1952)
Sandler, *De Lisle Psalter*	L. F. Sandler, *The Psalter of Robert de Lisle in the British Library* (London, 1999)
Scott, *Later Gothic Manuscripts*	K. L. Scott, *Later Gothic Manuscripts 1390–1490*, A Survey of Manuscripts Illuminated in the British Isles, 6, gen. ed. J. J. G. Alexander, 2 vols, I: Text and Illustrations, II: Catalogue and Indexes (London, 1996)
Sharpe, *Handlist*	R. Sharpe, *A Handlist of Latin Writers of Great Britain and Ireland*, Publications of the Journal of Medieval Latin (Belgium, 1997)
Warner and Gilson	G. R. Warner and J. P. Gilson, *Catalogue of Western Manuscripts in the Old Royal and King's Collections*, 4 vols (Oxford, 1921)
Watson, *Dated and Datable MSS British Library*	A. G. Watson, *Catalogue of Dated and Datable Manuscripts c. 700–1600 in the Department of Manuscripts The British Library*, 2 vols (London, 1979)
Watson, *Dated and Datable MSS Oxford*	A. G. Watson, *Catalogue of Dated and Datable Manuscripts c. 435–1600 in Oxford Libraries* (Oxford, 1984)

CHAPTER I

An English Modelbook for Nicholas of Lyra's *Postilla litteralis*

Of the many remarkable fifteenth-century English manuscripts that I have seen over the past forty years, MS Laud Misc. 156 ranks, for me, among the most interesting. The chief attraction of the manuscript is that it contains an unrecognized modelbook and, even more remarkably, a modelbook for a biblical commentary, Nicholas of Lyra's *Postilla litteralis super totam Bibliam* (see frontispiece and figs 1, 4, 11, 13, 15, 20, 21, 22). It does not contain the ladies, garlands, saints and dogs that artists often sketched in their personal notebooks (fig. 3), but rather it has plans and architectural features of the Temple of Solomon such as the lily capitals and cross-sections of entrances, and of implements and altars such as the Candelabra, Brazen Sea and the Altar of the Holocaust. In MS Laud Misc. 156, the miniatures are usually stacked one above the other in three unstructured registers (fig. 1), not distributed throughout the text, for there is no text of Lyra's *Postilla litteralis* in the manuscript, only inscribed titles and biblical references. But the images in the Laud manuscript can actually be found in another fifteenth-century copy of the *Postilla* at appropriate – and inappropriate – points in the text. Most importantly, MS Laud Misc. 156 is the only English modelbook whose images have been located in another manuscript.

Before embarking on a closer description of MS Laud Misc. 156, I want to comment briefly on the author and on the reception of his work.[5] Nicholas of Lyra (d. 1349) was a Franciscan scholar, theologian and professor at the University of Paris, who is 'widely regarded as the best-equipped Biblical scholar of the Middle Ages'.[6] He gave the *Postilla litteralis* first as lectures at the University in the 1320s and afterwards had them produced in book form that usually amounted to between three and five elephantine volumes. His work was intended to be a literal exegesis of the Bible, its unmediated meaning rather than an allegorical or other interpretation or sense imposed by a commentator; Lyra himself stated that he was writing in reaction to 'an excess of allegory'.[7] Lyra's study of the Bible, in fact, 'served as the basic source of practical information on scripture for the next two hundred years'.[8] This remarkable author almost certainly supervised the inclusion of 'literal' illustration, ground plans and diagrams that are inherent to his text, and specified the point at which they were to be placed; and scribes in fact usually followed Lyra's instructions by leaving blank spaces in their copy.[9] The translators of the Wycliffite Bible and Martin Luther are among those to have used Lyra's work.[10]

Lyra's sources for his illustrations of Temple implements and plans seem not to have been influenced by earlier Christian art, where the subjects were in any case infrequent;[11] nor were his renderings based, of course, on allegorical interpretations of the Bible. Lyra is said to represent 'the culmination of a movement for the study of

Hebrew and rabbinics',[12] and there can be no doubt but that he could read the Hebrew Bible[13] and that he was aware of illustrated Hebrew texts of the Old Testament, which, according to Nordström, did not become widespread until the thirteenth century.[14] The 'extraordinarily vigorous' rabbinical culture, with its 'great interest' in the Temple implements, seems to have influenced the iconography of the Hebrew Bibles.[15] But whether the Lyra programme of illustration was influenced by miniatures in Hebrew Bibles seems to be a moot issue. Lyra knew them, but because the Hebrew representations of the Temple implements occur on carpet pages in Hebrew Bibles and not within the text as in Lyra's *Postilla litteralis*, and because such care was taken in Lyra illustrations to 'transmit an accurate physical description', Kaczynski sees them as 'alien to the Hebrew Bibles, the interest of which was decorative rather than illustrative'.[16] Roth, on the other hand, believes that Hebrew Old Testament pictorial matter was taken over by Christians in their early book art,[17] and by Lyra in particular.[18] It is at least clear that, even though arranged on 'carpet' pages and placed at the head of the Bible,[19] the pictorial contents (usually the Ark of the Covenant, Tables of Stone, Candelabra, Table of Shewbread, Altar and Lavatorium) of the Temple in Hebrew manuscripts resemble, in some cases quite closely, those in Lyra manuscripts[20] and that the influence of Hebrew book art should not be dismissed without closer comparison.

Estimates of the number of surviving manuscripts of the *Postilla litteralis* vary between 'several hundred', 800, and over 1,200 manuscripts of all provenances,[21] but no separate count seems to have been made of the surviving English copies. I have identified eighteen manuscripts of the *Postilla litteralis* on the Old Testament, as well as three fragments (see Appendix B, Pt I),[22] but there could well be more copies yet to be found,[23] and, to judge from notices in library catalogues, wills and other documents, there would seem to have been a considerably larger number available in England in the fourteenth and fifteenth centuries (see Appendix B, Pt II). The Laud manuscript itself is made up of sixty-nine medieval parchment leaves, seven of which were originally blank. Quire 1 of six leaves contains on fols 2 and 3, possibly as an addition, the *tituli* of Lyra's *Questiones super bibliam*, as well as added outline drawings (fol. 4) of an unfinished left and right *manus meditationis*, i.e. without inscriptions. Folios 3v and 4v are blanks. The second item in the manuscript, the Lyra modelbook, begins on fol. 5 and ends on fol. 14v, with contemporary added material decorated by the colourist of the modelbook and extending to fol. 15; that is, the modelbook is self-contained in quires 2 and 3. The added items are a genealogy of Alexander the Great, who established the royal lines of Syria and Egypt (fol. 14v) and a genealogy of Antiochus Magnus (fol. 15). Folio 15v is blank. The scribal hand of the modelbook and that of the genealogical roundels on fols 14v–15 are not the same.[24] The modelbook is datable on stylistic grounds to around 1430–40.

The third item in MS Laud Misc. 156, a *tabula* or index to the *Postilla litteralis* of forty-four leaves (fols 16–60), was compiled by a different author, William Norton (fl. 1400), a Franciscan of the Coventry house. In this manuscript the Index was written by a scribe who signed himself '*frater* T.B.' on fol. 60 (fig. 5); fol. 60v is blank.[25] The 'T.B.' hand is not that of the modelbook section of the manuscript.[26] Although there are other 'T.B.' scribal monograms in English manuscripts and other signed scribes whose names would have the same monogram, it was not possible to identify

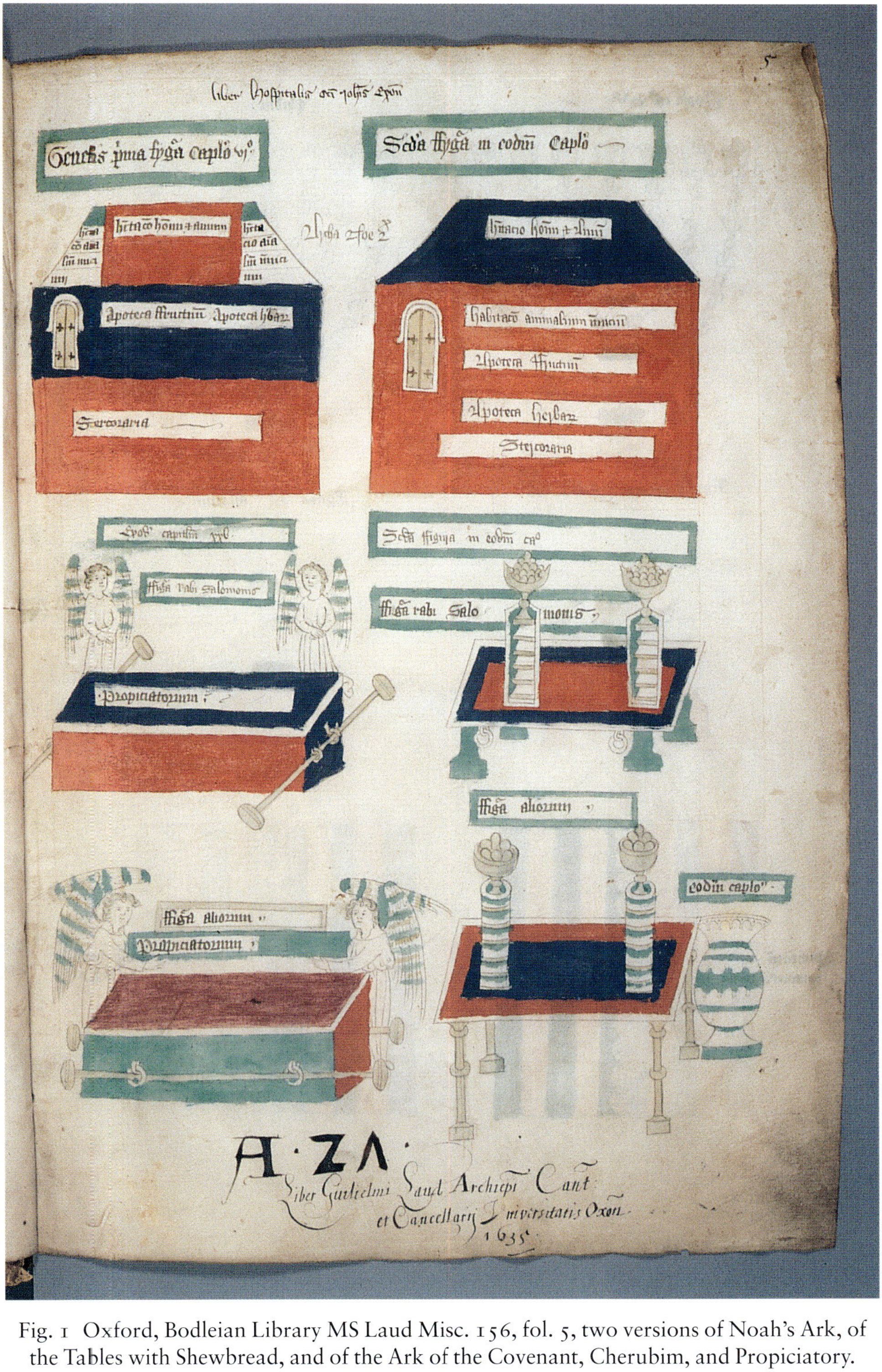

Fig. 1 Oxford, Bodleian Library MS Laud Misc. 156, fol. 5, two versions of Noah's Ark, of the Tables with Shewbread, and of the Ark of the Covenant, Cherubim, and Propiciatory. The Bodleian Library, University of Oxford.

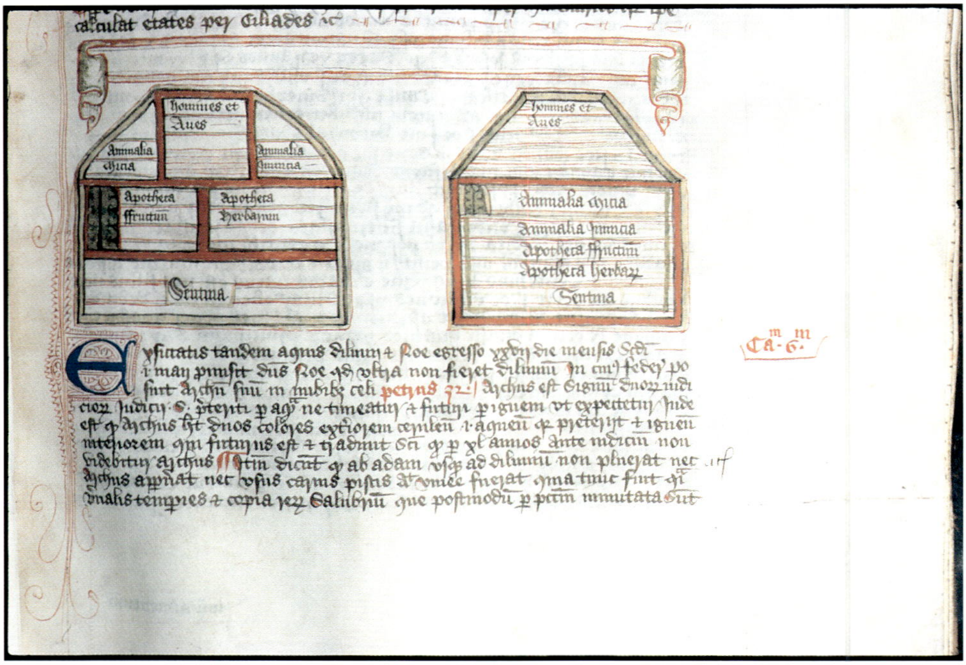

Fig. 2 Dublin, Trinity College MS 486, fol. 39, two diagrammatic versions of Noah's Ark from Ranulf Higden's *Polychronicon*. The Board of Trinity College Dublin.

any of these scribes as the hand of the Laud Misc. 'T.B',[27] even in a copy of the Lyra text with 't.b.' written in red in the introductory initial.[28] Copies of the Norton Index to the *Postilla* were routinely written separately from it; and Richard Sharpe has listed six other manuscripts containing this Index, four of which on examination proved to be either in composite miscellanies or in manuscripts composed only of indexes.[29] So while it was evidently not unusual for Norton's Index to circulate in its own right, MS Laud Misc. 156 is the only manuscript in which the Index occurs with miniatures for the *Postilla litteralis*; and, even more remarkably, I have as yet to find any surviving English manuscript that contains both the Index and the text of the *Postilla*.[30]

To return to the physical make-up of the Laud copy, the fourth and last item is a group of six leaves (fols 61–66v) that bear full-page tables and diagrams articulated with images (fig. 89) and trees;[31] these densely inscribed and sometimes illustrated diagrams are known as the *Speculum theologie* (see also Chapter V and Appendix F).[32] Thematically, they are a collection of items that were used for religious instruction in abbreviated form and/or as memory charts, and in the context of MS Laud Misc. 156 they are further evidence of the unusual nature of the manuscript as a container for items to be copied and employed elsewhere.[33]

Neither the modelbook nor the Index appear to have been separated from a complete manuscript of the *Postilla*, and are certainly not from the same one. Although the four main items in Laud are all physically discrete from one another, they nevertheless have certain important connecting features. The *tituli* in the first

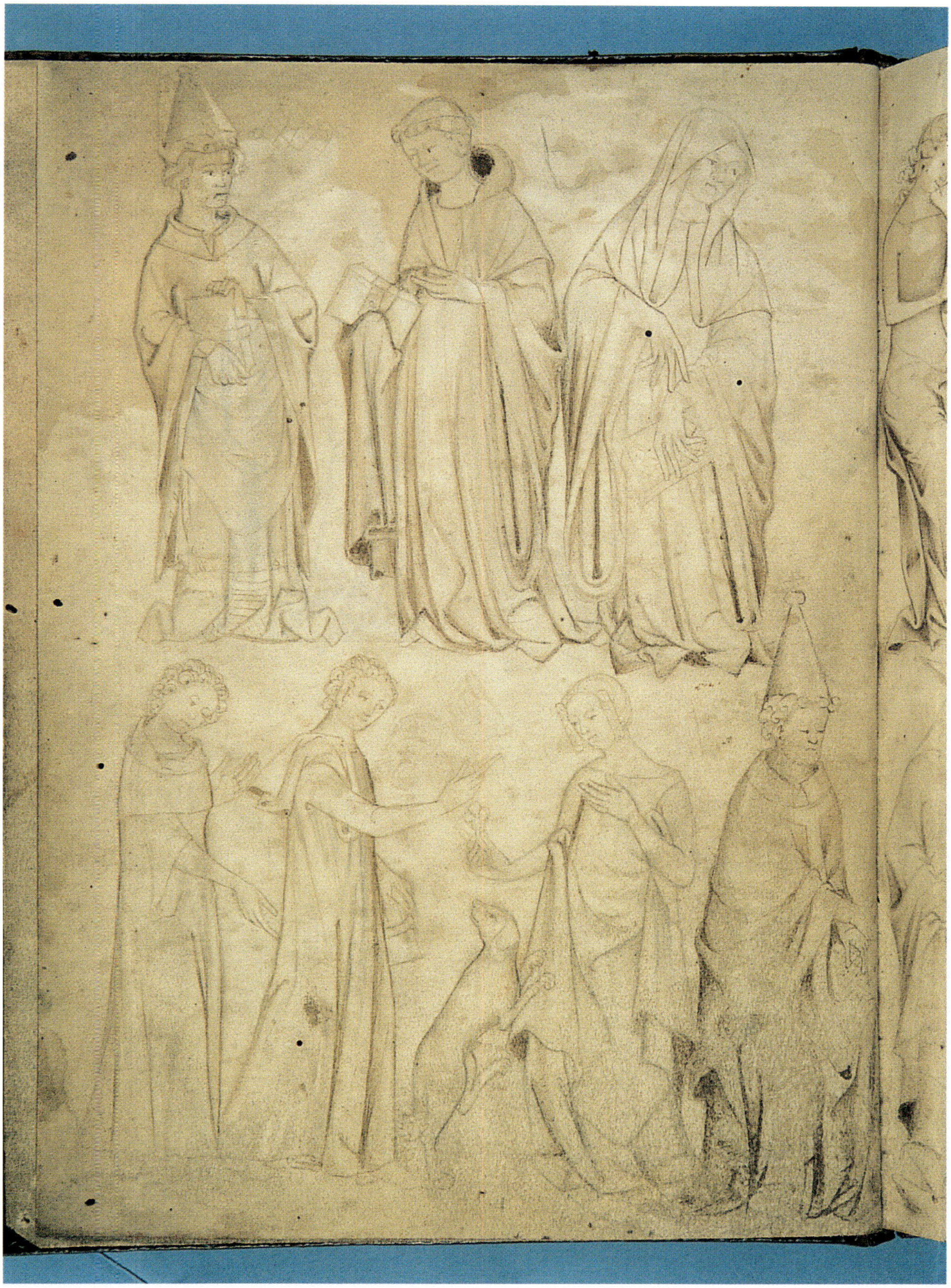

Fig. 3 Cambridge, Magdalene College, MS Pepys 1916, fol. 3v, modelbook page with saints, ladies, and dog. Pepys Library, Magdalene College, Cambridge.

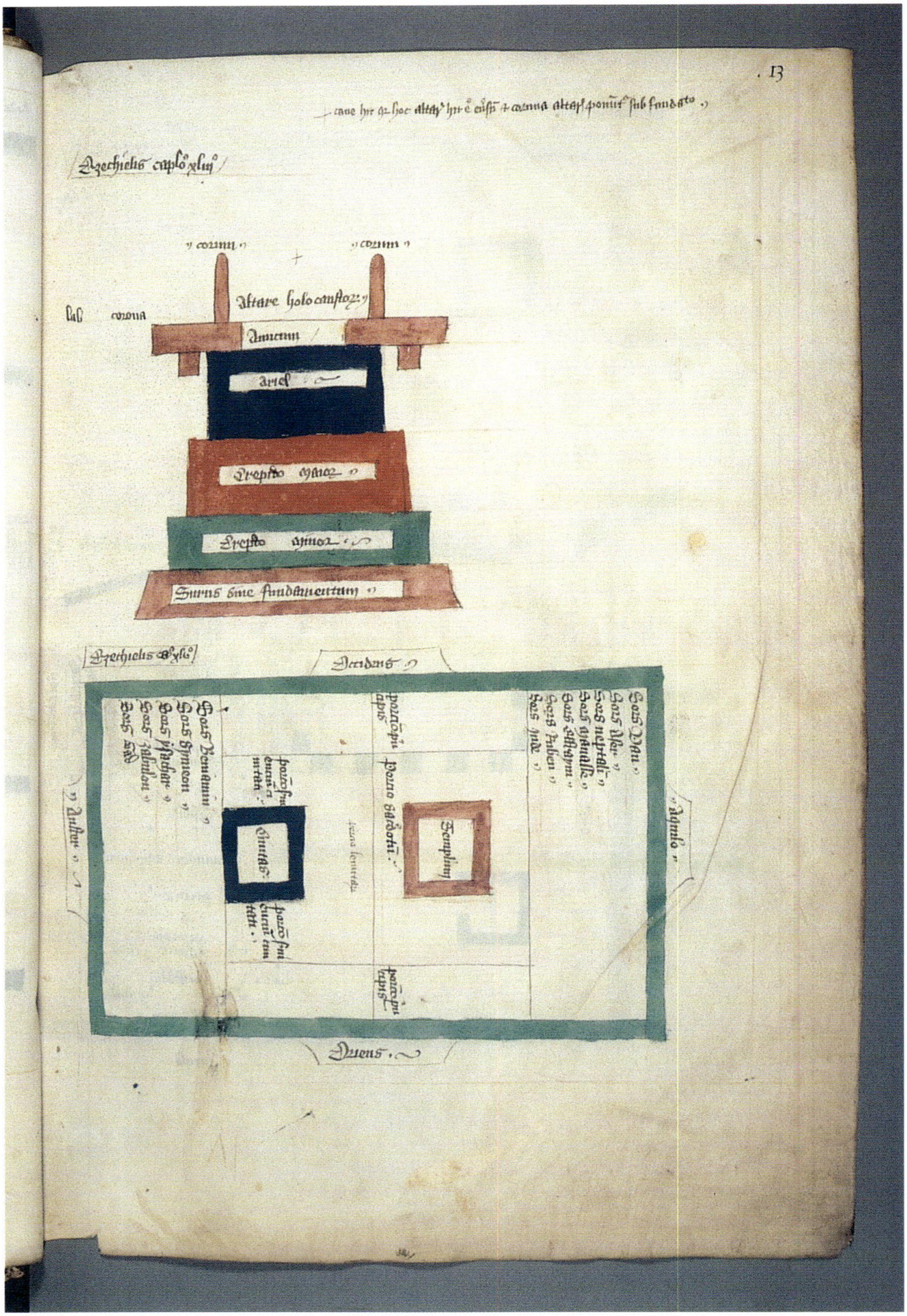

Fig. 4 Oxford, Bodleian Library MS Laud Misc. 156, fol. 13, Altar of the Holocaust; plan of the Temple. The Bodleian Library, University of Oxford.

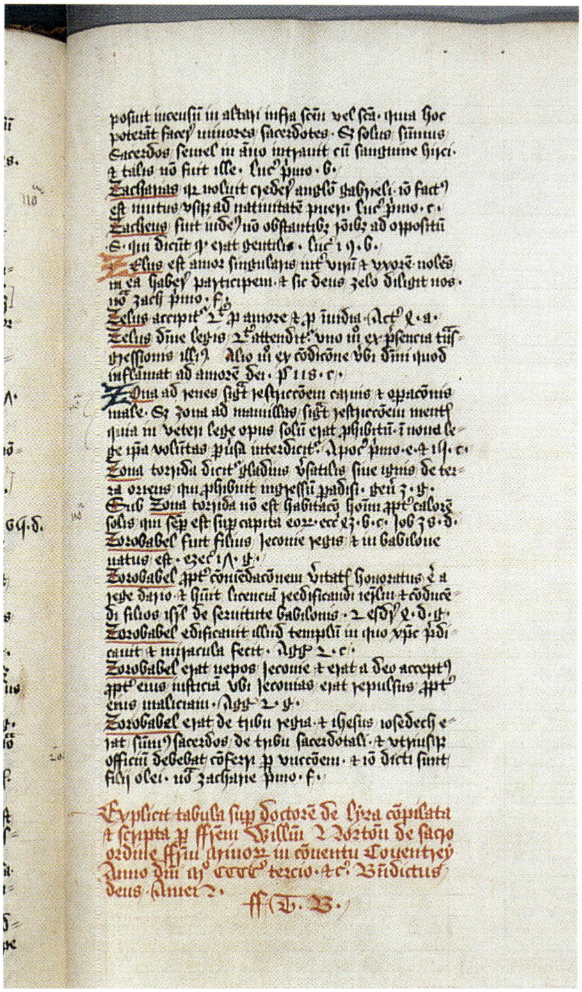

Fig. 5 Oxford, Bodleian Library MS Laud Misc. 156, fol. 60 (detail), signature of scribe, *frater* T.B., of William Norton's Index to Lyra's *Postilla*. The Bodleian Library, University of Oxford.

quire and the inscriptions in the modelbook were written by the same person, so quires 1–3 are connected through their production and locale and were certainly together from an early date. Similarly, the scribe, 'T.B.', of the third item, the Index, wrote and signed the inscriptions and text of the fourth item at fol. 60,[34] the *Speculum theologie*, again conclusively linking the last two parts. And it is also reasonable to link the second item, the *Postilla* miniatures with the third, the *Postilla* Index, on grounds of content. Although written by different scribes, they are of course material to the same text.[35] Each of the four items in Laud was, then, apparently conceived as appropriate to be retained by their producer, three of them on call for producing manuscripts of Lyra's works and the last one for transmission of a complex set of spiritual diagrams.

Another remarkable feature of MS Laud Misc. 156 is its size, which is approximately 430 x 230 mm, exceptional dimensions for a modelbook. The famous Pepys sketchbook in Cambridge, Magdalene College – Pepys MS 1916 (fig. 3) – measures, for instance, 250 × 181 mm, and the BL Sloane modelbook, MS 1448A, of English borders and alphabets is even smaller, at 220 × 144 mm.[36] Although larger, the Laud

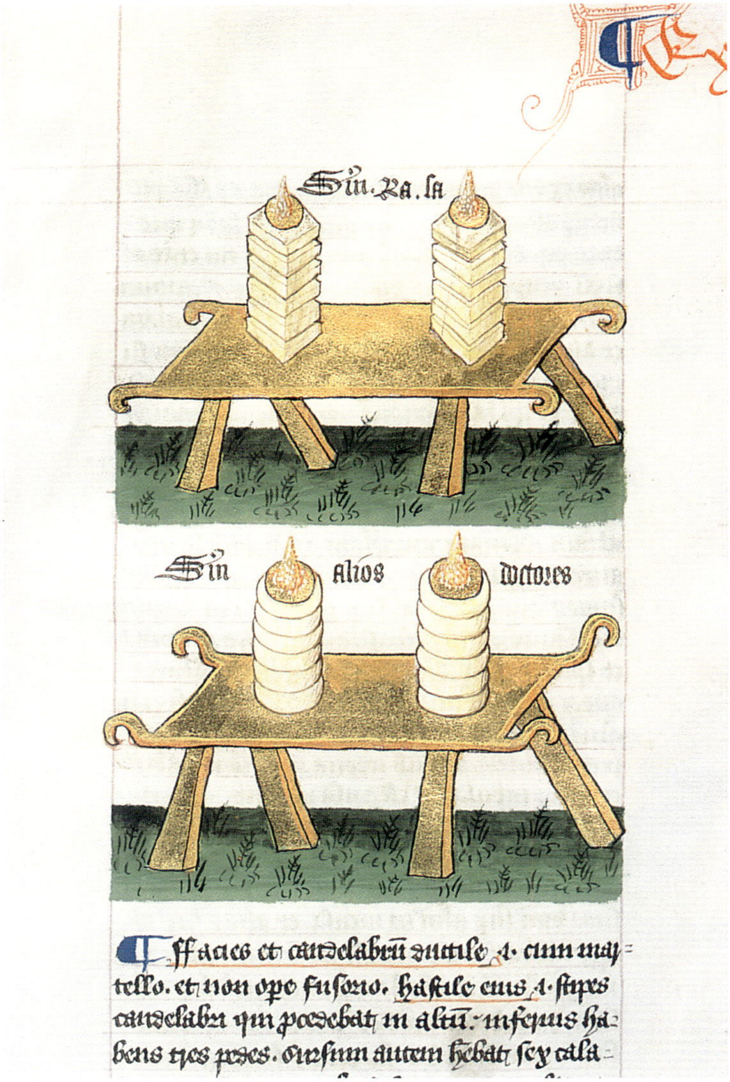

Fig. 6 Cambridge, University Library, MS Dd.7.7, fol. 79v (detail), Tables with Shewbread. By permission of the Syndics of Cambridge University Library.

modelbook has, on the other hand, fewer leaves than the others, with only sixteen. The more compact size of these other English modelbooks would have served for the travels of an artist or for placing the book on the same surface with his work, whereas the Laud modelbook would have required a separate lectern, in the manner shown in various English miniatures of the fifteenth century (fig. 26).[37]

In technique, the stored Laud images range between lightly tinted and heavily coloured drawings. These may occur as many as six to a page, as on fols 6 (fig. 13) and 8 (fig. 22), and on such pages are presented in pairs, showing two versions of the biblical text according to Hebrew and to Christian commentators, that is, according to Rabbi Shelomo ben Jishaq (Solomon ben Isaac) also called Ra-Sa and Rashi (1040–1105) and to Peter Comestor. On the other hand, some of the modelbook pages may show only two images (fols 7: fig. 20, 8v, 12v, 13: fig. 4) or only one (fols 9, 10v,

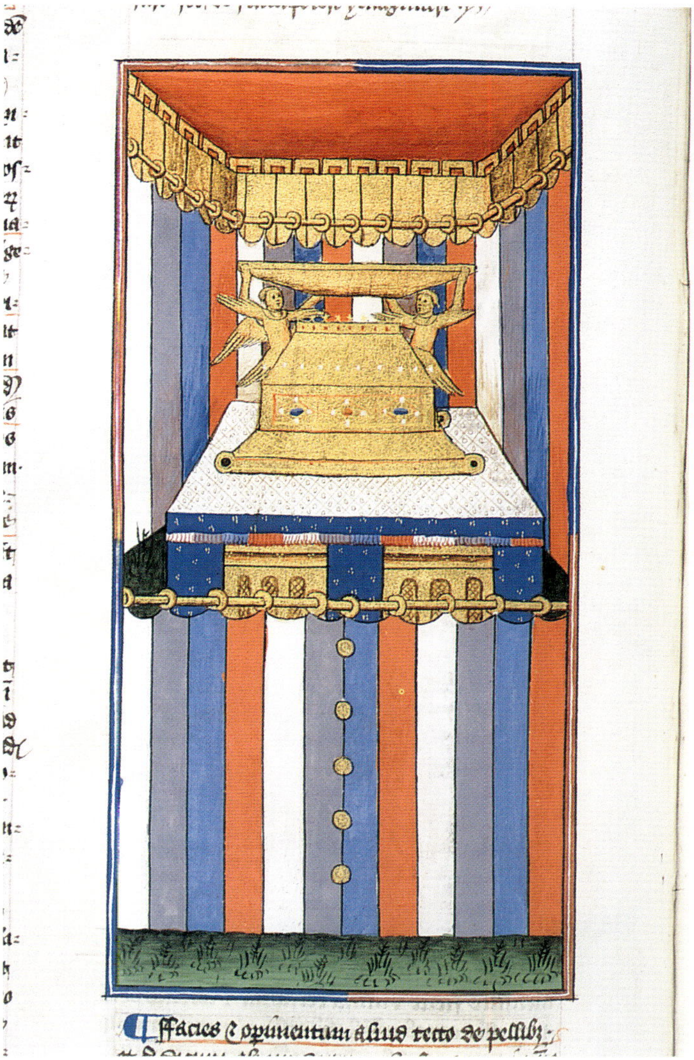

Fig. 7 Cambridge, University Library MS Dd.7.7, fol. 80v (detail), Boards of the Tabernacle; Ark of the Covenant, Cherubim, and Propiciatory. By permission of the Syndics of Cambridge University Library.

11, 12, 14v).[38] The first page (fol. 5) in the modelbook (fig. 1) shows two forms of Noah's Ark,[39] of the Ark of the Covenant with Cherubim and Propitiatory,[40] and of the Tables with Shewbread,[41] each subject in two different forms. The two box-like images of Noah's Ark at the top are *sui generis*. Other fifteenth-century renderings of the Ark, which are quite common, derive from entirely different iconographic traditions, i.e. full-fledged structures such as those from Ranulf Higden's *Polychronicon* in Dublin, Trinity College MS 486 (fig. 2), London, Society of Antiquaries MS 501, a genealogical chronicle of the kings of England, and BL Cotton Nero A.x, fol. 86v, the Gawain manuscript;[42] or more closely the diagrammatic images in chronicles such as BL Additional MSS 21219 (membr. 1), and 30509 (membr. 1), Lansdowne MS 456 (fol. 2v), Kings MS 395 (fol. 3), and Bodl. Lib. MS Bodley Rolls 6 (membr. 2).

The next page in MS Laud Misc. 156, fol. 5v (fig. 11) again contains two versions

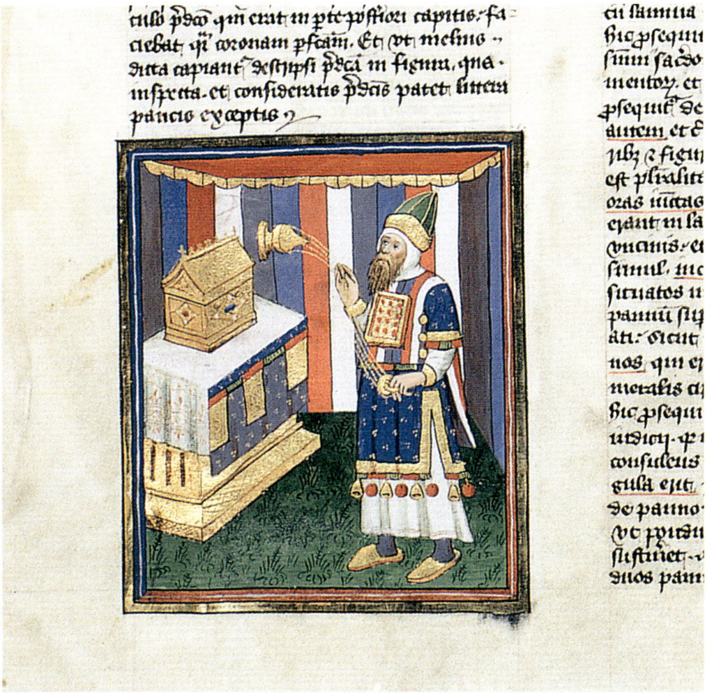

Fig. 8 Cambridge, University Library MS Dd.7.7, fol. 83v (detail), Aaron the High Priest with censer, before altar with Ark of the Covenant.
By permission of the Syndics of Cambridge University Library.

of Temple objects: the seven-branched Candelabra[43] and the Curtains of Linen of the Tabernacle.[44] Folio 6 (fig. 13) shows one side of the Tabernacle, with crenellated boards joined by three horizontal carrying staves passed through rings,[45] and two boards joined by the insertion of tenons in a crenellated socket at the bottom. Below are two versions of the Altar of the Holocaust[46] (Altar of Burnt Offerings) as described by Rashi and Peter Comestor; a *lavatorium* or laver on wheels[47]; and a remarkable figure of Aaron the High Priest (fig. 15), with fine detail of costume[48] including the biblical breastplate set with four rows of precious stones and held by chains, the ephod with stones on the shoulder, the 'curious' girdle,[49] an Old Testament mitre, and alternating golden bells and pomegranates around the hem of his gown. The verso of fol. 6 shows the Tablets of the Law[50] and a floor plan of the Sanctuary and Temple, and fol. 7 (fig. 20) has the disposition of the Levite camps[51] around the Tabernacle, as well as a cross-section of the Temple[52] as a half-timbered structure complete with chimney pots and lightening rods. Fol. 7v (fig. 21) shows cross-sections of the two sideposts of the entrance to the Temple,[53] a view of the facade of the Temple in the form of a Gothic window with tracery, crenellations and inscriptions concerning the height and width of the building, and a floor plan below of the inner court with the placement of three rows of stone columns[54] in the Hall of the Forest of Lebanon.[55]

Folio 8 (fig. 22) depicts two versions of the lily capitals made for the pillars of bronze,[56] as usual according to Rashi and Latin commentators, with three versions of the Brazen Sea, and, lastly, one version at lower right of the wheeled Base of Brass,[57] with the second version at the top of fol. 8v; the sundial of Ahaz[58] is below, and another version on fol. 9. With fol. 9v (see frontispiece) we come to the vision of

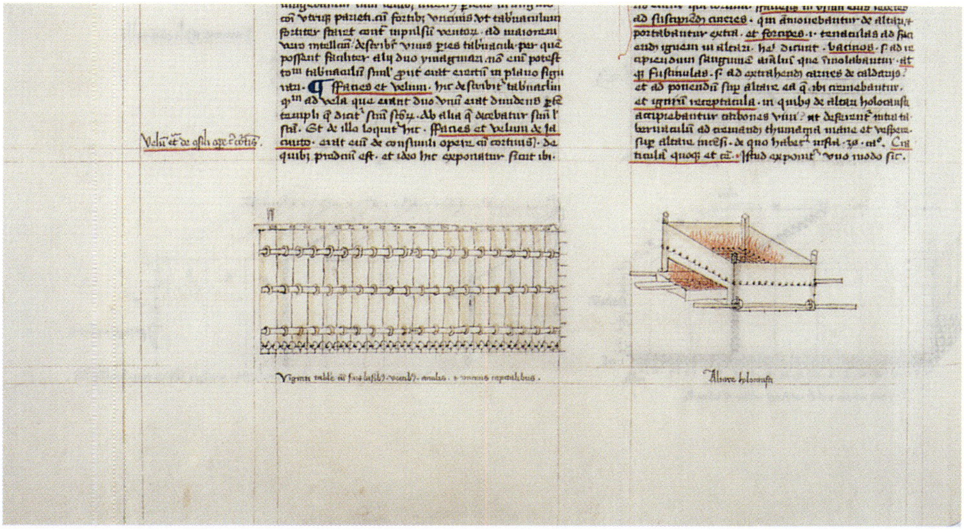

Fig. 9 Oxford, Bodleian Library MS Laud Misc. 154, fol. 49v (detail), Boards of the Temple; Altar of the Holocaust. The Bodleian Library, University of Oxford.

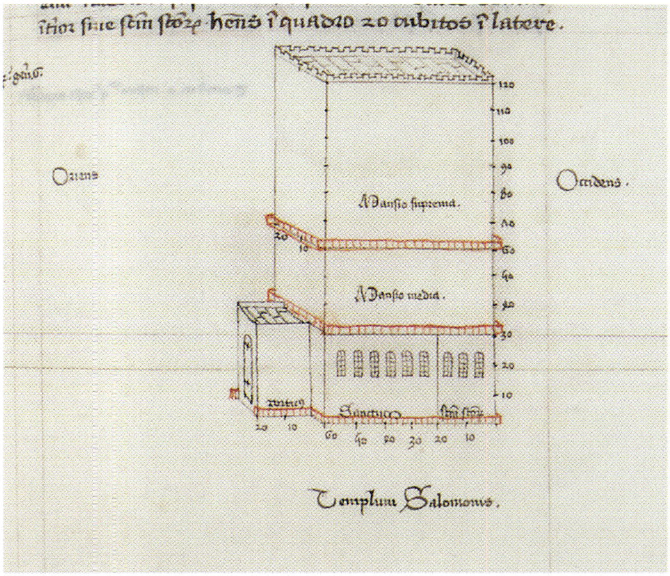

Fig. 10 Oxford, Bodleian Library MS Laud Misc. 154, fol. 138 (detail), Temple of Solomon. The Bodleian Library, University of Oxford.

Ezekiel, with its 'likeness of four living creatures' – that 'every one had four faces, and every one had four wings ... And their feet were straight feet; and the sole of their feet was like the sole of a calf's foot ... And they had the hands of a man underneath their wings on four sides ... As for the likeness of their faces, they four had the face of a man, and the face of a lion ... and they four had the face of an ox ...; they four also had the face of an eagle ... And they went every one straight forward.'[59] The circles below are unfinished, probably an attempt to render the wheels that flew about with the

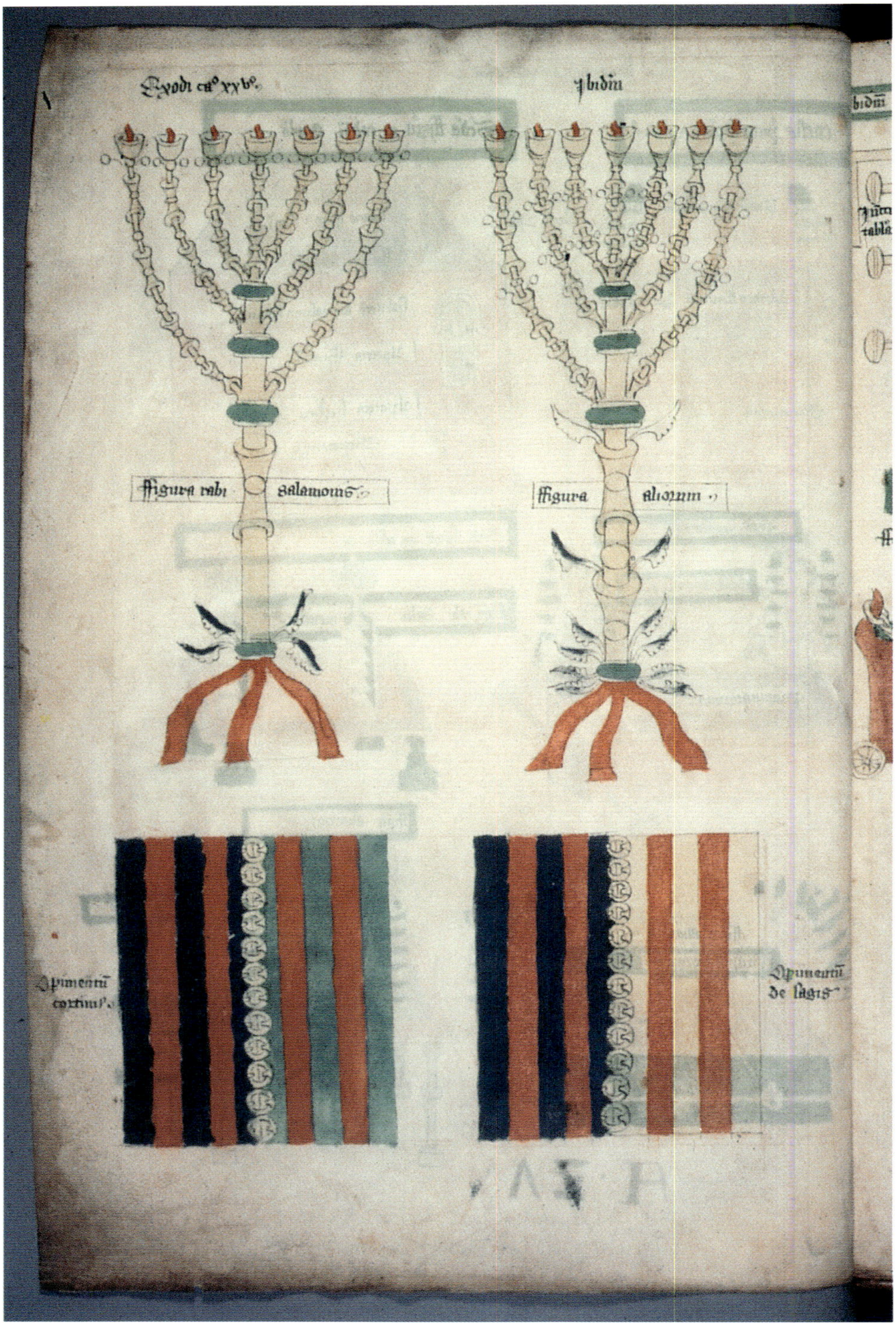

Fig. 11 Oxford, Bodleian Library MS Laud Misc. 156, fol. 5v, two versions of the Candelabra and of the Curtains of Linen for the Tabernacle. The Bodleian Library, University of Oxford.

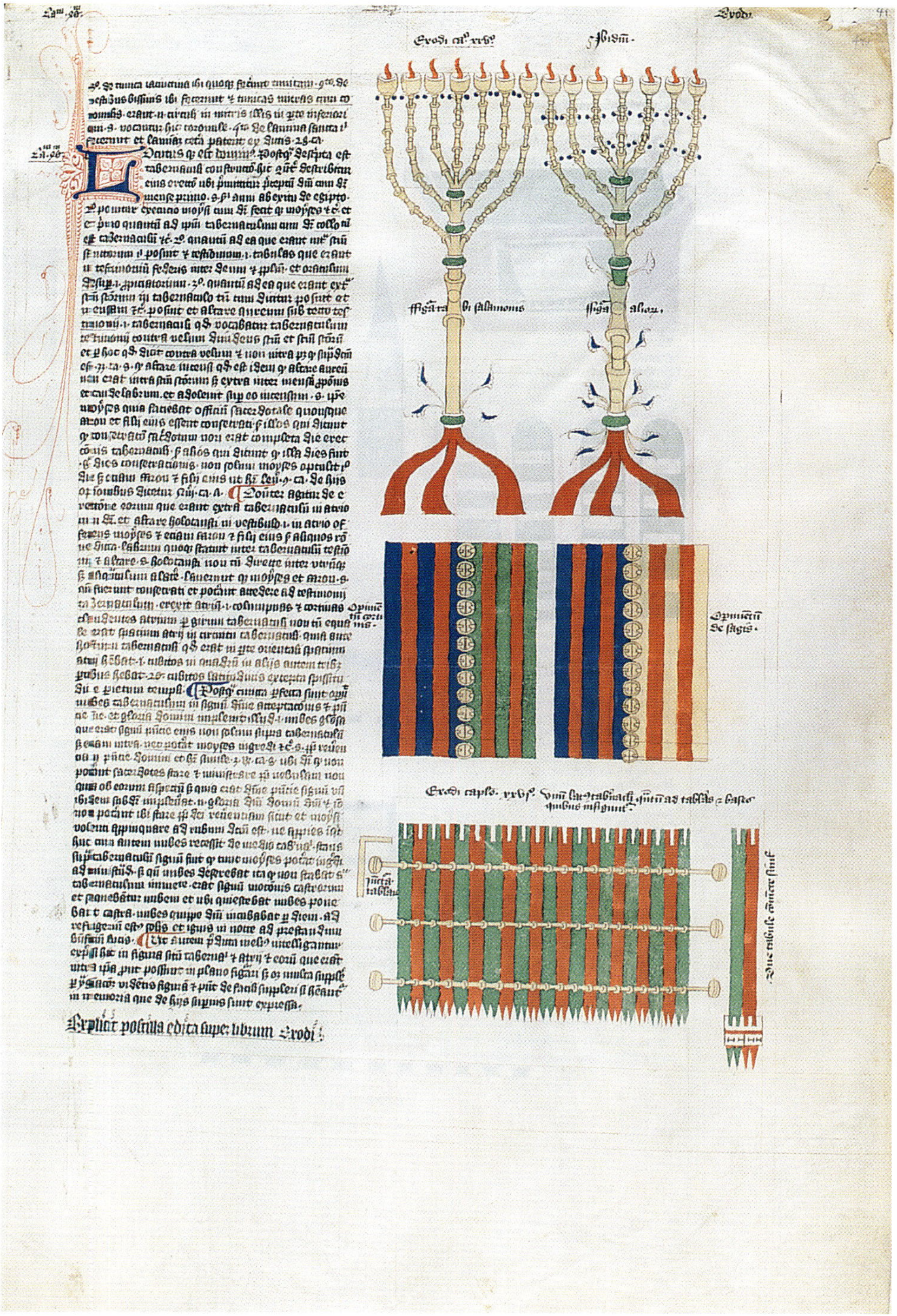

Fig. 12 New Haven, Yale University, Beinecke MS 640, fol. 40, two versions of the Candelabra and of the Curtains of Linen for the Tabernacle. Beinecke Rare Book and Manuscript Library, Yale University.

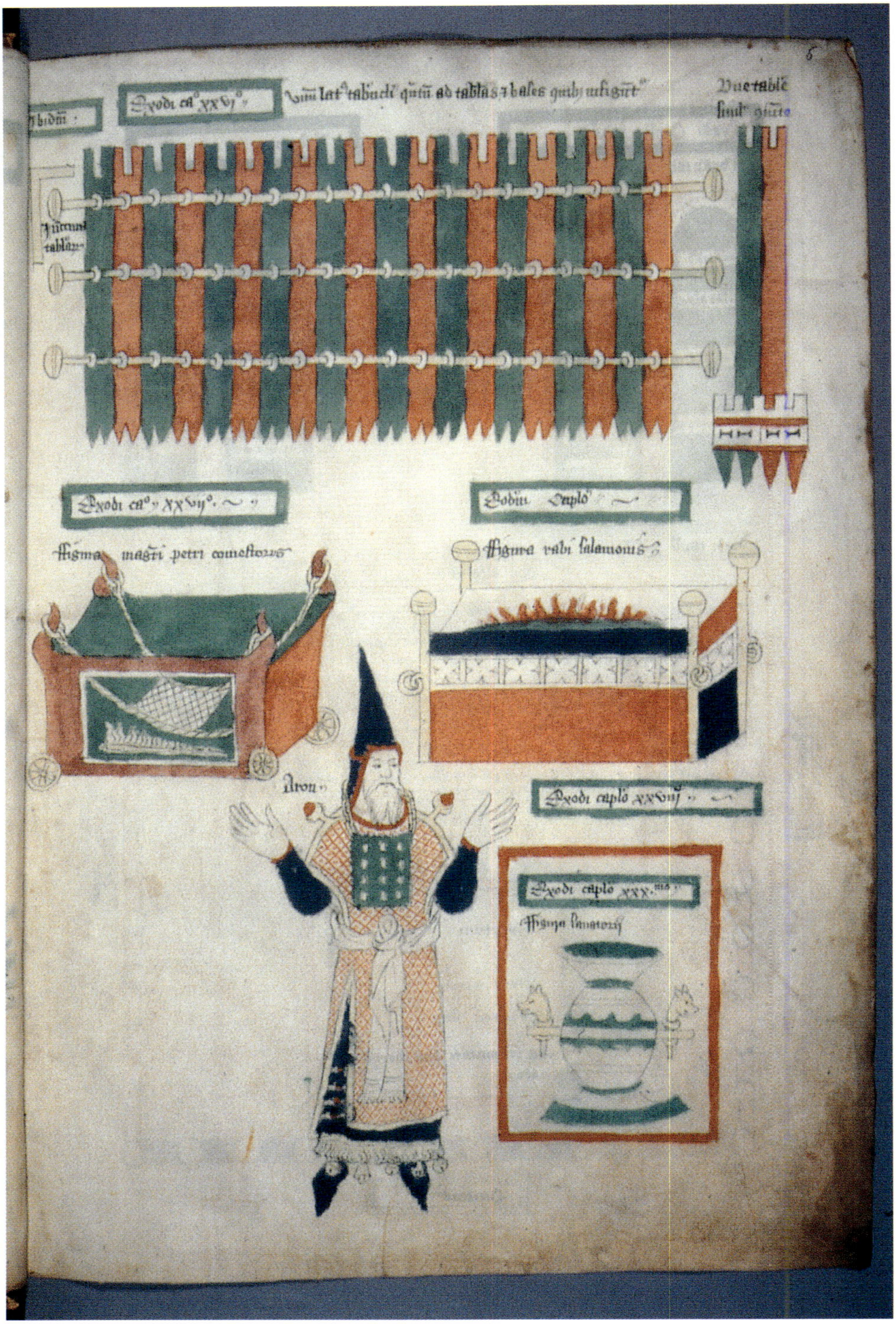

Fig. 13 Oxford, Bodleian Library MS Laud Misc. 156, fol. 6, Boards of the Tabernacle with carrying staves, two versions of the Altar of the Holocaust, Aaron the High Priest, and a *lavatorium*. The Bodleian Library, University of Oxford.

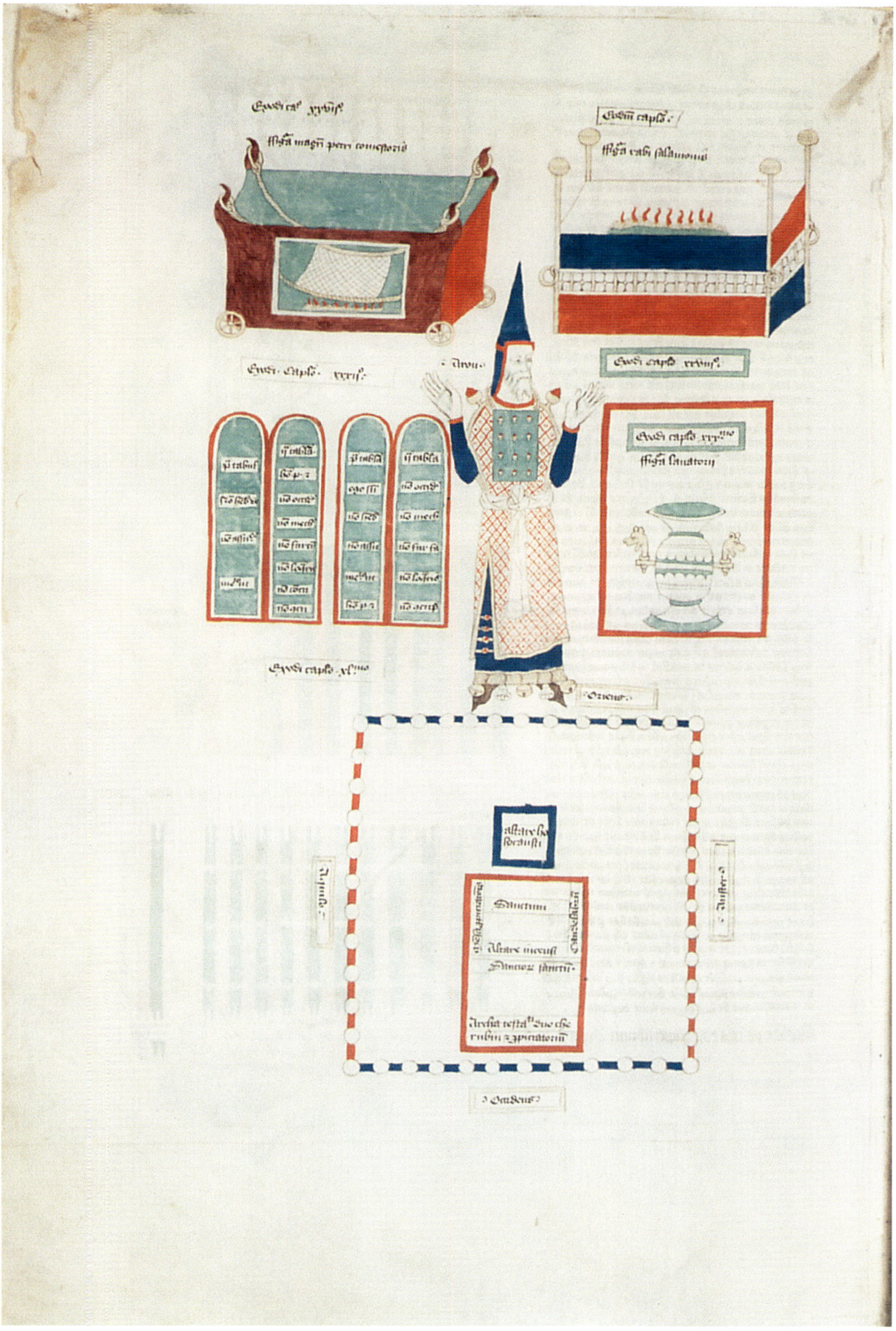

Fig. 14 New Haven, Yale University Beinecke MS 640, fol. 40v, two versions of the Altar of the Holocaust, Tablets of the Ten Commandments, Aaron the High Priest, Brazen Sea, plan of the Temple. Beinecke Rare Book and Manuscript Library, Yale University.

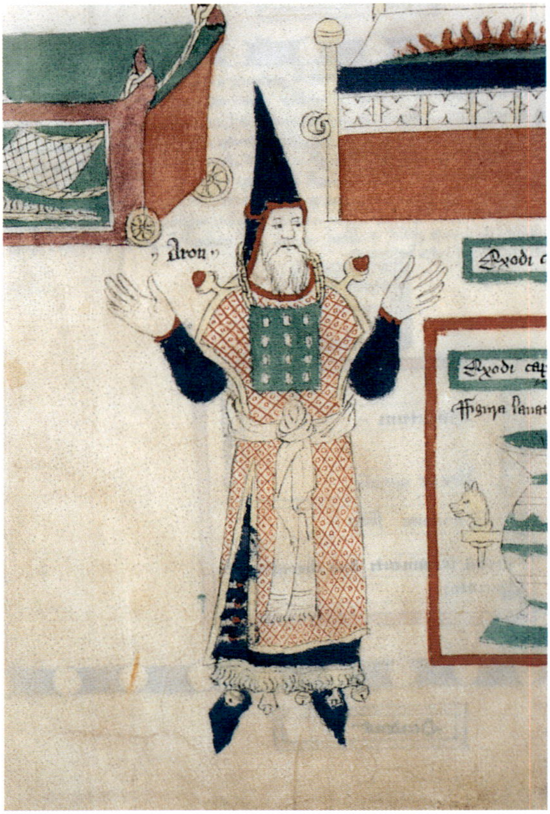

Fig. 15 Oxford, Bodleian Library MS Laud Misc. 156, fol. 6 (detail), Aaron the High Priest. The Bodleian Library, University of Oxford.

creatures,[60] though the artist was apparently uncertain about their meaning and how they were to be depicted. Folios 10, 11, 11v, 12, 13v–14, and 14v have ground plans of the Temple and precincts[61] according to Ezechiel, as well as tower-like portals with turrets of the Temple (fols 10v, 12v) developed to demonstrate its height in cubits.[62] On fol. 13 (fig. 4) we find a more elaborate drawing of the Altar of the Holocaust, i.e. for burnt offerings,[63] as well as a plan of the area around the Temple with the apportionment of land designated to the city of Jerusalem and to the tribes of Israel.[64] The modelbook section concludes with a drawing of the city of Jerusalem with its gates labelled and with a descent of the successors of Alexander the Great (fol. 14v); on the next page (fol. 15), there is a genealogy of Antiochus Magnus as related in Machabees, both descents possibly added at about the same time as the making of the modelbook but by a different scribe.[65]

Of the eighteen late fourteenth- and fifteenth-century English copies containing texts of Lyra's *Postilla* on the Old Testament and surviving in whole or in part[66] – but not including extracts or fragments of one or a few leaves – only three have illustrations. A few others have illuminated or coloured initials.[67] Eleven have spaces[68] and/or rudimentary sketches for miniatures, as in Oxford, New College MS 8,[69] one set has neither miniatures nor spaces,[70] and three are not relevant because they lack the early books of the Old Testament that would have contained the Lyra illustrations.[71] One of the three illustrated copies, a superb set of four volumes in CUL MSS Dd.7.7–10, was written by Stephen Dodesham[72] of the Carthusian priories of Witham

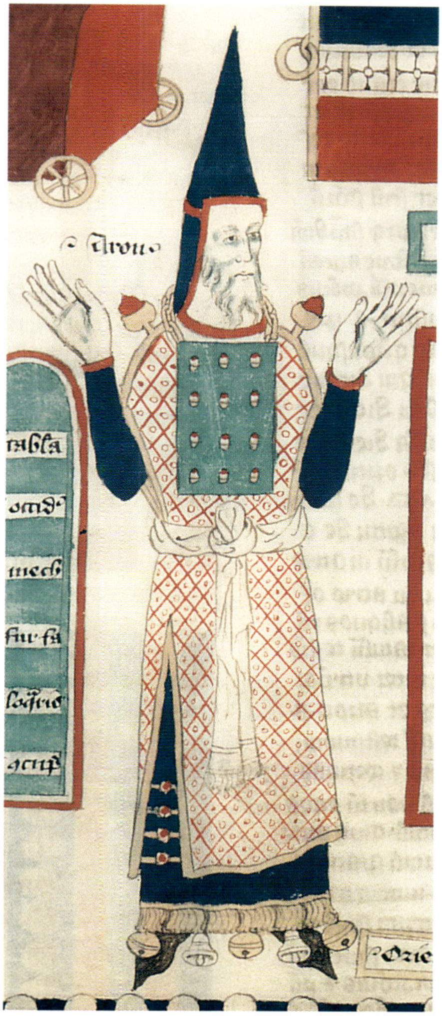

Fig. 16 New Haven, Yale University Beinecke MS 640, fol. 40v (detail), Aaron the High Priest. Beinecke Rare Book and Manuscript Library, Yale University.

and Sheen. This set was made around 1440 and was destined 'for the eventual ownership of St Albans Abbey',[73] and given in 1457. A second fine set, of two volumes, Bodl. Lib. MSS Laud Misc. 152 and 154, dated 1463, was written by Henry Mere and John Blacman and given by Blacman to Witham Charterhouse.[74] A third illustrated volume, recently acquired by Yale University, Beinecke MS 640, has another splendid series of miniatures, of the second quarter of the fifteenth century, but with no evidence for its destination.

It will be interesting to see what, if any, impact the Laud modelbook might have had on these three illustrated copies. I begin with the four-volume Cambridge set[75] of around 1440. These miniatures were of course integrated within the Lyra text in quite obvious contrast to the same images stored on the Laud page. A Cambridge miniature may occasionally in one or more spaces depict two, or even three[76] versions of images that look rather as if they were drawn from a modelbook. If however the Cambridge images are compared with the same subject in MS Laud Misc. 156, for instance, the Tables with Shewbread, it is clear from the much more elegant version in Laud that the

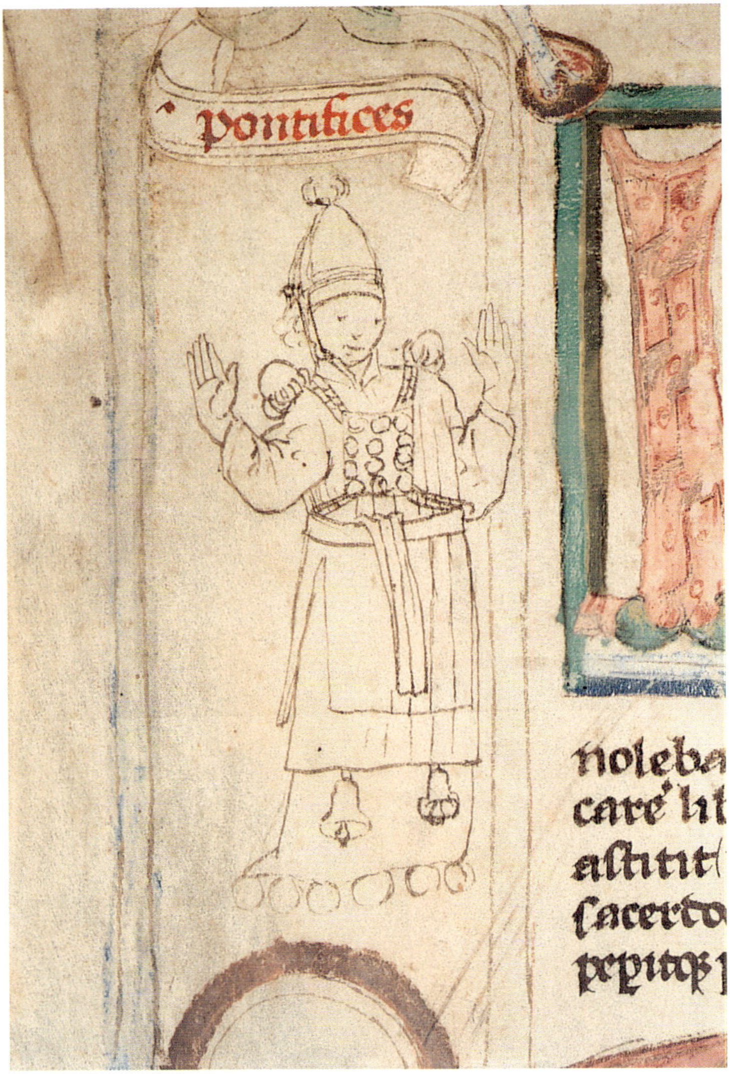

Fig. 17 British Library Additional MS 21219, membrane 3 (detail), Aaron the High Priest. The British Library.

two are not from the same source: the Laud version (fig. 1) is not at all comparable to the rough-hewn trestle tables in Dd.7.7 (fig. 6). In order to confirm the impression of two different iconographic sources, the Cambridge scene of the boards of the Tabernacle (fig. 7) should be compared with the Laud image (fig. 13). The Cambridge artist (or his exemplar) constructed a three-sided room from the boards and showed them enclosing the Ark of the Covenant with Cherubim and Propitiatory; he even included a canopy and dressed altar. The Laud artist, in contrast, depicted a simple, flat plane of attached boards (fig. 13): he was less interested in a reconstruction of their use than in the methods by which the boards were interlocked. The Cambridge artist or his exemplar showed same sort of invention in his miniature of the High Priest Aaron (fig. 8; cf. fig. 15), whom the miniature shows not only within a framed scene but also in a narrative episode, i.e. with Aaron in the act of swinging a censer before the Ark. Comparison with the Cambridge manuscript has, then, unexpectedly

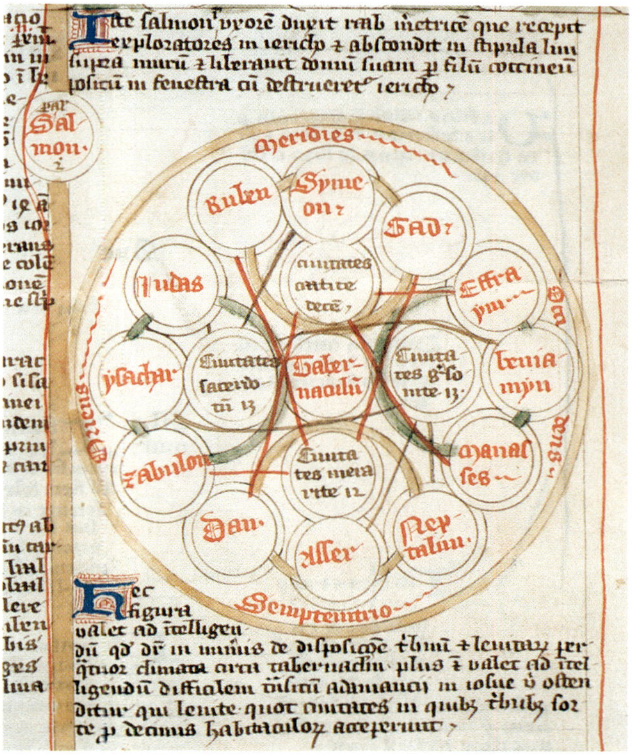

Fig. 18 Oxford, St John's College MS 58, fol. 4v (detail), diagram of the Disposition of the Twelve tribes of Israel around the Tabernacle of the Ark. By permission of the President and Scholars of Saint John Baptist College in the University of Oxford.

demonstrated that there must have been more than one illustrative programme for Lyra's *Postilla litteralis* being used or invented in England in the fifteenth century and that we cannot expect to establish the Laud modelbook as the ur-source of all of the illustrated English copies.

The second English set of illustrated *Postilla* is the copy comprised of MSS Laud Misc. 152 and 154.[77] These were produced much later in the century, in and just after 1463; the date is recorded in MS 152 at fol. 286v. The miniatures in MS Laud Misc. 154 (the Old Testament volume), which are lightly tinted drawings, differ profoundly from those in MS Laud Misc. 156. They are much reduced in size and extent of colouring, with yellow being the main tint, and were relegated to the lower and side margins, with the result that they no longer act as an immediate pictorial exegesis on the text. In a few instances, the iconography is similar to the Laud modelbook as with the boards of the Temple in a single plane (fig. 9),[78] but in other respects very different, as with the Temple of Solomon (fig. 10). Where the Laud Misc. 154 drawing (fol. 138) shows the upper stories of the Temple with cubits marked off precisely by tens, the Laud Misc. 156 (fig. 20) miniature merely has inscriptions within a cross-section and does not show the two upper stories of the Temple. In addition, MS Laud Misc. 154 does not have two versions of each image as clearly demanded by the text; the propitiatory (fol. 48), the mensa (fol. 48v), the Candelarum (fol. 48v), the Altar of the Holocaust,[79] the lavatorium (fol. 52), the lily capitals (fol. 139), etc., are all drawn in only one version, and the plans of the Temple and environs are less detailed than in MS Laud Misc. 156. For some reason, the scribes of this portion of the *Postilla*, Mere and Blacman, did not follow the textual prompts to leave spaces for figures, possibly

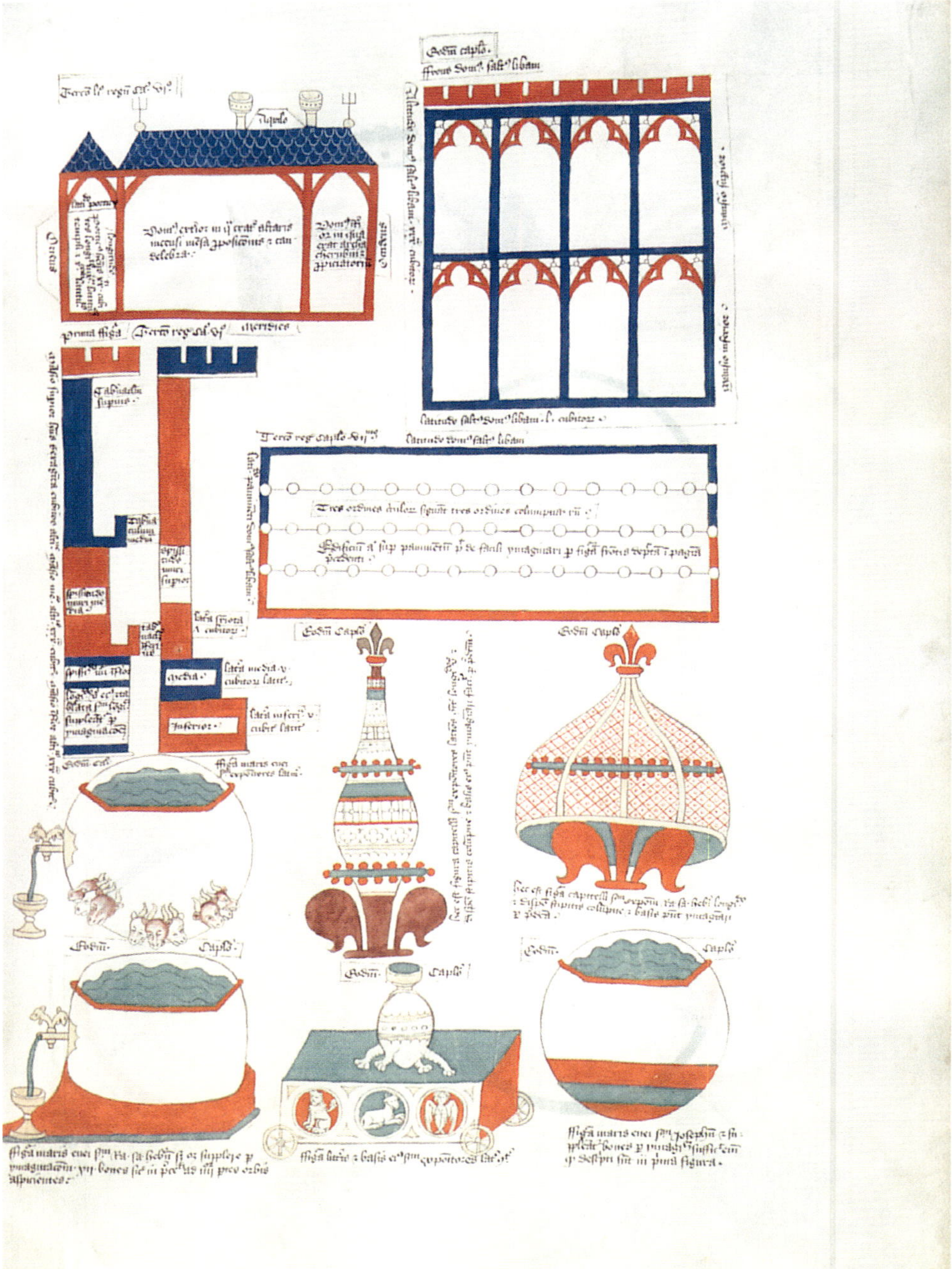

Fig. 19 New Haven, Yale University, MS 640, fol. 96, modelbook page with cross-section of the Temple, windows as facade of Temple, plan of columns, elevation of portals, two versions of the lily capitals, three versions of the Brazen Sea, and the Base of Brass on wheels. Beinecke Rare Book and Manuscript Library, Yale University.

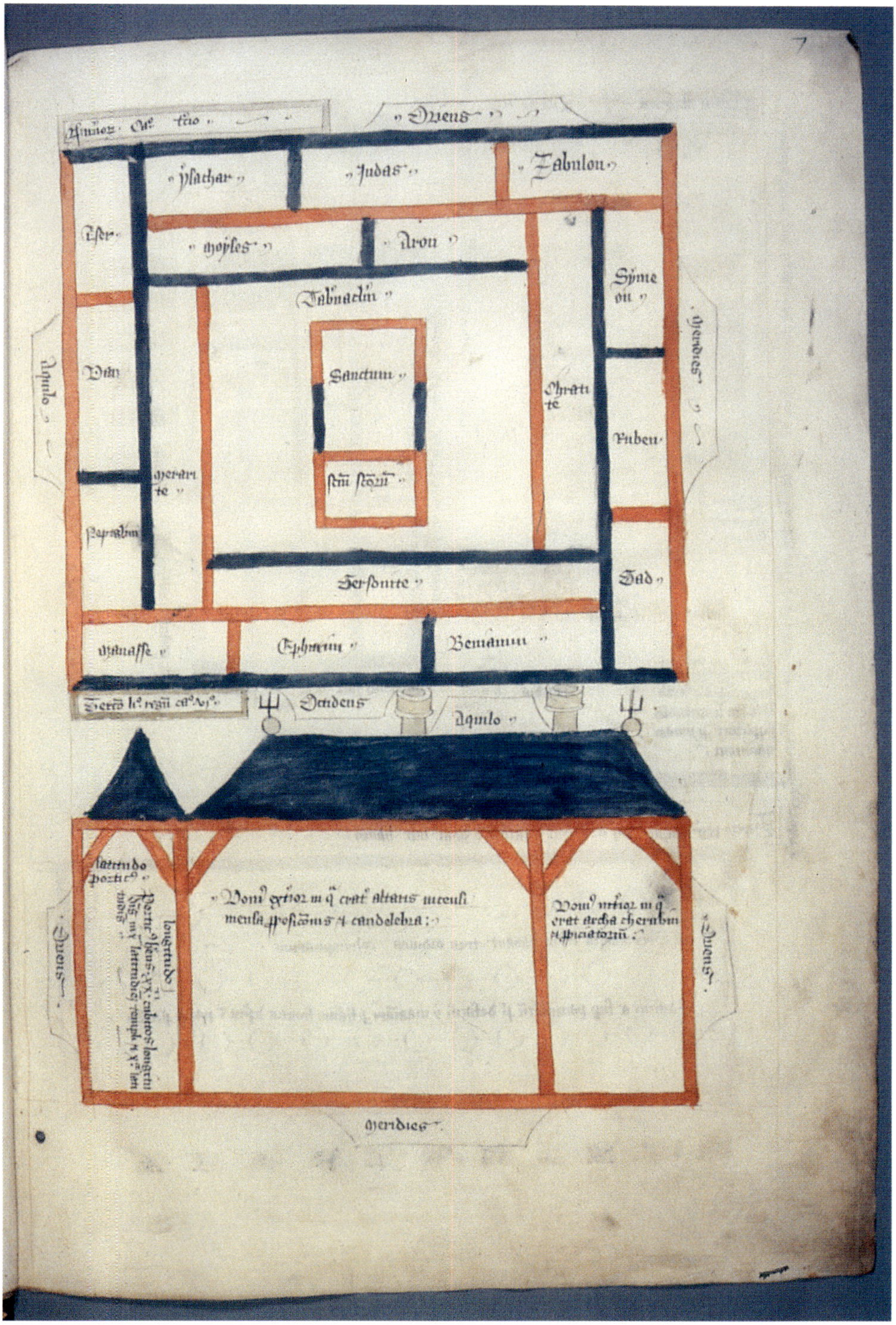

Fig. 20 Oxford, Bodleian Library MS Laud Misc. 156, fol. 7, diagram of the Levite camps around the Ark of the Covenant; cross-section of the Temple. The Bodleian Library, University of Oxford.

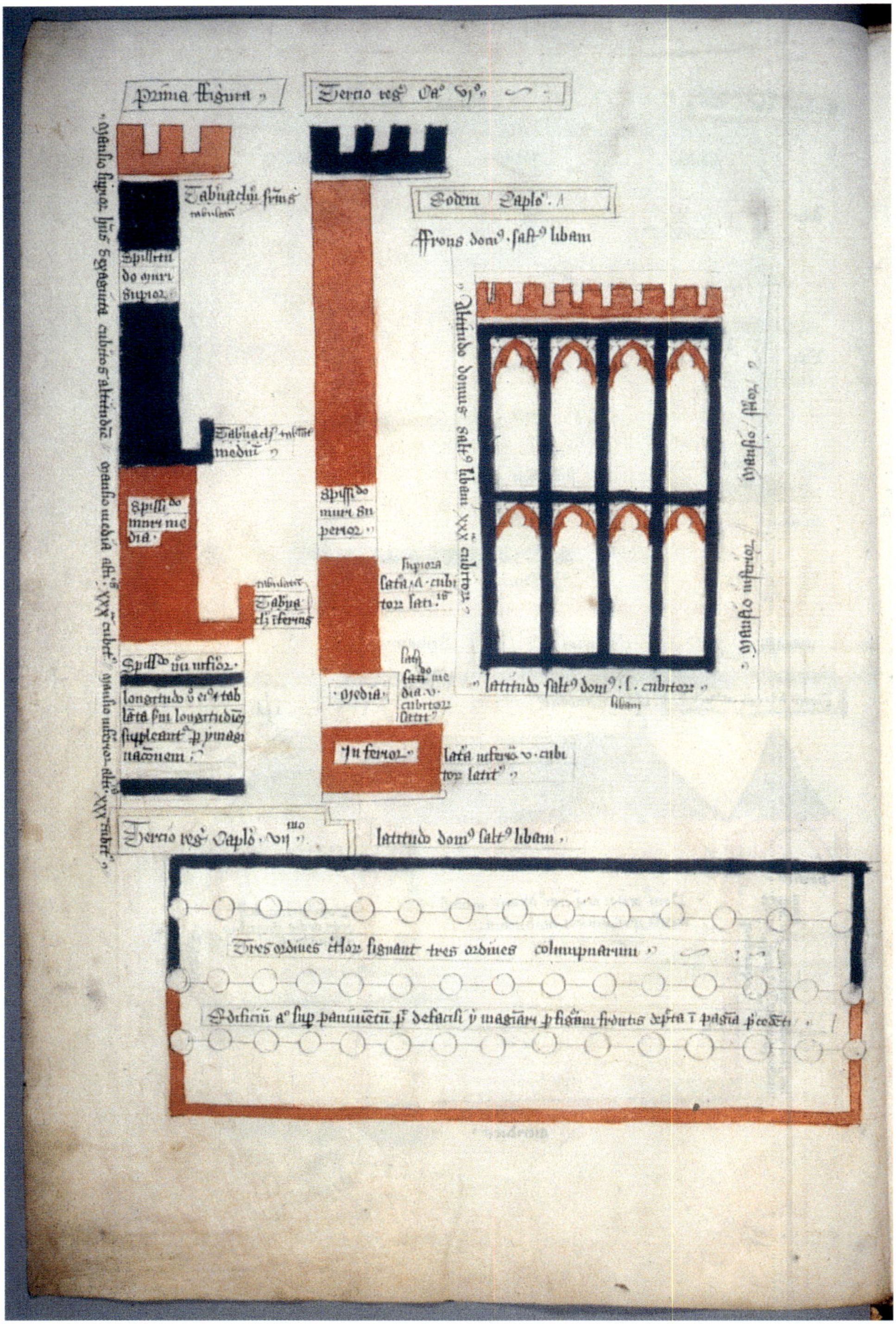

Fig. 21 Oxford, Bodleian Library MS Laud Misc. 156, fol. 7v, elevation of the portals, windows as facade of Temple, plan of columns. The Bodleian Library, University of Oxford.

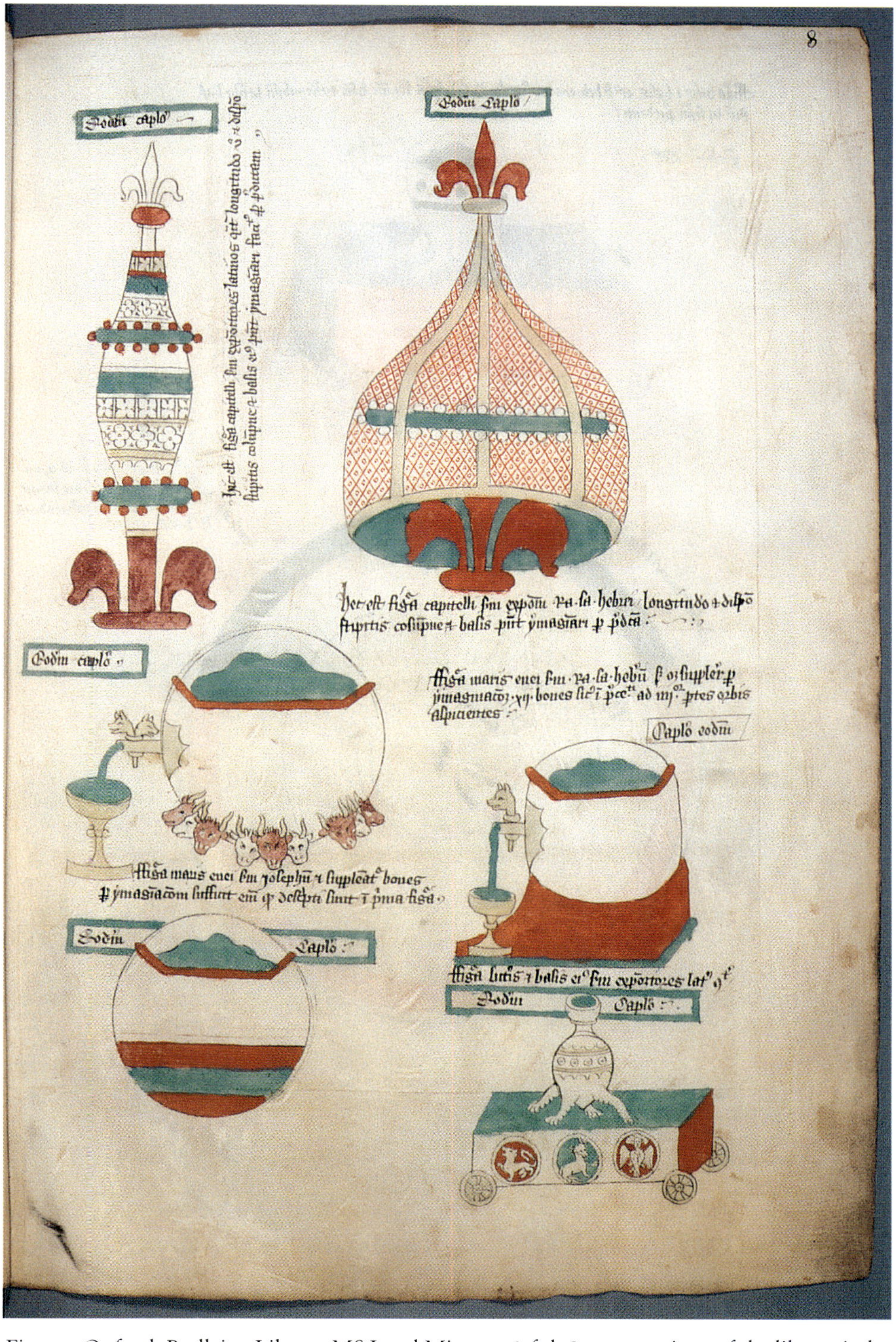

Fig. 22 Oxford, Bodleian Library MS Laud Misc. 156, fol. 8, two versions of the lily capitals, three versions of the Brazen Sea, the Base of Brass on wheels. The Bodleian Library, University of Oxford.

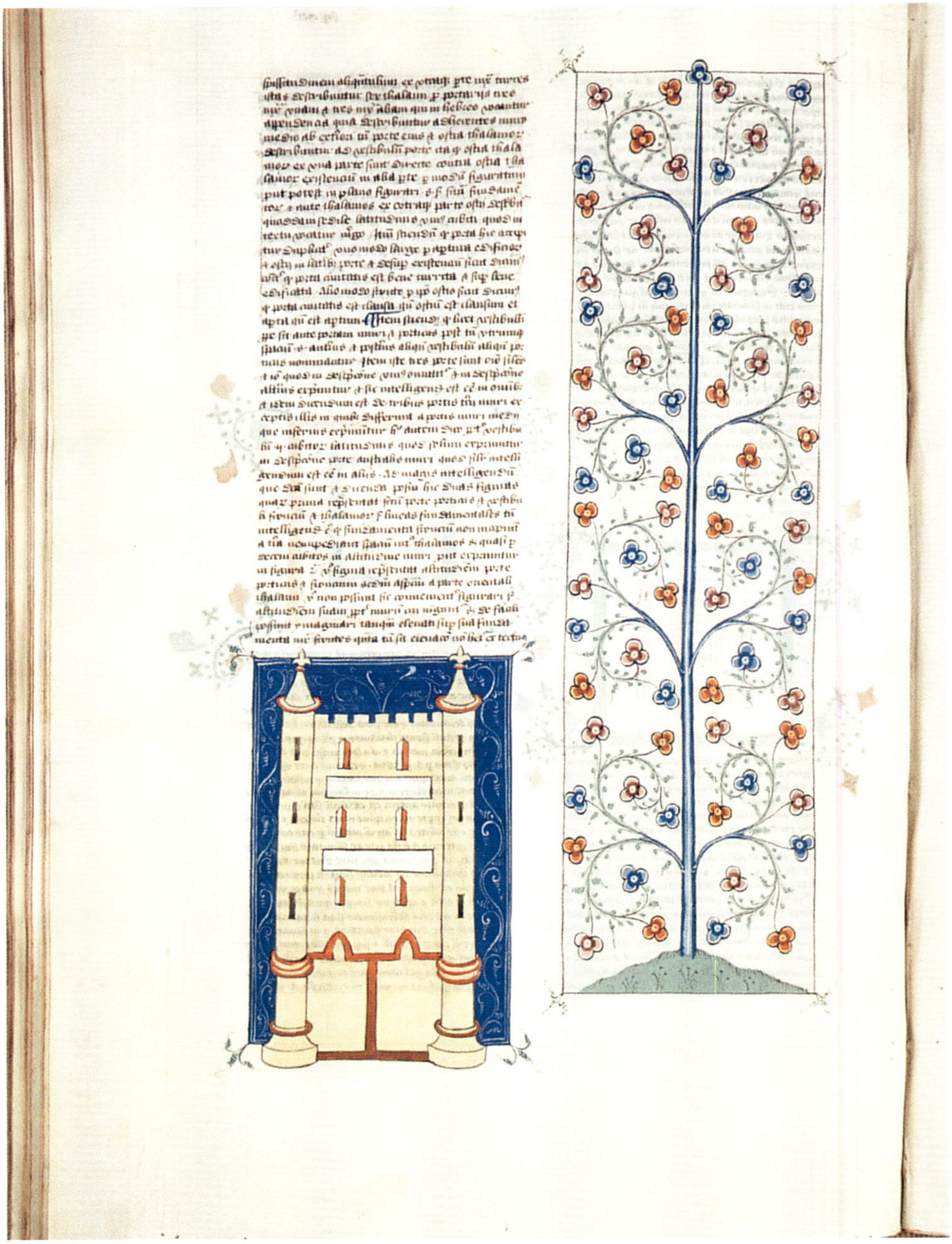

Fig. 23 New Haven, Yale University, Beinecke MS 640, fol. 196v, tower as facade of the Temple; carpet miniature with tree. Beinecke Rare Book and Manuscript Library, Yale University.

because their exemplar was not illustrated. Such a scenario would explain the placement of the drawings in the margins. Certainly Lyra's text itself was absolutely clear not only in prompting spaces for miniatures but in actually requiring the use of visual props. The difference in the iconography of miniatures in MS Laud Misc. 154, now a second variation from those in MS Laud Misc. 156, may again be attributed to a different exemplar or modelbook circulating in England. Given the draftsmanship-like precision of the Laud Misc. 152 and 154 drawings, this option – even though it requires the presence of a third exemplar (whether modelbook or illustrated text) – seems more likely than that of an artist acting on his own initiative for such a difficult programme of illustration. Whatever their source, the drawings in MSS Laud Misc. 152 and 154, like those in CUL MSS Dd.7.7–10, certainly did not derive from Laud Misc. 156.

With the Yale manuscript, MS Beinecke 640 (Appendix C),[80] of the second quarter of the century, there is, for the first time, a strong claim for a pictorial connection with MS Laud Misc. 156. Using two pages (figs 11, 12), those showing the Candelabra and Curtains of Linen, as comparative examples, it is possible to demonstrate at once that the figures resemble each other to a striking degree. They are like each other in details of drawing, as with the gold clasps on the boards, and in use of colouring, as on the tinted wings of the Candelabra. The lower boards, at the bottom of the Beinecke page, occur, however, at the top of the next Laud page (fig. 13); and on dropping farther down on the Laud page, we find those same four images at the top of the next Yale page (fig. 14) – in the like detail and colouring. The phenomenon of the same images progressing in the same order through both books, if shifted from top to bottom of the Laud page, occurs with other images as well: the pictorial material on fol. 96 of Beinecke (fig. 19) is spread, in this case, between three pages of the Laud manuscript: first, the cross-section of the Temple on fol. 7 (fig. 20), then the next three images on fol. 7v (fig. 21), and finally the capitals and Brazen Seas on fol. 8 (fig. 22). No other copies of the *Postilla* match, as I say, in the manner that these two do, and it is virtually certain that one was derived directly from the other or, at worst, both exactly from a common original.

Although the Laud and Beinecke artists were obviously trained in the same style, it is also evident, by comparing the facial renderings of the High Priest (figs 15, 16), that the two miniatures were not made by the same artist. We must, therefore, have one of two situations: either one in which the two artists were working in the same locale or one in which an exemplar circulated from one locale to another and was copied by a second artist. But the second scenario would not account for the close similarity in the style of the two artists, unless they were trained to imitate absolutely. Interestingly, the scribes of MS Laud Misc. 156 and of the Beinecke leaves appear to me also to have been trained in the same locale, and this combination of limners and scribes seems to indicate a single centre of some considerable importance.

A crucial point concerning the Beinecke manuscript is that the two leaves, fols 40 and 96, both of which contain a modelbook selection of images similar to those in Laud, were *inserted* in the Beinecke manuscript: they were not part of the original make-up of the book (see Appendix C). The first added leaf, fol. 40, has text and images from the last part of Exodus on the recto (fig. 12), as well as a full page of stored images on the verso (fig. 14). This leaf was, however, placed in a quire with com-

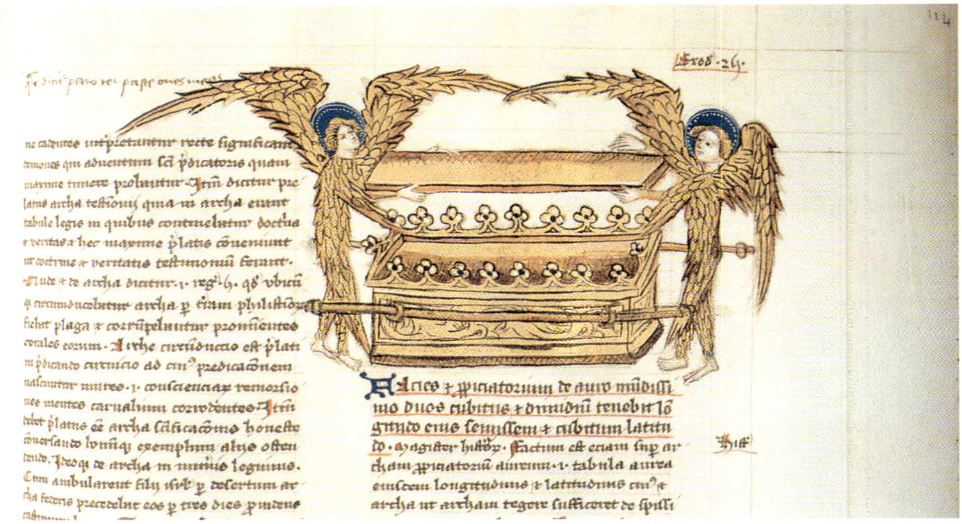

Fig. 24 Oxford, Bodleian Library MS Duke Humfrey b.1, fol. 114 (detail), Ark of the Covenant, Cherubim, and Propitiatory. The Bodleian Library, University of Oxford.

mentary on the Psalms. The second added leaf, fol. 96, has on the recto (fig. 19) images and diagrams for the illustration of 1 Kings by the same artist as fol. 40, yet there is no text of Kings in the Beinecke manuscript. Folio 96 verso has a set of images for Isaiah and is appropriately placed just before the book of Isaiah. These inserted folios were probably made originally for the same purpose as those in MS Laud Misc. 156, the storage of *Postilla* miniatures, but, where there was some sliver of a rationale for inserting fol. 96v before Isaiah, there can have been no reasonable motive beyond prettification for inserting fol. 40 with text and images of Exodus before the Psalms. And it should be said that the Beinecke manuscript was already quite attractive without the two added leaves; it contains highly decorative 'miniatures' that could be described as 'carpet' miniatures, as well as several true scenes (fig. 23).[81]

Because the Laud and Beinecke copies of the *Postilla litteralis* were made at about the same time, around 1430–40, and because the two folios added to Beinecke and the Laud modelbook-images are exceptionally similar in style, it would be useful to try to establish which set of images was made first. To my thinking, the most convincing argument for the chronological order is that MS Beinecke 640 has more images compressed on its two storehouse pages than were placed on pages with the corresponding images in MS Laud Misc. 156. The eleven images, for instance, on one page in Beinecke, fol. 96 (fig. 19), are spread over nearly three pages in Laud, fols 7–8 (figs 20, 21, 22). The Beinecke images are smaller and in one instance the shape of the image (the capital according to Rashi) has been considerably shrunk in order to accommodate it on the page. This reduction in size of the images is also true of the other storehouse page in Beinecke, fol. 40v (fig. 14). This page holds six images, whereas the same six are spread across one and one-half pages in MS Laud Misc. 156, fols 5v–6 (figs 11, 13, 15). It seems to me more likely that the compression of images would indicate that Beinecke was copied economically from Laud and, by the obverse

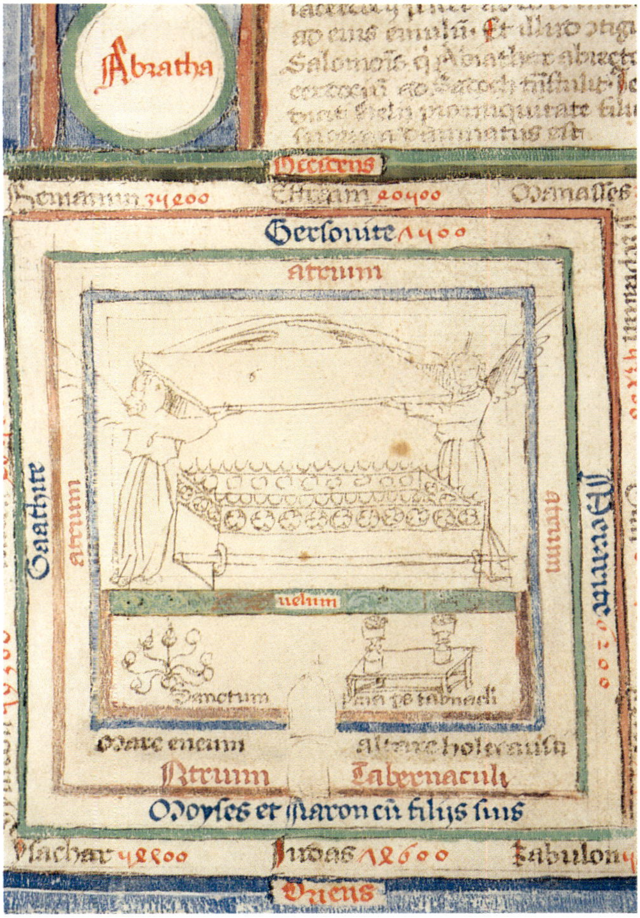

Fig. 25 British Library Additional MS 21219, membrane 3 (detail), (above) diagrammatic plan of Levite tribes with drawings of the Ark of the Covenant, Cherubim, and Propitiatory; (below) Candelabra and Table with Shewbread. The British Library.

token, that the lavish use of space on some of the Laud pages would suggest that it had been designed to be an archetypal exemplar. A more minor point is that the vision of Ezechiel scene in MS Beinecke 640 does not reproduce the circular diagrams in MS Laud Misc. 156, the artist perhaps not choosing to copy them in an incomplete state. Nevertheless, both the Laud modelbook and the Beinecke storage leaves must have been the result of exposure to an earlier English or Continental manuscript, and the Beinecke leaf must have been abstracted for a specific application similar to that intended for the Laud compilation of images.[82]

The scribe of the two added Beinecke leaves is not the only extraneous copyist in the manuscript (see Appendix C).[83] The first part with Psalms 1–150 on fols 1–95 (interleaved with the Exodus text on fol. 40), was written by one hand, whom I call Scribe A, and was decorated by one border artist, Hand A. The second part of Beinecke from fols 97–272 was written by a second scribe, Scribe B, and was decorated by a second border artist, Hand B. Ecclesiastes is missing between the end of Psalms in Part I and the beginning of Isaiah in Part II, and this fact, together with the two stray miniature pages inserted in the first part, is cause to wonder whether the entire first part of ninety-five leaves is not anomalous, if part of a different *Postilla* manuscript that was joined to Scribe B's much longer text. Scribe B's part of MS

Beinecke 640 might therefore be a second volume of one manuscript and the Psalms a separated part of another copy, with no intrinsic relationship between them. Instances of the second volume of the *Postilla litterales* beginning with the book of Psalms are in Oxford, Balliol College MS 171, Bodl. Lib. MS Laud Misc. 152, Lambeth Palace MS 9, and Worcester Cathedral Library MS F.27, probably evidence enough that someone was trying to add a first volume of the *Postilla* text to go with the more complete second part of MS Beinecke 640.

We should look not only at copies of the *Postilla litteralis* for instances of Nicholas of Lyra's pictorial subjects but also at any text whose illustration may have been affected by his cycle of pictures. There are two other noteworthy English fifteenth-century manuscripts that were possibly influenced by Lyra. The first is the exceptional manuscript of John Capgrave's *Commentarius in Exodum* (Bodl. Lib. MS Duke Humfrey b.1), the presentation copy to Humfrey, Duke of Gloucester, which has textual revisions in Capgrave's hand.[84] The composition was completed by 6 May 1440,[85] and the manuscript made about this time. Capgrave's literary output has been described as 'phenomenal',[86] and it is important to recall that Capgrave wrote commentaries 'on most of the books of the Old Testament'.[87] His work on Exodus in the Duke Humfrey copy is illustrated with images[88] that closely resemble those in the Lyra commentaries on Exodus. In particular, one should compare the scenes of the Ark with Propitiatory and Cherubim (figs 1, 24), as well as the boards of the Ark. The Capgrave miniatures are many fewer in number, only ten, than the number of images in the Laud modelbook, and some (fols 114: fig. 24, 118v, 122) are rendered in gold following the biblical descriptions of the illustrated items.[89] The Capgrave images are not by the Laud Misc. 156 artist, nor do they appear to have been copied exactly from the images in that manuscript, but it is worth pointing to the considerable resemblances and to the fact that the Capgrave manuscript was made shortly after the production of the two finely illustrated copies of the *Postilla litteralis* that I have mentioned: Laud Misc. 156 and Beinecke 640. One might even wonder if Capgrave's interest in writing commentaries on the Old Testament had been triggered by the recent production of these exceptional copies.

The second manuscript that shows influence of the standard images in Lyra's *Postilla litteralis super totam Bibliam* is BL Additional MS 21219, the *Compendium historie in genealogia Christi* of Peter of Poitiers. This manuscript of the third or fourth quarter of the fifteenth century is incompletely illustrated with unframed and uncoloured pen drawings, two of which show knowledge of the Lyra sequence: one is an image of the High Priest Aaron (fig. 17), and the other a diagram of the disposition of the Hebrew tribes around the Tabernacle, into the center of which has been added a drawing of the Ark with Propitiatory and Cherubim, with a candelabra and table with Shewbread below (fig. 25). It is likely that all of the drawings were either added or were preparatory sketches, especially the scenes of Adam and Eve (membr. 1) and Moses (membr. 3); and the spaces left for illustration (membrs 4, 5, 7, 8, 9) are also evidence of added or preparatory work. The manuscript concludes, however, with a well drawn *Lignum vite*, one of the frequent subjects in the *Speculum theologie* (see Chapter 4) and one which occurs in MS Laud Misc. 156 (fol. 61).[90] The large initials in Additional MS 21219 are elaborately finished in colours and in a style that suggests the date to be in the latter half of the fifteenth century.

Although there is no evidence for the provenance of MS Beinecke 640, MS Laud Misc. 156 contains evidence of its origin in a religious house in the signature of the scribe '*frater* T.B.' at the end of the Index to the *Postilla litteralis* on fol. 60 (fig. 5),[91] and fol. 5 (fig. 1) bears at the top of the page the following inscription in a fifteenth-century hand, Liber hospitalis s*ancti* joh*anni*s Exon*iensis*.[92] This *ex libris* refers to ownership by the Hospital of St John the Baptist, Exeter, but it is of course not a certain indication that it was produced there.[93] At the bottom of this page a monastic pressmark (in a display script), A.27, is certainly that of the Exeter Hospital.[94] There are similar Exeter inscriptions and shelfmarks in two other surviving manuscripts: BL Additional MS 38129, William of Malmesbury, *De gestis regum Anglorum* and Harley MS 3671, Ranulf Higden, *Polychronicon*.[95] The shelfmarks F.2 and F.7 in these manuscripts indicate a library of considerable size; they suggest 'the existence of several dozen volumes altogether, arranged in at least six chests, cupboards or shelves'.[96] In 1535 the Exeter hospital had an income of over 100 pounds per year and was the 'sole house in the region which could be called large and complex in its activities'.[97] In the first quarter of the fourteenth century the hospital had been given income to support twelve scholars and in 1535 it still supported nine.[98] One use (among others mentioned below) for a manuscript such as MS Laud Misc. 156 may have been as a visual aid in teaching or study.

It is also possible to associate most of the other surviving English copies of the *Postilla litteralis* with religious houses: among these are Durham,[99] Rochester,[100] St Albans,[101] Witham Abbey,[102] and Bury St Edmunds,[103] as well as the cathedral libraries of Hereford and Worcester.[104] Copies were also owned by prominent religious persons: Thomas Langley, bishop of Durham,[105] Richard Colling, Vicar of St Lawrence Jewery,[106] and William Courtney, Archbishop of Canterbury.[107] Various copies are recorded, if not yet identified with surviving manuscripts, as belonging to the Austin Friars of York, the London Franciscans, and to at least four Benedictine houses (see Appendix B, Pt II). Given the accumulation of this and other evidence concerning the ownership and readership of Nicholas of Lyra's *Postilla super totam Bibliam*, I think it virtually certain that the modelbook in MS Laud Misc. 156 was conceived or copied in a well-endowed religious house of some kind rather than in a commercial shop. This production site would seem to have had some on-going special interest in producing illustrated copies of the *Postilla* as well as, apparently, in farming out apparatus for their production. In fact, the Laud manuscript, in spite of its size, may have been expressly made not only as an item to be copied but also to circulate: without a text there would seem to have been little other reason for its production. Evidence for this kind of lending can be found in a copy of the *Postilla litteralis* on the New Testament in the Fisher Library of the University of Sydney, New South Wales (MS Nicholson 1).[108] This manuscript, dated 1436, bears an inscription by the scribe, Robert Makworth, stating that he had received his exemplar from the prior of the Augustinian Priory at Repton.

However, although a function can be posited for such a modelbook, we still must ask why the text and illustrations were not simply kept together and transmitted as a whole? Perhaps by way of response I may refer here to something Ralph Hanna said in another context: 'Exemplar poverty motivates much of the literary record'.[109] What we have in the Laud modelbook may be a *forestalling* of pictorial exemplar poverty.

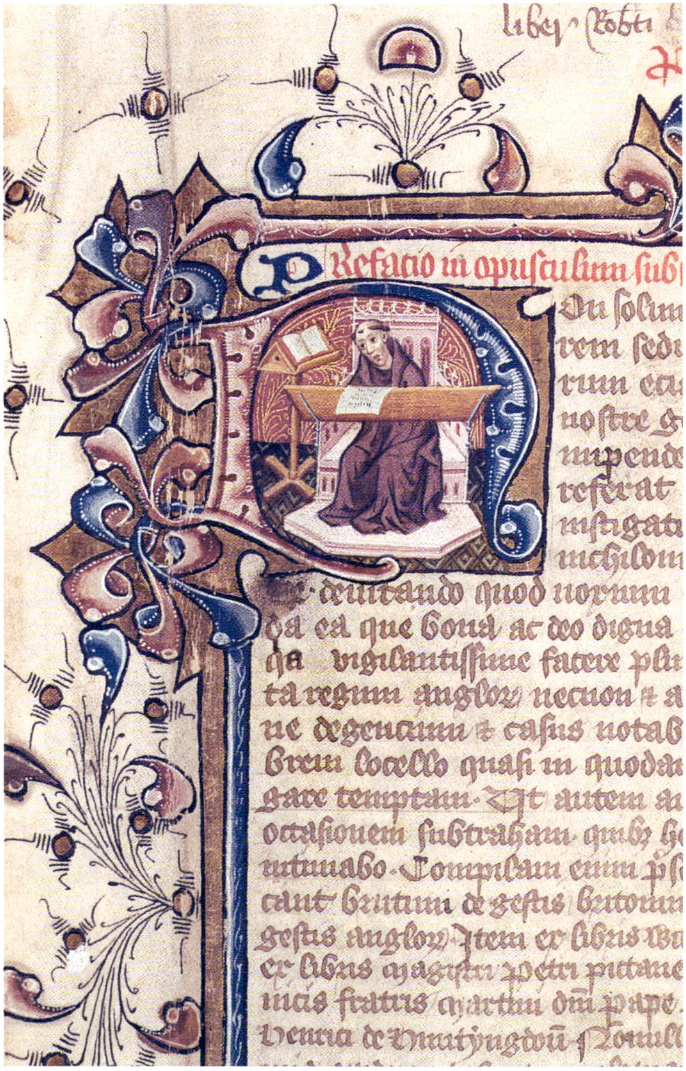

Fig. 26 Oxford, Queen's College, MS 304, fol. 1 (detail), monastic scribe with writing board; lectern with exemplar. The Provost, Fellows and Scholars of the Queen's College Oxford.

The difficult and precise versions of Hebrew and Christian pictorial readings of the Old Testament were evidently stored up against the lack of an illustrated exemplar or the lack of what was perceived to be the correct exemplar. The contemporary shortage of an illustrated exemplar can be demonstrated through the eleven English *Postilla* manuscripts with blanks where the pictures were meant to be (see Appendix B, Pt. I). These illustrations could not be supplied by guesswork, substitution, or local creativity: they were meant to depict exactly how the Hebrews described a Temple capital and how it varied from the Christian version (fig. 22). We have, moreover, witnessed differences in the iconography of the three illustrated *Postilla litteralis*, all presumably perceived to be correct by their makers. It is hard, then, to doubt the necessity of a modelbook for miniatures of such complexity and importance to the text.

It would normally be assumed that illustrations were placed in English medieval manuscript-books either for functional reasons such as emphasis at divisions in a text, locating passages of a text, or for dramatic purposes, for the enjoyment of violent narrative action scenes such as a martyrdom of St Edmund or the self-immolation of Dido.[110] We may even go so far as to assert that illustrations 'intervene to structure particular readings' of the text.[111] Illustrations, together with borders and large initials, do indeed aid the reader in finding his way around larger blocks of text, and there is no doubt that they can provide pleasure or change the balance of the reader's perception of a text. But some medieval authors appreciated that words were not enough to create understanding in a reader, and that some direction had to be given for the illustration of a text in order to understand it. Many examples of this phenomenon can be found in later English manuscripts, and one example in Middle English can be brought forward from BL Harley MS 674 (fols 111v–112): here the anonymous author instructs us that '... the names of þees children ... scholen be knowen by þis figure þat foloweþ'. The figure on the page opposite the text, not the text, transmits the names of Jacob's sons, organized by the relevant wife, and the author obviously believed the chart easier to comprehend than a recitation in his text.

When relationships became too complex or when the subjects described were too obscure or alien for the reader, an author might direct that an image should be made at a certain point in the text as a specific visual aid to the text. This seems to me to go beyond giving instructions to an illuminator and beyond an author supervising the presentation copy of his book:[112] where the author wrote into his text the necessity for an illustration, it was a matter of comprehension not a question of getting the pictorial content right. In such cases an author may state explicitly that a 'figure', by which either a diagram or image could be meant, has preceded or will immediately follow in order to clarify what was just described in words.[113] Peter of Poitiers in his *Compendium historie in genealogia Christi* has the following sentence after a circular table (fig. 18): 'Hec figura valet ad intelligendum quod dicitur in Numeris de disposicione tribuum leuitarum per quatuor climata circa tabernaculum.'[114] And Petrus de Alliaco expressed the following remarkable statement in his *De concordancia theologie et astronomie*: 'Et hec que dicta sunt clarius patent ex subscripta figura.'[115] Here, for the author, the images were implicitly as important as the author's own words.

The difficulty in visualizing musical instruments, especially for some reason, the monochord, is another instance, moderately widespread, where the author states his dependence on an image. Both John of Tewkesbury in the *Quattuor principalia musicae* and, more unexpectedly, Ranulph Higden in the *Polychronicon* have language to address this issue. In the former the phrase used is 'super instrumentum hic figuratur',[116] and in the latter for an illustration often the only one in the manuscript, 'Sicut patet in presenti figura inferius depicta'.[117] An anonymous author in Bodl. Lib. MS Bodley 842, a musical miscellany, uses the following phrase before his delineation of a harp: 'Et sic patent nomina secundum boycium notarum tam per figuram predictam quam eciam per cytheram.'[118] Another anonymous example of the necessity of illustration as an aid to the text is in BL Egerton MS 827, Wyse Book of Phylosophe, fol. 18: 'per istum circulum cognosces naturas elementorum', which occurs before a three-quarter page diagram of the four elements. John of Arderne was also explicit in requiring (and perhaps devising) illustration in his medical writing, especially the *Practica* for fistula-in-ano of 1376 for an 'understanding of the operation itself'.[119] Even 'John Mandeville' felt that he had to sustain his assertion concerning the language of the Caldees with a demonstration of their alphabet: 'And yir er þe figures of þar lettres'.[120] In sum, it is probably fair to say that modern scholars have not adequately emphasized the fact that a medieval author might overtly depend on illustrations for an understanding of his text.[121]

A variation on this theme is Thomas Hoccleve's insistence that a true-to-life portrait of Geoffrey Chaucer accompany his verses of praise to his great mentor. Hoccleve was concerned that Chaucer's image not be forgotten, so 'of his persone I haue here the likenesse do make'. And Hoccleve's personal direction in having Chaucer's portrait painted in his text has influenced our mental image of Chaucer to this day, not to speak of illuminating his stanzas in praise of Chaucer with an image that dramatically complemented his words.

Nicholas of Lyra in the *Postilla litteralis* took the notion of requiring and emphasizing illustrations even further. He not only wrote commentaries on the difficult passages of Exodus, Kings and Isaiah, and brought together later conflicting versions of them, but he also made allowance verbally and spatially within the text for the inclusion of numerous miniatures and diagrams. Various examples will demonstrate Lyra's determination to make his point through images. The Worcester Cathedral Library manuscript F.26 states (before a blank space): '... ad hoc facilius intelligendum ponitur hic figura' (fol. 181v); CUL MS Dd.7.7, before two versions of the Ark with propitiatory: '... oportet quod ymanginacio inspicientis suppleat illud quod non potest figurari hoc modo' (fol. 78v); Peterhouse MS 19, before the Brazen Sea: 'Figura maris enei secundum Josephum & supleatur bones per ymaginaciones sufficit enim quod descripti sunt in prima figura' (fol. 163); CUL MS Dd.7.9, before a third variation of the Altar of the Holocaust: 'Sciendum tamen quod cum altare sit quadrum equilaturm non potest totum figurari in plano. Sed unum satus tamen alia vero tria sunt per ymanginacionem inspicientis supplenda' (fol. 157v); and MS Beinecke 640, before the vision of Ezekiel, 'Ad facilius capiendum praedictam visionem ymanginariam posui his figuras praedictorum secundum descripcionem latinorum & eciam hebreorum. Sciendum tamen predicta non possunt sufficientur in plano describi sed oportet per ymanginacionem inspicientis multa supleri' (fol. 175v). Not Lyra's own words of commentary, those of other authors, or those of the Bible could do justice to the plans, measurements, architecture and implements of the Temple, and illustrations had to be included in order to clarify the imagery of obscure items as well as the contradictory interpretations of earlier commentators. It is even more extraordinary that Nicholas of Lyra also states repeatedly in his text that the reader should supply or supplement through his imagination those things that cannot be adequately written or pictured; the phrase occurs three times alone on fol. 8 of MS Laud Misc. 156 (fig. 22). Even the pictures had to be 'suppliatur per imaginacionem',[122] and Lyra also refers, at various places, both to his own use or to an artist's use of the imagination.[123] Lyra's statements are an implicit judgment on both text and illustration, on their deficiencies in communcicating information, and it is the reader who in *his* mind composes the final version of the biblical text. The intensity, moreover, with which fifteenth-century makers of the *Postilla* copied, decorated and illustrated the commentary, leaves no doubt as to the reception of Nicholas of Lyra's 'imaginary' illustrations.

CHAPTER II

The Enigma of All Souls 10

CERTAINLY the most mysterious of the manuscripts described here is a New Testament in the collection of All Souls Library, Oxford, MS 10. This book was produced in England, probably between 1415 and 1430 and probably in London. It is the work of two scribes following the same exemplar,[124] a late fourteenth-century French version of the New Testament. This version combined part of the Old French Bible of the thirteenth century with the fourteenth-century *Bible historiale* of Guiart des Moulins: this text was, itself, a French translation of a twelfth-century University text book, the *Historia scholastica* of Peter Comestor.[125] This composite Bible was later named the *Bible historiale complétée* by the nineteenth-century scholar, Samuel Berger.[126] It was usually copied in two volumes, Genesis to Esther from the *Bible historiale* and Proverbs to Apocalypse from the Old French Bible.[127] The text surviving in All Souls MS 10 was frequently part of a second volume and is possibly all that survives of a two-volume set of the full *Bible historiale complétée*.

The manuscript is of parchment, i + 204 medieval folios of 294 × *c.* 201 mm at fol. 57. The text space is laid out in two columns of thirty-nine lines, with ruling in lavender. Titles, running titles, incipits and explicits are in red, and the text is further decorated at chapter with one-line blue and gold paragraph signs with red and blue flourishing, with blue or blue and gold line endings, and with two-line champ initials, i.e. gold letters on a rose/blue ground with sprays of green feathering and gold motifs. At the table of chapters and at prologues, there are three- and four-line coloured letters infilled with a monochrome motif on a gold ground, with sprays containing gold and coloured motifs.[128] At book divisions there are three-sided borders with sprays having gold and coloured motifs (fig. 27).[129] The same artist worked throughout on the borders, with a change of design and care at fol. 181v; this artist also made the spray initials.

Where might the French exemplar for All Souls 10 have come from? And who in England in the fifteenth century would require a fourteenth-century French version of the Bible, when there were plentiful Vulgate and Wycliffite versions available?[130] The All Souls text is, however, embedded in an undeniably English decorative setting (fig. 27) – line endings, small initials, spray initials, borderwork and miniatures, despite the fact that the scripts of both scribes show French influence.[131] Clive R. Sneddon, the authority on medieval French Bibles, has confirmed that there are no other copies, either of the Old French Bible or of the *Bible historiale complétée,* like All Souls MS 10 surviving from the fifteenth century in England; the All Souls manuscript is in fact 'unique in having been written in England'.[132] The manuscript was clearly made under special circumstances and for a very particular reason.

Malcolm Parkes has suggested that the second scribe of BL Royal MS 19.B.xvi, *Le mirouer des dames*, dated 1428,[133] might be Doal, the second scribe of All Souls 10

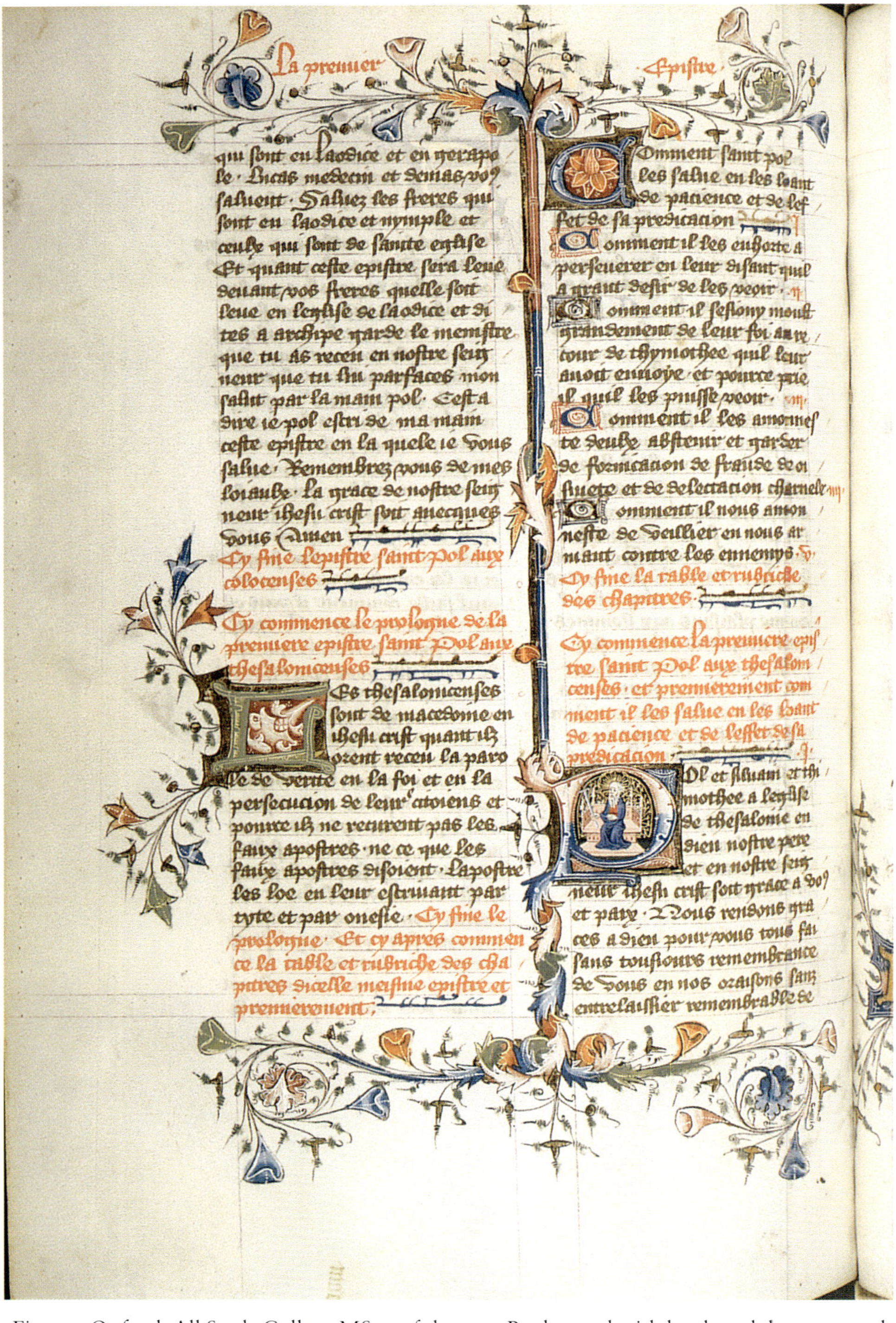

Fig. 27 Oxford, All Souls College MS 10, fol. 140v, Paul seated with book and down-turned sword; mid-column border. The Warden and Fellows of All Souls College, Oxford.

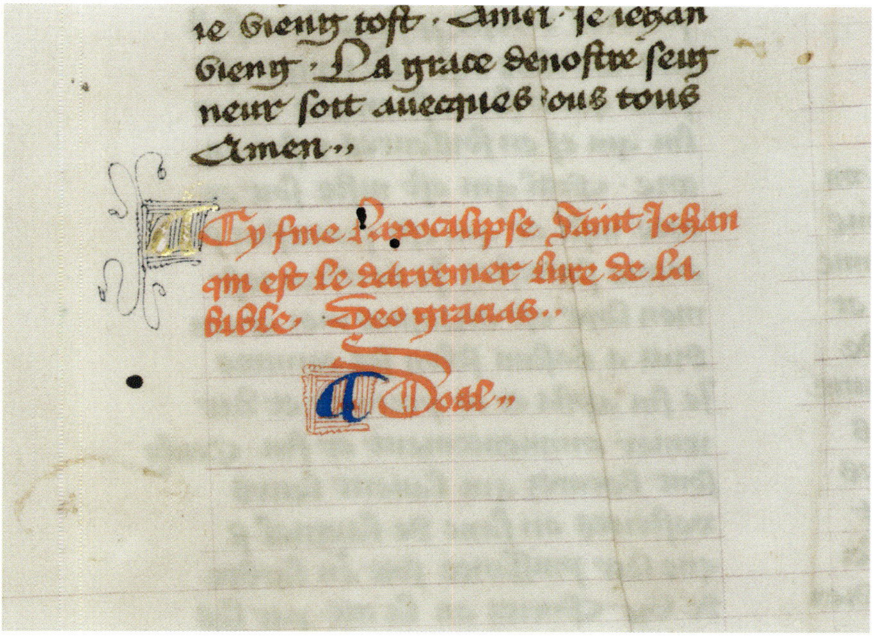

Fig. 28 Oxford, All Souls College MS 10, fol. 204v (detail), script and signature of scribe, Doal. The Warden and Fellows of All Souls College, Oxford.

(fig. 28). Although, according to Parkes, the handwriting in Royal is less formal than in MS 10, the minim strokes and stems of other letters are close to the vertical, and the ratio of pen-width to minim height is the same. The same distinctive scribal practices appear in both manuscripts: 1) the letter **l** traced with a broken stroke at the base of the stem and with a curved hook at the top of the ascender, especially at the beginning of words; 2) the letter **g** with a horizontal stroke which closes the lobe and connects with the following letter; and 3) the letter **b** with a large lobe.[134] The flourishwork initials in this manuscript are French work, and this suggests that, if the hand is Doal, he was working in France when the manuscript was made. I am not convinced that this scribal hand is Doal because I see several consistent differences that make the identification doubtful.[135]

The identity of the artist of the sixteen historiated initials (see Appendix D) in All Souls 10 is less mysterious than the questions surrounding the selection of this French text for production in an English shop. His work or his direct influence on other artists is known in a half-dozen other manuscripts. He was an important artistic presence on the English limning scene of the first and the second quarters of the fifteenth century, having patrons of noble and possibly royal status. Leaving aside the illustration of books of Hours and Missals, the artist's work in the All Souls manuscript contains an assemblage of favourite English pictorial subjects of the period, but these are presented with considerable differences from standard English iconography. It will be the task of this study to examine these iconographic variations and to demonstrate the implications for ownership of both text and miniatures.

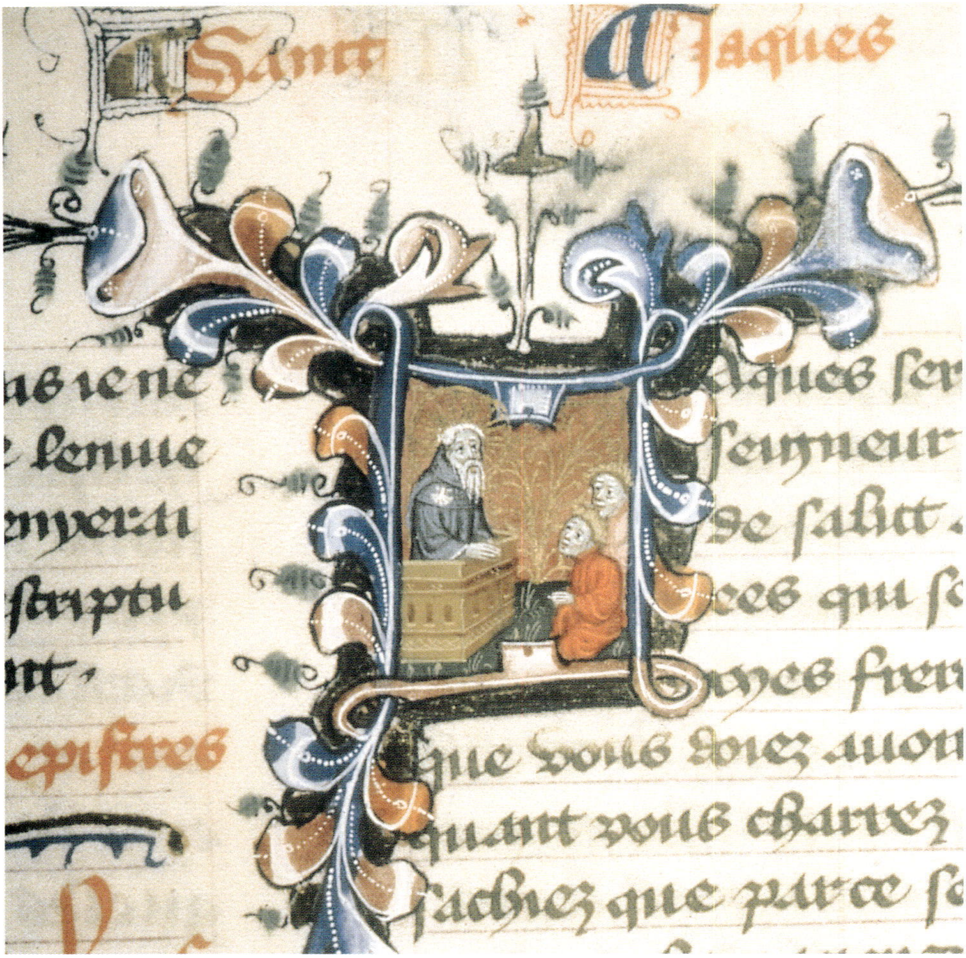

Fig. 29 Oxford, All Souls College MS 10, fol. 181v James the Greater in pulpit, preaching to seated young men. The Warden and Fellows of All Souls College, Oxford.

According to Samuel Berger,[136] MS 10 belongs to a textual group of eleven manuscripts of the *Bible historiale complétée*, all French in origin, and all of the late fourteenth or early fifteenth centuries. Nine of the copies can be dismissed immediately as not relevant to All Souls 10 because they contain a version of the Psalter, of Jean de Blois, not in MS 10. Otherwise, the text in All Souls is nearly identical to Bibliothèque nationale de France MSS français 3 and 4, a two-volume *Bible historiale* of the late fourteenth to fifteenth centuries.[137] MS fr. 3 has ninety miniatures and fr. 4 sixty-three, whereas All Souls MS 10 survives with only sixteen historiated initials, and with twelve or thirteen more perhaps once present on ten excised pages. The All Souls manuscript would thus have had about thirty fewer than the BnF manuscript of the New Testament (fr. 4). The subjects of the Paris miniatures are related to those of All Souls MS 10 (fig. 29) only by broad iconographic strokes, as

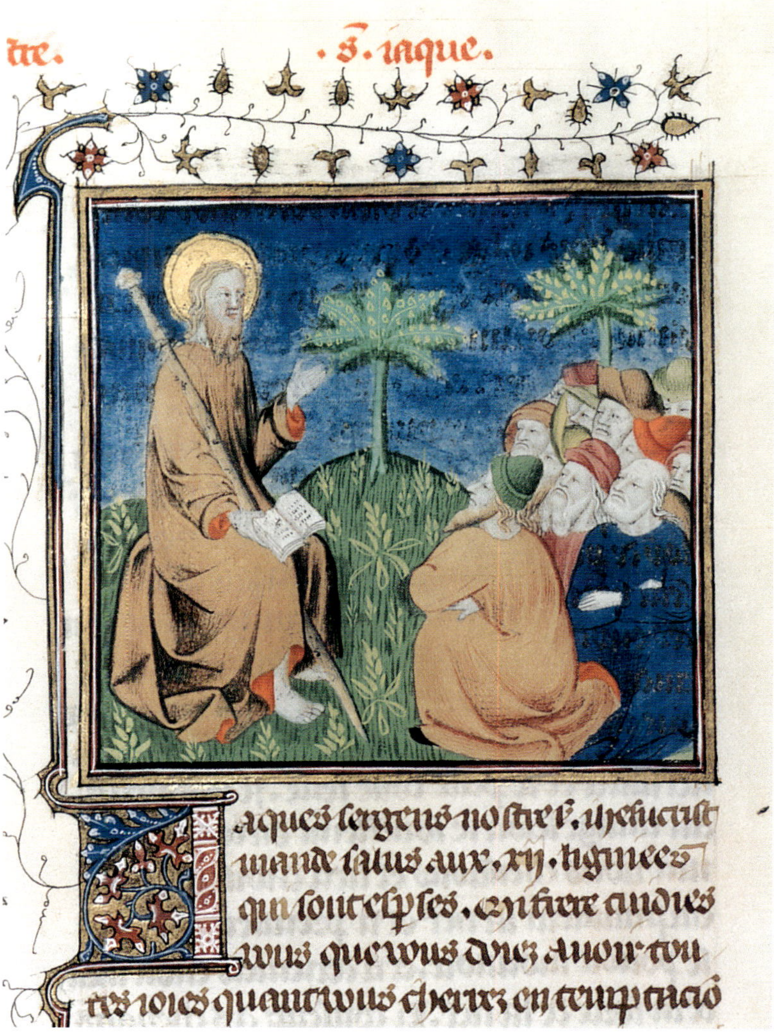

Fig. 30 Paris, Bibliothèque Nationale MS français 4, fol. 248v (detail), James with open book, preaching to a group of seated men. Bibliothèque nationale de France.

is obvious by comparison with the miniature of St James in BnF MS fr. 4 (fig. 30). But even tangential relationships will come to be seen as an influence on the All Souls manuscript.

Before conducting a search of French Bibles, it was first necessary to examine English-made Bibles approximately contemporary with All Souls MS 10 for a source of the illustrations, but there was little cheer. Only two English Bibles of the later period have an extensive series of illustrations: one is BL Royal MS 1.E.ix, the Vulgate 'Big Bible' of around 1410, which has 143 historiated initials.[138] Unfortunately, the scenes in the Big Bible have no relationship at all to the All Souls initials; they concern either biblical stories depicted in single or multiple narrative scenes or the author of the prologues, Saint Jerome. Another fine English Bible, a Wycliffite translation of the last decade of the fourteenth century, in the Herzog-August-Bibliothek, Wolfenbüttel, Germany, Cod. Guelf.A.2 Aug.20, belonged to Thomas of Lancaster (d. 1421), son of Henry IV.[139] This copy has historiated initials, some of whose subjects depict half-

and full figures of the Apostles; but it seems nevertheless not to have any compelling iconographic connection with the All Souls miniatures, possibly partly because of its location in a royal library.

The only other illustrated English Bibles of this period are also Wycliffite. One, CUL MS Dd.1.27, of *c.* 1450, has a series of small roundels of narrative scenes of the Creation on the first leaf;[140] and the other, BL Royal MS 1.C.viii,[141] of the late fourteenth century, has only one miniature, oddly alone at the opening of the gospel for John (fol. 325v). The first leaf of this book was replaced in the late fifteenth century by one decorated with a contemporary border and the arms of Henry VII; the original first leaf might, then, have had an introductory biblical miniature – but the design of the book would still be odd. Having mentioned these Wycliffite Bibles, it should be noted that Wycliffite production is the most important context – or anti-context – for All Souls MS 10, in that the widespread use and production of Wycliffite versions far outnumbers that of any other Bible in late medieval England, and that the (as-a-rule) unillustrated Wycliffite Bibles in English cast into clearer relief the oddity of the illustrated All Souls manuscript in French. The over 250 surviving copies of Wycliffite translations of the Bible are notable – while often nicely decorated with illuminated or flourishwork borders – for their lack of illustration.

The closest to a context for All Souls MS 10, as far as similarity in production is concerned, would be a *Histoire de la Bible*, a narrative 'of an unusual type ... more like a chronicle than like an abridged Bible',[142] in Boston, MA, Public Library MS 1482. Like All Souls MS 10, the Boston manuscript is written in French by an English scribe and decorated with (seventeen) historiated initials,[143] secondary illuminated initials with sprays, flourished initials, and line endings by English limners (fig. 31). The scribe, artists and border artist are not those of All Souls MS 10, but the illustrator of the historiated initials and the artist of the secondary initials can be identified as a limner who worked on BL Additional MS 50001, the Hours of Elizabeth the Queen.[144] The date of the Boston manuscript would then be 1420–1430, the same approximate time of the making of All Souls 10; like All Souls 10, the original owner of the book is not known – though surely a person of means and of similar interests as the patron of All Souls MS 10.

So, if there is little or no contemporary English context for the biblical miniatures of All Souls, it is at least possible to demonstrate that their subject matter is not unusual when used within other texts in English manuscripts. Some fifteen of the sixteen surviving pictorial subjects are relatively common in English book illustration of the fifteenth century, but the iconography of the All Souls subjects does not correspond to standard English iconography for the same subjects. Those subjects used three or four times in All Souls MS 10 are authorial writing, reading and preaching scenes; each was an important item in the English limner's repertoire, being often designated for the head of a text and frequently the only miniature in a manuscript. But, as we have seen, this selection of subjects is not found in the two surviving English Bibles of the period, and now we shall also see that the manner in which these English scenes are rendered is uncommon.

In order to demonstrate how the extraordinary iconography shows itself in ordinary subjects, I begin with the All Souls miniatures of writing scenes. The image of Mark (fig. 32) depicts the author as a cleric seated at a writing board supported by

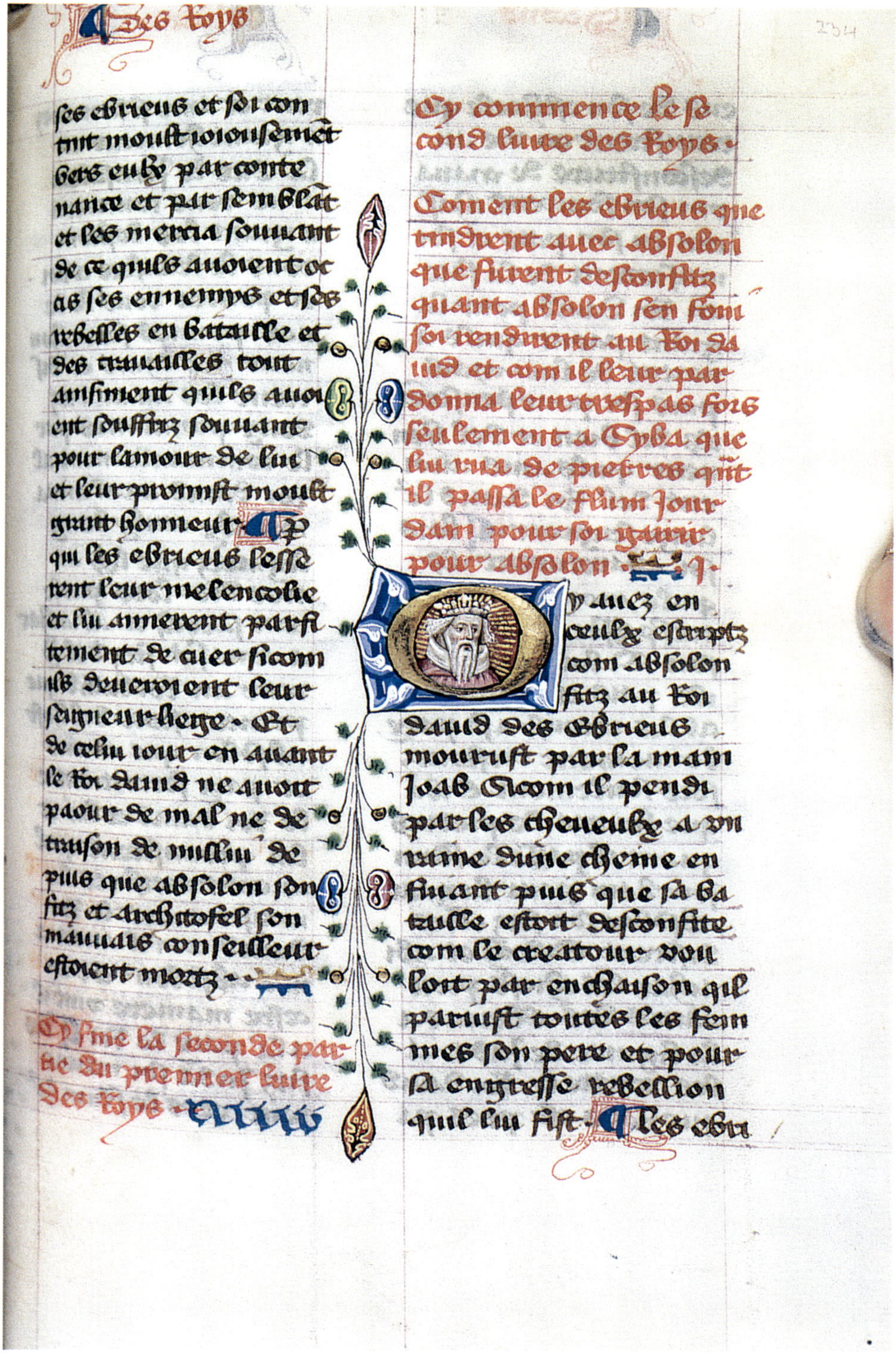

Des Roys

234

ses ebrieus et si con
tint moult ioiousemēt
vers euls par conte
nance et par semblāt
et les merci a souuant
de ce quils auoient oc
cis ses ennemys et ses
rebelles en bataille et
des trauailles tout
ainsiment quils auoi
ent souffirz souuant
pour lamour de lui
et leur promist moult
grant honneur ¶ P
qui les ebrieus lesse
rent leur melencolie
et lui amerent parfi
tement de cuer sicom
ils deueroient leur
seigneur liege. Et
de celui iour en auant
le Roi dauid ne auoit
paour de mal ne de
traison de nullui de
puis que absolon son
filz et architofel son
mauuais conseilleur
estoient mortz..

Cy fine la seconde par
tie du premier liure
des roys.

Cy commence le se
cond liure des Roys.

Coment les ebrieus que
tindrent auec absolon
que furent desconfitz
quant absolon sen fui
si vendrent au Roi da
uid et com il leur par
donna leur trespas fors
seulement a Syba que
lui rua de pierres quāt
il passa le flum Jour
dain pour soi garir
pour absolon. ¶ J

ly auez en
ceulx escriptz
com absolon
fitz au Roi
dauid des ebrieus
mourust par la main
Joab. Et com il pendi
par les cheuuls a vn
raime dune cheine en
fuiant puis que sa ba
taille estoit desconfite
com le creatour vou
loit par enchaison qil
pariust toutes les fem
mes son pere et pour
sa engresse rebellion
quil lui fist. ¶ Les ebri

Fig. 31 Boston, Public Library MS 1482, fol. 234, bust of king in spray initial. Boston Public Library/Rare Books Department. Courtesy of the Trustees.

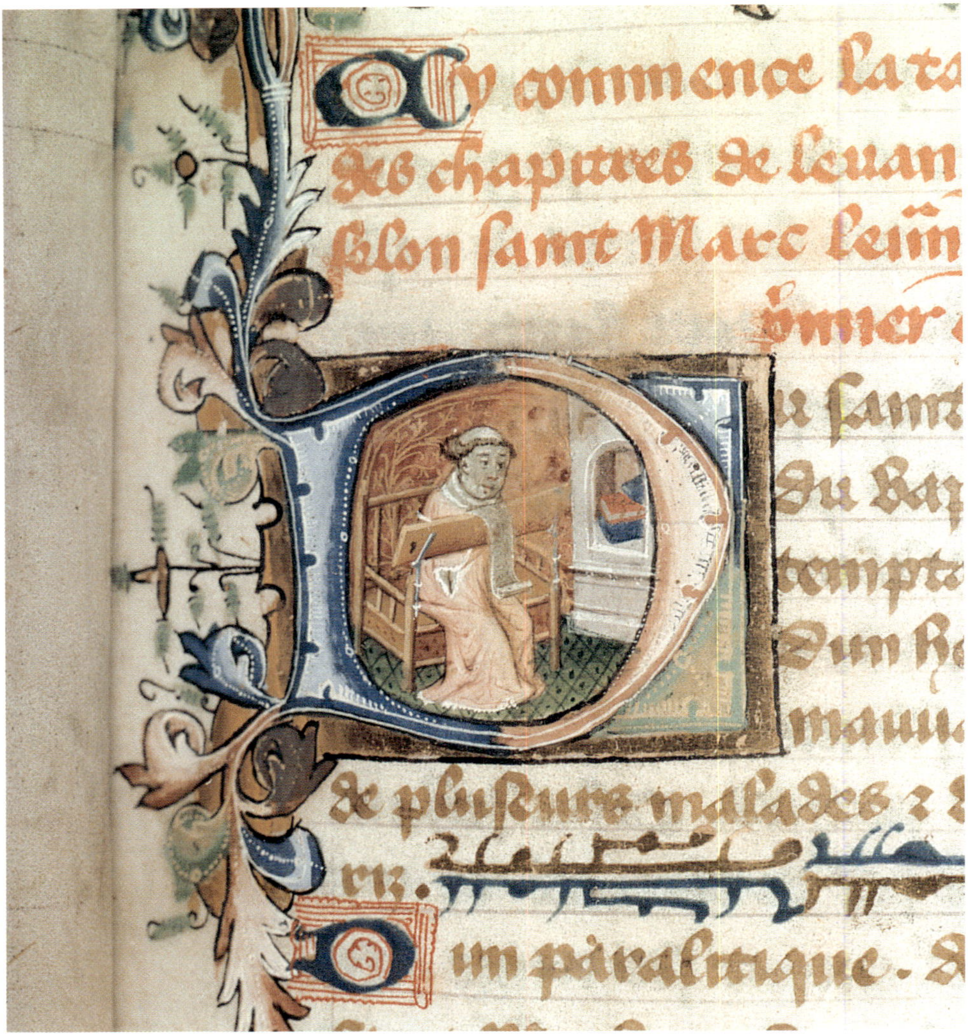

Fig. 32 Oxford, All Souls College MS 10, fol. 2 (detail), Mark as cleric, writing. The Warden and Fellows of All Souls College, Oxford.

brackets that slot into rings attached to the chair, with a single sheet hanging over the board, a pole-backed wooden chair, a pen holder on the rear of the board. The scene is realistic in intent as a description of one contemporary manner of writing and is a scene similar to others in contemporary English book art.[145] The miniature of Luke either writing or reading (fig. 33), in contrast, is wholly unrealistic and unlike most other English representations. Apart from reporter-scribes, such as in Bodl. Lib. MS Rawlinson A.386 (fol. 83),[146] authors are not shown sitting on the ground, nor were symbolic creatures used as their writing support. The scene of Luke is not ordinary but no source for it is known, whereas the image of Mark is what can be acknowledged as representative of the English author-writing scenes that were current throughout the

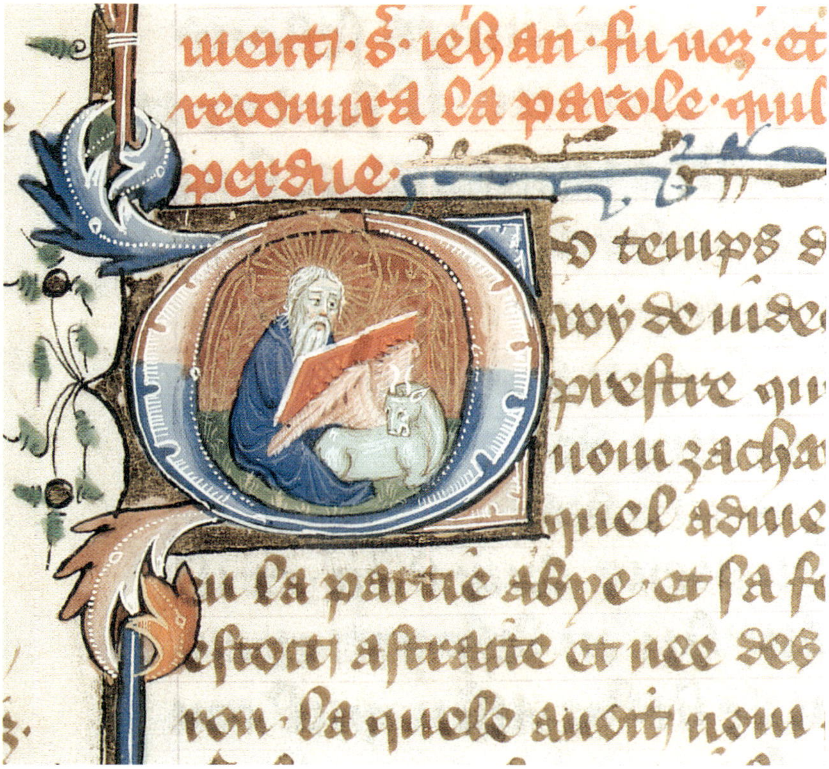

Fig. 33 Oxford, All Souls College MS 10, fol. 49 (detail), Luke reading or writing. The Warden and Fellows of All Souls College, Oxford.

century, nearly a hundred of such scenes having been recognized to date.[147]

Reading scenes were apparently of somewhat less importance for the late medieval English artist and his patron, and I have found that such scenes were depicted mainly by three artists working in England in the fifteenth century. The illustrator of All Souls 10 made four such scenes in the manuscript, two of them with an interesting variation. The two conventional scenes are those of Paul (fig. 34) and of Simon Peter (fig. 35); each is depicted as seated on a stone bench, the former obviously reading, the latter either paused in reading or farsighted. The second artist who seems to have delighted in portraying persons reading was the Caesar Master, an Italian illustrator who worked in England around 1450[148] and who scattered his borders and initials with half-figures of readers (fig. 36). The third artist who specialized in this theme was probably a monk of Glastonbury, who was active around 1405 and who worked together with a fellow monk and scribe, John Merylynch.[149] Several of the historiated initials from the Glastonbury chronicles in Queen's College, Oxford, MS 304, show readers who went at the task with considerable intensity – though I doubt that the monk illustrated in fig. 37 bedded down every night in such canopied comfort.

Apart from miniatures by these three artists, only a few other reading scenes survive in English book art: among these are St Jerome in BL Royal MS I.B.ix (fol. 230);[150] an

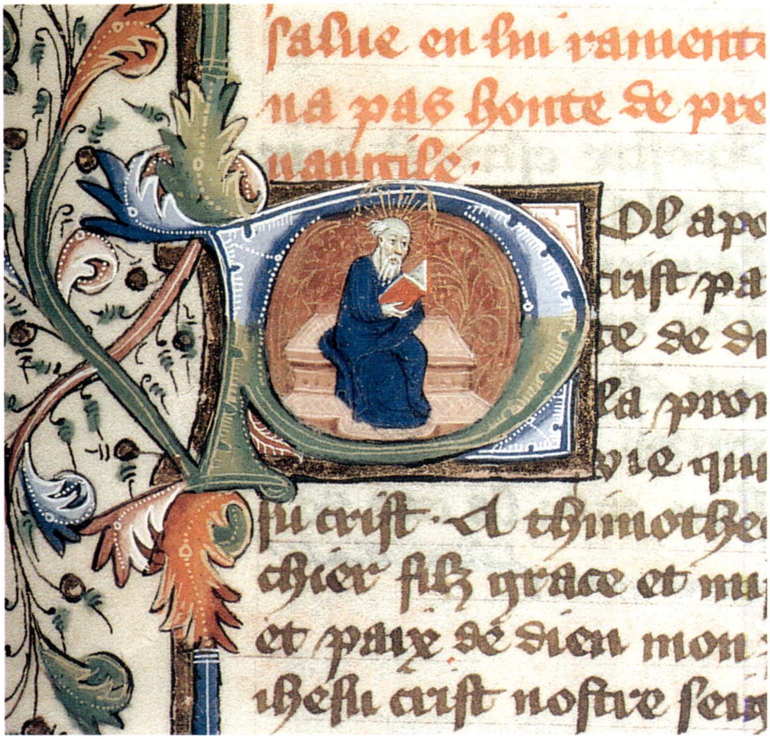

Fig. 34 Oxford, All Souls College MS 10, fol. 145v (detail), Paul reading.
The Warden and Fellows of All Souls College, Oxford.

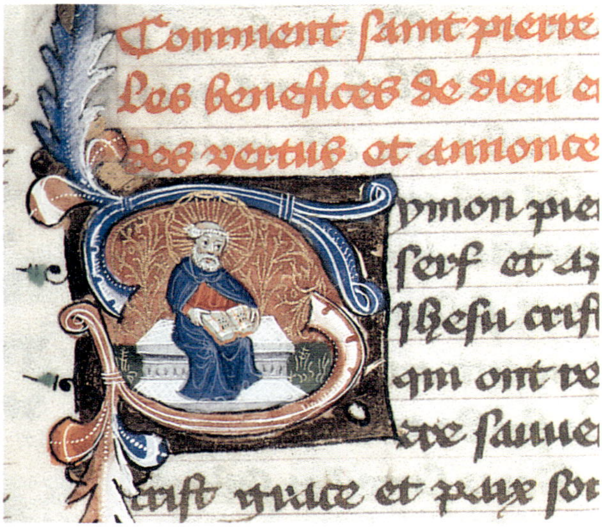

Fig. 35 Oxford, All Souls College MS 10, fol. 186v (detail), Simon Peter, ?reading.
The Warden and Fellows of All Souls College, Oxford.

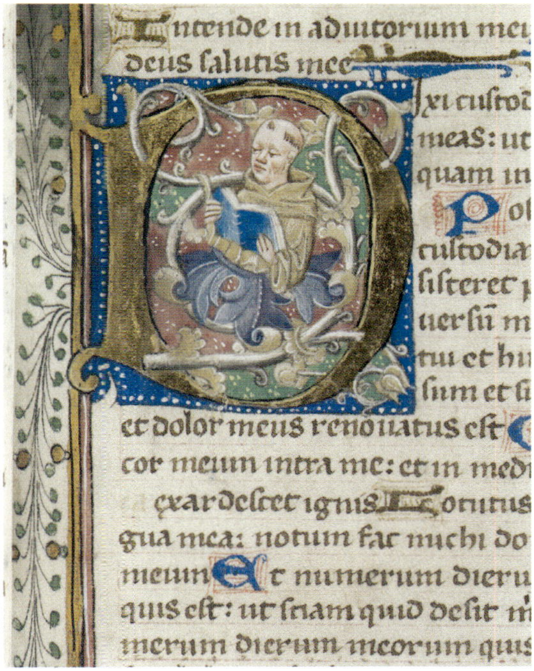

Fig. 36 Oxford, Bodleian Library MS Lat.liturg.e.48, page 59 (detail), monk reading. The Bodleian Library, University of Oxford.

apostle in Bodl. Lib. MS Digby 227, Missal (fol. 207v); a prophet with open book in Oxford, Brasenose College MS 16, Psalter (fol. 2); and the miniature of an abbot standing at an open cupboard in BL Cotton MS Claudius E.iv, *Gesta abbatum monasterii Sancti Albani* (fig. 38), as well as several other similar scenes of an abbot seated or standing, reading or writing.[151] The scene of a reader walking with his guardian angel (BR MS IV.1095, Hours, fol. 27v) is particularly charming.[152] Thus far, all the miniatures that I have mentioned are of a solitary reader rapt in the words on the page before him. The scenes show a private experience, and one during which the reader might pause to contemplate.

Yet, when we come to the two unconventional miniatures of readers in All Souls MS 10, the depiction shows a different kind of experience. In the later Middle Ages reading could also be spoken and communal in nature, indeed was probably more often than not a social practice, and in the All Souls initial of Saint Paul, the saint is shown apparently reading aloud to a young man kneeling at his feet (fig. 39). Although they do not look directly at each other, reader and listener cannot help but be aware of each other; here the act of reading is shared, if only between two people. The subject is quite rare in English book illustration of the period: I know in fact of only three or four other scenes that might be construed as one person reading to another. The first is a tête-à-tête scene from Peter of Herenthal's Commentary on the Psalter in St John's College, Oxford, MS 14 (fol. 1), late fourteenth century, a bishop with a cleric, both grasping an open book between them, the bishop by his gesture and the scroll, even though blank, indicating that he is speaking and very probably reading from the book.[153] Probably the best representation of communal reading that survives

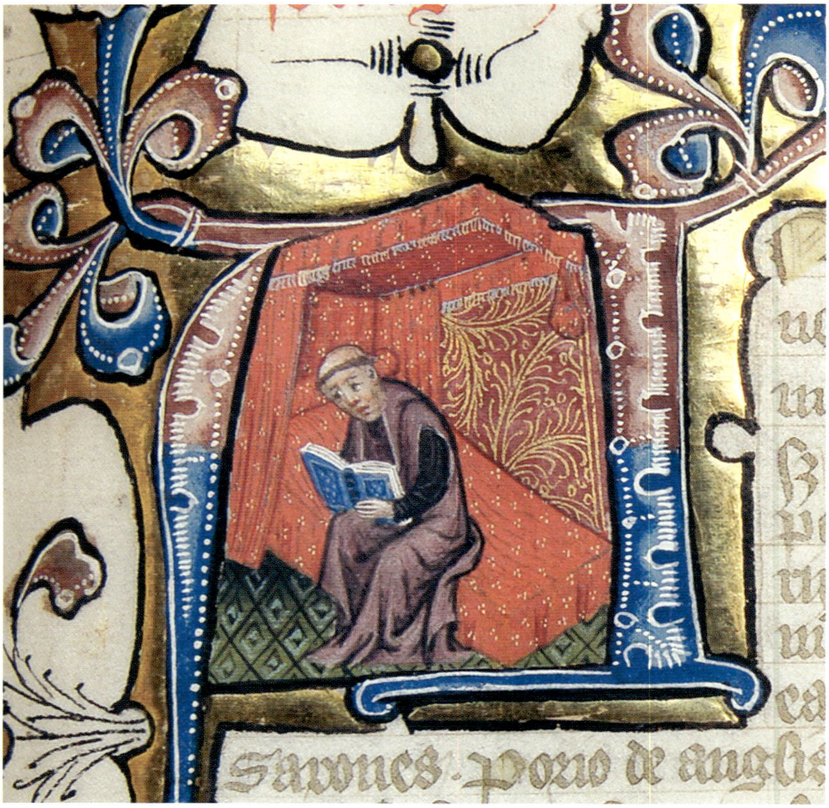

Fig. 37 Oxford, Queen's College MS 304, fol. 49 (detail), monk reading on canopied bed. The Provost, Fellows and Scholars of the Queen's College Oxford.

in an English manuscript is the historiated initial in London, Lambeth Palace MS 69 (fol. 1), *c.* 1410, of Archbishop Chichele instructing his clerics from an open book.[154] The third scene of this type is in CUL MS Dd.9.18 (fol. 45v), *c.* 1460, showing figures in university dress, including Aristotle with an open book, apparently reading to two students.[155] Although couched in differing pictorial languages, these miniatures of a person reading record a societal experience more common in the Middle Ages than it is today.

The illustration for the book of Acts in All Souls MS 10 shows the second unconventional reading scene (fig. 40). In this initial an Apostle is seated on the ground, reading in the midst of the entire assemblage of Apostles, if looking a bit sheepish about it. Because the scene shows the Virgin Mary as well, it may have been adapted from an English Pentecost scene, where the Virgin often appears,[156] or it may have come from a French model: a Pentecost miniature also appears at the beginning of Acts in the *Bibles historiales complétées.*[157] I am, however, reasonably certain that there is no other such scene with a seated, reading Apostle in an English illustration of the Pentecost produced in the fifteenth century. An Apostle may be depicted seated on a bench,[158] but he is not distracted from the main event. However, the French scene in

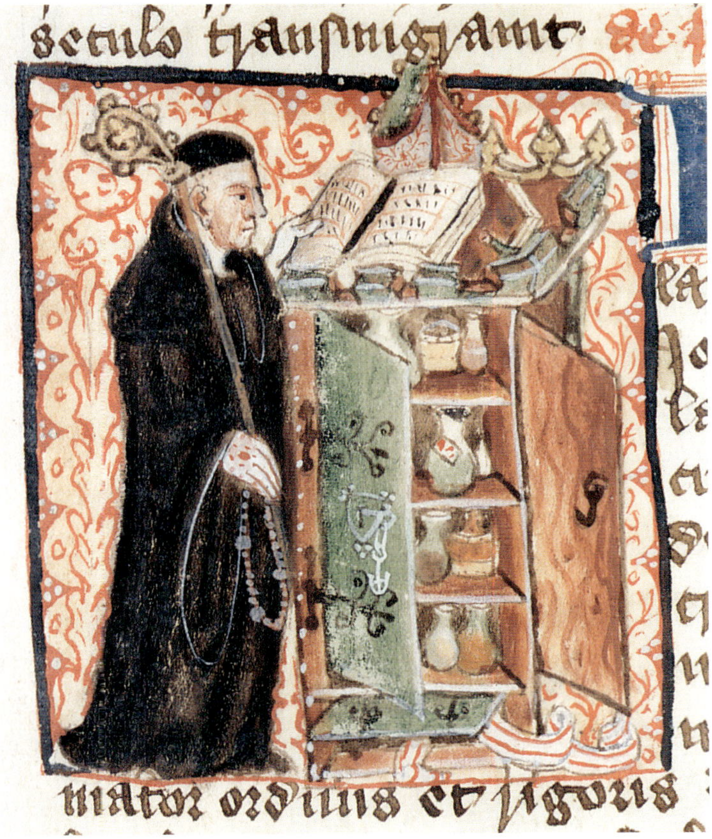

Fig. 38 British Library Cotton MS Claudius E.iv, fol. 129v (detail), Abbot Johannes de Cella with crosier, standing at open cupboard, reading from slanted top. The British Library.

BnF MS fr. 10, *Bible historiale*[159] (fig. 41), shows an Apostle in the left of the scene, holding a book and not really paying attention. I take this figure as a hint at a non-English, presumably French, source of this All Souls miniature.

The next pictorial subject from All Souls MS 10 to examine briefly is the preaching scene, a subject relatively common in English book art. The scene occurs twice in the All Souls manuscript, and both iconographies are unique in English book illustration. One shows a bearded, haloed man in a pulpit, speaking to several men seated on the ground (fig. 42), a scene which is meant as a visual introduction to Paul's Epistle to the Hebrews. Here the standard form for preaching iconography in England in the fifteenth century is depicted, a figure in a pulpit with a few people listening. It is, nevertheless, *not* standard to depict an *Apostle* in a pulpit, though many other medieval characters were so depicted: friars (Bodl. Lib. MS Laud Misc. 740, fol. 20);[160] a bishop with a glamourous audience (BL Royal MS 8.G.iii, fol. 2);[161] priests (Hatfield House, MS Cecil Papers 300, fol. 70v); monks (Durham, University Library MS Cosin.V.III.5, fol. 1); academic doctors (BL Stowe MS 39, fol. 10v); John the Baptist (BL Additional MS 29704–5, fol. 136v);[162] and, not least, Christ (Göttingen, Universitätsbibliothek, Cod. theol.107r, fol. 93v). These figures are all shown in a pulpit, but not, as already noted, an Apostle. It is, however, not uncommon to find

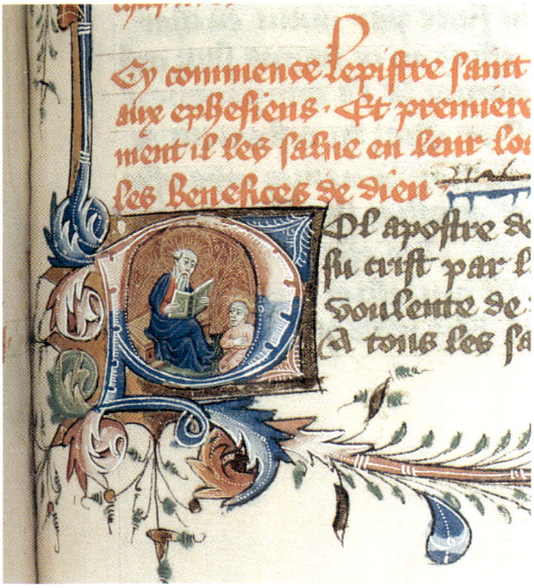

Fig. 39 Oxford, All Souls MS 10, fol. 134 (detail), Saint Paul reading to young man. The Warden and Fellows of All Souls College, Oxford.

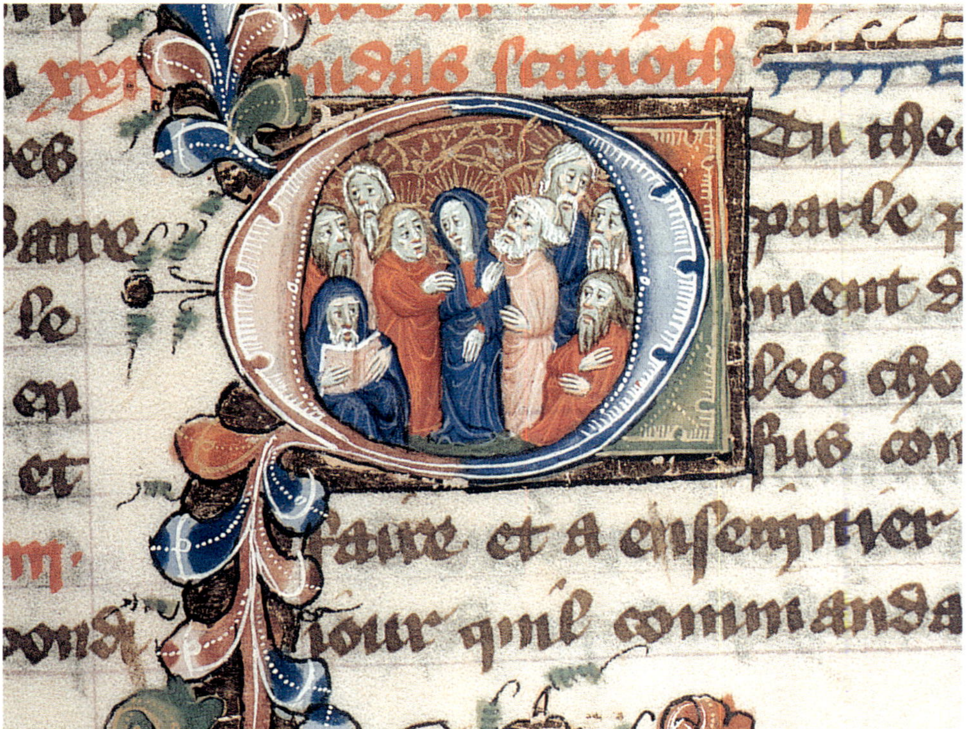

Fig. 40 Oxford, All Souls College MS 10, fol. 156 (detail), Pentecost, with seated Apostle reading. The Warden and Fellows of All Souls College, Oxford.

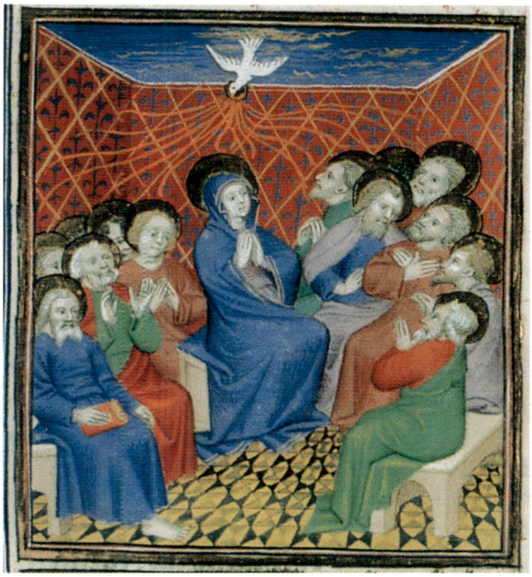

Fig. 41 Paris, Bibliothèque Nationale MS français 10, fol. 572 (detail), Pentecost, with Apostle holding book. Bibliothèque nationale de France.

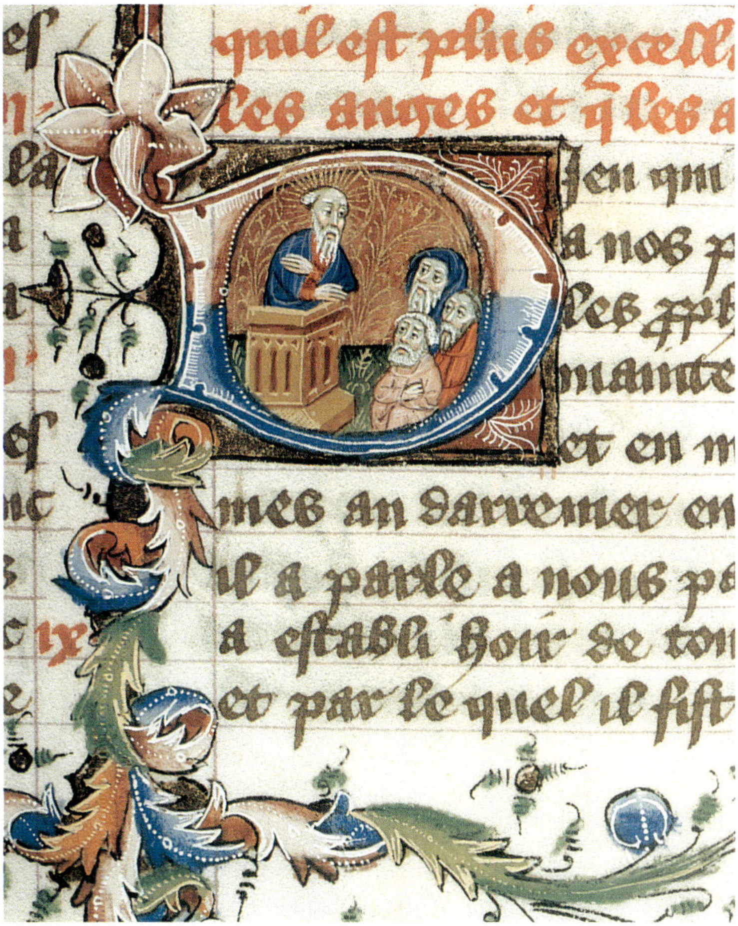

Fig. 42 Oxford, All Souls College MS 10, fol. 147v (detail), Saint Paul in pulpit, speaking to seated men. The Warden and Fellows of All Souls College, Oxford.

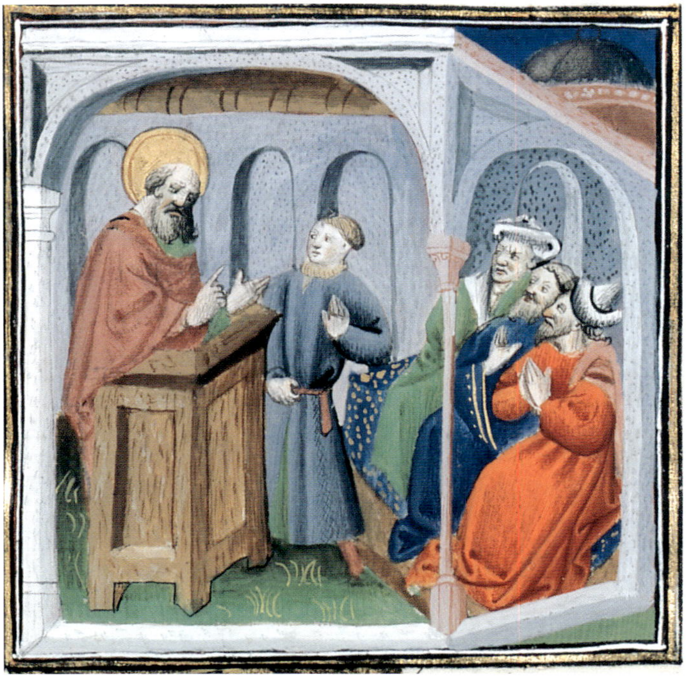

Fig. 43 Paris, Bibliothèque Nationale MS français 20088, *Bible historiale*, fol. 548 (detail), Saint Paul preaching. Bibliothèque nationale de France.

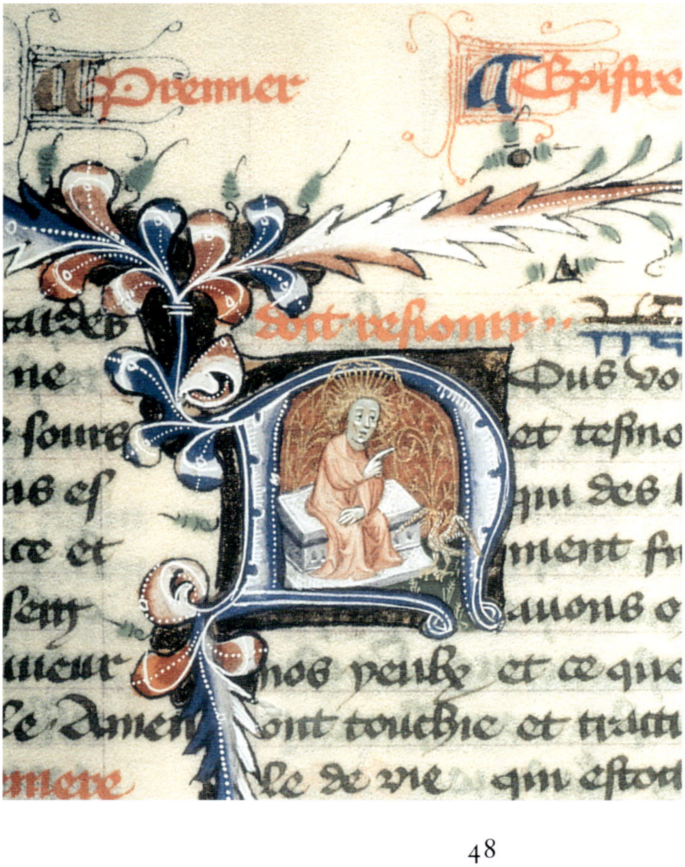

Fig. 44 Oxford, All Souls MS 10, fol. 188v (detail), Saint John the Evangelist seated, pointing, with eagle beside. The Warden and Fellows of All Souls College, Oxford.

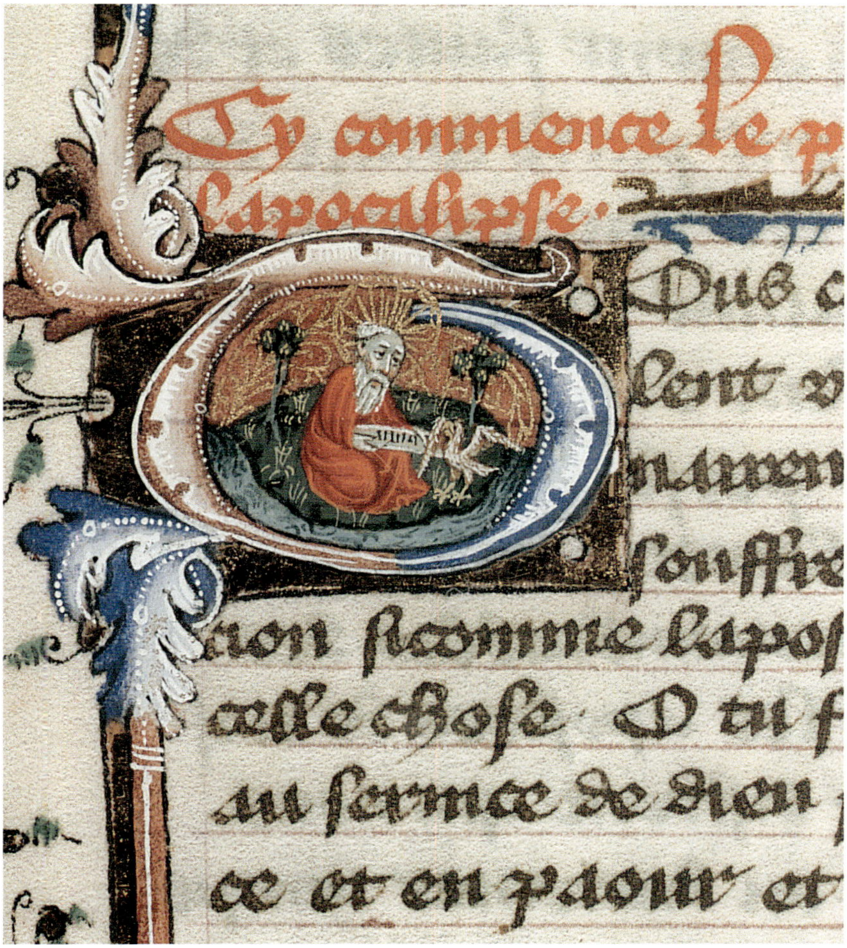

Fig. 45 Oxford, All Souls MS 10, fol. 191v (detail), Saint John on Patmos, with eagle beside. The Warden and Fellows of All Souls College, Oxford.

an Apostle preaching from a pulpit in later fourteenth- or fifteenth-century French manuscripts; see, for examples, BL Additional MS 15247, *Bible historiale* (Genesis-Apocalypse), fol. 283v, Paul in pulpit, gesturing to a group of men; BL Royal MS 19.D.ii, *Bible historiale* (fol. 499v), Paul teaching from a pulpit with people, including two bishops, seated on the ground;[163] and BnF MS fr. 20088, *Bible historiale* (fol. 548), Paul in a pulpit before three elders and a youth (fig. 43). Saint Paul is normally depicted seated or standing with either an up- or down-turned sword. In one other initial in All Souls 10 (fol. 140v), Paul holds a down-turned sword (fig. 27), if oddly by the blade, which the majority of English miniatures show.[164]

Now, in mentioning the second preaching image from All Souls 10 (fig. 29), of Saint James the Greater, it must be reiterated that, apart from this manuscript, there are simply no other miniatures of an Apostle standing in a preacher's pulpit in English fifteenth-century manuscripts. Such iconography is, however, not unusual in the *Bibles historiales complétées* made and illustrated in France in the fifteenth century (as

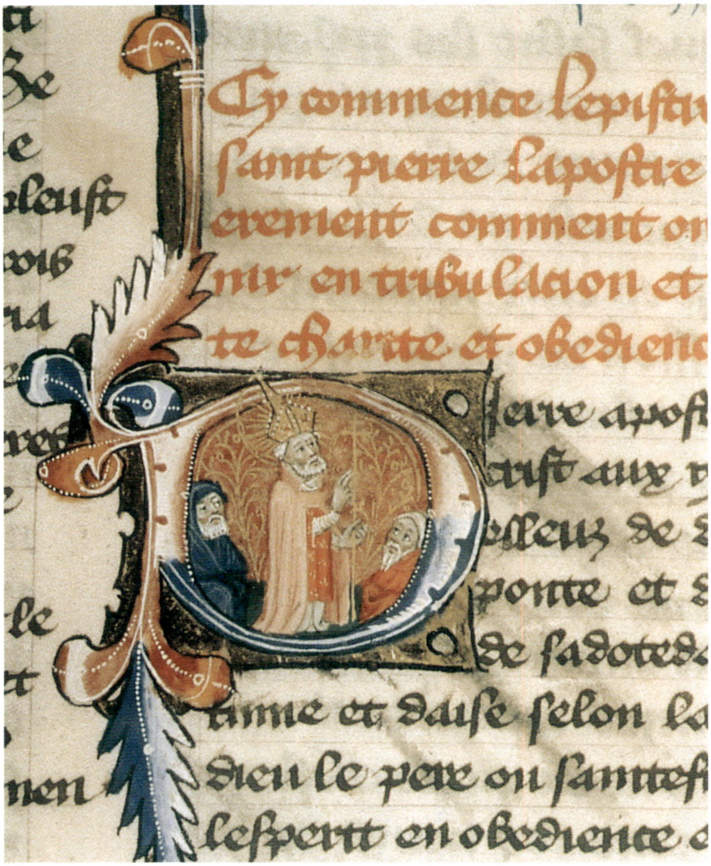

Fig. 46 Oxford, All Souls MS 10, fol. 184 (detail), Saint Peter in tiara with cross, holding cross-staff and blessing seated men. The Warden and Fellows of All Souls College, Oxford.

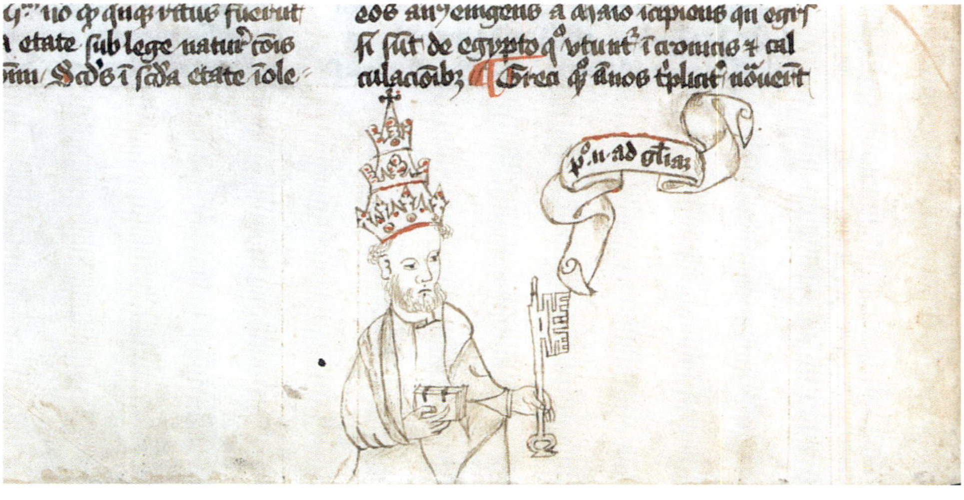

Fig. 47 Oxford, Magdalen College MS Lat. 97, fol. 10v, (detail with catchword) Saint Peter in papal tiara, with book and key. The President and Fellows of Magdalen College Oxford.

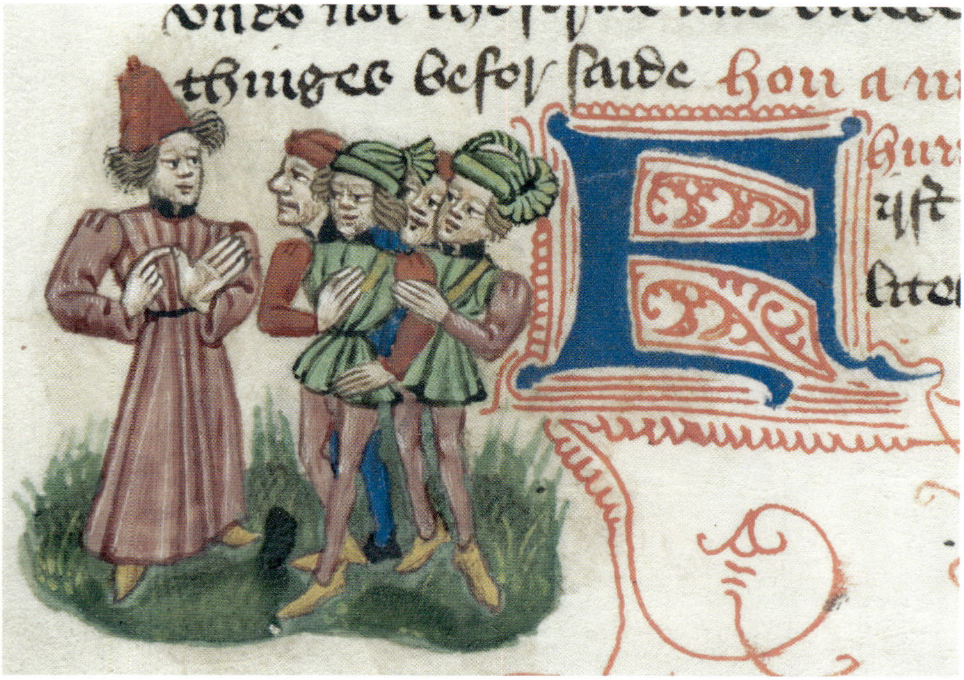

Fig. 48 Oxford, Bodleian Library MS Douce 335, fol. 45v (detail), Master of Game teaching group of young men. The Bodleian Library, University of Oxford.

just mentioned), and the scene in MS 10 may be a reflection of those models. English miniatures invariably show Saint James standing or walking, wearing a pilgrim's hat and cockle shell and carrying a pouch and staff.

The remaining miniatures of Apostles in All Souls MS 10 are also not typical of English iconography. On fol. 188v (fig. 44) the young John the Evangelist is seated with an eagle and pointing towards the text, whereas in other English manuscripts he is shown in one of three attitudes: standing and pointing to a chalice, at a desk as the Gospel writer, or as an older man seated on the ground, writing on Patmos. It would appear that the All Souls artist knew the conventional pointing gesture often employed with this saint in the first instance, but for some reason decided to show the Apostle pointing to the text rather than to a chalice. The third common depiction, of John on Patmos, is also in this manuscript (fol. 191v), at the prologue to Revelation (fig. 45). Here, again, the All Souls artist deviates from the norm, if only slightly, by showing John without a pen, merely holding rather than writing on a scroll. Because the All Souls artist is not known in his miniatures in other manuscripts for unusual iconography, the evidence is accumulating that he was being influenced by models outside the formulae of contemporary English artists.

The last Apostle picture in the All Souls manuscript, though not the last miniature, is of Saint Peter dressed as pope, blessing, holding a cross-staff and wearing a mitre that has evolved into something approximating a triple crown (fig. 46); he is pictured with two seated men, as if addressing them, in what is probably a unique iconography.

This miniature is once more not composed of the customary English components: Peter is conventionally shown in a nondescript robe, standing with a key and book.[165] In only two other English instances in the fifteenth century does he wear a triple crown; one is, of all places, in a catchword (fig. 47), the other in Cambridge, Corpus Christi College MS 251, *Chronicon Buriense* (fol. 1). I keep emphasizing the abnormality of the All Souls miniatures because the fact is obviously relevant for a consideration of the origin of its pictorial sequence.

A third scene used by the All Souls artist is what I believe to be a teaching scene. As usual with this artist, the scene does not stick in every particular to pre-established English 'teaching' iconography. The components of this subject are usually a person of some superior rank who makes a characteristic gesture, that of the forefinger of one hand pressed to the thumb of the other, and who has in his presence at least one attentive person, if more often a group of several listeners. Such scenes encompass a variety of social types: the Carmelite Missal shows Edmund Rich, Archbishop of Canterbury, instructing prelates of the church and lay people;[166] the *Turba philosophorum* shows a schoolmaster and his pupils, the teacher with the appropriate hand gesture;[167] in Bodl. Lib. MS Douce 335 a Master of Game instructs his apprentice in the ways of the hunt (fig. 48),[168] and in University College, Oxford, MS 85, p. 70, Aristotle is found tutoring Alexander.[169] The ambiguity about the All Souls scene of Saint Paul apparently teaching the Corinthians (fig. 49) is that he is *not* making the gesture that would correctly go with the rest of the scene. The artist's motives are uncertain, but he may have wished to tone down – or even deliberately eliminate – the explicit teaching theme based on a reading of the biblical text. Paul exclaims in 1 Corinthians: 2, that 'I came not with excellency of speech' and continues in the same chapter, 'Knowledge puffith up, but charity edifieth'. It is possible that the artist or his patron took these statements to heart and decided to render a muted theme, even if it was not easily expressed pictorially: its absence implicitly acknowledges the conventional gesture.

The final miniature in All Souls 10 illustrates the book of the Apocalypse (fig. 50). This scene, which was placed after the prologue, shows the Apocalyptic Christ clothed in a long gown and standing in a partially enclosed garden, in the midst of the seven golden candlesticks that represent the seven churches of Asia. Apart from the gown and candlesticks, the figure is not biblical. He does not wear the biblical 'golden girdle', nor are his head and hair white as wool, nor his feet like fine brass, nor does he hold seven stars in his right hand or a two-edged sword in his mouth. The garden, an enclosing hedge or *hortus conclusus*,[170] in which the apocalyptic figure stands, is also not biblical. The same scene in the Big Bible (fig. 51) contains many more of the biblical elements, including a seated figure of John of Revelation, the seven stars, the sword and, quite literally, the seven churches of Asia. In the Sherborne Missal the scenes are separated, and John has fallen at the feet of the Christ-like figure, also a reference to the biblical text.[171] These three scenes, and two further small initials in the Sherborne Missal (BL Add. MS 74236), are the sum total of representations of the subject depicted in English manuscripts. Although produced throughout the thirteenth and fourteenth centuries, illustrated Apocalypses were not made, to judge by survival, in the fifteenth century,[172] and those illustrated in the previous two centuries might include a prologue initial of Saint Paul[173] but not Saint John, as in All Souls MS 10; or they might have scenes from a life of Saint John.[174] Again, I want to emphasize the differences between the All Souls scene and other versions of the subject made in England.

I must also question the presence of a *hortus conclusus* in the scene. Why would this image appear in an Apocalypse miniature? It seems that unusual pictorial ideas came to this artist either from his own innovation or, more likely, from an alien exemplar. In English manuscripts the enclosed garden occurs in a different set of iconographic situations: with a Virgin and Child, Saint Anthony, Anne teaching the Virgin, the Garden of Gethsemane, the Garden of Virtues, and Paradise; and it may be depicted as a green hedge,[175] a brick wall,[176] or, in the *Speculum humanae salvationis*, a crenellated stone wall enclosing a plot with a locked well,[177] as from the Song of Songs: 'A garden enclosed is my sister, my spouse; a spring shut up, a fountain sealed (4:12).' Perhaps the generally unspecified use of the *hortus conclusus* in English miniatures may account for its appearance in the All Souls subject, as well as the notion that it would be appropriate to an illustration of the Apocalypse.

In spite of my insistence on the oddness of the iconography in All Souls MS 10, there is actually one aspect of the manuscript that does not present a puzzle, and that is the corpus of the artist of the sixteen historiated initials. I have, in the past, identified his work in three other manuscripts and a single-page fragment.[178] The most impressive of his pictorial sequences is in an Hours of the Virgin and the Cross, in Trinity College, Cambridge, MS B.11.7,[179] datable between 1413 and 1422. This manuscript contains forty-three miniatures and twenty-four historiated roundels, and there can be no doubt about its sumptuousness. B.11.7 was commissioned by a man and woman from the higher ranks of nobility, and because of the woman's coronet, chased as jewelled, worn over her headdress, she should be identifiable as a duchess.[180] It is also possible that the patron and patroness had the book made for the king, who is represented in prayer at the prayer for peace; at this time the monarch was Henry V (d. 1422). Nicholas Rogers has suggested an identification of the patrons on the basis of mottoes in the Trinity miniatures as Sir John Cornwall, Lord Fanhope, and his wife Elizabeth (d. 1425), sister of Henry IV.[181] If so, this commission to the All Souls artist tells us, then, a great deal about his status in the book-producing community of England, in particular among noble book-commissioning patrons who may still have used French as a court or as a second language.

Another manuscript which contains work by the All Souls artist is, again, an elaborate Book of Hours, Paris, Bibliothèque Mazarine MS 469, made in Paris around 1415 in the atelier of the Boucicaut Master.[182] Our artist's work here consists of a miniature added on an unfinished French border page. The manuscript also contains a Veronica head worked on leather, in an English style, at the front, and the book was undoubtedly taken to England, unfinished, after 1415 and completed there.

A third manuscript that has a miniature by the All Souls master is Karlsruhe, Badische Landesbibliothek, St Georgen 12, a copy of Part I of the *Sanctilogium salvatoris*.[183] This book was largely written by Stephen Dodesham, monk of Witham and Sheen Charterhouses, probably before 1439.[184] Only the first miniature is by the All Souls artist: it shows a monk seated on a pillow, writing, strangely, on the cover of a book.[185]

MS Sanct Georgen 12 was made for the Brigittine bretheren of Syon Abbey, Isleworth, which was founded in 1415 by Henry V,[186] and the person virtually certain

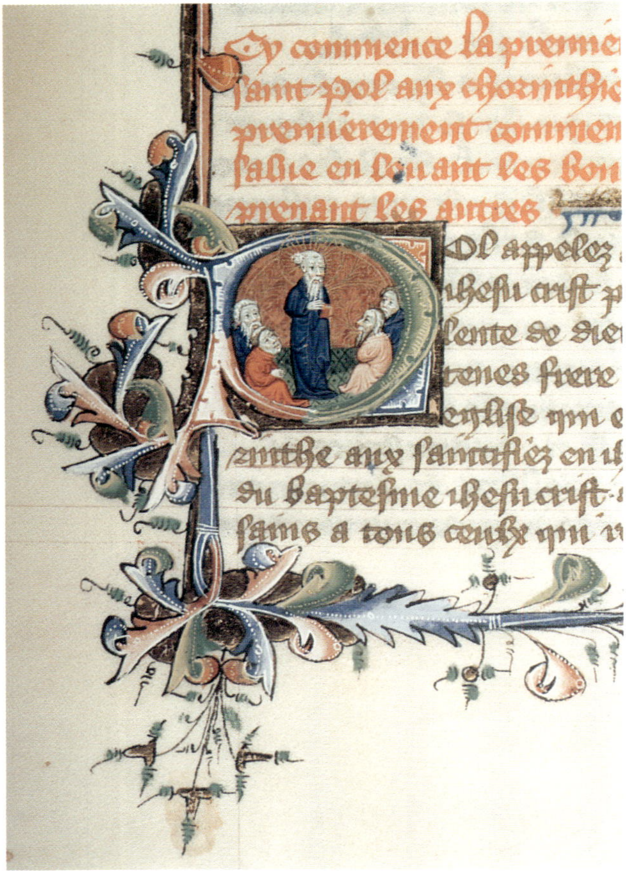

Fig. 49 Oxford, All Souls MS 10, fol. 114v (detail), Saint Paul teaching group of seated men. The Warden and Fellows of All Souls College, Oxford.

to have been the donor of the *Sanctilogium* to Syon was Margaret Holand, Duchess of Clarence, who died in 1439. She was twice married to brothers of kings, first, John Beaufort, half-brother to Henry IV, and afterwards – before July 1412 – to Thomas, Duke of Clarence, brother of Henry V. Margaret had an association with Syon comparable only to that of Henry V, the founder. Her most recent chronicler, George Keiser, has demonstrated that '[f]rom a very early time in Syon's history, [Margaret] was a supporter and benefactor of [the] royal foundation'.[187] She had even received permission from the Pope to live near the Abbey, to have her confession heard there, to be administered the sacraments and, not least, to be assisted by the brothers in making her will.[188] In fact, the Duchess's name appears as donor of six books in the medieval catalogue of Syon Abbey;[189] among these is listed a two-volume copy of the *Sanctilogium Salvatoris*, and there appears to be direct evidence in the Karlsruhe manuscript that it is volume I of the copy given by the Duchess to Syon.[190] So, we have another manuscript illustrated by the All Souls artist that can be connected to nobility.

Margaret, Duchess of Clarence, is also known to have commissioned an expensive book of Hours made in the second quarter of the fifteenth century, not illustrated by the All Souls artist. Once owned by Major J. R. Abbey, it is now in the collection of

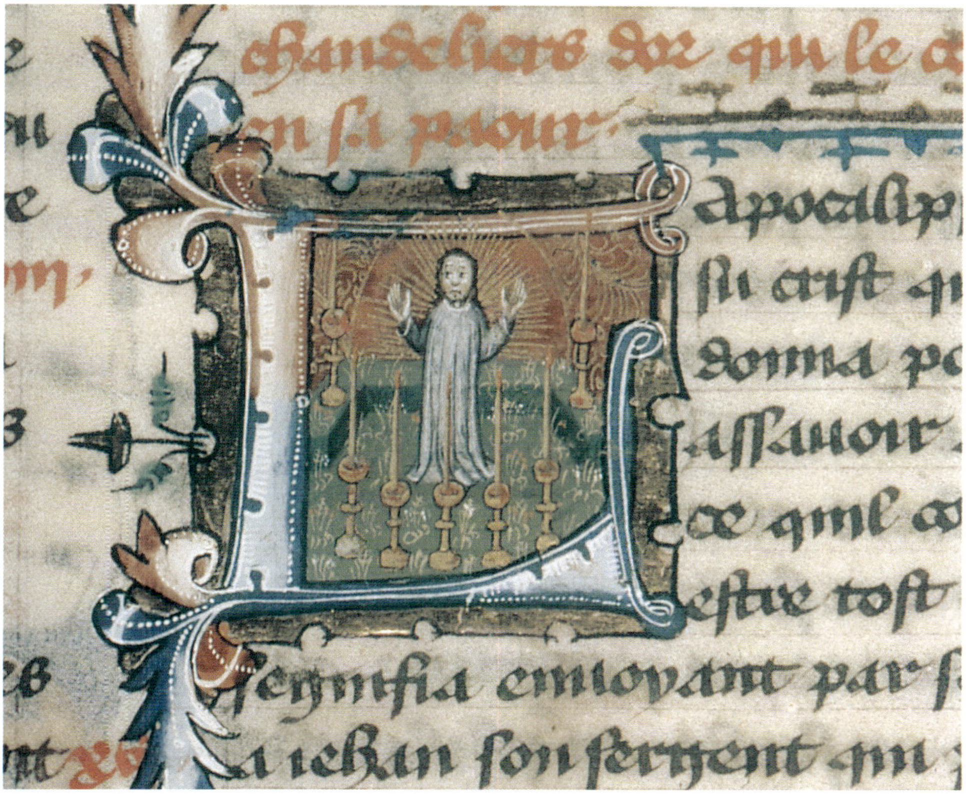

Fig. 5c Oxford, All Souls College MS 10, fol. 193 (detail), Apocalyptic Christ in *hortus conclusus*, with seven candlesticks. The Warden and Fellows of All Souls College, Oxford.

Renate König, on deposit at Kolumba, Diözesan Museum, Cologne.[191] The Hours of the Duchess of Clarence was produced with eight full-page miniatures, eleven half-page miniatures, two historiated initials, and elaborate borders. Further evidence of the Duchess's activity in the book world are the several copies of a life of Saint Jerome that were expressly translated for Margaret from the Latin *Legenda aurea*,[192] and the fact that around 1430 the Duchess gave money for the purchase of a Bible for Syon Abbey: the volume purchased was a mid-thirteenth-century Bible written in England, now BL Additional MS 40006.[193] Margaret was a substantial force in the market for fine books in the 1420s and 1430s, and she was the type of English patron who might have been interested in owning a copy of the *Bible historiale complétée* and who might have commissioned an elegant book such as All Souls MS 10.[194]

There is, nevertheless, another way of looking at, or for, the patron of this strange All Souls manuscript. Rather than assume that we need to find a French-reading or French-speaking *English* person as patron, we might also consider a French person living in England. Putting aside such transients as officials, wine merchants, messengers and other persons who were in and out of London, two prominent French patrons of books were actually in forced residence in England in the 1420s and 30s.

They were Charles d'Orléans and his brother, Jean d'Angoulême. Charles was captured by the English on St Crispin's Day, 1415, when he was twenty-one, and three years before, when he was thirteen, Jean had been handed over to the English as a guaranty for a large sum of money owed to various English lords.[195] During their twenty-five and thirty-three year captivities in England, both men bought English books and had books made for them by English scribes and illuminators. An example of the latter is a beautiful prayer book (BnF MS lat. 1196[196]) made for Charles in England, with historiated initials and partial borders, that is to say, with decoration at about the same level as All Souls MS 10.

While in captivity, Charles was also regularly in touch with France through his various officials and servants – he was, after all, the senior French prince – and he had access through them to the library at his castle of Blois and had books brought to him in England.[197] The Blois collection, assembled by Charles's father, Louis d'Orléans, contained ninety-one volumes, including several Bibles in French, as we know from an inventory made in 1417.[198] At the death of his mother, Valentine Visconti of Milan, Charles acquired a Bible in French in two volumes,[199] and in 1410 he authorized, after an interval of twelve years, continuation of work on the translation and production of the 'Grande Bible' or 'La Bible de Jean de Sy' begun for the French king, Jean le Bon, Charles's grandfather.[200] According to a listing of his books made around 1440 just as Charles returned from captivity in 'l'ennuyeuse Albion',[201] he brought with him 101 books, which were individually noted as 'apportés d'Angleterre'.[202] This number is impressive, and especially so because it includes four Bibles, two of which were recorded as in French.[203] Pierre Champion, who compiled a list Charles's books from three inventories, those of 1417, 1427 and *c.* 1440, registered a total of seven Bibles owned by Charles, four in French and three in Latin.[204] One of the French versions, now BnF MS fr. 157, of before 1417, was the second volume of a Bible with miniatures. Unfortunately, unlike All Souls MS 10, MS fr. 157 begins with the book of Solomon, and its miniatures did not prove to be relevant to those in MS 10. So, at very least, we can be certain that Charles was both interested in the production of Bibles and, more significantly, had a French Bible in England that could have been passed to an English stationer as an exemplar for All Souls MS 10.[205]

Jean d'Angoulême shared a love of books with his older brother and, like Charles, is known to have had more than one regular copyist during his captivity (1412–45)[206] and to have acquired books made in France at an earlier date.[207] It is also of possible importance that Jean was placed in the custody of Thomas, Duke of Clarence, and that, after the death of Clarence in 1421, he was transferred to the keeping of Margaret, Duchess of Clarence, whose interest in books I have just described. Whether she put Jean in touch with her illuminator, we can only imagine. It may be unlikely, because she has been said to have treated Jean 'more harshly than her husband did',[208] and she was described by Jean's biographer as among those most devious and rapacious in negotiating his release.[209] At the same time, the duchess has also been described as having 'a motherly feeling towards Jean'.[210] What is the truth? The only Bibles recorded as owned by Jean are, however, an incomplete Bible in Latin[211] and a *Bible historiale*[212] previously owned by his brother, whose miniatures are, as already noted, not related to those in All Souls. Jean is, to my mind, less likely to have commissioned the All Souls manuscript.[213]

What I have chosen to call the enigma of All Souls 10, with regard to its illustrator, is that this artist was a widely known, highly professional craftsman who normally worked in the mainstream of English iconography[214] but who nevertheless in this manuscript did not follow the English pictorial conventions of the 1420s and early 1430s. His pictorial ideas were supplemented from non-English sources, either by a patron who specifically requested deviations from the standard mode of picturing Apostles in England or by an exemplar with miniatures, perhaps – in a wild surmise – the one used by the two All Souls scribes. Although this exemplar is not extant, its influence would be the better guess. Surviving French-produced texts of this version of the Bible have miniatures similar enough to those in All Souls MS 10 to suggest direct French influence in some manner. It is also important that ten of the sixteen surviving miniatures in All Souls 10 have the same pictorial subjects as in manuscripts of the *Bible historiale complétée*.[215]

The enigma concerning the manuscript of All Souls 10 – a thirteenth-century French Bible in its evolved fourteenth-century form as the *Bible historiale complétée* – concerns its patronage. Given the absence of any other extant copies either of a French New Testament or of a *Bible historiale complétée* from an English workshop, we can be reasonably confident that All Souls 10 was not made as an archetype for general circulation and that it is equally unlikely to have been made as a speculative venture. The decline in the use of French and of the production of English books in French over the first half of the fifteenth century adds to the mystery of the All Souls manuscript.[216] This quandary concerning its patronage could be resolved by positing a French-reading patron resident in England long enough to need and to commission such an item. Such a supposition would, as discussed, exclude transient officials and merchants, but would include an English patron who was a French reader. Apart from other more arcane possibilities, one would imagine, however, that the patron's basic need was for simple, comprehensible access to the biblical text, which may have been denied to him or her because of lack of facility in Latin or, perhaps, by lack of complete fluency in English or, if it was an English person, from apprehension about using a Wycliffite translation.[217] Within this premise, personal devotion was probably the over-arching motive for such a commission, as Sneddon has suggested was the motive for the original translations into French in the thirteenth century.[218] It seems unlikely that the patron was a member of the clergy, since he would presumably have been capable of using a Bible in Latin.[219] The patron or patroness would seem, therefore, almost certainly to have been a lay person, and he or she probably had available a copy of this version of the Bible, since it is unlikely that an English stationer would have had one on hand. This hypothetical person presumably wanted the English shop to re-do the exemplar, either in a more 'modern' form or in a form more socially compatible with his or her current circumstances. This person must also have been affluent enough to afford a book with at least twenty-seven miniatures, counting the twelve or so that were excised,[220] and scarcely guessing at the number in a hypothetical first volume with an Old Testament perhaps an original companion volume to All Souls MS 10, that is, possibly about another forty-one historiated initials.

These qualifications would best fit, if not exclusively, one of the French princes held captive in England for so many years, and, in particular, I like the idea of Charles d'Orléans,[221] who had in hand several Bibles in French while he was in England and –

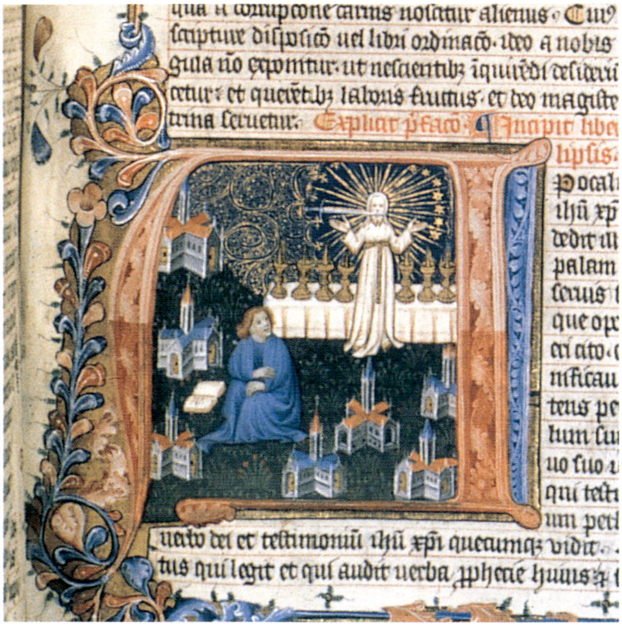

Fig. 51 British Library Royal MS 1.E.ix, Big Bible, fol. 319 (detail), John of Revelation with Apocalyptic Christ, seven churches, and seven candlesticks. The British Library

it is important – who while in England commissioned a book of prayers, BnF MS lat. 1201, with a border (fig. 52) by the same artist as in All Souls MS 10.[222] Charles's certain knowledge of this limner is as close to certain knowledge of his commission as we are likely to get. As for the motive for such a commission, I would suggest that, since Charles presumably had little need of a French Bible himself, he had it made as a gift, perhaps even for one of his sympathetic keepers.[223] Two good prospects present themselves. The better one might be, on the face of it, William de la Pole, Earl of Suffolk, who had spent close to seventeen years in France and was a known Francophile. At his own request, Suffolk became Charles's keeper for four years and, like Charles, Suffolk was bilingual,[224] a lover of letters, and perhaps a sometime poet;[225] and, above all, the two were on good terms, possibly even close friends.[226] Suffolk was also involved in the effort to secure the release of Jean d'Angoulême, a matter that had long been of utmost importance to Charles, and Suffolk was actually the signator of the treaty of release for Jean on 12 May 1444.[227] And in April of 1444 Suffolk visited Charles at Blois.[228] But would Charles have had a *Bible* made for this particular friend?

The other prospect as recipient of a fine gift from Charles would be Sir John Cornwall, Lord Fanhope, who 'apparently had always had some kind of overall responsibility for the keeping of Charles'.[229] Cornwall was in fact the 'only one of the keepers of Charles present at his wedding to Marie de Cleves' after Charles's return to France in 1440,[230] and, according to Ouy, the period of Charles's stay with Cornwall was the only time during which his younger brother Jean was allowed to live with him.[231] More importantly, Cornwall and his wife Elizabeth probably commissioned the splendid book of Hours, Trinity College, Cambridge, MS B.11.7, illustrated by the artist of All Souls MS 10, and Cornwall could presumably have directed Charles to

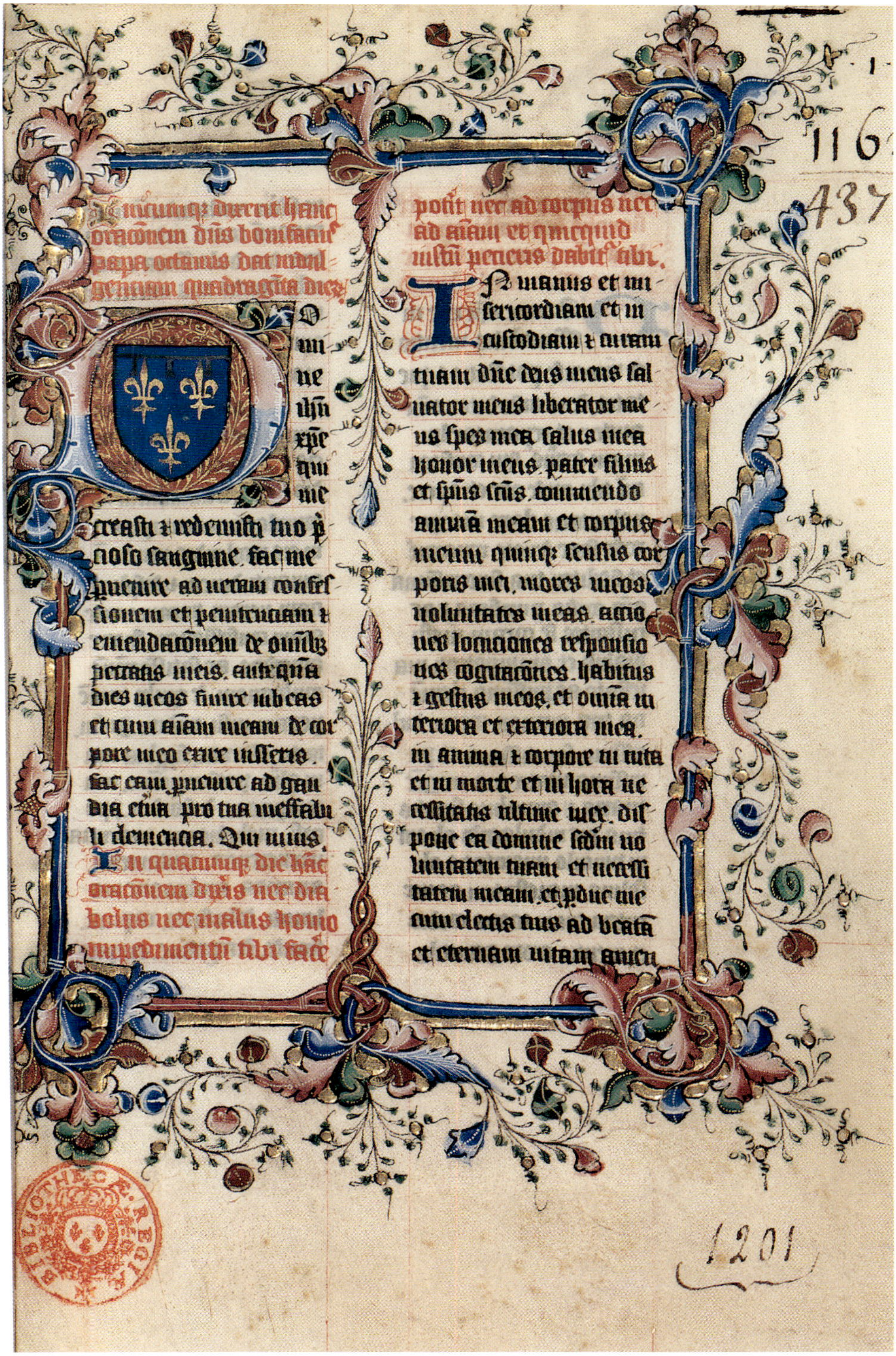

Fig. 52 Paris, Bibliothèque Nationale MS lat. 1201, fol. 1, full-page border by All Souls border artist. Bibliothèque nationale de France.

this illustrator. The dates are not impossible in that MS B.11.7, if made for John Cornwall and Elizabeth, is likely to have been finished by 1425, when she died; and Charles was placed in Cornwall's custody in December of 1429, to remain there until 1432.[232]

Unfortunately, I have been unable to penetrate the core of the All Souls enigma, to provide my reader either with the name or even the homeland of the patron of this exceptional manuscript or with a certain motive for its production, but, as far as the French source of the miniatures is concerned, I hope to have untangled a few skeins from around one mystery concerning All Souls 10.

CHAPTER III

The Unique Pictorial 'Afterpiece' to the *Abbey of the Holy Ghost* in BL Stowe MS 39

THE subject of this chapter is a manuscript of many contexts. The text, the *Abbey of the Holy Ghost*,[233] is a Middle English treatise of spiritual guidance for those living a mixed life – in the world and of the spirit. It has been described as among 'the absolute classics of English vernacular spirituality'.[234] Derived from a French tract of the mid-fourteenth century,[235] the English translation, of the third quarter of the same century, was influenced by the mystical thought of Richard Rolle.[236] The narrative line of the text is shaped by an extended metaphor of the structure and activities of an abbey, a 'figure of interiority', which stands for the human conscience.[237] The abbey is populated by nuns who represent allegorical figures, mostly virtues, figures who take on the offices and chores necessary to the successful running of a nunnery and, by implication, the management of a clean conscience. The audience for this tract was, as the author says, the laity who wished to pursue the contemplative life but who could not because of the realities of secular life, such as poverty or the bonds of marriage; it was for those who found themselves in a mixed active and contemplative life.

As it is a rather short work, the text was consistently produced in anthologies, apart from Stowe MS 39, where it is together only with a fine illustrated version of the *Desert of Religion* and a brief poem, a Debate for a Soul.[238] The same artist produced the miniatures for all three texts in Stowe 39. The *Abbey* was often copied with the unrelated and much longer *Charter of the Abbey of the Holy Ghost*,[239] and also with the *Prick of Conscience*, lives of saints, the works of Richard Rolle, and a few times even with works of Chaucer. The *Abbey* survives in whole or in part in twenty-five manuscripts[240] and was printed three times by Wynkyn de Worde, twice in 1496 and once in 1500, in a conflated form together with *The Charter of the Abbey of the Holy Ghost*.[241] The Stowe copy, written in the second quarter of the fifteenth century, was made for a Benedictine nunnery with a dedication to the Virgin, almost certainly in the north of England,[242] but the arms (*argent* a saltire *gules*) in the manuscript have not been identified as belonging to a religious house[243] (fig. 55).

The Stowe manuscript measures *c.* 265 × *c.* 195 mm at fol. 9; it has no signatures or catchwords. Folios 1 and 2 are of modern paper; fol. 3 is a medieval ruled blank. Folios 4–9 contain the prose *Abbey* text; fol. 9v is blank; fol. 10 contains a miniature of the Virgin and Child with kneeling nun and with the unidentified coat of arms. Folio 10v begins the *Desert of Religion*, in long lines of two verses to the line; this text ends on fol. 31. The text on fol. 32 begins 'I wende to ded clerk full of skill' and with a miniature at left of a bishop, king and knight standing before a figure of Death; at right there is a scene of a debate over a soul before an angel, Christ, the Virgin and God the

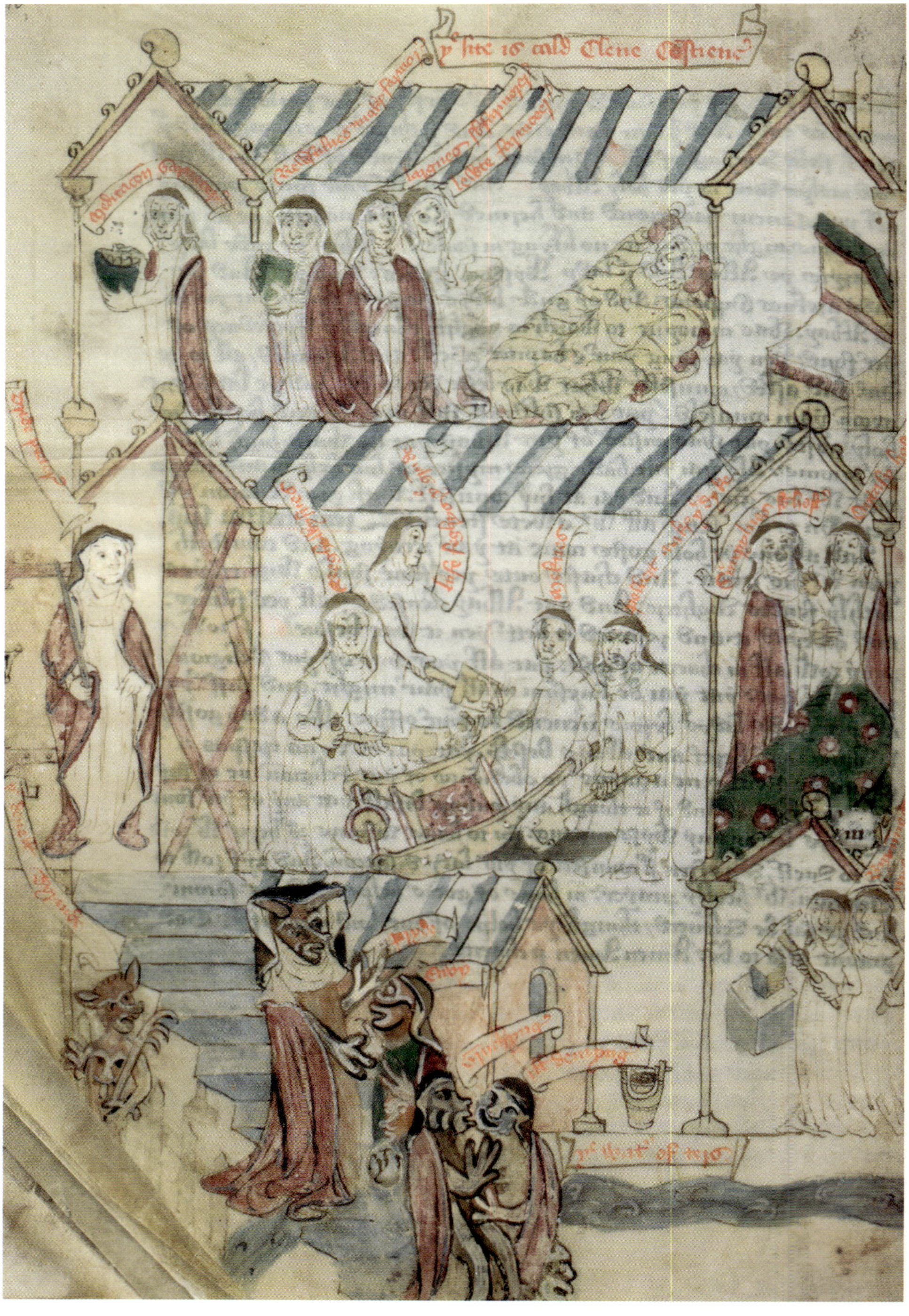

Fig. 53 British Library Stowe MS 39, fol. 8v, Abbey of the Holy Ghost (first afterpiece). The British Library.

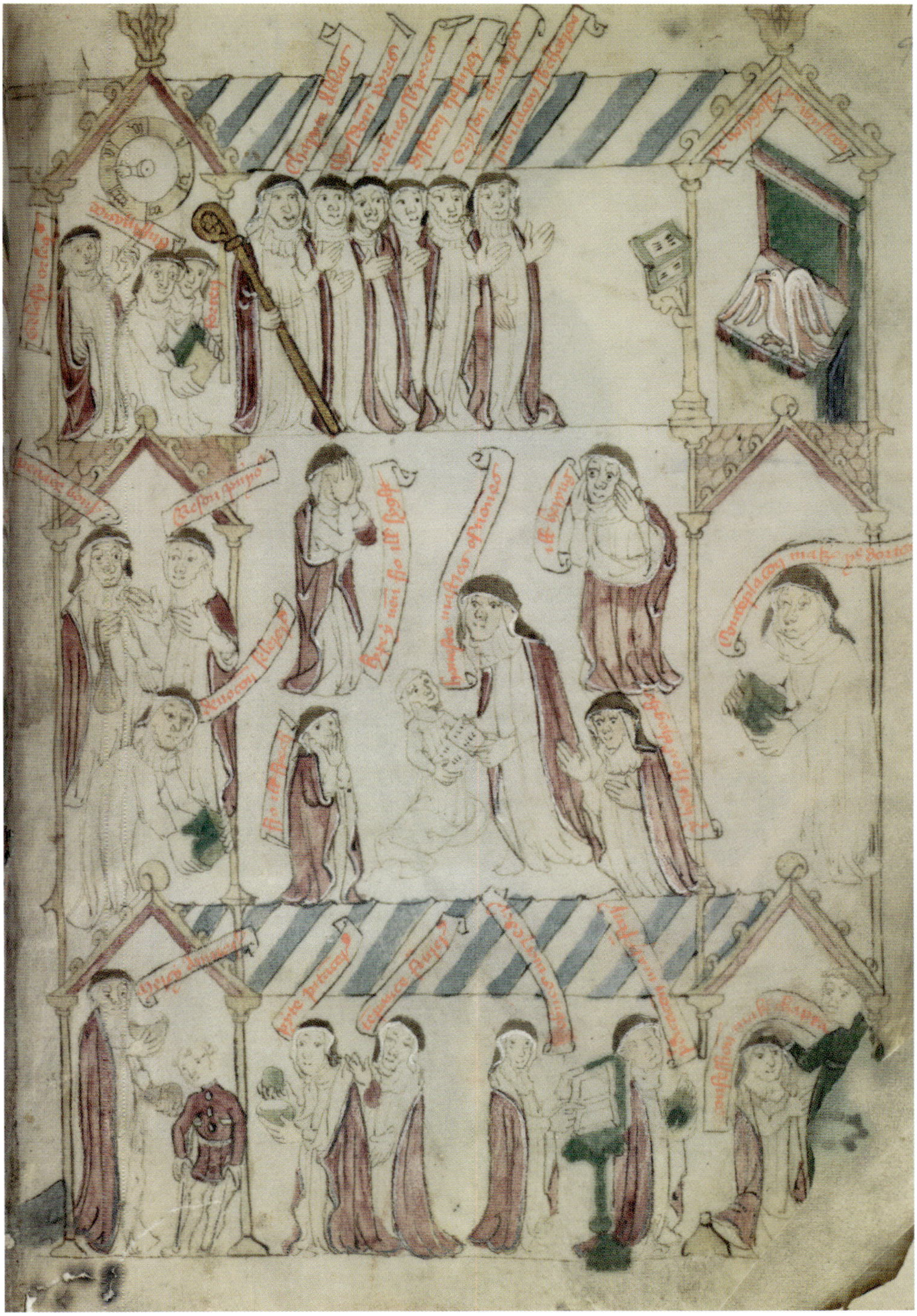

Fig. 54 British Library Stowe MS 39, fol. 9, Abbey of the Holy Ghost (second afterpiece).
The British Library.

Father. The known provenance of Stowe MS 39 is that it was given to Richard Greene, an apothecary of Lichfield, by a Reverend Gastrell in 1767. Greene gave the book to the British Museum in 1767. The name of the antiquary, Thomas Astel, appears on fol. 1v with the date 'Jan. 7th 1768'.

The illustration of Stowe MS 39 is innovative among fifteenth-century English manuscripts because of both its form and its content. The illustration consists of two full-page miniatures in three registers, one on the verso of the last text page and the other on the facing recto (figs 53–54). This 'afterpiece', as I have decided to call it by pictorial analogy with a frontispiece, is unique in being the only full-page illustration in any English copy of an *Abbey* manuscript,[244] one of only two illustrated *Abbey* texts, and in being an opening planned to follow its text. 'Afterpiece' is conventionally a word which refers to a farce or short piece after a play; but I feel that it may appropriately be adapted to the present usage, also by analogy with 'afterword' a 'relatively brief concluding section' of a text that typographically may be treated like a chapter, foreword or preface, i.e. as beginning on a new page.[245] The opposite of 'frontispiece' would be, to use a Latin derivation, 'postpiece', a less attractive coinage, and 'postscript' too trivializing.

A few other English manuscripts have miniatures at the end of a text, all much smaller scenes that were, as a rule, not planned for that position. A miniature (fol. 68v) in CUL MS Ii.4.9, a miscellany, seems to have been an afterthought rather than afterpiece; and the drawing in Bodl. Lib. MS Bodley 100 (fol. 72v), Walter Hilton, Treatise on the Active and Contemplative Life, was certainly not planned. Only the drawing in BL Egerton MS 847 (fig. 56), astronomical miscellany, including the *Practica geometrie* (fols 54–56v) was, to judge by the space left before the explicit, actually anticipated; even so, it is not extensive enough to be comparable to Stowe MS 39.[246] The only comparable facing set of miniatures with full-page illustration appears at the end of a fine early sixteenth-century copy of the *Speculum humanae salvationis* in BL Harley MS 2838, made for Henry VII.[247] Here, each page shows three registers with six compartments of miniatures of dialogue scenes, beginning on fol. 51v on the last recto of the *Speculum*. The facing folio (52) is followed by three blank pages (fols 52v–53v) and a blank endleaf. The Harley miniatures do not, therefore, illustrate a text, either before or afterwards; they would have been a reference to a *following* text and intended as the frontispiece to that text. Each compartment of the Harley miniature depicts a nimbused figure, almost certainly an Apostle, with a blank scroll, apparently speaking with a secular male, possibly an Old Testament prophet, also with a blank scroll. If these Harley figures represent types and archetypes of Apostles and prophets just as the scenes in the *Speculum humanae salvationis* are types and archetypes, then it is possible that the two facing pages are a genuine afterpiece as in Stowe MS 39.

Although the Stowe opening was demonstrably planned to be in the end position, I intend to look upon it, for purposes of comparison, as a sort of misplaced frontispiece: by necessity, because frontispieces are the only other comparable sites for a similar opening. And for present purposes I take as my definition of a frontispiece and, by association, of an 'afterpiece,' as one or more full-page illustrations that either precede the first text page or that follow immediately on the end of the text and that are related in some way to it. This definition, of course, describes mainly where the illustration occurs, not what its function may be.[248] I shall first place the Stowe 'afterpiece' in the context of other manuscript copies of the *Abbey*, then in the context of fifteenth-century English frontispieces, and finally in relation to thirteenth-century French illustration of the *Abbey*. In order to determine its function for the medieval user of the Stowe copy, it will also be useful to describe the narrative movement of its pictorial opening on fols 8v and 9 with respect to the structure of the text.

Nothing will give a clearer notion of the importance of Stowe MS 39 than a comparison with the opening pages of other *Abbey* manuscripts. Folio 156v of BL Egerton MS 3245 (fig. 57), fol. 1 of Tokyo, Takamiya MS 65,[249] and fol. 139 of Bodl. Lib. MS Douce 141 all have introductory pages with pen-flourished letters and are the unexciting norm for *Abbey* manuscripts. A manuscript such as BL Harley MS 1706 (fig. 58) represents the lower end of *Abbey* production: not entirely terrible but nothing like the Stowe 'afterpiece'. Longleat House MS 4, with sermons and other texts, in contrast, is a fine, large manuscript with illuminated initials and partial borders; this copy introduces the *Abbey* with an illuminated initial and spray of daisies and shows the run-on manner in which the text may appear in a miscellany.[250] The closest it is possible to come in an English manuscript to the quality of Stowe MS 39 is the half-page tinted drawing of the elevation of an abbey in Bodl. Lib. MS Douce 323 (fig. 59), an illustration that is also, oddly, at the end of the text but which is not iconographically related to the Stowe manuscript. The only other image with an *Abbey of the Holy Ghost* in the surviving manuscripts is a male profile head in an initial in Corpus Christi College, Oxford, MS E.155, perhaps an addition and anyway not an illustration of the text.

The pictorial afterpiece in Stowe MS 39 (figs 53–54) is organized into three registers, each one of which depicts a superstructure supporting three cross-sections of the elevation of the building. The supporting structures consist on each level of a roof, exposed beams and pointed gables with crockets, these in turn being held up by slender columns with capitals. The lowest register on the verso illustration (fig. 53) shows an external half-view of the Abbey consistent with its position on a river bank but inconsistent with the free-standing column and gable at right. Apart from this level, the columns divide each register or story of the abbey into one larger and two smaller compartments that, as a rule, show activities unrelated to each other. The perspective of the end of each building is distorted in that the ends are turned forward on a plane with the central room in order to create a framed space for the two outer episodes. The distortion does not imply an incompetent artist, for it was relatively common to show the west or east side of a church on or nearly on a single plane with its long side.[251] The cut-away architectural frames of the Stowe compartments were also very commonly used to open up one room for a single scene.[252]

The figures within the architectural frames are labelled, allegorical nuns shown constructing the nunnery and carrying out its daily tasks. Depictions of nuns are generally speaking infrequent in fifteenth-century English book illustration, and even fewer allegorical figures are depicted as a nun. Among these last few are 'Reason' in scenes from one of the Chaundler manuscripts[253] and several figures in miniatures from a fine manuscript of the *Pilgrimage of the Life of Man*.[254] Otherwise, nuns appear occasionally as patrons (figs 55, 60),[255] as representatives of an order,[256] as a saint in the habit of an order (fig. 61),[257] as a generalized figure,[258] and of course in the

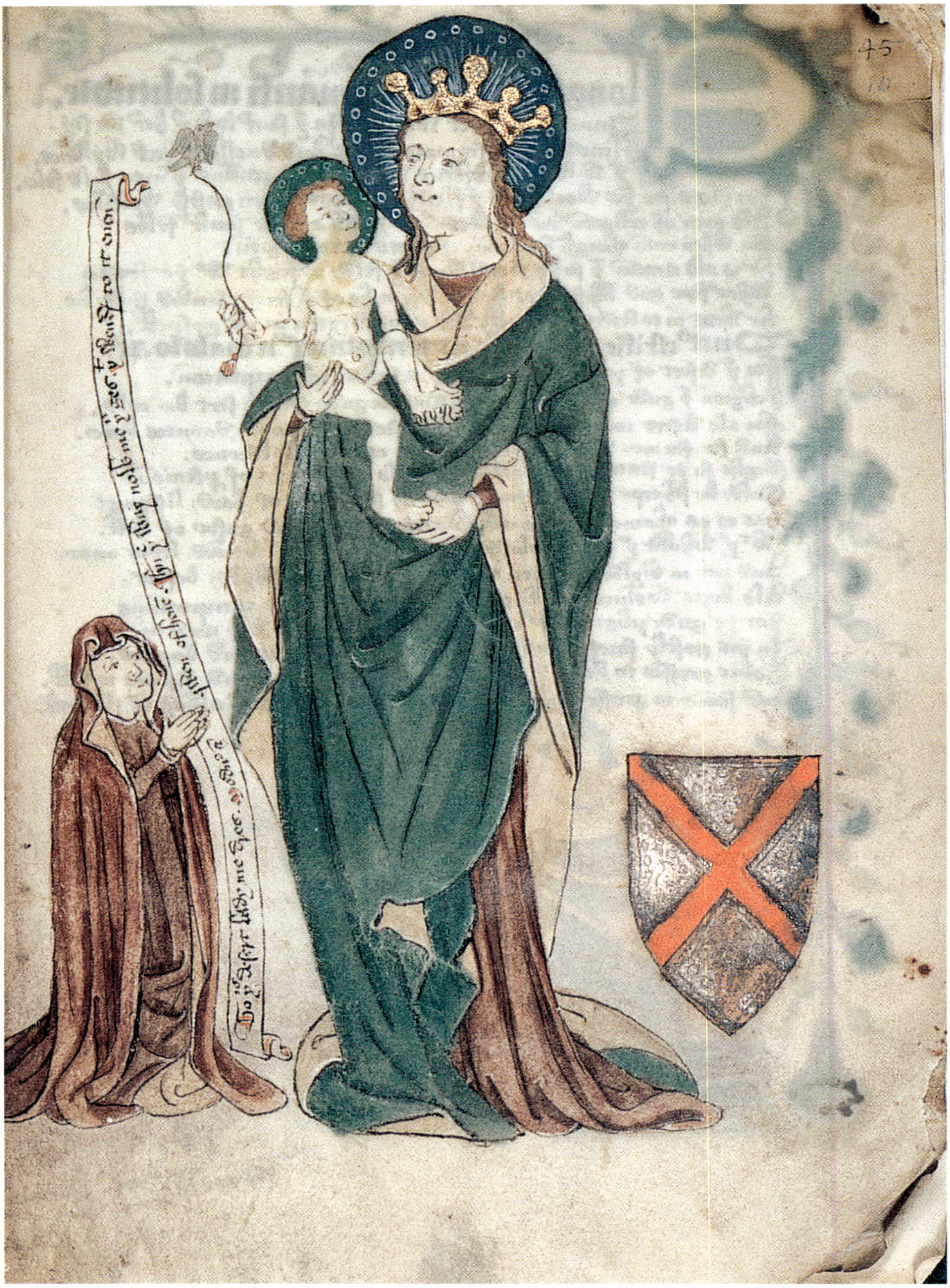

Fig. 55 British Library Stowe MS 39, fol. 10, Virgin and Child, with bird on string; kneeling patron-nun; unidentified coat of arms. The British Library.

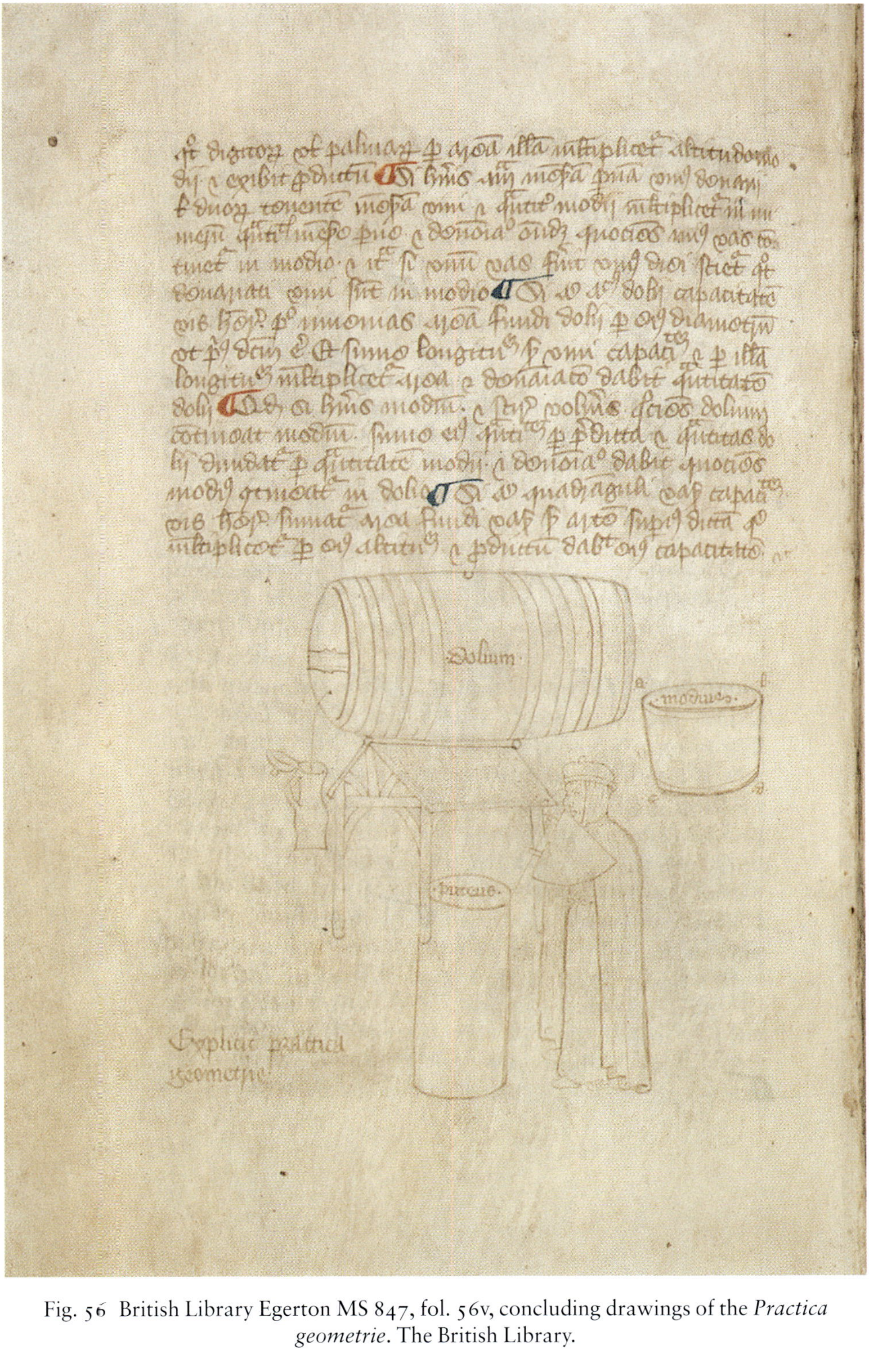

Fig. 56 British Library Egerton MS 847, fol. 56v, concluding drawings of the *Practica geometrie*. The British Library.

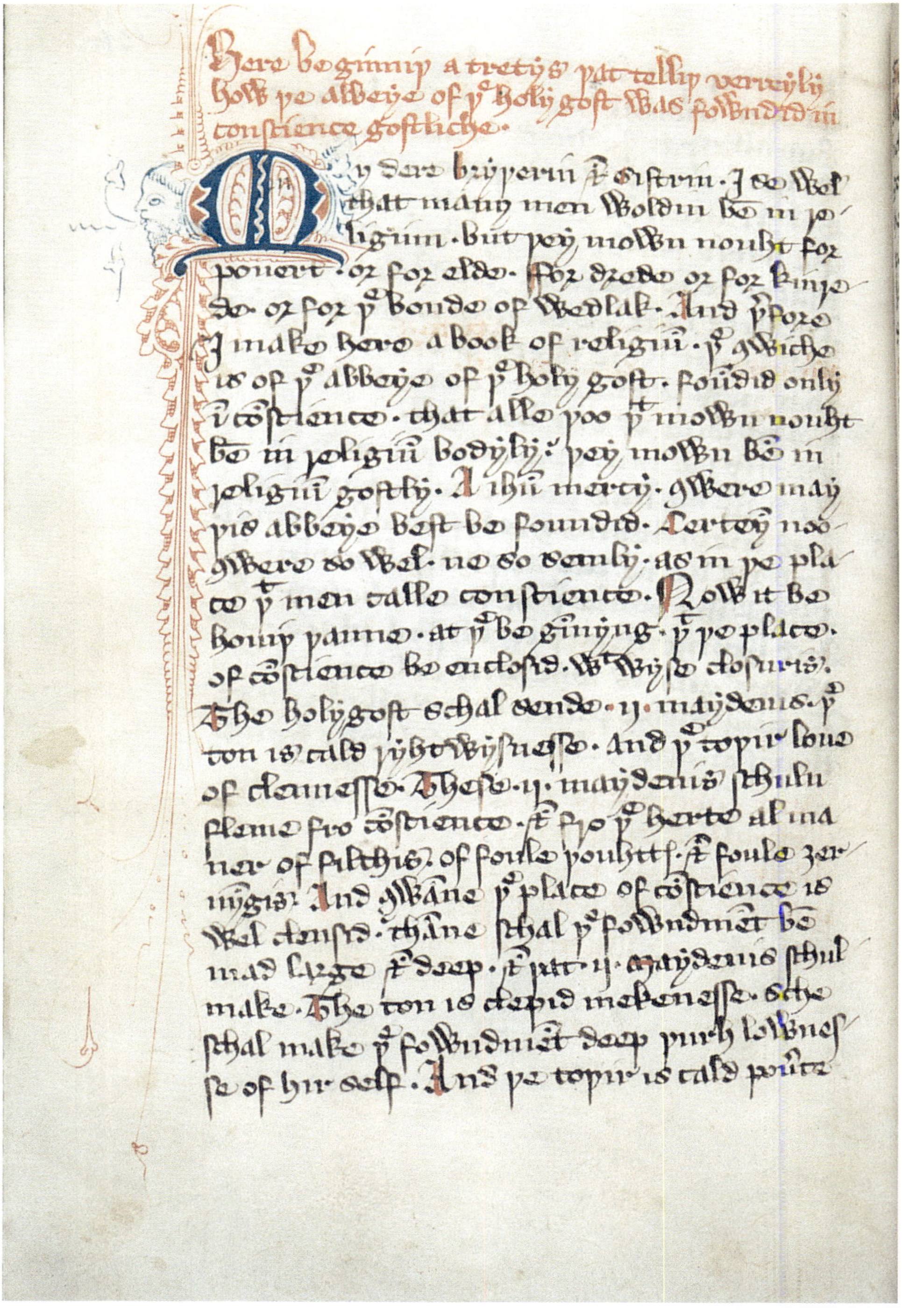

Fig. 57 British Library Egerton MS 3245, fol. 156v, opening page of the *Abbey of the Holy Ghost*, with flourished initial. The British Library.

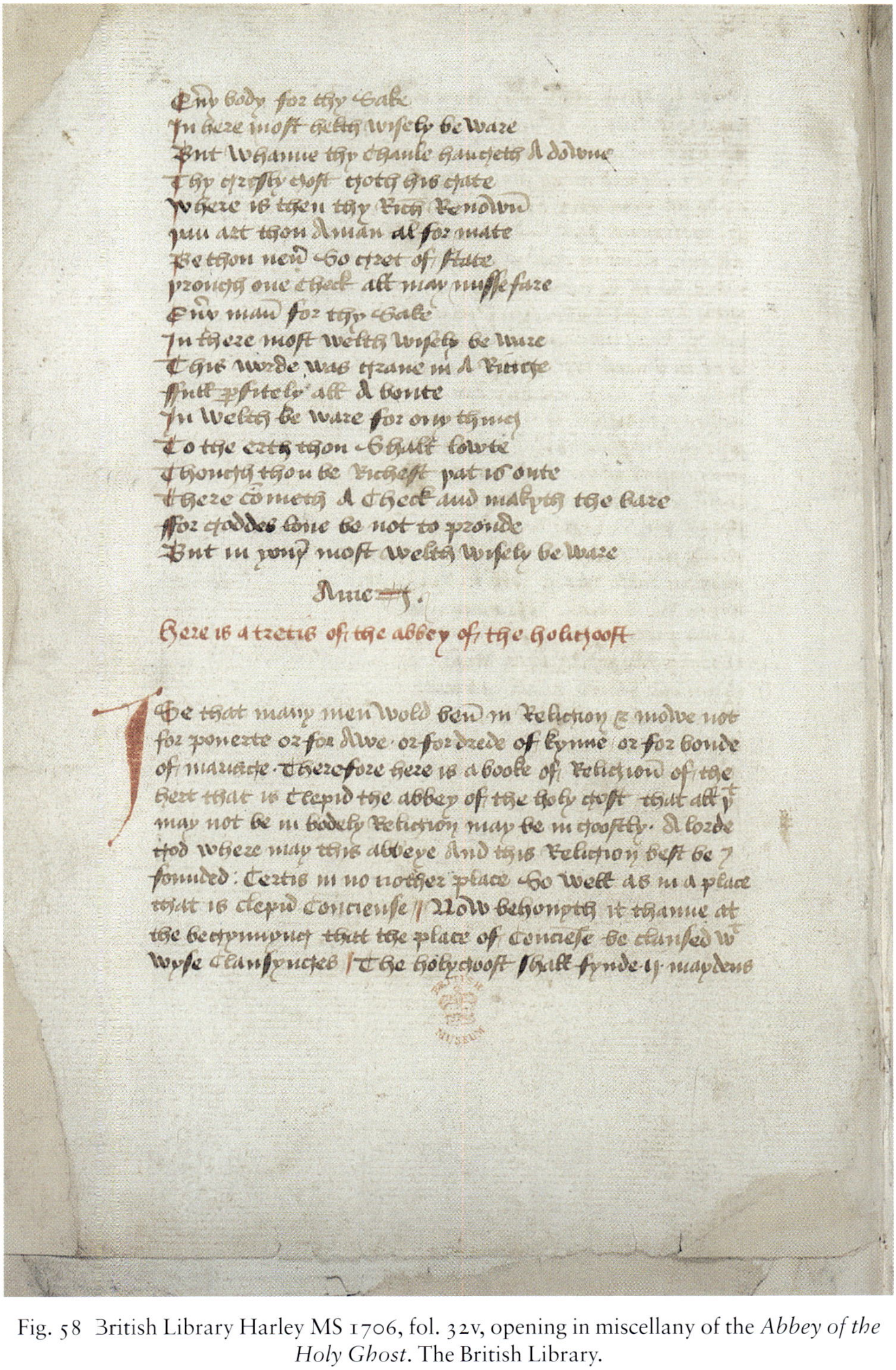

Fig. 58 British Library Harley MS 1706, fol. 32v, opening in miscellany of the *Abbey of the Holy Ghost*. The British Library.

Canterbury Tales.[259] The sustained pictorial representation of nuns is, then, another exceptional feature of the Stowe afterpiece.

It is furthermore unknown in English miniatures, as far as I am aware, to find women depicted in physical labour such as shovelling dirt and lifting blocks of stone[260] (fig. 62). And the grotesquely caricatured nuns shown as handmaidens to the devil are also, to my knowledge, unknown elsewhere in English book art of this period. The final oddity that needs to be mentioned is the fence at the top and inside of each page, apparently as a some sort of enclosure (figs 53–54). It may be an attempt at giving a naturalistic locale to the Abbey building or perhaps it is the suggestion of a *hortus conclusus*, an enclosure for a particularly holy spot such as a clean conscience; but a practical guess relative to the design of the scene would be that the fence was meant to link the two pages visually, just as the river crosses over from the left bottom register to the right.

It is important to locate the Stowe afterpiece in the context of other English miniatures, in particular, of frontispieces, and subsequently to mention it with regard to the only surviving French illustration of the *Abbey*. The issues here are whether facing, full-page illustrations like those in Stowe MS 39 were used as frontispieces; whether the allegorical subject matter appeared in English frontispieces; and whether their presentation corresponds to the Stowe opening. In answer to the first of these issues, there are, as it happens, two other surviving facing pages employed as frontispieces. One is a very attractive opening that occurs before a short treatise called the *Vado mori* at the head of a copy of the *Desert of Religion*,[261] just as the *Abbey* occurs with the *Desert* in Stowe MS 39. Another such opening was created in a Missal by moving the Crucifixion page to the front of the book and facing it with a patron page.[262] Elsewhere, such openings at the head of a text in an English manuscript may run to a sequence of four or as many as twelve full-page miniatures.[263] So, if the opening in Stowe 39 were a frontispiece, its format would not be exceptional.

In order to clarify the second issue, that of pictorial subject matter, I have sorted the conventional subjects of English frontispieces into the following categories: 1) depictions of authors under various circumstances;[264] 2) renderings of patrons and donors, either literally or through their coats of arms;[265] and 3) a single pictorial reference intended to capture either part of or the entire theme of the text, under which I would include maps.[266] Further examples of this thematic mode would be the portrait of Saint Patrick used as introduction to the text of *Saint Patrick's Purgatory*[267] (fig. 63) and that of William the Conqueror granting the Honour of Richmond to Alan of Brittany at the head of the grant.[268] The frontispiece of Noah's Ark in Dublin, Trinity College MS 505 (fig. 64), the Ark here being a quite splendid Onassis-like vessel, refers, by contrast, only to the opening part of a Brut chronicle that covers the chronological period from Noah to Edward IV. Similarly, a full-page scene of the Annunciation may precede a Book of Hours, while actually announcing only the opening part, Matins.[269] It is clear from this listing that the literal content of ordinary types of English frontispieces is radically different from the sequence of allegorical scenes of the 'afterpiece' in Stowe MS 39, even granting that it reproduces the text. The only frontispiece grouping of folios whose subject matter is expressed in allegorical figures is the Chaundler text, the *Liber Apologeticus*, in Cambridge, Trinity College MS R.14.5.

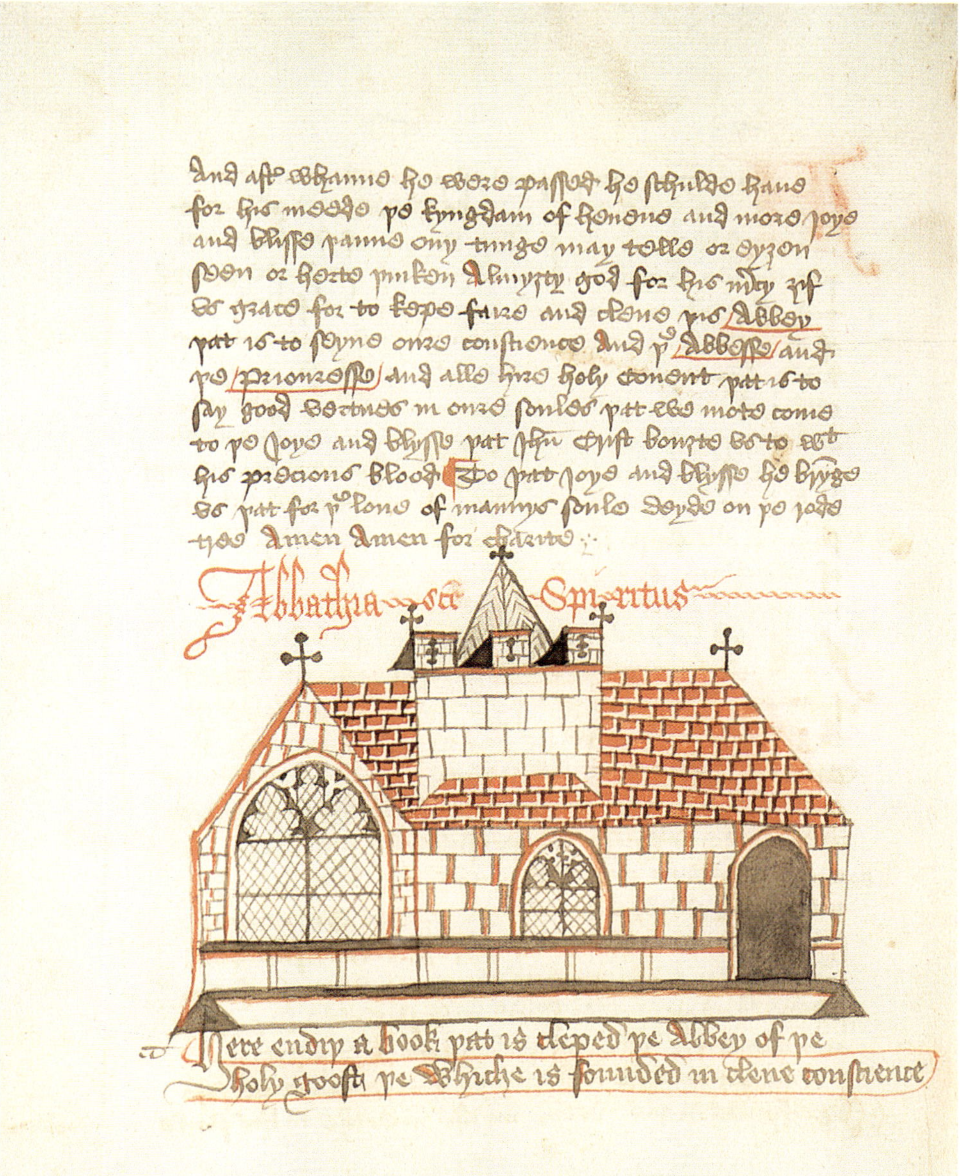

Fig. 59 Bodleian Library, MS Douce 323, fol. 159v, tinted drawing of the Abbey of the Holy Ghost. The Bodleian Library, University of Oxford.

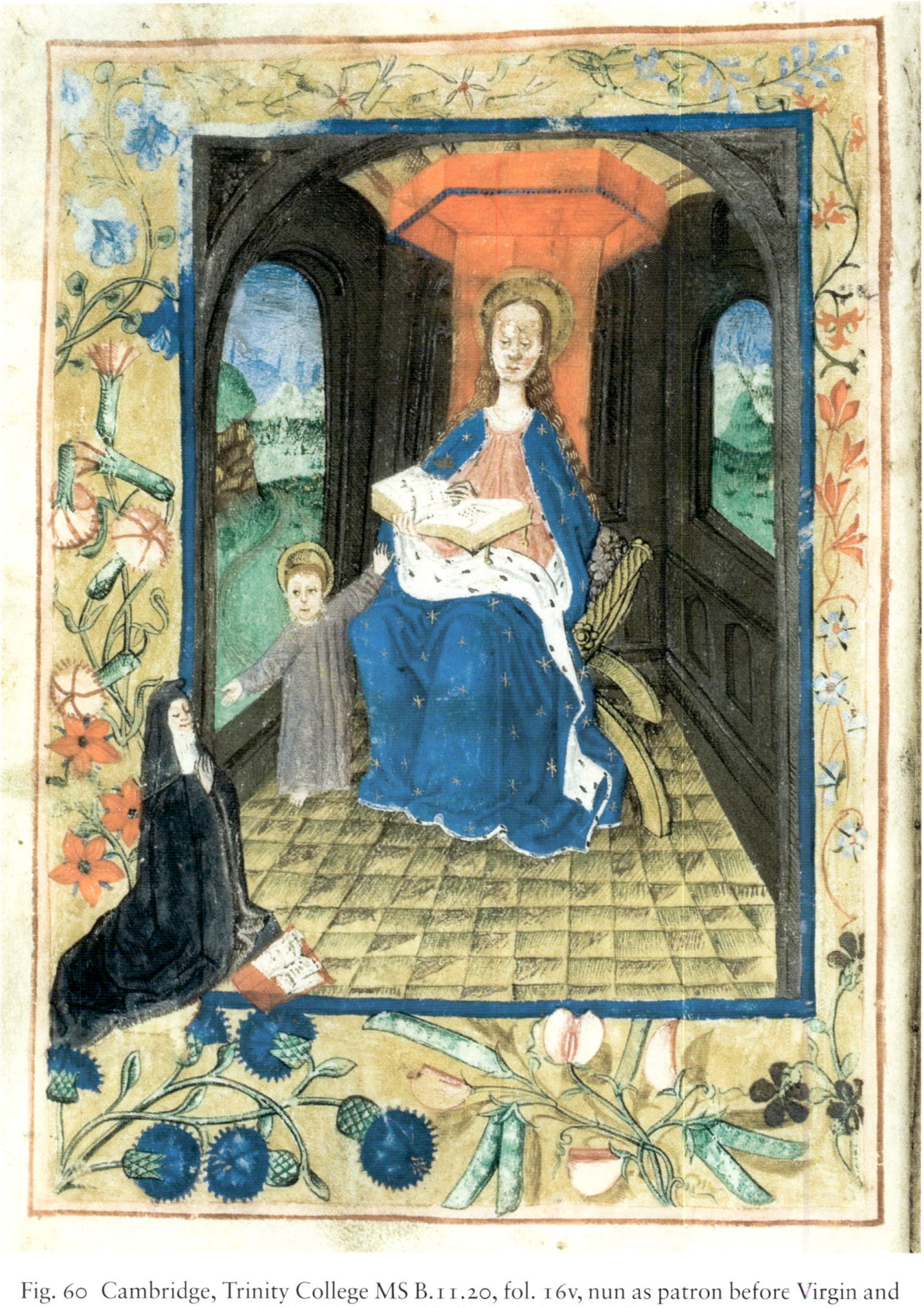

Fig. 60 Cambridge, Trinity College MS B.11.20, fol. 16v, nun as patron before Virgin and Child. Master and Fellows, Trinity College.

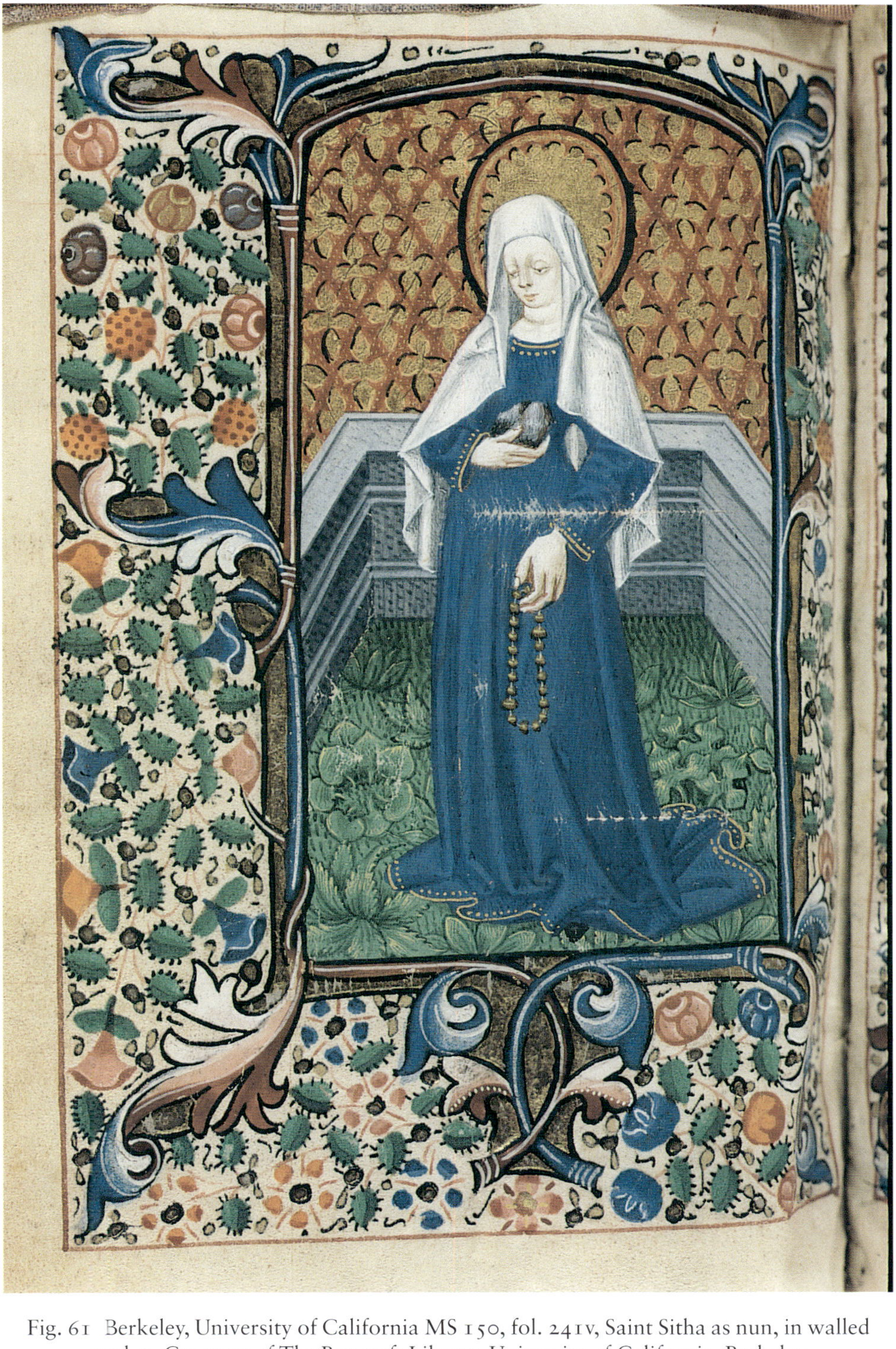

Fig. 61 Berkeley, University of California MS 150, fol. 241v, Saint Sitha as nun, in walled garden. Courtesy of The Bancroft Library, University of California, Berkeley.

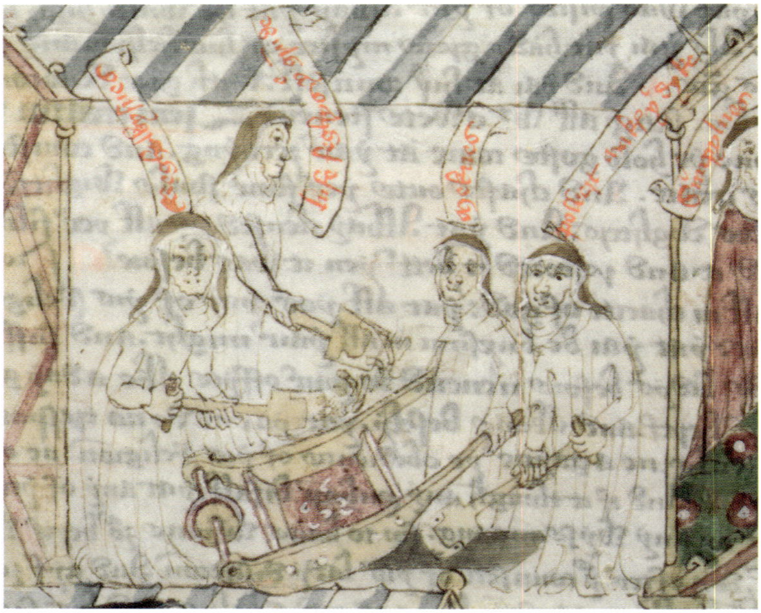

Fig. 62 British Library Stowe MS 39, fol. 8v (detail), working nuns. The British Library.

Three other English manuscripts contain single frontispieces that are, however, more obviously comparable in their presentation to that of the Stowe miniatures. The frontispiece in Bodl. Lib. MS Fairfax 16 has three compartments divided by pictorial not structural framework, with one space unequal in size to the others:[270] beyond format, however, the Fairfax page is not comparable in that its subject matter refers only to the two opening poems, 'The Complaynt of Mars' and 'The Complaynt of Venus', at the head of the manuscript anthology and would, to my mind, belong in the classification of a single thematic reference rather than a recreation of a full poetic episode. The frontispiece in Bodl. Lib. MS Bodley 263 is compartmentalized by amorphous land masses, curving rivers, a sea, and various cut-away architectural structures similar to those in Stowe MS 39.[271] The text is John Lydgate's *Fall of Princes*, a series of separate stories and histories illustrating the theme that what goes up must come down. The designer of this frontispiece chose to render the moment of the downfall from selected 'historical' episodes rather than to summarize visually the entire sequence of episodes, and he chose to function through a cumulative effect rather than through the solitary impact of one story.

The frontispiece in Bodl. Lib. MS Bodley 264 has more in common in presentation with the afterpiece in Stowe MS 39 than any of the others mentioned thus far. This manuscript had a leaf added early in the fifteenth century to illustrate one of its fourteenth-century contents, a *Romance of Alexander* in French (fig. 65).[272] The miniature is divided into two registers of two equal compartments, and the picture spaces are partitioned by thin columns that support a molded cornice; in other words, the framing is architectural in concept and execution. The pictorial matter in MS Bodley 264 is also akin to that in Stowe MS 39 in showing scenes that reproduce events from a single textual narrative, the life of Alexander. It is not allegory, but this

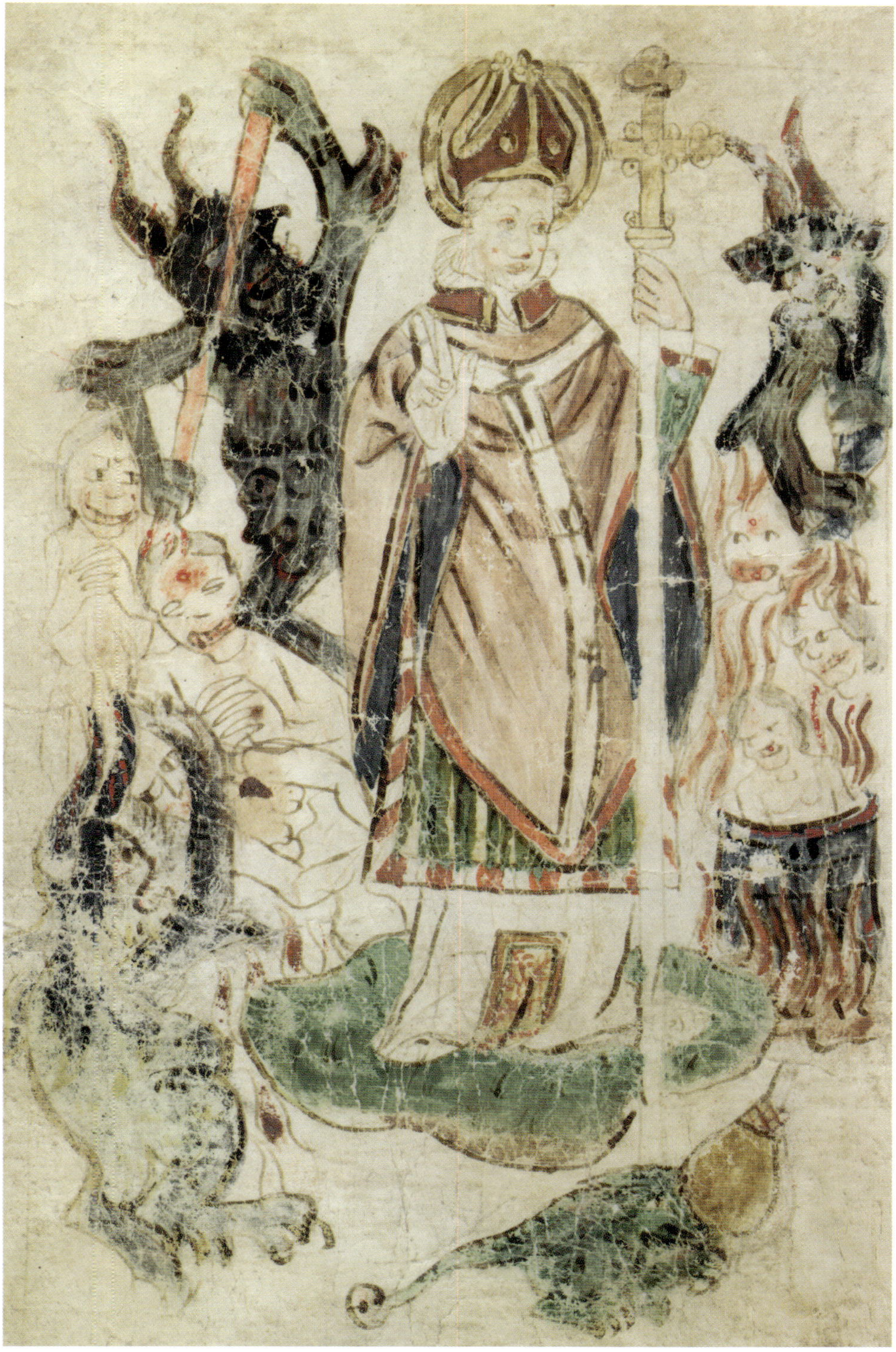

Fig. 63 British Library Royal MS 17.B.43, fol. 132v, (frontispiece) Saint Patrick in Purgatory. The British Library.

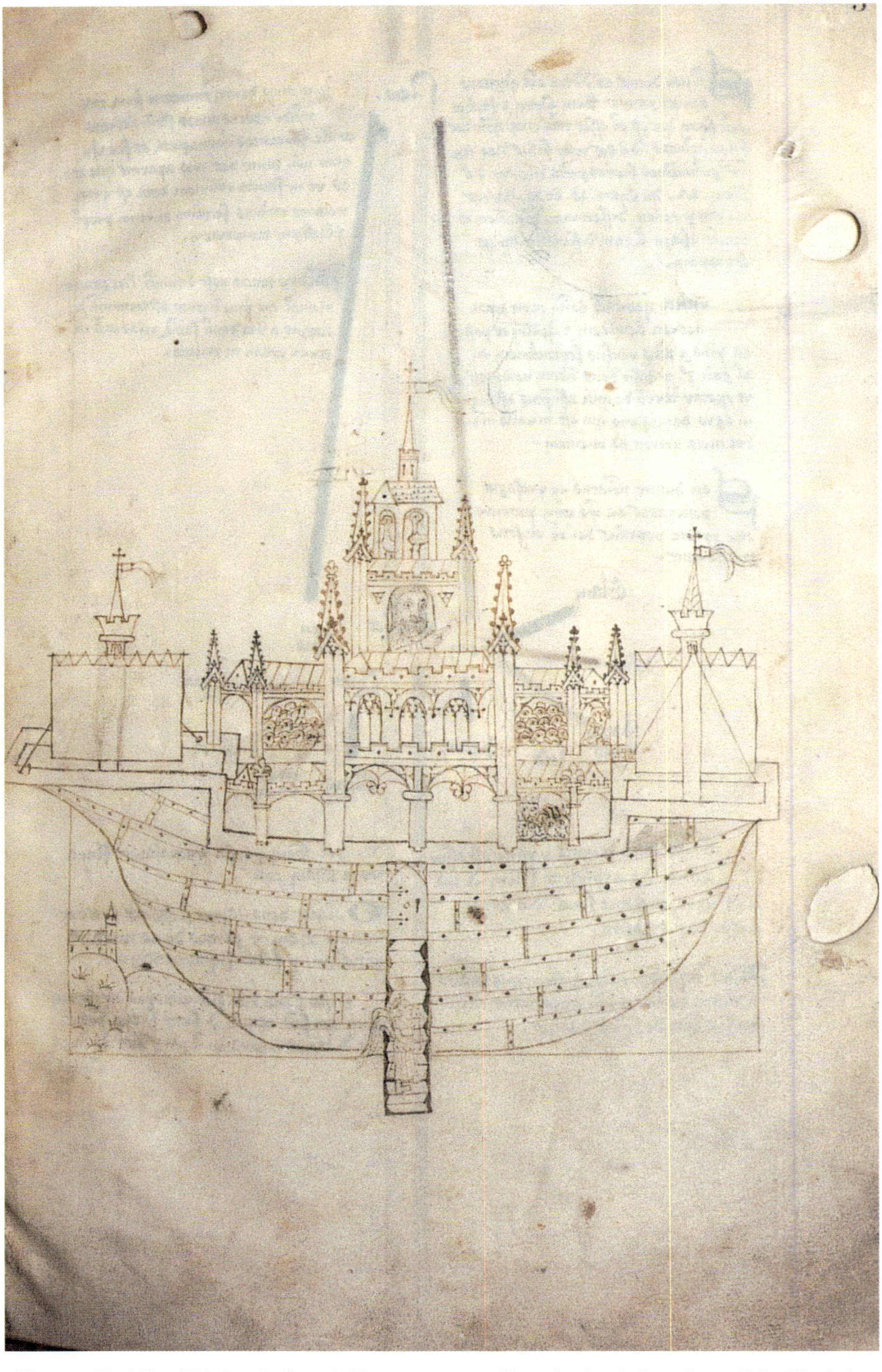

Fig. 64 Dublin, Trinity College MS 505, page 5, (frontispiece) drawing of Noah's Ark. The Board of Trinity College Dublin.

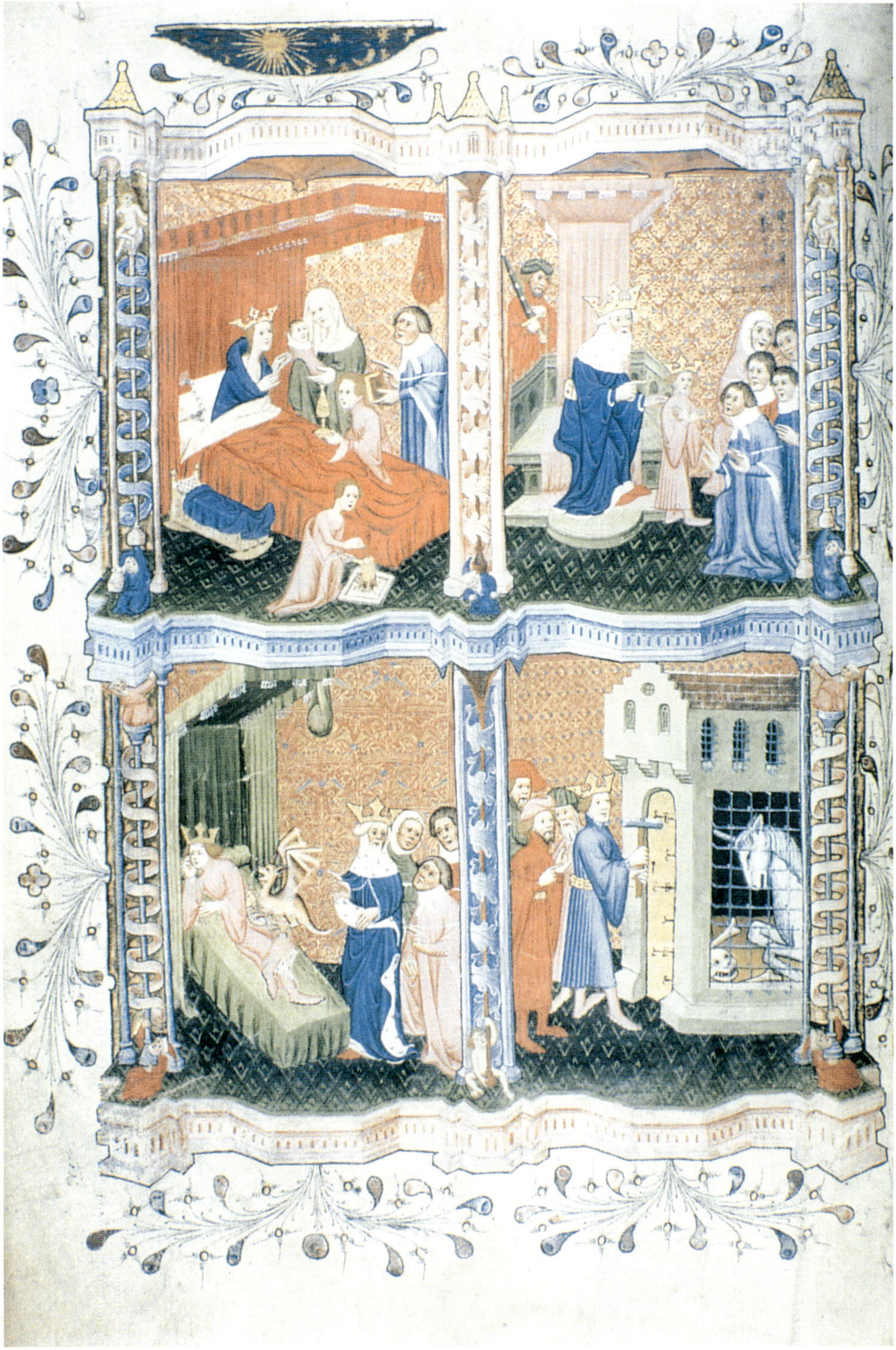

Fig. 65 Oxford, Bodleian Library MS Bodley 264, fol. 2v, (frontispiece) episodes in the life of Alexander. The Bodleian Library, University of Oxford.

frontispiece begins in one place, proceeds in chronological manner through life episodes, and leaves the viewer presumably more informed of the linear development of the story.[273] The concept, then, of dividing an illustrated page into registers was certainly not new, nor was the notion of recording pictorially the chronology of a text, and in these regards the Stowe artist worked well within English conventions.

The French version of the *Abbey*, *L'Abbaye du Saint Esperit*, survives in four different states in nine manuscripts:[274] one dating from around 1300, five from the fourteenth century, and three from the fifteenth.[275] Two are beautifully illustrated, Bodl. Lib. MS Douce 365, dated 1475, in a devotional miscellany made in Ghent for Margaret of York, Duchess of Burgundy,[276] and BL Yates Thompson MS 11 (BL Additional MS 39843), of around 1300–1320.[277] The Douce copy has only one miniature associated with the *Abbaye*, that of four standing allegorical figures (Truth, Purity, Humility and Poverty portrayed as women), and it bears no illustrative relationship to the miniatures in Stowe MS 39. The Yates Thompson manuscript has, like Stowe MS 39, two full-page miniatures that illustrate the *Abbaye* (figs 66, 67), if not on facing pages. Although made 130 to 150 years earlier by a French artist, these illustrations bear a clear resemblance to those in Stowe MS 39 in the structuring of pictorial elements on the page, as well as in a few of the figural groupings. The entire upper part of the first Yates Thompson miniature-page – fol. 1 – with God the Father as part of a Trinity[278] in a mandorla does not appear in any form in Stowe MS 39, nor do the supporting figures in architectural niches beside the Trinity, of angels, the Virgin, St Peter and saints. The lower part of this page is divided into two abbey-like structures with cutaway compartments, and they show at left a grouping of nuns that is thematically similar to the middle group on fol. 9 of Stowe MS 39 (fig. 59), that is, the French scene shows Courtesy with a birch and (standing) novices, two with an open book, a grouping comparable to Courtesy teaching a (kneeling) novice with open book in Stowe. The opposite scene at lower right of this first French miniature depicts the abbess and a nun kneeling in adoration of the Trinity, not a theme that occurs in either of the Stowe pages.

The second of the Yates Thompson miniature-pages (fig. 67) is more impressive as a possible archetype for the second miniature-page in Stowe MS 39 (fig. 54). Both miniatures are contained within an architectural setting and have spatial divisions created by columnettes into which nuns are disposed. The French miniature (fol. 6v) at the same time shows notable differences: it is divided into only two registers, and the tower feature is differently placed and more elaborate than in the Stowe miniature, having a rose window and two pinnacles; and the French scene also shows a smaller tower with bells rather than with a clock face as in Stowe 39. Both scenes have, however, a row of nuns with the abbess at the far left of the row, and there are two similar groupings of two nuns in each miniature. On the whole, the earlier French scene places more emphasis on the role of clerics in the Abbey: in the upper register a priest with two deacons (rather than nuns as in Stowe MS 39), one holding a fan, is depicted saying mass at a dressed altar with chalice (not with the Holy Spirit as in Stowe 39) and in the lower register a priest with a cleric and an acolyte with cross take part in a procession which seems to head the row of nuns. In the Stowe manuscript, the only priest shown is hearing the confession of the allegorical figure of Confession. Apart from Penitence or possibly Courtesy with a birch, the French pictorial interpret-

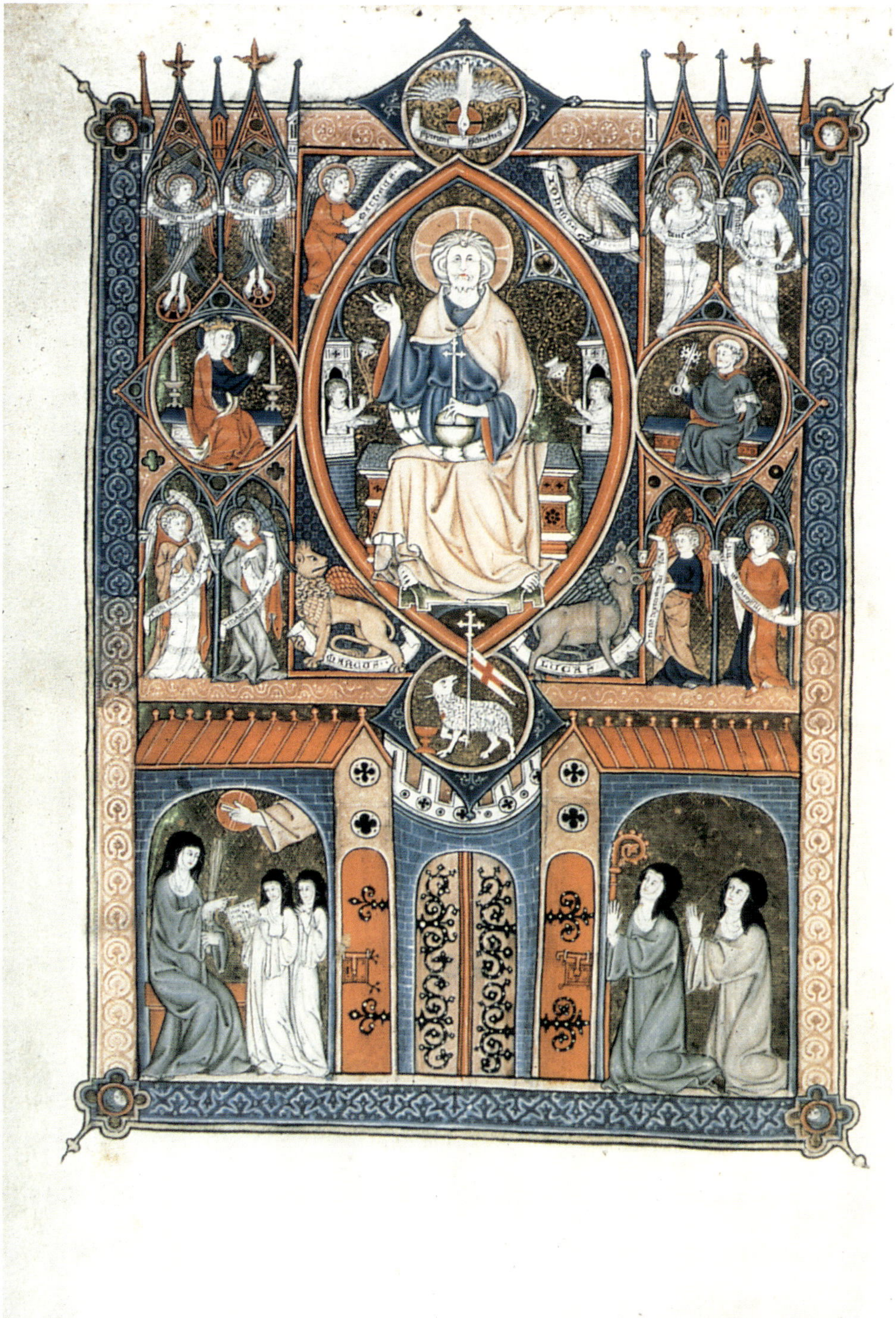

Fig. 66 British Library Yates Thompson MS 11, fol. 1v, Abbey of the Holy Ghost, with mandorla of God the Father. The British Library.

ation of the text shows little or no interest in identifying the nuns as individual allegorical figures or in depicting their labours in constructing the Abbey, guarding it, carrying out charitable acts, or even in the appearance of the Holy Ghost, not to speak of the daughters of the Devil. All in all, there is little likelihood of a direct connection between the French miniatures of *c.* 1300 and the Stowe scenes of the fifteenth century, and, if there was an intermediary, it is apparently lost. The rough liveliness of the Stowe scenes would suggest a dynamic and sympathetic creation by the artist and his supervisor, that the scenes are *their* individual adaptation of the text, not that of a model.

It may be useful now to offer a more substantial account of the text of the *Abbey* and its relationship to the sequence of images in the afterpiece. The text in this manuscript begins with an address to 'My dere systirs',[279] and then speaks more precisely to those women who would be 'in religion' but may not because of poverty, age, fear of kin, or the bond of marriage. For these, the author promises to make 'a book of the religion of the heart' so that, if not possible to be bodily in religion, these women may be so in spirit. In the miniature on fol. 8v the scroll above the structure at the top begins with the location of the narrative in an inscription that states, 'þe site is cald clene Conscience' (fig. 53), and we know at once where we are: in a Christian edifice of a spiritual significance that is pictorially grounded in reality yet emblematic of a religious state. The textual narrative concerning the Abbey follows on immediately from the address, with the Holy Ghost sending down two maidens, Righteousness and Love-of-Cleanness, to cast all manner of foulness from the abbey. But the miniature depicting this passage does not show the Holy Spirit and contrariwise labels these figures 'Meditation' and 'Rewfulness'; and they are depicted with non-textual baskets, presumably to carry away the filth. So, from the outset there are several deviations from the text.

The first register of the miniature (fig. 53) further shows a nun sick in bed and an empty altar, neither of which occur in the text. The textual chronology goes on to the digging of the foundations by two maidens called Meekness and Poverty, who in terms of the Stowe afterpiece are at the right of the middle register of fol. 8v (fig. 53), and the text then tells us that the Abbey is founded beside a 'good riveer of teeres', which is placed in the third or lowest register of the miniature. Obedience[280] and Mercy arrive to raise the walls (they are at right of the third register), and in the top register of the second page (fig. 54) Patience[281] and Fortitude erect the pillars.

The text then follows with a listing of further allegorical figures: Confession with a priest, at lower right of the third register on fol. 9 (fig. 68), Preaching (behind Confession), Prayer,[282] Contemplation, and Devotion lifting a block, at left of the middle register on fol. 9, and Meditation. Only after these virtues have built their various sites in the Abbey of Conscience, only after they have prayed and sung 'Veni creator spiritus', only then does the Holy Ghost visit the Abbey, pictured on the altar, at the right of the first register of fol. 9. At this point the text has a rather long disquisition concerning Charity the abbess (upper register of fol. 9, with crosier), Wisdom the prioress (next to Charity), Meekness the subprioress (next along), then Discretion the Treasurer, Prayer, and Jubilation, all of whom constitute the row of nuns. Textually, Penance is next, then Temperance and beside her Soberness, then Pity and Mercy, Fear of God[283] as porter of gates to the cloister, which is pictured back at

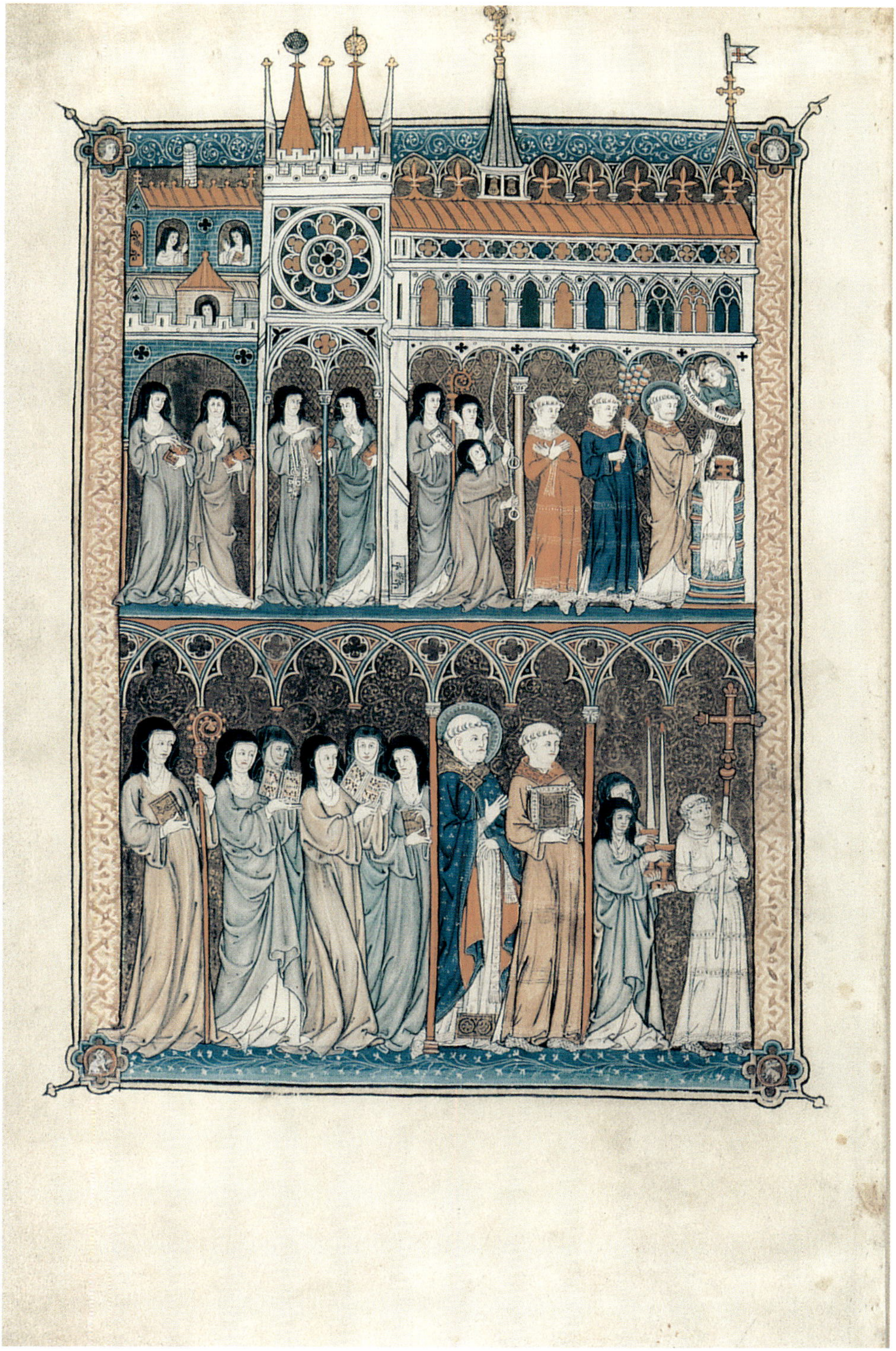

Fig. 67 British Library Yates Thompson MS 11, fol. 6v, Abbey of the Holy Ghost, in two registers. The British Library.

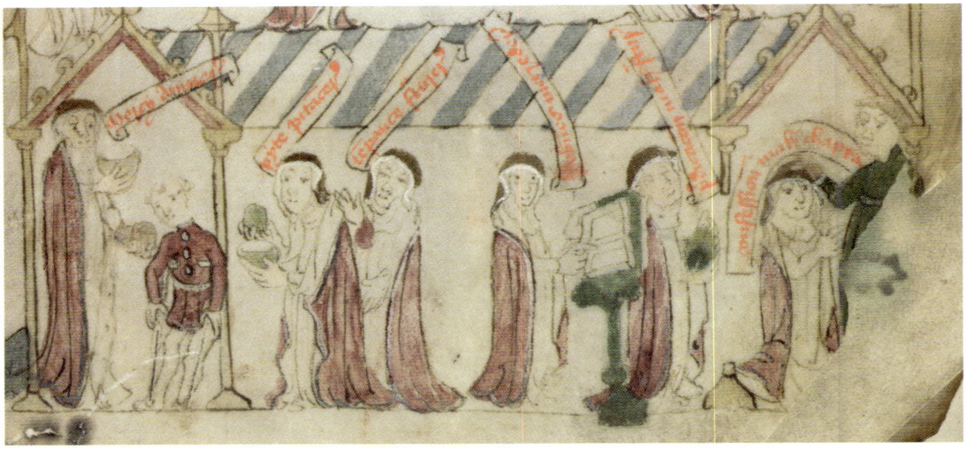

Fig. 68 British Library Stowe MS 39, fol. 9, (detail, lower register) (left) Mercy and Pity, each offering bread and drink to a young man with crutches; (right) Confession with a priest; etc. The British Library.

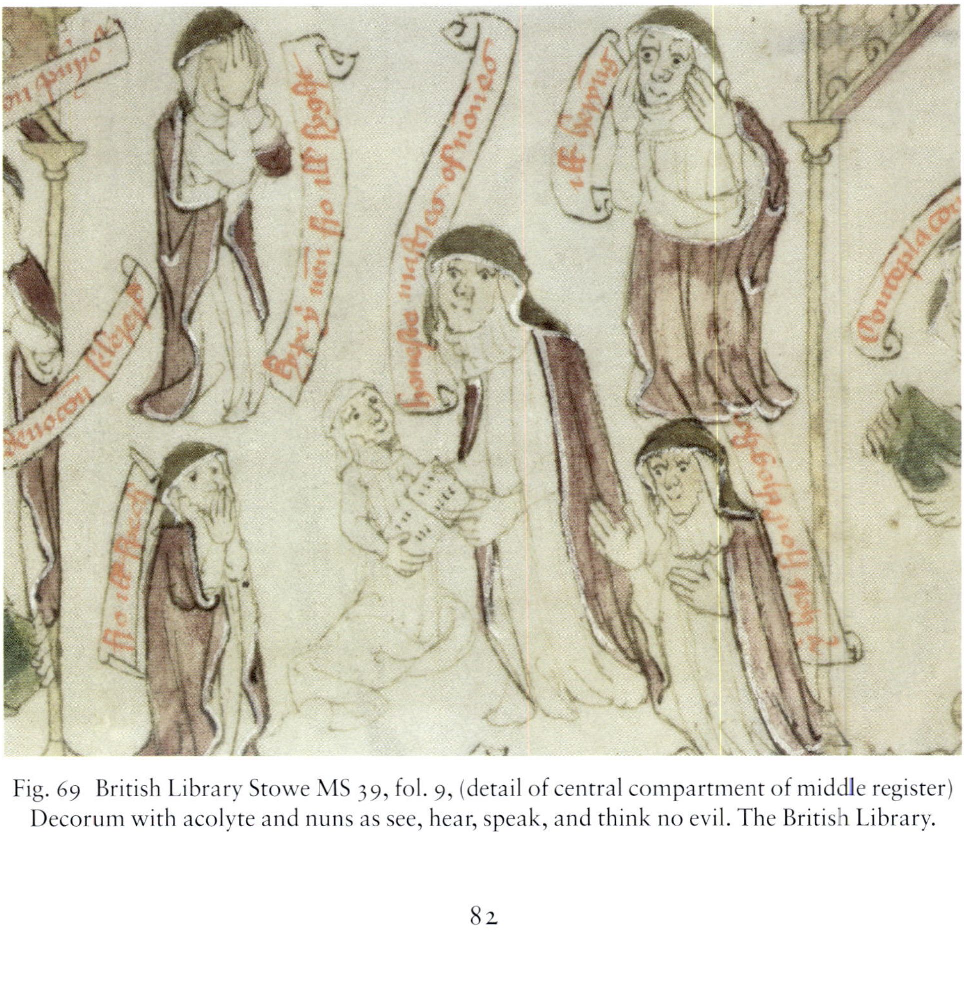

Fig. 69 British Library Stowe MS 39, fol. 9, (detail of central compartment of middle register) Decorum with acolyte and nuns as see, hear, speak, and think no evil. The British Library.

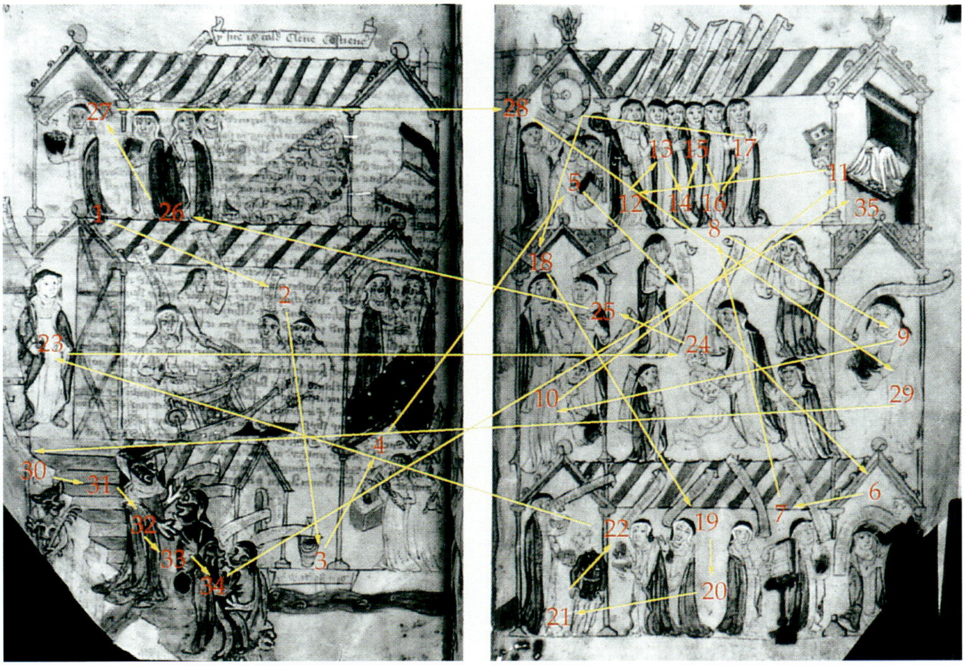

Fig. 70 British Library Stowe MS 39, fols 8v–9, diagrammatic relationship of the text of the *Abbey of the Holy Ghost* and the Stowe afterpiece. The British Library.

the front of the second register of fol. 8v (fig. 53), and Decorum,[284] mistress of novices, with two damsels, Courtesy and Simplicity. In the miniature (fig. 69), by contrast, Decorum is accompanied by four figures and a kneeling acolyte. Textually, Reason follows, then Service,[285] and a second mention of Meditation, with a long disquisition on this subject, the 'principal English interpolation into the French text'.[286] The last two figures named in the text are Bellringer,[287] who wakes the convent for Matins, and Zeal, the nun who wakes the zealous *before* Matins.[288] At this point in the narrative, the Devil introduces into the Abbey his four ugly daughters, Envy, Pride, Grudging and False Judgement. A chapter meeting is called by the Abbess, and Discretion counsels an appeal to the Holy Ghost through prayer. The Spirit arrives, drives out the foul daughters, and the Abbey is restored to its former state. The text ends with the author's plea to whomever reads or hears of this religion to keep the good ladies of the Abbey spiritually in their heart.

As is obvious by now, the relationship between the text of the *Abbey of the Holy Ghost* and the pictorial afterpiece in Stowe MS 39 is very complex as far their mutual chronologies are concerned. The relationship is in fact an excellent example of 'systemic rivalry' within books[289] in that the Stowe pictures are anything but a mimetic reading of the *Abbey* text. They are a second, uncertain text in relation to the written one rather than a pictorial recreation. They are an artistic approximation, with the text broken up for use as building blocks that can be arranged or omitted to suit the pictorial delimitations of a page as well as the intellectual selection of the planner or artist. The Stowe miniatures have, moreover, in themselves neither an internal nor an external rationale. As an example of the former, we can see the porter-nun standing at the abbey gates, in the middle register of fol. 8v, chronologically before the foundation has been laid or the walls erected; and the hideous daughters of the Devil (fol. 8v) are driven out pictorially before the Holy Ghost is summoned (fol. 9). I have tried to embody the remarkable external disengagement of the miniatures from their text by superimposing onto the two allegorical miniatures numbering and lines of direction to indicate the order in which they actually occur in the text and to indicate, of course, how fully they disagree (fig. 70).[290]

Because the pictorial scenes do not appear in a sequential reading and are not a faithful visual reproduction of the text, we must ask why the course of the allegorical chronology was disarranged? Why were attributes added to accompany the allegorical figures? Can these pictorial revisions help us to understand the function that was intended for the miniatures? And is the position of the illustrations at the end of the text related to a possible special function?

The first issue that one must always raise in such a text/picture situation is the possible intervention of the mind of the artist between the text and its pictorial rendering or the possible intervention of instructions, either of which might be responsible for a mistranscription of the text. If the artist could read and had been left with freedom to interpret the text – both of which are shaky assumptions – then he was the interventionist. And if so, design and production constraints would have been his main interests; that is, the artist might think about how many pictorial episodes he could squeeze onto the size of leaves that he had been given and whether the scenes were more or less what his patron required. If, though, the artist could not read and was given instructions, then the instructing person was the intermediary, and we might assume here that he or she had reasons beyond painterly structuring for rearranging the textual narrative. In this case, we would also have to assume that the artist was working from memory of oral instructions, a notoriously fallible approach. Such instructions must have taken the form of a moderately long listing of figures, such as those noted earlier, or of separate components of the text, such as a nun with building blocks or a nun at a lectern, but not, apparently, of a strict narrative chronology. It is also likely that the instructing person might see the concepts of cleaning filth from the nunnery and of the altar of the Holy Ghost as properly placed, respectively, at the beginning of the text and in an upper register, whereas the concepts of the river of tears and the evil daughters of the Devil would belong implicitly or aesthetically in the lower portion of the page. With such components as these fixed in place, the artist's problem would then have been to fit the rest into a ground plan, elevation, or other scheme of an abbey. Since a page is normally characterized by its height and an abbey more by its horizontal length, the artist may have been led to the decision to present six registers of abbeys or of an abbey, with a further breakdown into compartments to give a notional habitation to the figures. Hence, an organized framework but a disorganized ordering of the allegory.

Apart from the textual chronology and one or two other interpretations, the artist managed very well the feat of assembling and clarifying the many pictorial elements through separation by columns and through placement of figures, either facing each other in groups or standing back-to-back to form an internal articulated scene, as in the lower register of fol. 9. At very least, we can say that separate elements were, as a rule, kept separate, and that the pictorial organization made the two pages very readable, if the order of the text is not taken to be of first importance.

Another device apparently intended to make the miniature pages more comprehensible was the addition of attributes, props, and non-allegorical human figures that identified a location, an activity, or the function of an allegorical figure. Without such items as stone blocks, chisels, spades, a crosier, clock, sword, or a lectern, as well as a non-allegorical figure such as the priest/confessor, it would have been more difficult to understand the significance of certain figures and activities. The figure of Pity is, for example, much helped by the presence of a crippled young man as a 'prompt ... to tender offices'.[291] Fear of God as guardian of the gate is pictured with a sword that is not mentioned in the text, and Conscience is drawn as a non-textual sick nun. The designer of the Stowe 'afterpiece' went even further in his or her self-assumed task of clarifying the text by omitting its digressions, even though two of them, concerning King David and Nebuchadnezzar, might themselves have translated well into standard visual images.

As an explanation for the two pages of illustration in Stowe 39, it is reasonable to suggest that meditation or reflection on the allegory of the Abbey may have been objectives involved in the presentation of the miniatures. Although the figures are small, their separateness and clarified functions were probably intended to provide the impetus for thought on the different qualities that contribute to a clean conscience. In other words, the 'afterpiece' may have been an attempt to cause the viewer to respond differently, as we would put it, to the text. Instead of a linear reading through the *Abbey*, one can drop in at will on the scenes and contemplate any one of them for its own independent meaning. It is a computer-like manner of reading in which one clicks on a word and follows a non-linear hyperlink to an expanded rumination on a subject.[292] In the miniatures one could click, as it were, on 'Fear of God' and then perhaps on 'Preaching' without concern for the sequential textual path from one to the other. My son assures me that the movement of the Stowe scenes is similar to that of cyberspace and surprising, to him at least, in that the scenes so much predate the modern technology. In both cases, however, it is the user who determines how the pictures are read or 'navigated' rather than the chronology of the text.

It is therefore evident that the person responsible for the Stowe 'afterpiece' was someone who was more interested in the allegory and themes of the *Abbey of the Holy Ghost* than in its narrative form, and more interested in emphasizing and refining certain aspects of the text rather than in reproducing the text as a final authority. The central metaphor of the human conscience as a built structure was without doubt taken up with enthusiasm, being repeated as it is in six stories on the two pages. Equally, the allegorical figures were seen as an important method of communicating the truths of the text, but where the truths were not self-evident or according to the liking of the designer, this person was not above changing the import of the text. The pictorial handling (fig. 69), for instance, of Decorum, mistress of novices, demonstrates this kind of change. Textually, Decorum is there to teach novices 'alle cortesye', how they shall 'speken, gon, sitten, and stonden'. These phrases sound like instructions for manners from a courtesy book, but in the picture they are translated into quite a different concept: the see-, hear-, speak- and think-no-evil dictum, here pictorialized as figures with gestures more appropriate to this morality than to good manners. Inscriptions on the relevant scrolls also fit the pictorial concept, not that of the text. The overriding means of communicating this interventionist version of the text was, of course, the fundamental decision to include miniatures at all, at the same time as the agenda of the designer of the miniatures was to supplement the narrative of the text by his or her innovative reinterpretation of it in picture.

The position of the pictorial opening at the end of the text also contributed to the designer's purpose of emphasizing certain selected themes. The two pages of miniatures constitute a 'summary reading' that could be looked at by those who did not read or that could be used as a supplement by those who could read or had only heard the text. I see this supplementary 'summarizing' function also present in frontispieces with multiple compartments, as well as in sequential series of frontispieces. The frontispiece series of two openings each divided into three registers in Bodl. Lib. MS Douce 546 constitutes, for instance, an encapsulated version of the text, *Master of Game*, showing the different types of dogs used in hunting, and deer antlers of various types or at different stages of development.[293] These miniatures (fols 1v–3r) immediately precede the text, and they are witness that frontispieces could be conceived as summarizing more or less technical information. This kind of function is also applicable to pages that depict a series of narrative events. I have mentioned earlier the compartmentalized scenes in Bodl. Lib. MS Bodley 264 (fig. 65), which summarized an extensive narrative text, and MS Bodley 263, which showed in separate pictorial blocks the theme of a larger sequence of unrelated episodes. 'Summarizing' frontispieces might, then, have learning, teaching and memorial functions as much as, or even more importantly than, a pleasurable purpose; and they, indeed, supplement the imagination of the textual narrative and of its author.

However, because Stowe MS 39 concludes with the pictorial opening, these scenes, even disordered as they are relative to the text, may also be considered a review of the *Abbey of the Holy Ghost*. The text was brief enough to be appropriate for reading aloud at meal or other times in a nunnery,[294] and the miniatures may have been particularly useful in working with novices and children boarded at the nunnery for schooling,[295] namely, as an ABCs of the means for entering into a clean conscience – spelled out in pictures. Apart from the usual surviving records of children in medieval religious houses, there is rather nice evidence for my hypothesis in these lines from *Piers Plowman*:

> Abstinence the abbesse myn a.b.c. tauȝte
> And Conscience com aftur and kennide me betere.[296]

Reginald Pecock has said that 'summe extractis or out drauȝtis be maad into smaler bokis and tretices proporcianable and euere meet to ech mannys mesure of receyvablenesse'.[297] 'Ech mannys mesure of receyvablenesse' is a fine phrase, and the 'receivableness' of novices and children sets in place an appropriate social context for the pictorial opening at the end of Stowe MS 39 and explains the need for a supplement. For this purpose the immense truths of the text had to be rendered in reduced size, in line and tint, rather than in the complexity and ambiguity of an allegorical concept.

CHAPTER IV

The Genealogical Genre: BL Royal MS I.B.x

British Library Royal MS 1.B.x (Part I) contains the *Compendium historie in genealogia Christi,* a summary of biblical history by Peter of Poitiers, Chancellor of the University of Paris from 1193 until his death in 1205. The *Compendium* was written in the form of a diagrammatic genealogical succession that traced Christ's descent from Adam and Eve; it also included notice of biblical figures who did not enter into the genealogy.[298] The work is further interpolated with 'a great number of passages' borrowed from the *Historia scholastica* of Peter Comestor.[299] It is possible that this Poitiers text was written 'as a teaching tool' for training clerics.[300] The majority of Poitiers' chronicles made in England in the fifteenth century and earlier were written in rolls, and the Royal manuscript is unusual in being a codex.[301]

The *Compendium*, on fols 8–33v, was added in the second quarter of the fifteenth century, together with four other items, at the front of a thirteenth-century Jerome Bible. The other added items are the *Speculum theologie* (fols 1–7), Tables of the Epistles and Gospels (fols 34–39), a Table of the first words of each Psalm (fols 40–41), and a concordence of the Gospels (fols 41v–43v), the last three of which are not illustrated.[302] A fifteenth-century annotator added *nota bene* signs both in the Bible and in the four added texts, confirming that both parts of the Royal manuscript were together by then.[303] The *Compendium* is on thirty-three folios and ends incompletely – in mid-stroke of the genealogical descent as far as the artist was concerned – less than a third of the page down on fol. 33v.[304] Comparison with thirteenth-century copies of the text shows, however, that not much is likely to be missing. The Royal text is interwoven with a dense programme of pen-and-ink drawings of a high quality and often a highly unusual subject matter.[305] It is these drawings that are the focus of this chapter, together with the drawings in the seven preceding folios, the *Speculum theologie*, which contains full-page tables, diagrammatic trees, and images and tables of a religious nature. These and the other added articles in Royal MS 1.B.x were written by the same scribe, and the *Compendium* and *Speculum* were illustrated by the same artist.

The fifteenth-century part (fols 1–43v) of the Royal manuscript is constructed of parchment quires of eight sewn onto modern paper strips in such a manner as to leave the centre string visible. The size of the first text leaf at fol. 8 is *c.* 290 × 210 mm, and the total number of folios including the thirteenth-century Bible is 291. There are no signatures or catchwords either in the *Compendium historie* or in the *Speculum theologie*. A non-medieval hand, probably sixteenth-century, has written 'p. 4' at the top right of fol. 1, suggesting the presence of missing leaves before the present first folio; this hand also wrote 'I.B.x'. Folio 1v bears 'Emeria in aliquibus Exempl', as well as the couplet: 'Tres trib*us* Arma viris fertur peperisse Marial; Quas duxere viri,

Ioseph, Alpheus, & Zebedeus'. On fol. 3v hand of the previous couplet wrote: 'Memoriae [Miae] quoad A*nim*am consule, Castiga, Solare, Remitte, fer, Ora/ quoad corpus Visito, poto, Cibo, Redimo, tego, Colligo, Condo.'[306]

Many of the Royal pictorial subjects (see Appendix E) do not occur in other Poitiers' manuscripts, and often not in any other fifteenth-century English manuscript. It will, however, be possible to give only an oversight of the unusual or prominent scenes in Royal MS 1.B.x and to mention only those that establish the innovative nature of this copy of the Poitiers' text. The opening page of the Royal *Compendium* has two miniatures: a partly finished scene of the Fall of Man (fig. 71), as it is possible to judge from the outlines in crayon of the serpent, the Tree of Knowledge, and a figure standing opposite Eve; in the space below The Fall, there is a scarcely begun sketch of Adam delving and Eve spinning. The former subject occurs frequently in English manuscripts, but the latter is rare.[307] A tinted drawing from an English *Speculum humanae salvationis* (fig. 72) of the early fifteenth century,[308] Oxford, Corpus Christi College MS 161 is reproduced here as a fully rendered example of the subject. The scene is not known in any other fifteenth-century English Poitiers' *Compendium* but does occur in a few thirteenth-century copies (see below) and in a quite different form in a roll containing Roger Alban's chronicle, i.e. as Adam standing (not digging) with a spade.[309] The genealogical descent (*Linea genealogie*) in Royal MS 1.B.x starts just below these two unfinished miniatures, with inscribed roundels for the lineages of Cain and Seth.

Before proceeding with a survey of the rest of the pictorial subjects in Royal 1.B.x, it would be useful to to give some sense – based on the opening page of the Royal *Compendium* – of the pictorial chasm between surviving thirteenth-century English Poitiers chronicles and this mid-fifteenth century copy. The opening membrane of BL Additional MS 24025 has, for instance, as its first miniature, a roundel of the Creation of Eve at the top and below a series of four roundels in a foliate panel with Old Testament scenes[310] followed by a rectangular miniature of Adam delving and Eve spinning (fig. 73). The same thematic arrangement of subjects with very similar iconography is in BL Additional MS 14819, both sequences undoubtedly based on the same model. Somehow, the last scene, of Adam and Eve at labour, in these thirteenth-century sequences survived down to Royal MS I.B.x, suggesting that an older illustrated copy of the text was available to the makers of the Royal manuscript.

Another type of thirteenth-century copy opens with a miniature of the Fall of Man,[311] and it must have had in this regard the most far-reaching influence, since the majority of the fifteenth-century versions of the *Compendium* have the Fall of Man as their only miniature. BL Lansdowne MS 456 and BL Harley Rolls C.9 (fig. 74) are examples of the conventional late medieval presentation of the text and contrast in format and number of miniatures not only with earlier copies but also with Royal MS 1.B.x. Thirteenth-century copies show even further variation: Bodl. Lib. MS Lat. theol.b.1 begins with Christ in a mandorla supported by angels and a seven-branched candelabra just below. BL Royal MS 8.C.ix (fol. 3), and Bodl. Lib. MS Laud Misc. 270 (fol. 1), open with separate 'portrait' scenes of Adam and Eve, and the latter has only one diagram of Noah's Ark, where normally two or three versions are drawn. The thirteenth-century Poitiers manuscripts have, however, pictorial subject matter that agrees with the full figural drawings (in contrast with the small roundels) in Royal MS

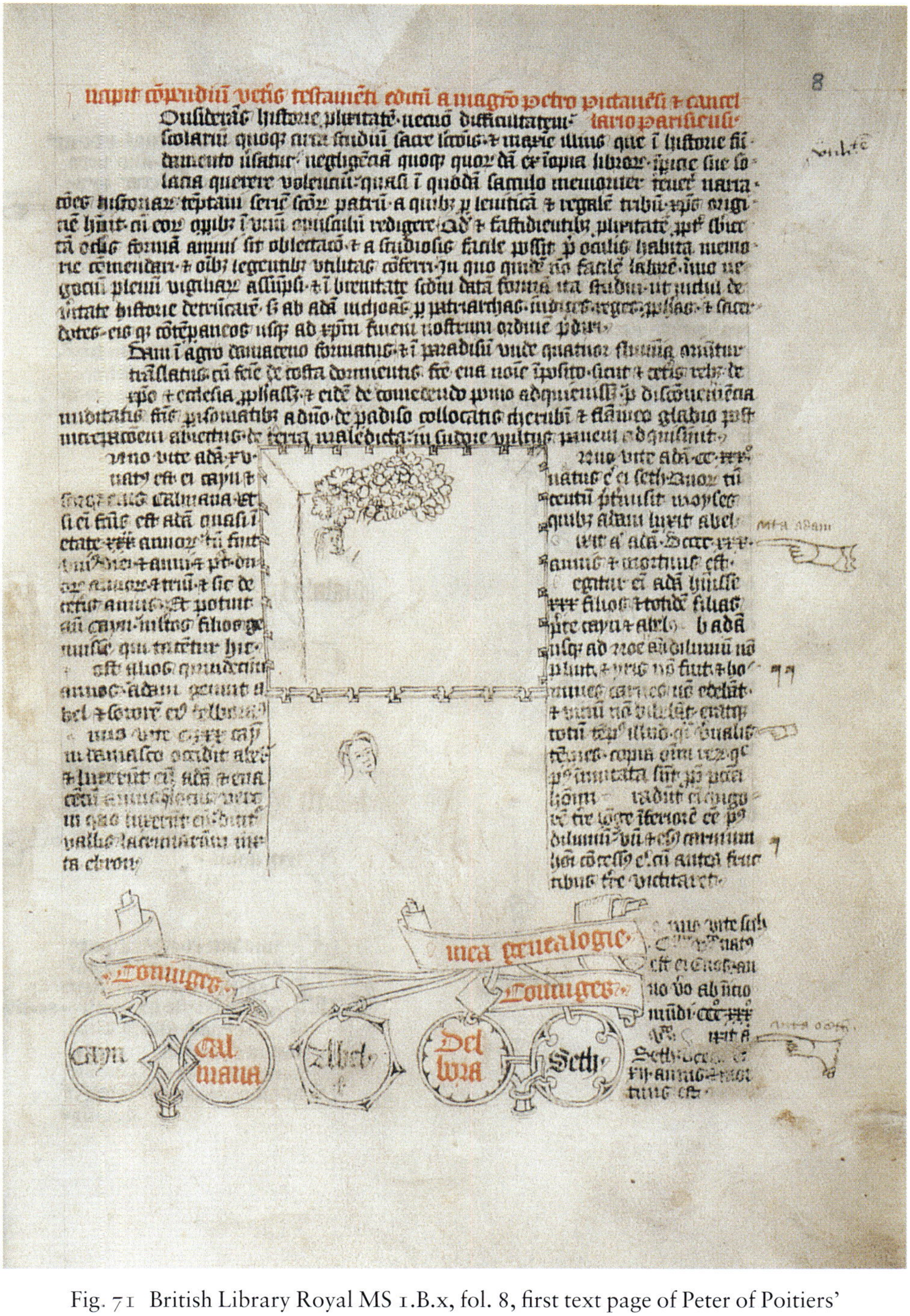

Fig. 71 British Library Royal MS 1.B.x, fol. 8, first text page of Peter of Poitiers' *Compendium historie in genealogia Christi*, with unfinished miniatures of the Fall of Man and Adam delving and Eve spinning; *nota bene* hands. The British Library.

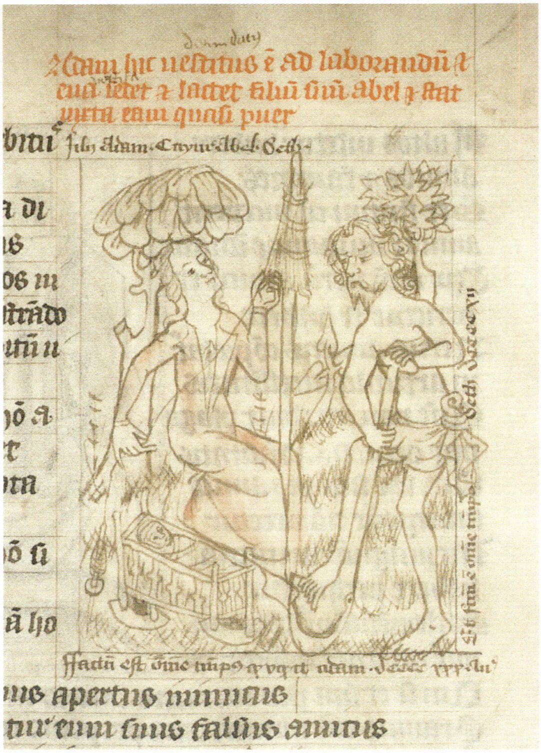

Fig. 72 Oxford, Corpus Christi College MS 161, page 7 (detail), tinted drawing of Adam delving and Eve spinning. By permission of the President and Fellows of Corpus Christi College, Oxford.

1.B.x in only two or three other instances: the Fall of Man, Noah's Ark, and King David harping. It is, then, not possible to look to the earlier versions for a precisely equivalent source of the Royal manuscript but to them for only selected pictorial subjects.

In the pictorial sequence in Royal MS 1.B.x, we find, following the unfinished Adam and Eve scenes, an exceptional rendering of Noah's Ark (fig. 75). Here the names of the voyagers, unusual in itself, are inscribed and there is an uncommon but convivial collection of animals, exact details of the poop deck and rudder, a well defined prow, and a remarkable underwater view of an eel, swordfish and other fish, a crab, tree trunks, drowned towers and spires, a dead cow and goat, and corpses, including a child in swaddling clothes, all in all, an imaginative, snorkel-like view of the sea beneath the fortunate Ark. The artist even includes an allusion to a proverb, at right: 'Big fish eat little fish'.[312] As I have already noted in Chapter 1, conventional English renderings of Noah's Ark take two different forms in the fifteenth century: either an unframed diagrammatic image or images[313] (figs 1, 2) or an actual boat with a small cabin on board, sometimes partly diagrammatic, with only the heads or half- figures of Noah and his wife, and sometimes the other lucky few survivors.[314] Thirteenth-century English renderings of the Ark in Poitiers manuscripts also depict it in two versions, either in the diagrammatic form[315] or more rarely in the shape of an actual vessel, as in the fine copy in BL Royal MS 14.B.ix.[316] The closest contemporary representation of a Ark to that in Royal MS 1.B.x is in BL Kings MS 395 (fol. 3), of

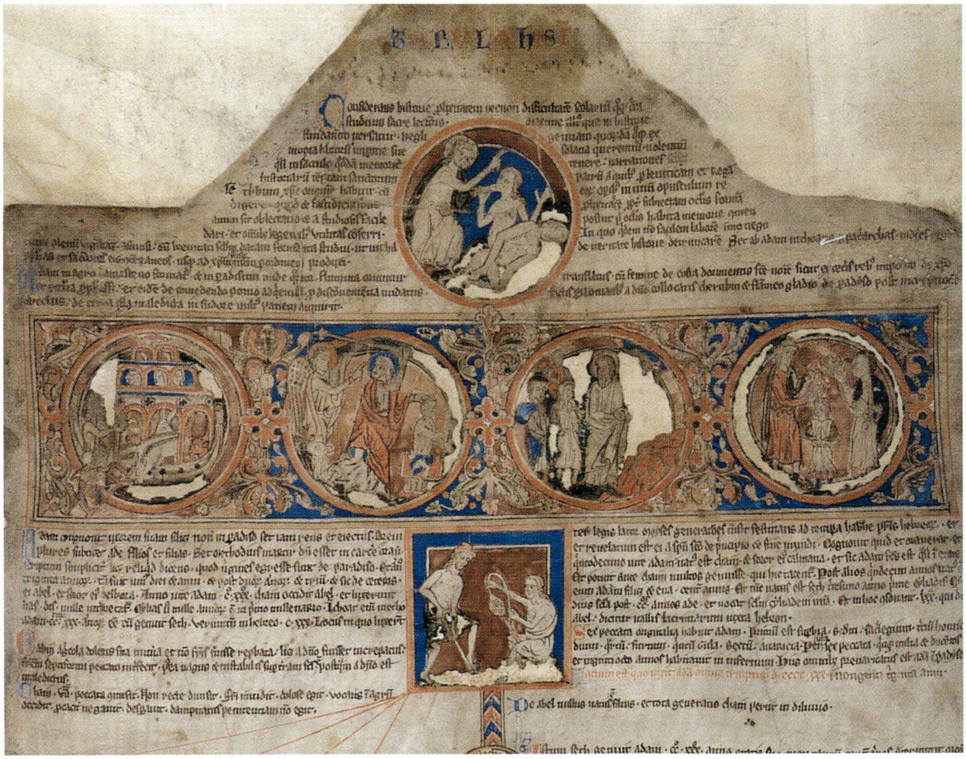

Fig. 75 British Library Additional MS 24025, top of membrane (detail), Old Testament scenes, (below) with Adam delving and Eve spinning. The British Library.

the early sixteenth century, and, even so, its main point of comparison is the unusual inclusion of fish in the lowest partition of a diagrammatic Ark.[317]

After the Ark drawing, the next two pages in Royal continue with a descent of Noah, and fol. 10v (fig. 76) is shown in order to indicate the typical complexity of a page, the intense interaction between text, diagram, and miniature-drawing, and the attention lavished on scrollwork. Throughout this Poitiers manuscript, the page design varies between one, two, three and five columns of text of no standard width. The text 'columns' are usually divided from one another by drawings of branches and of stone pillars that support roundels, plaques and scrolls inscribed with the name or the image of a biblical figure. The roundels are linked or looped to each other by pipe-like tubes or by branches with loops, and surmounted by mitres, crowns, and triple crowns. The manuscript easily has the most intricate decorative design found in a fifteenth-century English chronicle. Folio 10v (fig. 76) also shows a miniature of a crenellated tower made of blocks of stone and finished with turrets, pinnacles and crockets, a hinged door, and portcullis, a structure that represents the Tower of Babel, if without any sign of life.[318] This image does not occur in any other English Poitiers chronicle and is rare elsewhere in English manuscripts. In fifteenth-century manuscripts I can point to only two with a Tower of Babel: Edinburgh, National Library of

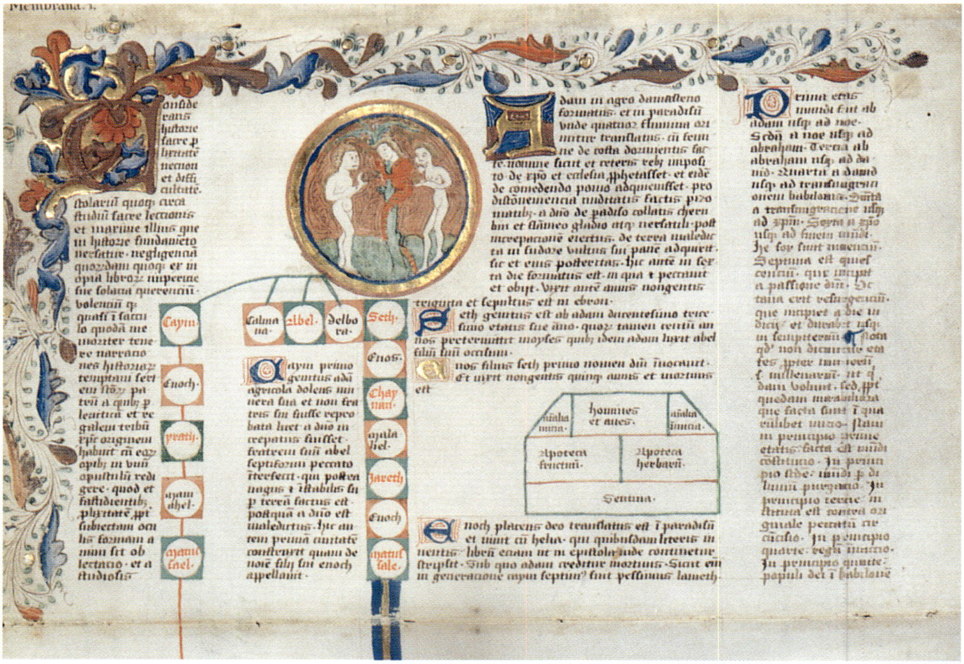

Fig. 74 British Library Harley Rolls C.9, top of roll (detail), roundel with Fall of Man, diagrammatic Ark of Noah, and border. The British Library.

Scotland MS 33.3.1, a *Scala mundi* (fol. 20v), and BL Additional MS 37049 (fol. 9v), a largely Middle English Carthusian miscellany of verse and prose with bizarrely formatted illustration.[319] These two subjects are similar to the Royal Tower of Babel in not showing any human activity, but the structure of the buildings has no iconographical connection with the Royal image.

Next, the Royal manuscript presents us with seven more blank spaces for miniatures,[320] but because the titles of the miniatures were inscribed, we know what the pictures were meant to be (see Appendix E). Only two of these, the Sacrifice of Isaac and the Israelites crossing the Red Sea, can be found in early copies of the Poitiers chronicle[321] and only the Sacrifice of Isaac in other fifteenth-century copies. Folio 15v offers a demonstration of the manner in which the scribe prepared spaces for miniatures by stepping his lines down the text column. He seems to have known exactly what the artist had to insert, and if the scribe knew, then it follows that he was working from an illustrated manuscript, making it possible for him to count the lines needed for any given picture space. Why the artist did not fill in all of the miniature spaces is a mystery, since he and/or the scribe apparently had an exemplar for the completed drawings. It would appear that the artist's job was interrupted for some reason rather than that he had an incomplete exemplar. Even stranger is that all of the blanks for miniatures occur in the first quire and on the first leaf of the second quire, as if the artist had worked backwards through the quires to be illustrated – or, perversely, as if he had begun work in the second quire. He was almost certainly not

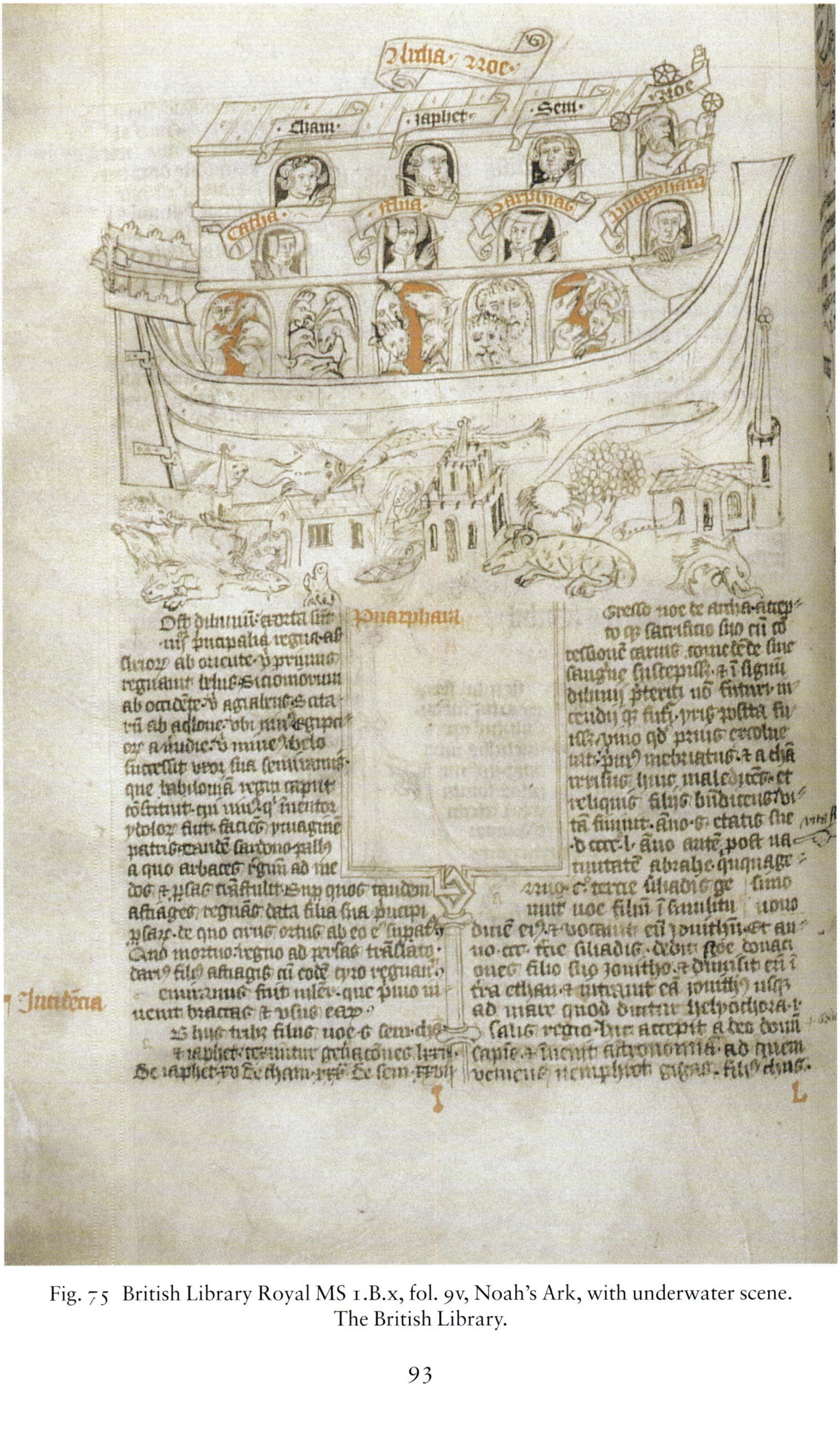

Fig. 75 British Library Royal MS 1.B.x, fol. 9v, Noah's Ark, with underwater scene. The British Library.

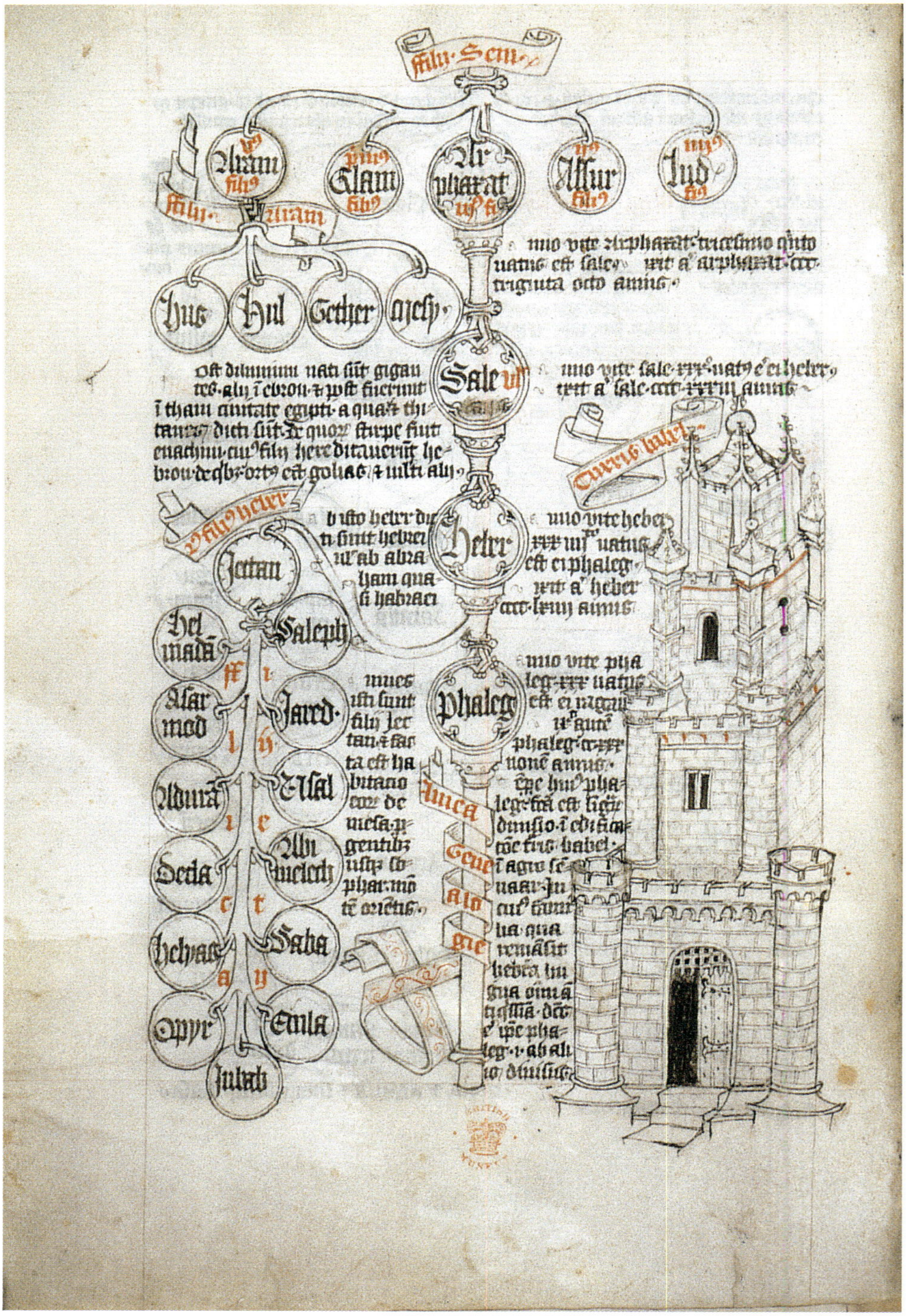

Fig. 76 British Library Royal MS 1.B.x, fol. 10v, Tower of Babel; lines of descent with stone roundels and branches; inscribed scrolls. The British Library.

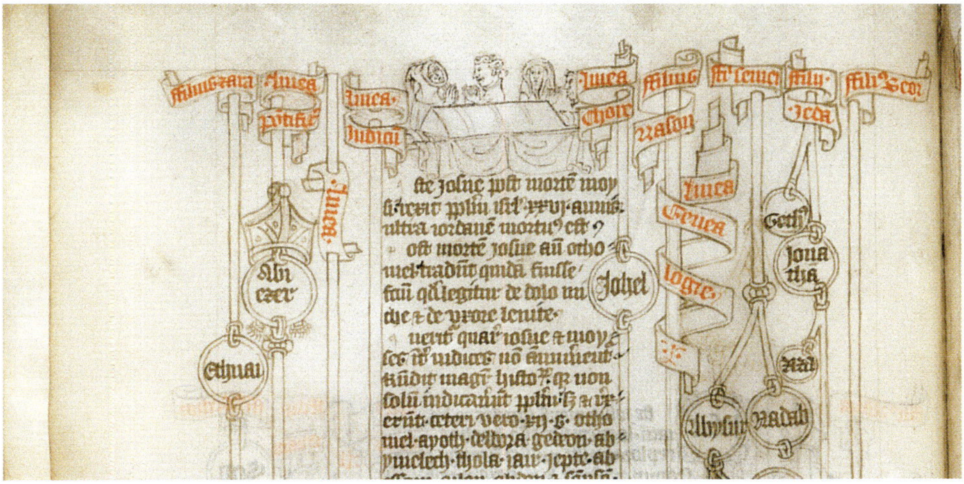

Fig. 77 British Library Royal MS 1.B.x, fol. 16v (detail), death of Moses. The British Library.

leaving these blanks for a second illustrator – pen artists simply did not work that way, that is, they did not collaborate,[322] and, in any case, the Royal artist himself had already worked on some of the pages with blank spaces.

Drawings on the next few pages of Royal 1.B.x are mainly smaller, emblematic items that required less space: a mitre to indicate the *Linea pontificales*, a urine flask with Apollo's name, and garlands with four roses for the *Linea iudicum*. A tiny miniature, with figures lamenting over the draped bier of Moses, occurs at the top of fol. 16v (fig. 77), a rendering adapted from funeral scenes for the Office of the Dead in Books of Hours, but, with respect to Moses, a subject not known elsewhere in English book illustration. On the facing page (fol. 17), there is, oddly, a hurdy-gurdy as the emblem of Mercury, even though the instrument is referred to as a *lyra* in the text (fig. 78). Mercury (Hermes) – messenger of the gods, god of science and commerce, and thief – was also an inventor: relevant here is that he is credited with the invention of the lyre and of music. The *Linea Iudicam* on fol. 17v leads to a small roundel of Samson slaying the lion and finally we arrive at an extravagantly crowned but smallish roundel on fol. 19 of David seated on a bench, harping, with his descendants and relations looped around him. The iconography of David harping is conventional in English illustration generally and in roll chronicles specifically.[323] David harping was in fact a widely employed subject in England in the fifteenth century, mainly in Psalters,[324] and its use even extended, rather crazily, to catchwords, as in Oxford, Magdalen College MS Lat. 97 (fol. 60v).

With a representation of the Temple of Solomon on fol. 20 (fig. 79) we are back to larger scenes and, as frequently in the Royal manuscript, to an image completely different from those usually in Poitiers chronicles. Temple scenes usually show either a plan of the Temple[325] or a cross-section,[326] not an actual structure (see, however, fig. 10). To compound the oddness, this scene has diagrammatic steps that are inscribed with the first words of the fifteen Gradual Psalms.[327] The Royal artist was particularly gifted in rendering architecture, so we can assume that he deliberately drew the portal

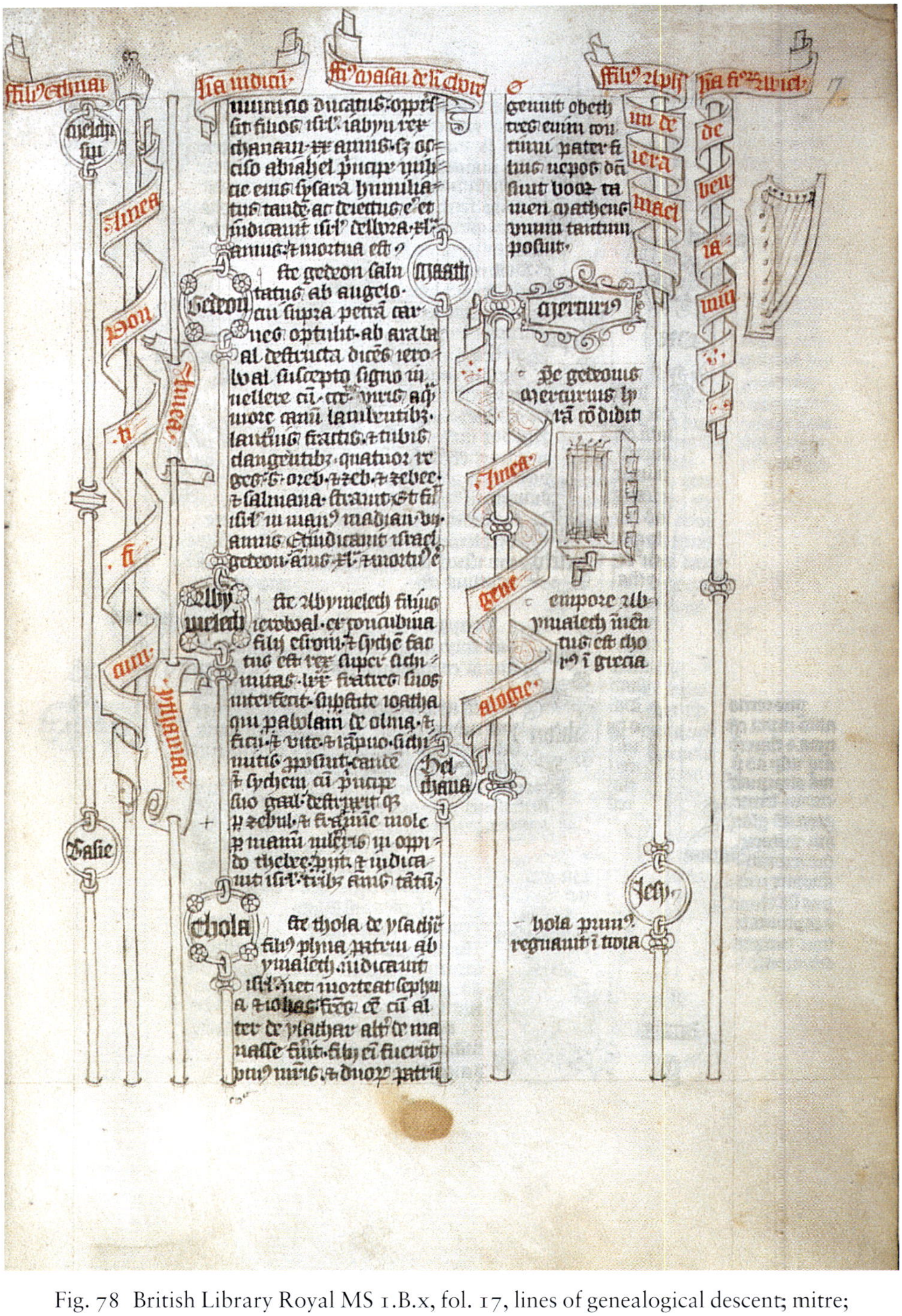

Fig. 78 British Library Royal MS 1.B.x, fol. 17, lines of genealogical descent; mitre; hurdy-gurdy; harp. The British Library.

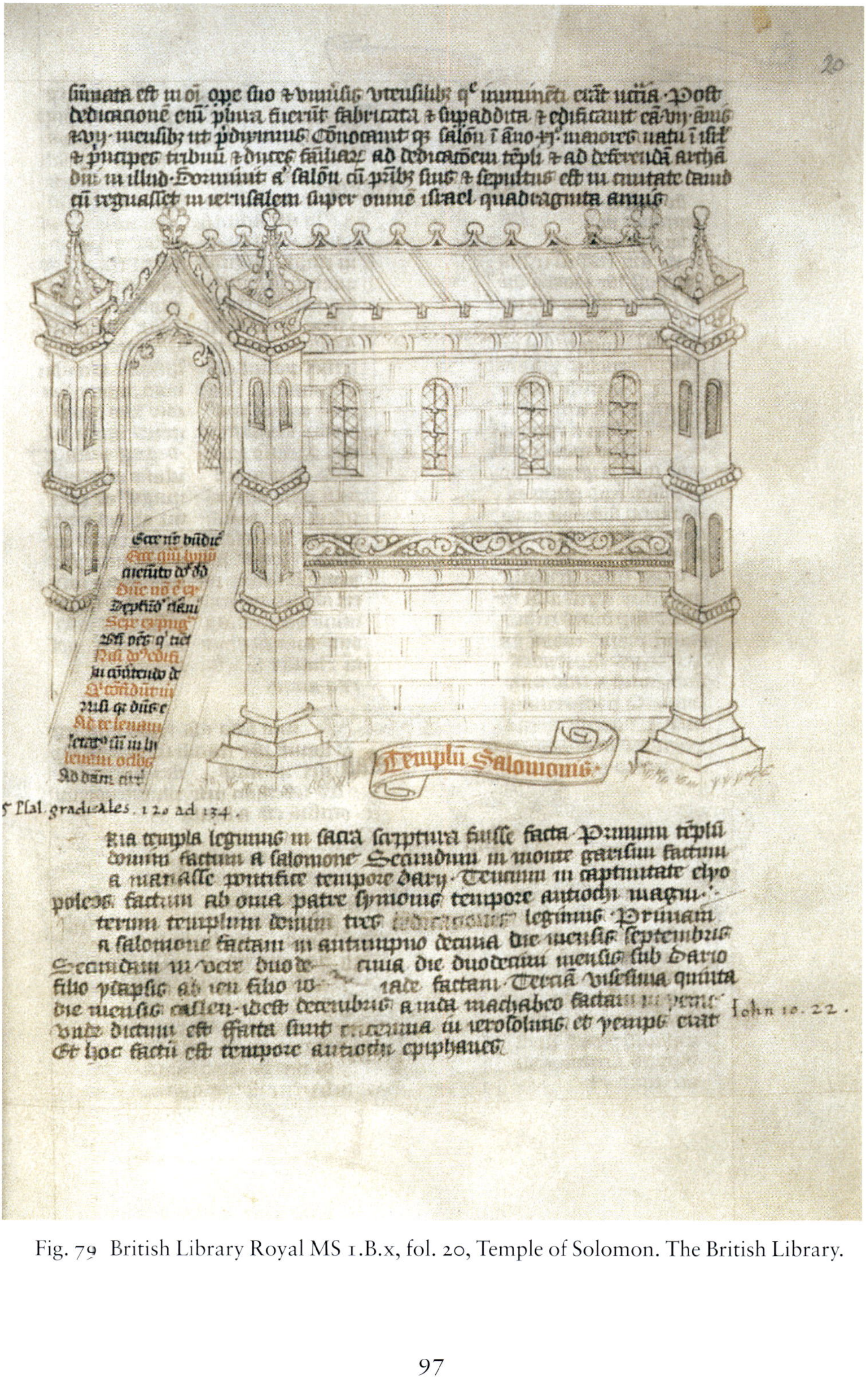

Fig. 79 British Library Royal MS 1.B.x, fol. 20, Temple of Solomon. The British Library.

and supporting towers skewed around to the front in order that the doors and far tower would be fully visible. This was not an uncommon practice, but a charming insistence on seeing the west window of a church.[328]

Another passage considered important enough to illustrate with a full scene was that of Jonah leaving the whale's mouth. The subject is not known in other copies of the Poitiers *Compendium*; it is otherwise found mainly in English copies of the *Speculum humanae salvationis*, if in a very different composition, and only occasionally in Psalters and books of prayers.[329] After this scene, the Royal manuscript continues with heads of biblical personages in small roundels and, more notably, a drawing of Rome with chimney pots and an hexagonal church. A depiction of Rome is again an uncommon subject, apart from a presence on world maps of the period – as in BL Additional MS 37049 and in an unusual copy of Higden's *Polychronicon* illustrated throughout with pen drawings.[330]

Several leaves further, on a splendidly designed page, fol. 26v, there is a small miniature of Judith with the head of Holoferenes (fig. 80), and on the opposite page Esdras seated at a slanted desk with writing board,[331] both, as ever, not in any other English Poitiers chronicle. Judith's gown with rounded neck and hugely draped sleeves (without dagging), and her heart-shaped headdress are nonetheless helpful in dating the manuscript. These styles were in use between *c.* 1425 and *c.* 1440 and would place the book in the second quarter of the century.[332] This scene of Judith is also very rare in English manuscripts with other texts, being found only in an early fifteenth-century book of Prayers, BL Additional MS 22720 (fol. 86); in the Big Bible, BL Royal MS 1.E.ix (fol. 129); and in two copies of the *Speculum humanae salvationis*.[333] None of these scenes is related iconographically to the drawing in Royal MS 1.B.x.

The next exceptional page in Royal 1.B.x is an overhead view of the city of Jerusalem (fig. 81) rendered as a flattened hexagonal series of walls, six gates, and a central space for the king and holy men, with two outer walls defining spaces for nobility and populace; the middle walls are shown with buttresses and crenellations, and the outer walls with turrets and slits for defence. In other Poitiers manuscripts this scene is largely diagrammatic with only a few realistic elements, e.g. BL Cotton MS Tiberius D.iii (fig. 82).[334] Apart from the Nicholas of Lyra manuscripts described in the first chapter, pictorial representations of Jerusalem seldom occur in fifteenth-century book illustration. One rare instance is a coloured drawing of a walled city in the Carthusian miscellany;[335] another is a scene of the Lamentation of Jeremiah in the Big Bible (BL Royal MS 1.E.ix, fol. 206); and a third in the *Speculum humanae salvationis* (e.g. Yale University, MS Beinecke 27, fol. 34v). The aerial view of Jerusalem by the Royal artist is undoubtedly impressive, but may possibly be a concept evolved from the diagrams of the city in earlier Poitiers manuscripts such as BL Cotton Tiberius D.iii.[336]

The scene of Jerusalem is followed by a series of four drawings that are almost certainly unique in English manuscripts: those of Socrates drinking the hemlock, of Diogenes in a teaching posture,[337] of Aristotle teaching Plato, with Hippocrates in a roundel beside and, below in roundels, of Demosthenes and Aristotiles disputing (fig. 83). Below these figures is, as the text says, the temple that Manasses had built on Mount Garizim, again a church with its portal turned to the viewer (fol. 28v). On the

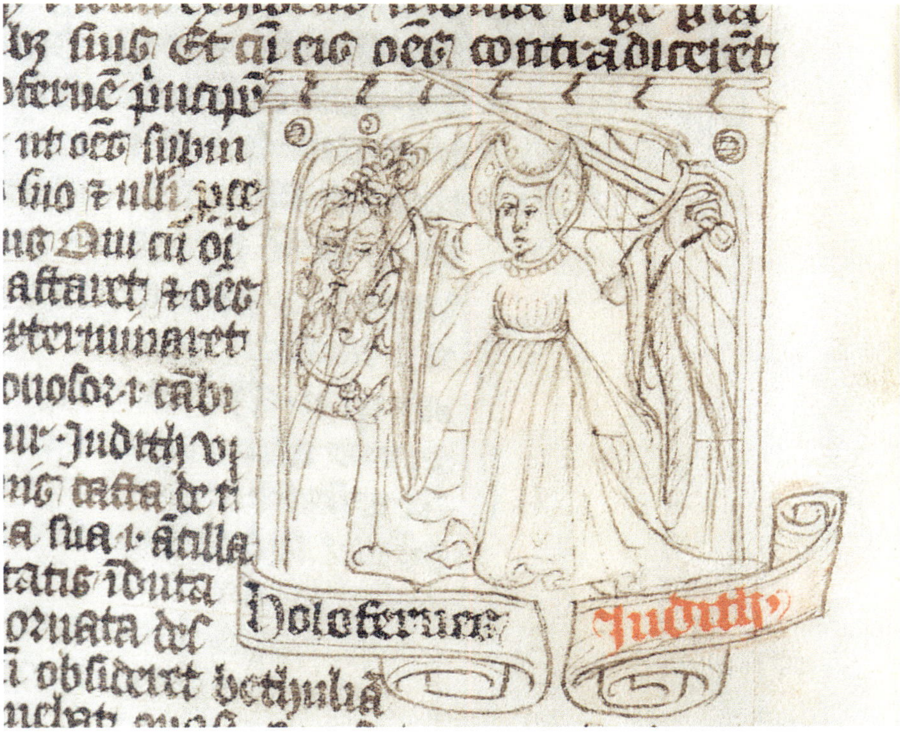

Fig. 80 British Library Royal MS 1.B.x, fol. 26v (detail), Judith with the head of Holofernes. The British Library.

facing page, there is a rare scene of Alexander with upturned sword, seated on a cushion and being drawn by two griffons. Then there comes a plentitude of heads in roundels, of crowns, mitres, and scrolls, until the final scene in the manuscript on fol. 33, a Nativity of the Virgin, rendered in the iconography of the Nativity of Christ (fig. 84), even to Joachim leaning on a cane in the style of Joseph.[338]

On the page following the Nativity (fol. 33v), both text and pen drawings of roundels end, as I have said, abruptly with no indication of the cause. This truncation leaves the impression that scribe and artist were working almost simultaneously and that they might have been the same person. A good many of the thirteenth-century English Poitiers chronicles also end with inscribed roundels,[339] or with roundels and illustrations of the Apostles,[340] but not with a sense of incompleteness.

Thus far the Royal *Compendium* has proved to be both a typical and an atypical chronicle, that is, both traditional and innovative. The design is typical in having inscribed and pictured roundels surmounted by crowns and mitres and in its notion of joining all these by genealogical lines of descent; the subject matter is typical in depicting several traditional scenes: the Fall of Man, Noah's Ark, and David harping. But the manuscript is noticeably atypical in its extensive use of scrolls for titles, in the lines of descent drawn as stone columns, in the large number of scenes not found in other English copies of the Poitiers chronicle, in the absence of diagrams of the forty

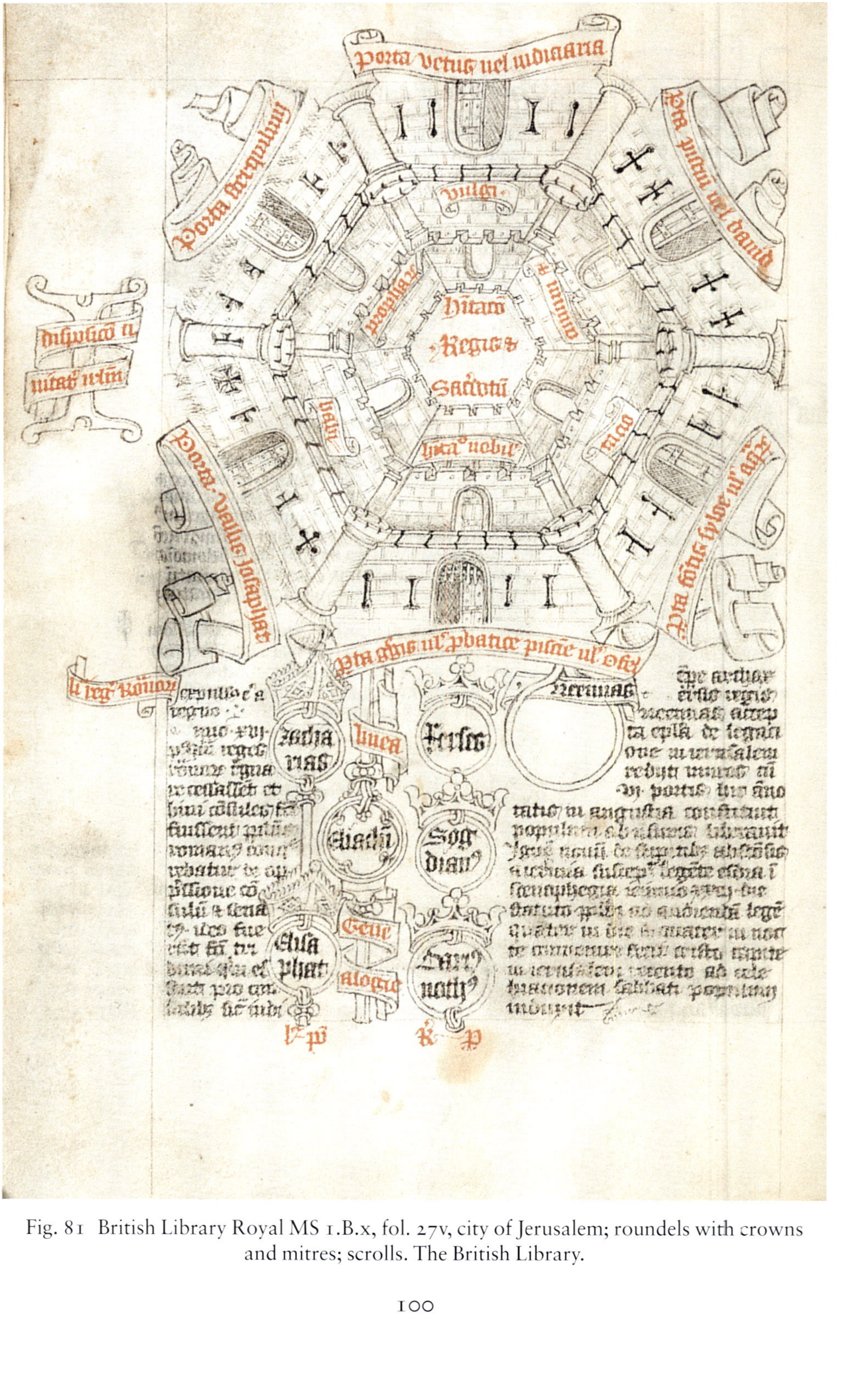

Fig. 81 British Library Royal MS 1.B.x, fol. 27v, city of Jerusalem; roundels with crowns and mitres; scrolls. The British Library.

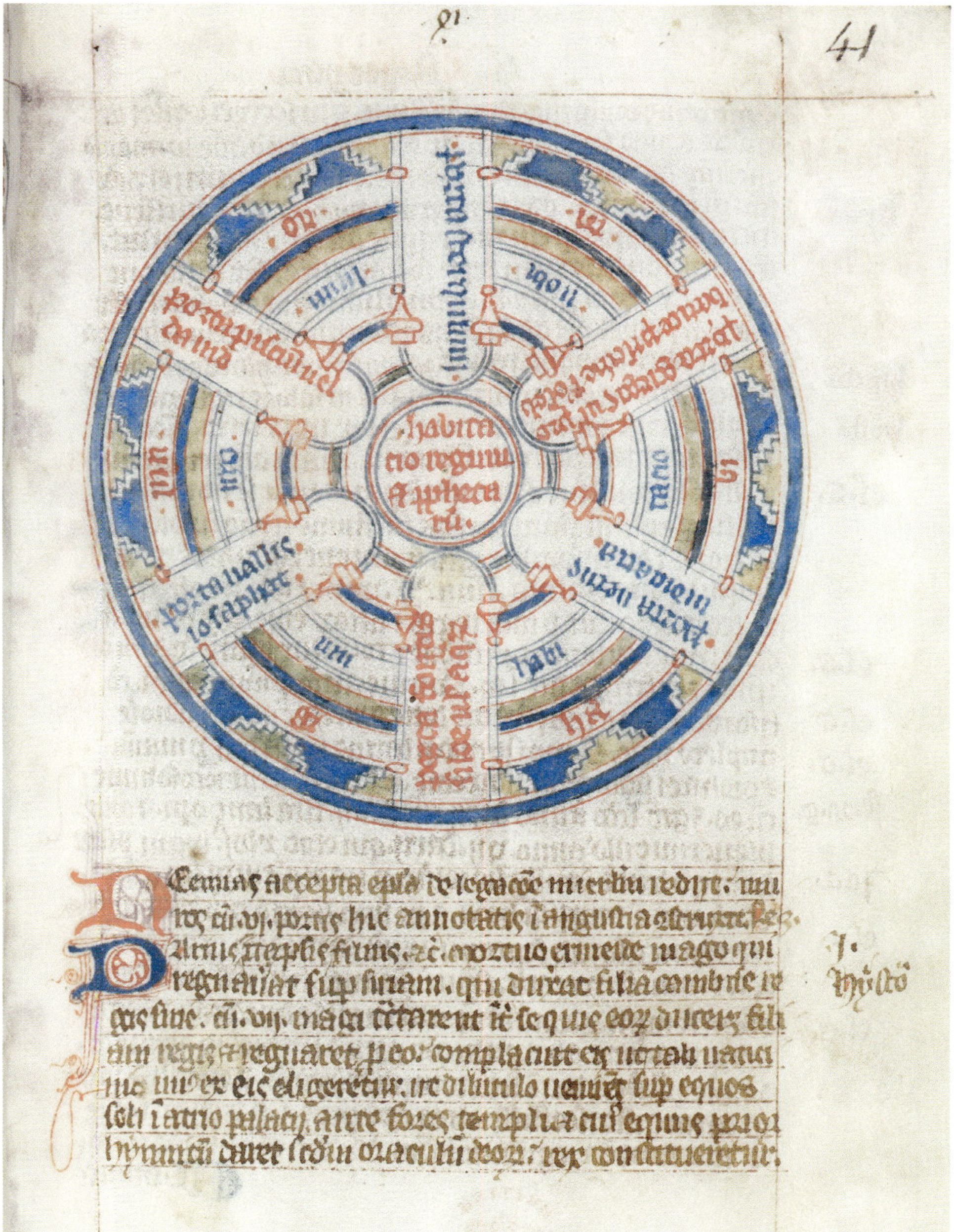

Fig. 82 British Library Cotton MS Titus D.iii, fol. 41, diagrammatic city of Jerusalem. The British Library.

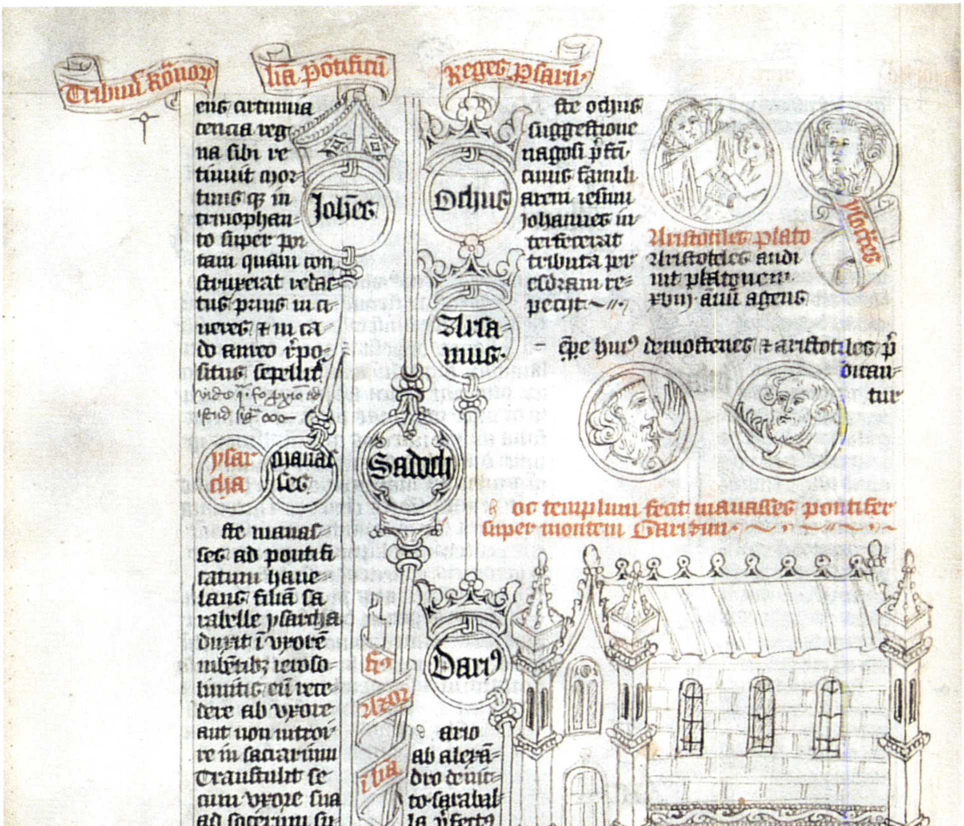

Fig. 83 British Library Royal MS 1.B.x, fol. 28v, roundels with Aristotle and Plato, Hippocrates, Demosthenes, and Aristotiles; Manasses' temple on Mount Garizim; roundels with mitre and crowns. The British Library.

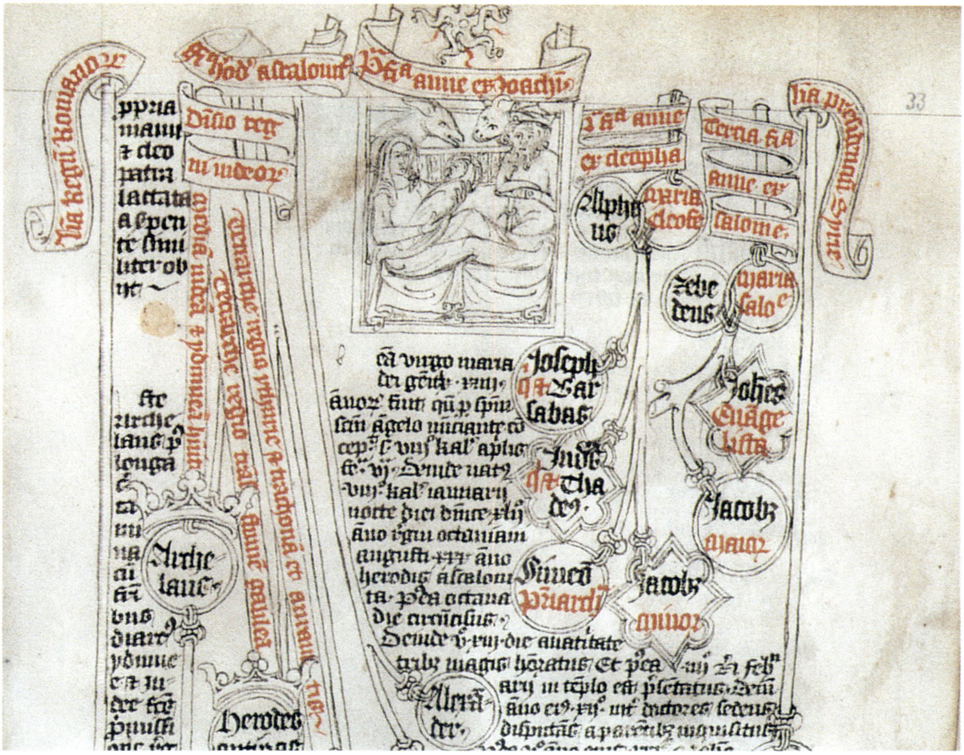

Fig. 84 British Library Royal MS 1.B.x, fol. 33 (detail), Nativity of the Virgin.
The British Library.

resting places of the Hebrews and of a circular diagram of the Hebrews' camps around the Tabernacle of the Ark, and in its lack of colours and gold. The majority of illustrated Poitiers chronicles made in England in the fifteenth century were painted and illuminated, such as that in Bodl. Lib. MS Lyell 33 and BL Harley Rolls C.9 (fig. 74).[341] But though most were illuminated, not pen drawn, they differ even more notably in having only one miniature, that of the Fall of Man, to which format the Royal manuscript stands in arresting contrast.[342]

In addition to the many atypical illustrative features of Royal is the fact that the text of the *Compendium* is preceded by a quire of seven leaves and a stub[343] containing the *Speculum theologie*.[344] The *Speculum* is a collection of moral, devotional and theological tables, and diagrams compiled by John of Metz, a Franciscan, who was 'active in Paris during the last quarter of the thirteenth century'.[345] Such diagrams have been described as '"fixes" for memory storage', as well as 'cues to start the recollective process'; they are open-ended sites for meditation and rumination.[346] The idea of moral diagrams associated with the Poitiers *Compendium* was not in itself new. There had been single diagrams with the text since the thirteenth century, *viz* BL Royal MS 14.B.ix (membr. 9), a Wheel of Vices.[347] And occasionally, stray diagrams from the *Speculum theologie* were attached to fifteenth-century copies of the Poitiers

Compendium, one instance being BL Additional MS 21219, with a large drawing of the *Lignum vitae* at the end (membr. 9). The Royal *Speculum* contains five tables[348] and eight diagrammatic or representational charts whose relationships are clarified by scrolls, columns, roundels, medallions, links of chain, and interlace designs, as well as by representational trees and even the wing feathers of a cherub. The *Speculum* diagrams as a set are not found in any thirteenth-century English copy of Poitiers' *Compendium*, but they do appear in four fifteenth-century English manuscripts, two of which also contain the *Compendium*.[349] The four manuscripts with the Poitiers' *Compendium* and *Speculum* diagrams in common with Royal MS 1.B.x are: CUL MS Dd.3.56, with two (Tree of Virtues, Tree of Vices); London, Gray's Inn MS 9, with three (Table of the Twelve Articles of the Faith, Tree of Virtues, Tree of Vices) and two stubs with the visible remains of four further diagrams torn away; St John's College, Oxford, MS 58, with five (Table of the Ten Commandments, Table of the Twelve Articles of the Faith, Table of the Seven Requests of the Lord's Prayer, Tree of Virtues, Tree of Vices); Bodl. Lib. MS Laud Misc. 156, the modelbook for Nicholas de Lyra's *Postilla litteralis* (see Chapter 1), with six *Speculum* diagrams in common with Royal 1.B.x (Cherub, Tree of Virtues, Tree of Vices, Table of the Seven Acts of the Passion, Table of the Ten Commandments, Table of the Twelve Articles of the Faith).[350] No set of diagrams in the four English fifteenth-century manuscripts with the *Speculum* agree, however, with each other or have the same diagrammatic contents as those in Royal MS 1.B.x.

The first of these full-page *Speculum* drawings in Royal shows a Tree of Sciences. This so-called Tree, which is a breakdown of *Sciencia* or knowledge into its constitutent parts or branches, as the pictorial metaphor here would have it, into *Philosophia*, *Eloquencia*, *Poetria* and *Mechania*, appears in only one of the other thirty-eight surviving *Speculum theologie*, in a fourteenth-century copy from the Rhineland,[351] presumably not related to the Royal copy.[352] On the verso of fol. 1 (fig. 85) the diagram in genealogical form is called *Parentes Anne* or the kinship of Saint Anne. Again, of the thirty-eight copies of the *Speculum* that Sandler located, not one other includes the genealogical tree of Saint Anne, and there would seem to have been a compelling reason for its presence in this set of diagrams. A particular devotion to Anne would obviously have been the determining factor, but her cult was very widespread in England in the fifteenth century; only the Dominicans have been mentioned as perhaps especially in her service.[353] This matrilineal descent of Christ is thought to have flourished in the fifteenth and sixteenth centuries as a kind of rebuttal to the patriarchal descent in the form of the Tree of Jesse that had been obscuring the 'formerly central role of the Virgin'.[354] But this observation does not take us much further with respect to its purpose in Royal MS 1.B.x.

The *Speculum* next follows with a series of seven moral tables. The first (fol. 2) concerning the Ten Commandments is conceived pictorially as a column linked by scrolls to roundels that end in tassels. This central column is looped around by the Ten Commandments and aligned to the right with the Abuses of the World and to the left with the Ten Plagues of Egypt. This diagram is one of the few to occur in another contemporary English manuscript, i.e. St John's, Oxford, MS 58,[355] with Peter of Poitiers' *Compendium* and five tree diagrams, but in a quite different tree format; here scrolls are not used as the aligning feature, and there is variation in the wording of the

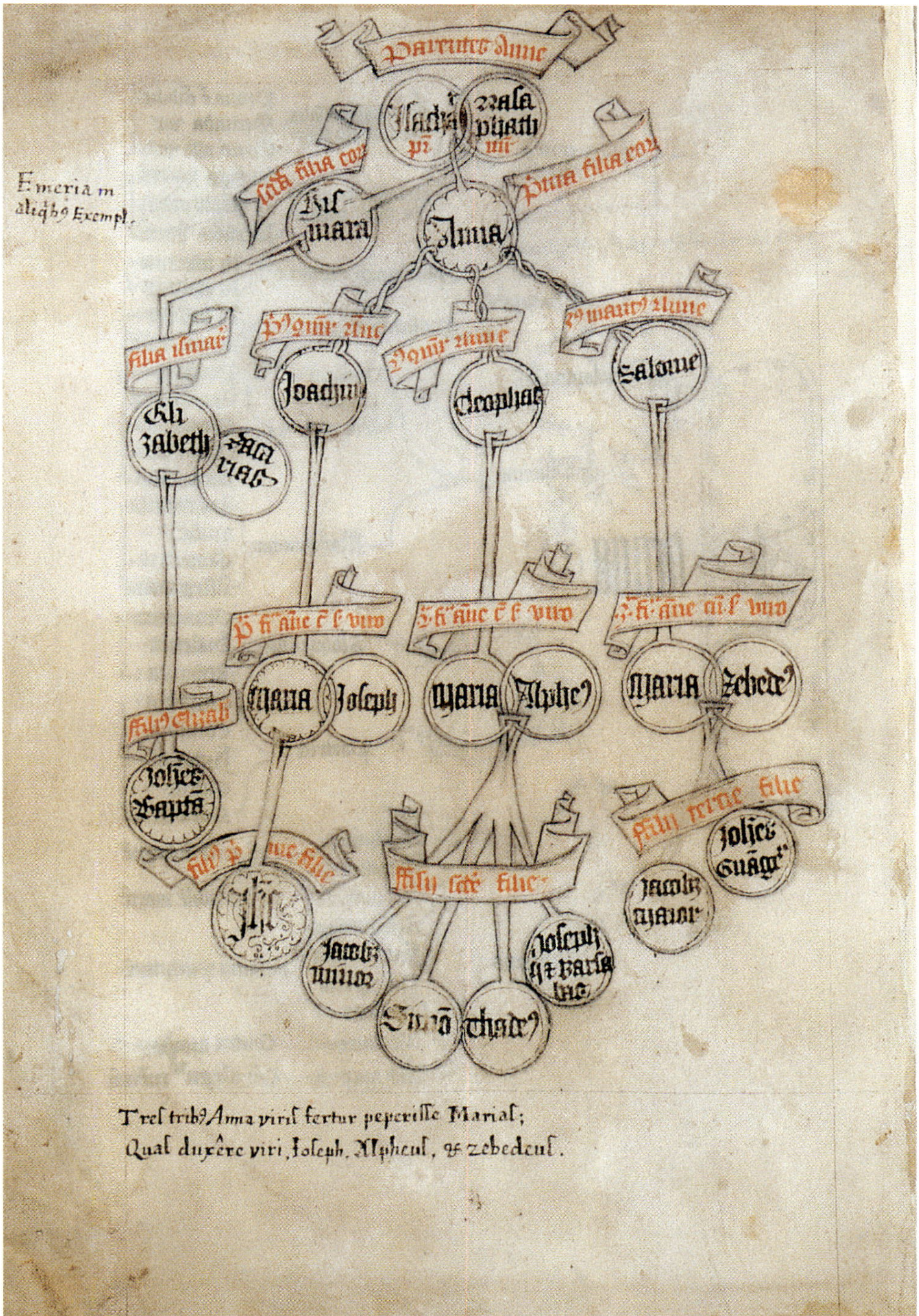

Fig. 85 British Library Royal MS 1.B.x, fol. 1v, diagram of the *Parentes Anna*. The British Library.

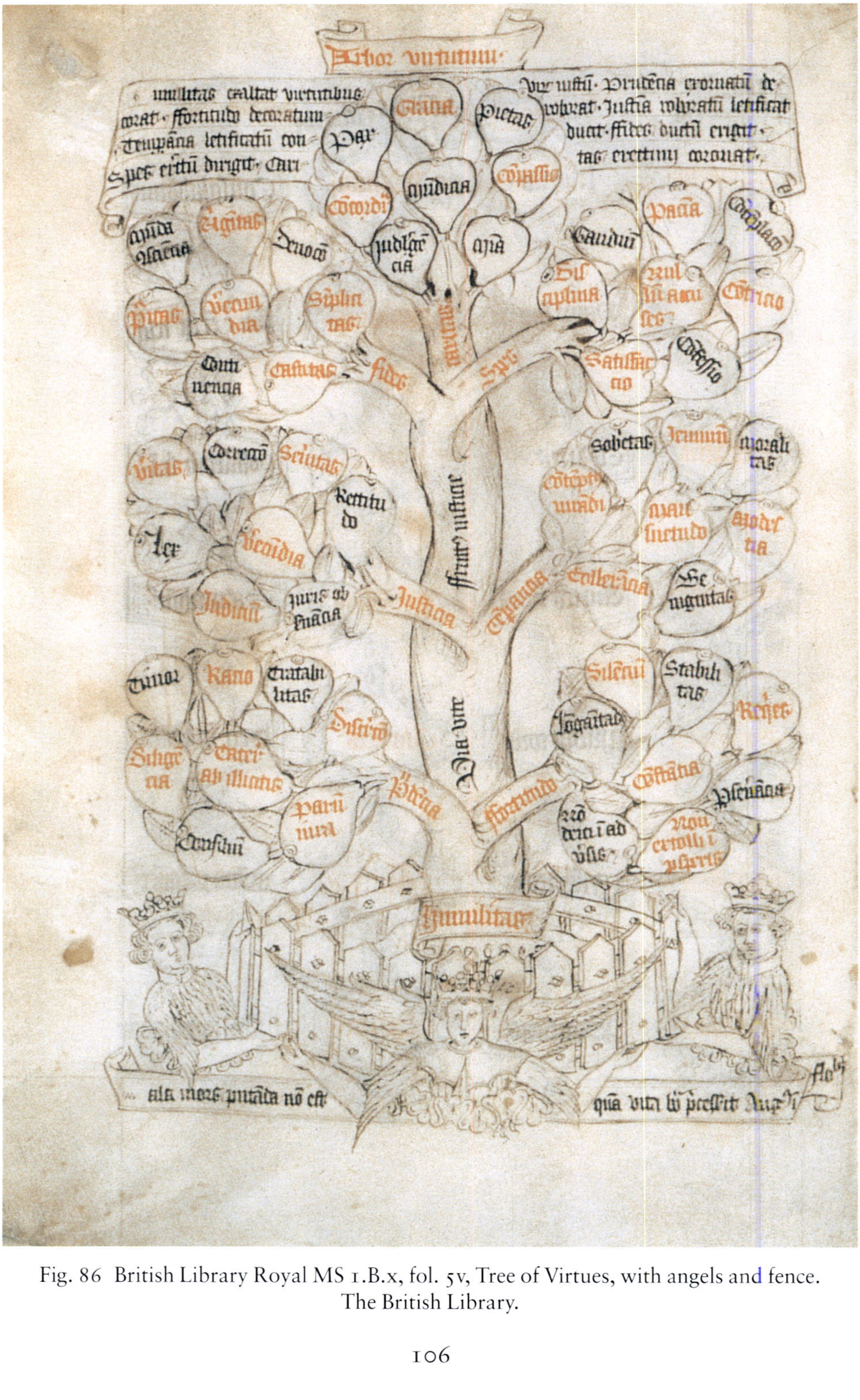

Fig. 86 British Library Royal MS 1.B.x, fol. 5v, Tree of Virtues, with angels and fence. The British Library.

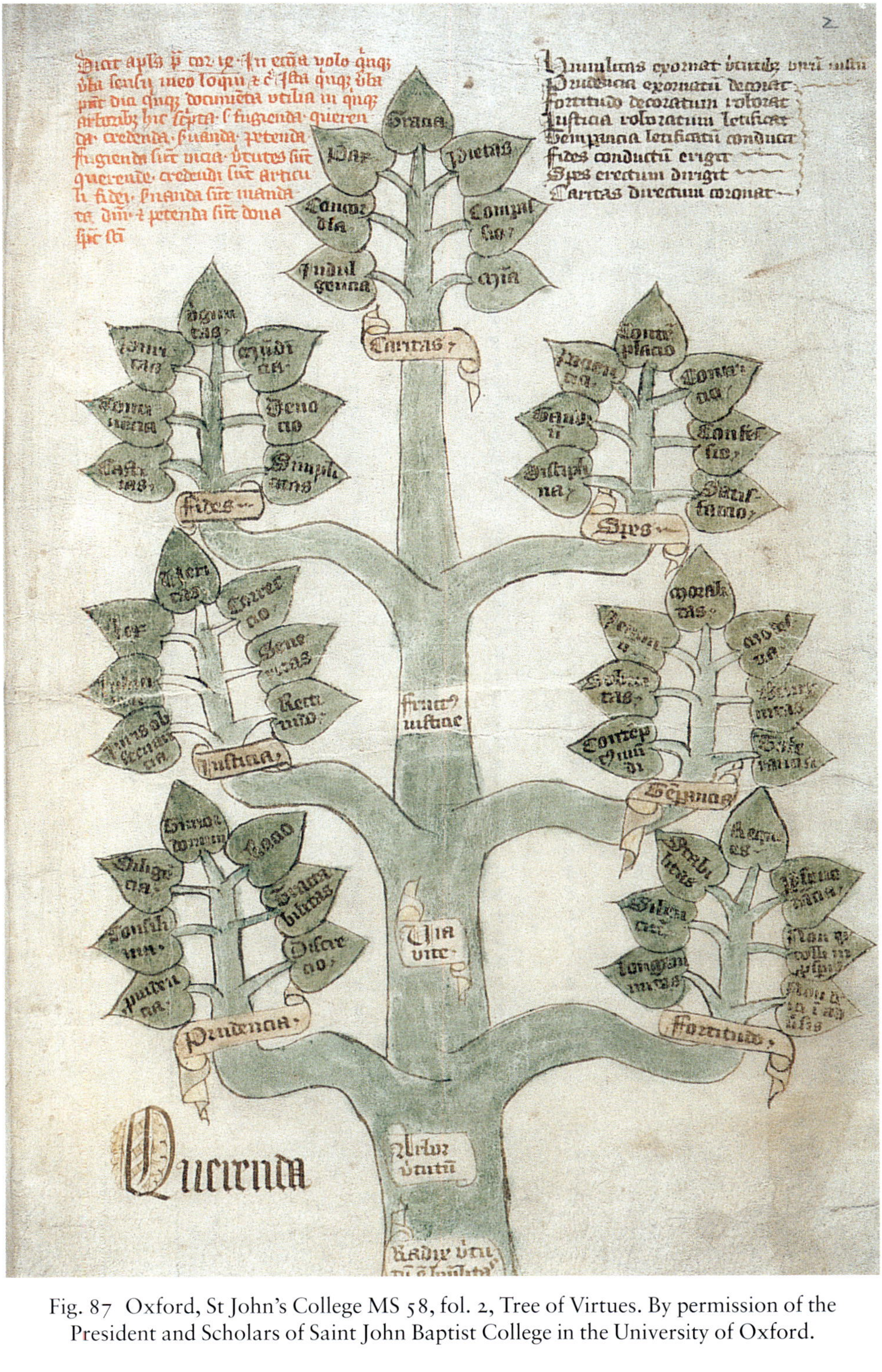

Fig. 87 Oxford, St John's College MS 58, fol. 2, Tree of Virtues. By permission of the President and Scholars of Saint John Baptist College in the University of Oxford.

titles. Folio 2v in Royal shows the Twelve Articles of the Creed with plaques bearing the names of the Apostles traditionally associated with each phrase of the Credo and the twelve prophets with their words predictive of the revelation. Again, there is an analogous tree diagram in St John's MS 58, but it also shows rubrics not in the Royal version, suggesting that the two sets of the *Speculum theologie* are unlikely to be directly related.

Folio 5v[356] (fig. 86) of Royal shows in a literal representational style an *Arbor virtutum*, a Tree of Virtues, that takes its roots in Humility and is protected by three angels and a fence suggestive of a *hortus conclusus*. With its leafy branches and their pear-shaped fruits the Royal Tree is a particularly fine example of this allegorical image. The guardian angels and the enclosing picket fence of this Tree are unknown elsewhere and were probably either additions by the artist or derived from his lost exemplar. Together with the Trees in CUL Dd.3.56 and Laud Misc. 156, the only other fifteenth-century Tree of Virtues comparable in quality to the Royal drawing is in BL Cotton MS Faustina B.vi, Part II (fol. 4), with a *Desert of Religion* which contains some of the finest miniatures made in England in the period, as well as twenty diagrammatic trees. But however fine, the Cotton Tree of Virtues was not based on the same textual or pictorial model as the Royal Tree, and the text of the Cotton tree is in Middle English as are the other contents. The Tree of Virtues in St John's MS 58 (fig. 87), which Hanna attributes to London or Westminster in the 1470s and so later than Royal MS 1.B.x, is the only such Tree to have a connection with Royal through displaying a jingle that begins 'Humilitas exornat virtutibus' (fol. 2).[357] MS 58 has, however, also a quotation from 1 Corinthians 14, which is not with the image in Royal MS 1.B.x; nevertheless, while clearly not of the same iconographic source, the two manuscripts may share some aspects of a textual tradition. No other English Tree of Virtues of this period has with it either the excerpt from Corinthians or the jingle.

The next leaf in Royal MS 1.B.x, fol. 6 (fig. 88), has the pictorial pièce-de-résistance of the diagrammatic images, a wonderful full-page Cherub holding crown and upturned sword and standing on part of a wheel. Its wings and feathers are employed as sites to record the forms of virtuous behaviour: confession, purity of mind, purity of body, love of God, love of one's neighbour, and Giving Satisfaction.[358] The Cherub in Royal 1.B.x differs from earlier versions in lacking a fully realized wheel with spokes inscribed with the Seven Works of Mercy.[359] Originally deriving from a treatise by Alan de Lille, *De sex aliis Cherubim*, the Cherub was later altered by the compiler of the *Speculum theologie*, John of Metz. The figure is rare in fifteenth-century book illustration,[360] and it does not occur in the *Speculum theologie* in the two other fifteenth-century English manuscripts with the Poitiers' genealogy (Oxford, St John's MS 58 and CUL MS Dd.3.56).[361] The image is, however, in the modelbook in Bodl. Lib. MS Laud Misc. 156 of Nicholas de Lyra's *Postilla super totum Bibliam*, discussed in the first chapter, but the Laud Cherub is not of the same pictorial and textual traditions (fig. 89) as the Royal version.

The imagery and rendering of the Royal Cherub are extraordinary in the shading and drawing of the figure, in its well-delineated hair, face and body, and in the almost baroque movement of the scene created by the wings and the sword raised obliquely above the head. Its attributes of crown and sword and the heavenly display of the radiant sun, clouds and fiery storm do not appear in any other English rendering,

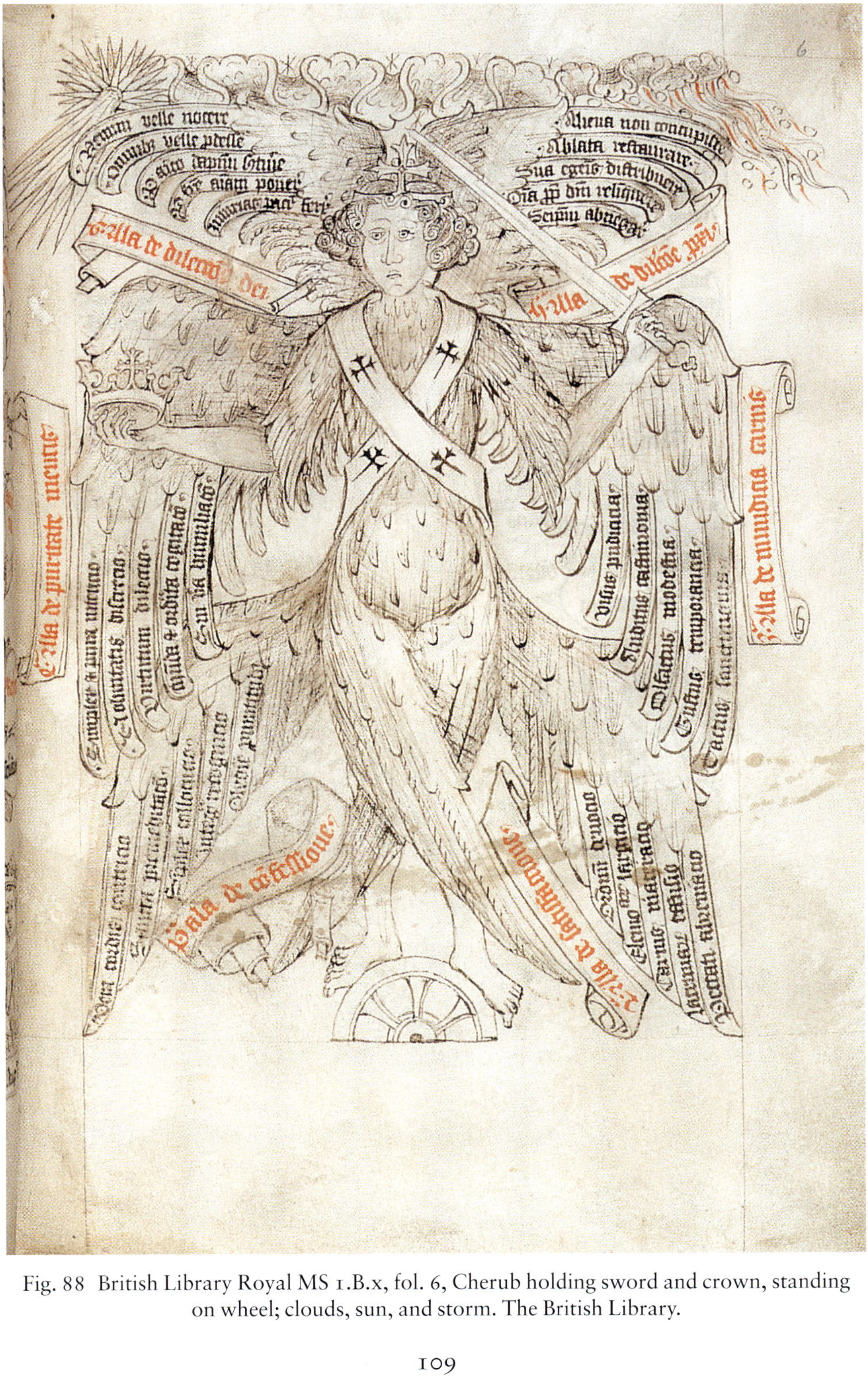

Fig. 88 British Library Royal MS 1.B.x, fol. 6, Cherub holding sword and crown, standing on wheel; clouds, sun, and storm. The British Library.

earlier or later, of this subject. These attributes would, as with the unusual features in the Tree of Virtues scene, seem to be the addition of an innovative artist or exceptional exemplar, intending allusions beyond the thirteenth-century versions that are notable for their rigid, upright wings, no visible body and a strictly forward-facing head.[362]

The page following the Cherub in Royal MS 1.B.x returns to the arboreal theme, with a Tree of Vices (fig. 90). The roots of this tree grow from a Hell-mouth wherein a horned devil with flesh-hook resides, apparently awaiting a sinner. The yawning jaws of Hell do not appear with any other known English Tree of Vices, but the drooping branches of the Seven Deadly Sins and the leaves of the subsidiary sins are not an unknown iconography with a Tree of Vices. The Royal artist drew the leaves in a somewhat amorphous kidney-bean shape in deliberate contrast to the pear-shaped fruit of the Tree of Virtues (fig. 86) and set them against a shaded black background. He also drew a number of stubs on the branches of the Tree of Vices, as if to say that growth from evil is incomplete, stunted, lopped off. There are no such stubs on the Tree of Virtues, and it is evident that this artist did not miss any relevant or possible detail that would communicate his intentions. The Tree of Vices (fol. 1v) in St John's MS 58 (fig. 91) projects a similar droopiness and is accompanied by the same jingle at top as in Royal MS 1.B.x,[363] although, oddly, this Tree bears heart-shaped leaves. But because St John's MS 58 has only five of the thirteen diagrams in Royal, I would not claim that they are related through place of production but that they may have come from the same source. The Tree of Vices from Bodl. Lib. MS Laud Misc. MS 156 (fol. 63) is, on the other hand, a much less realistic rendering and clearly from a different pictorial tradition.[364]

The final table in the Royal sequence of the *Speculum theologie* is presented in 'bewegt' scrolls and angled and curvilinear tree trunks: it concerns the Twelve Worldly Abuses of the centuries, with sub-texts aligned on branches (fig. 92). The diagram of Abuses does not appear in any of the other fifteenth-century English sets of the *Speculum theologie*, nor in any of the five fourteenth-century English versions of the text,[365] nor is it in any of the known continental versions. The only remotely similar version that I have been able to locate is once again in BL Cotton Faustina B.vi, containing a *Desert of Religion*.[366] The Cotton diagram, with the inscription, 'Þer er þe twelve abusiones herde/þat er growande in þe werlde', offers however a translation only of the central column of scrollwork on the Royal page and is not pictorially relevant to its counterpart in Royal MS 1.B.x.

Why, then, was the *Speculum theologie* conceived as an appropriate adjunct to Poitiers' *Compendium historie in genealogia Christi*? A possible answer would seem to lie in the composition of the *Compendium*, which is an encapsulation of biblical history, just as the *Speculum* is a distillation of extended thinking on Christian morality. Poitiers actually states in his opening sentence that he is making the edition for students because of its length and difficulty, and in one Poitiers manuscript even the 'heaviness' of sacred history is mentioned. So why not match such a history with a sequence of diagrams that reduce aspects of Christian thought and morality to a more compact form? Perhaps the motive was instructional: diagrams are said to have been 'a common feature of medieval classrooms',[367] and it is thought that Poitiers himself invented the concept of hanging rolls with diagrams in the classroom in the manner of a modern-day teaching aid.[368]

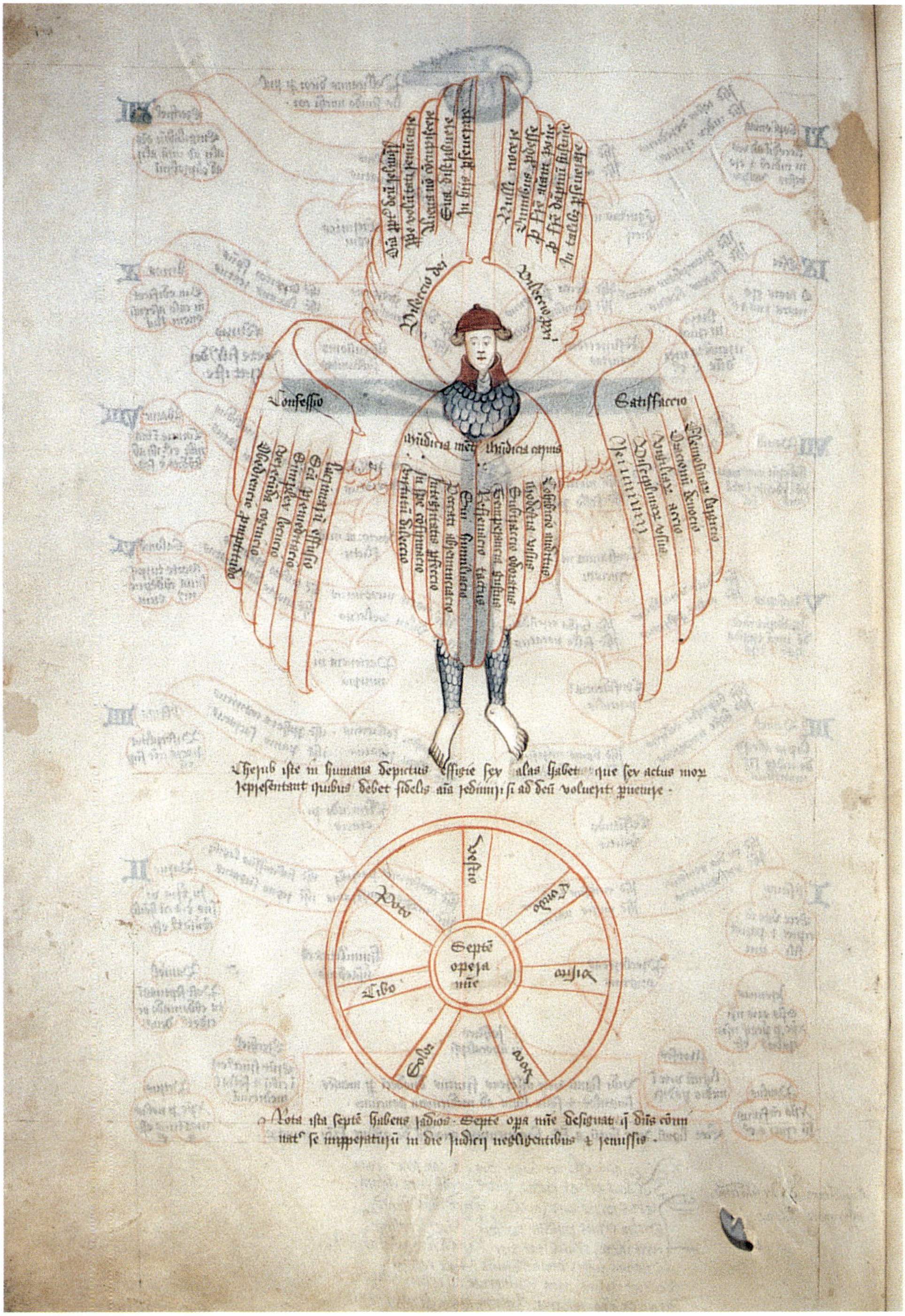

Fig. 89 Oxford, Bodleian Library MS Laud Misc. 156, fol. 61v, Cherub with wheel. The Bodleian Library, University of Oxford.

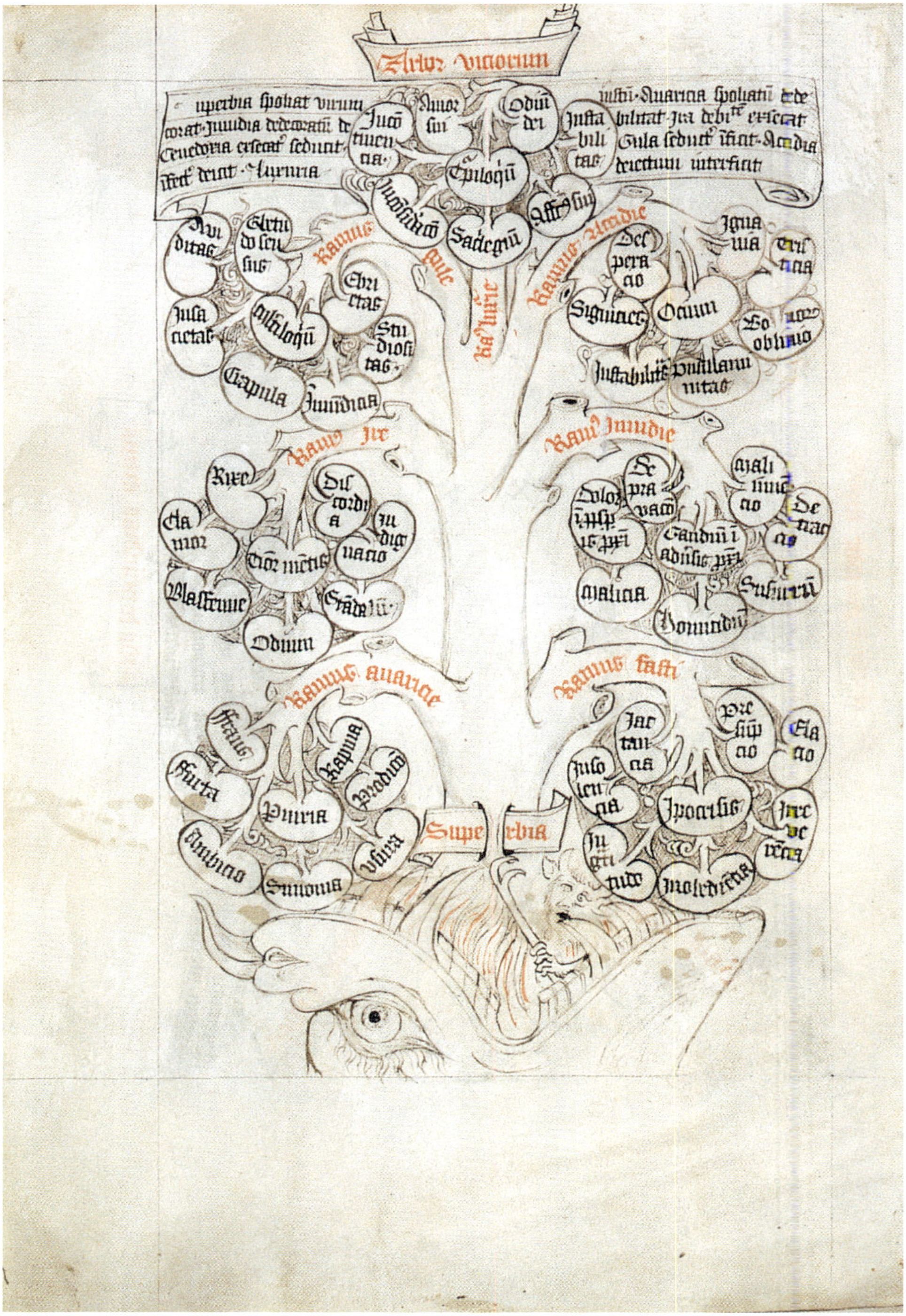

Fig. 90 British Library Royal MS 1.B.x, fol. 6v, Tree of Vices, with Hell-mouth and devil. The British Library.

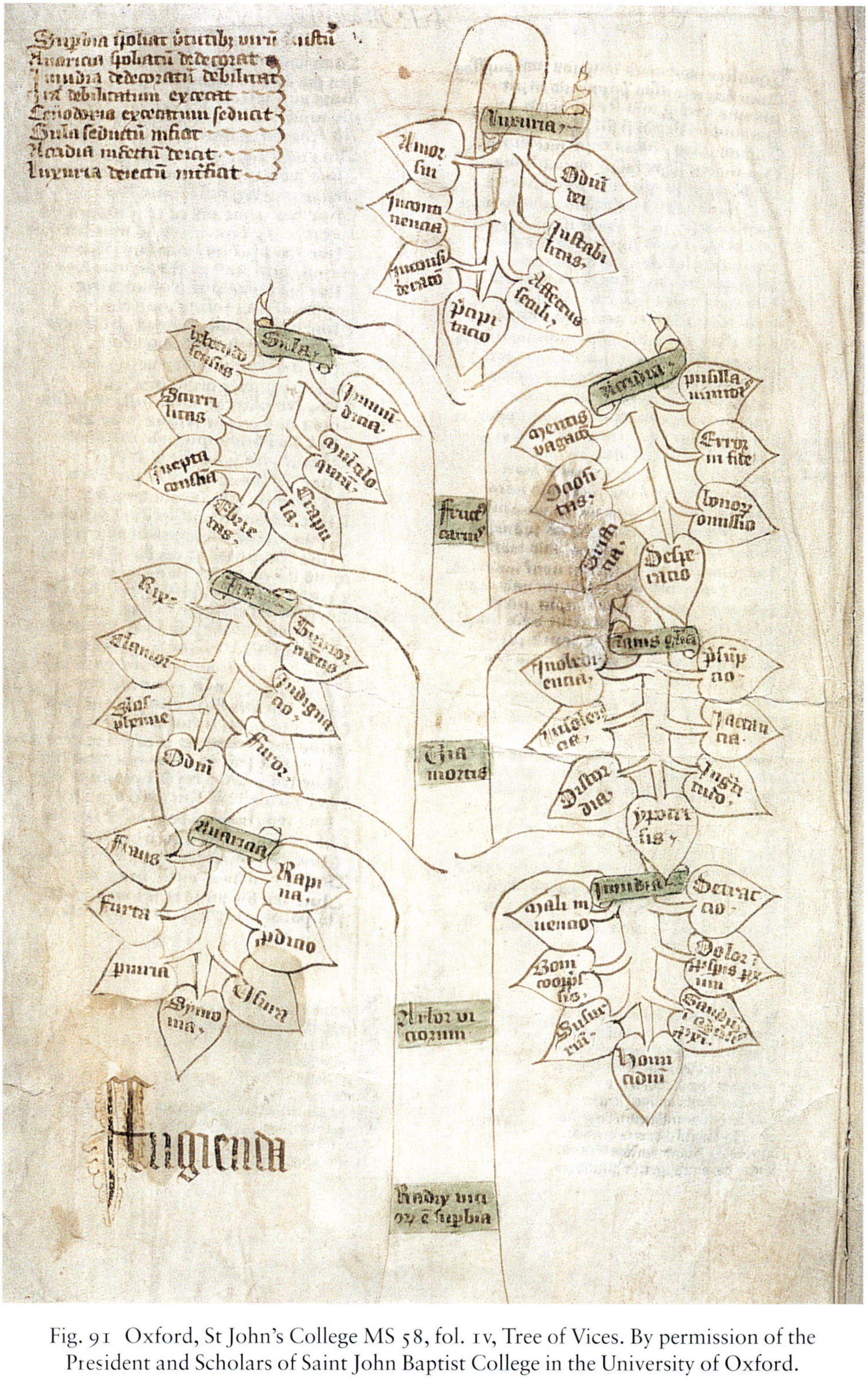

Fig. 91 Oxford, St John's College MS 58, fol. 1v, Tree of Vices. By permission of the President and Scholars of Saint John Baptist College in the University of Oxford.

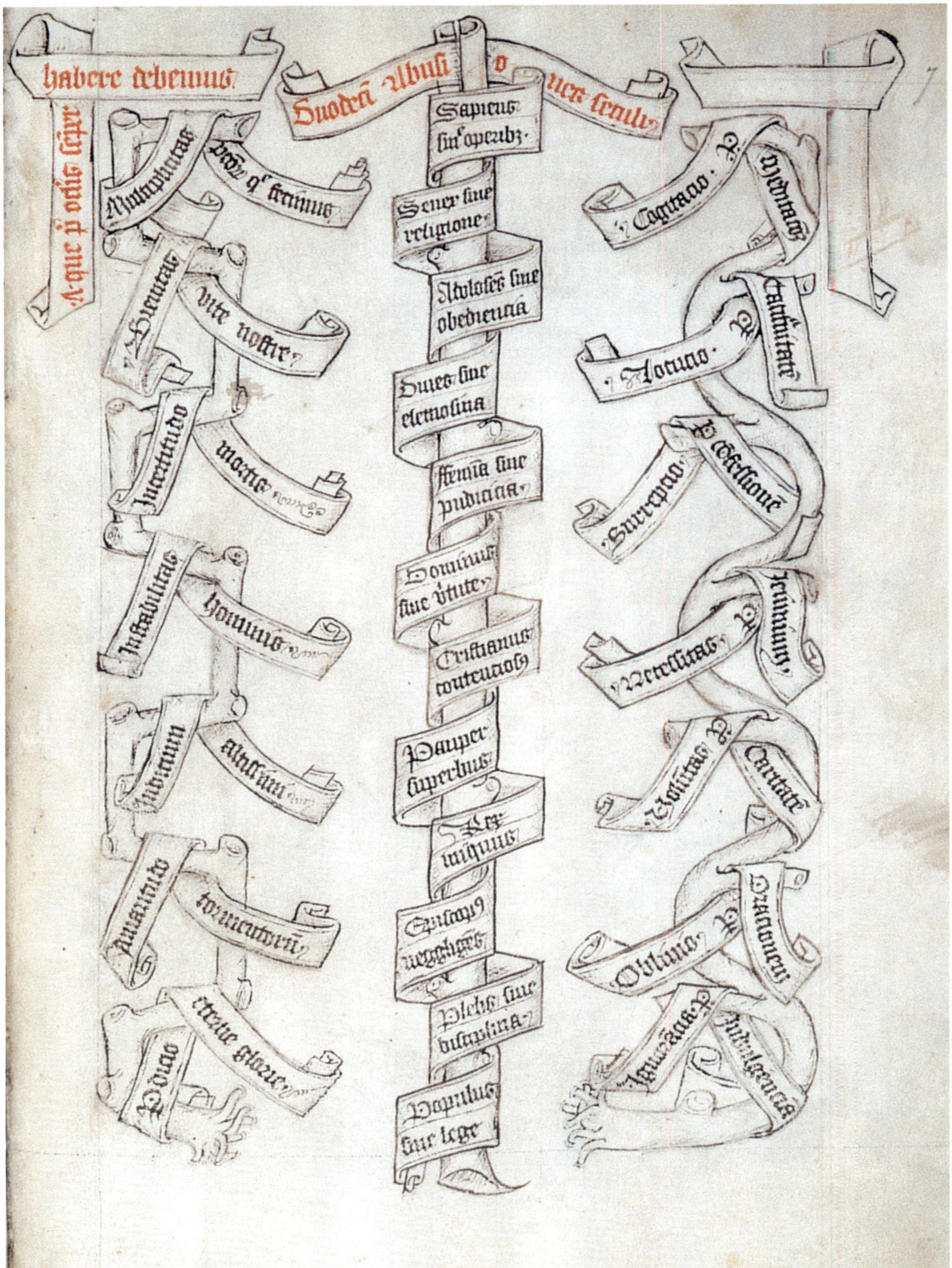

Fig. 92 British Library Royal 1.B.x, fol. 7, Table of Twelve Seven Worldly Abuses.
The British Library.

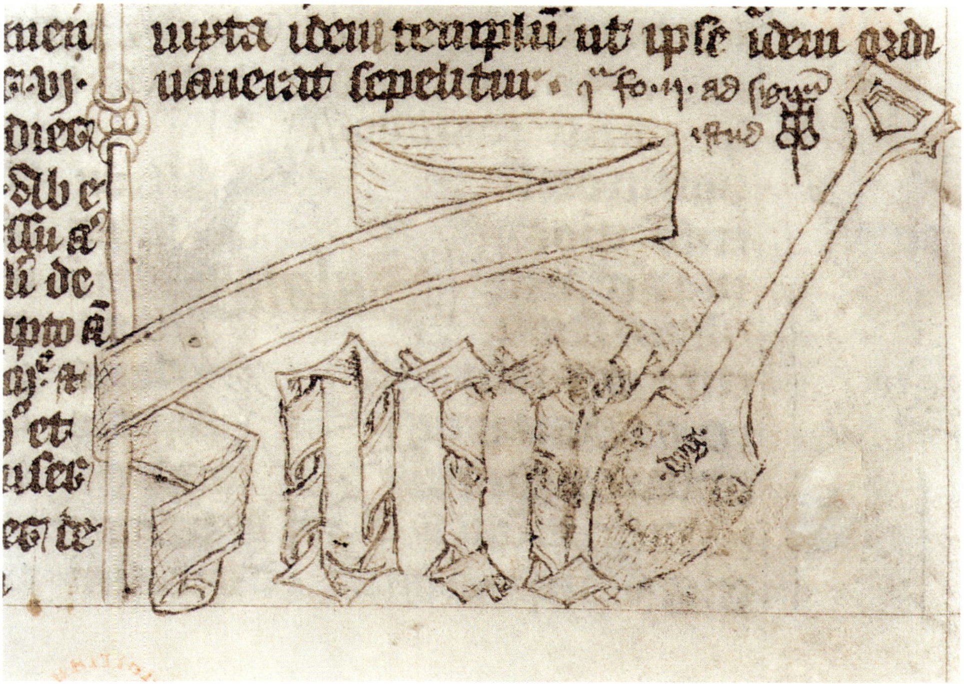

Fig. 93 British Library Royal 1.B.x, fol. 25v (detail), rebus of John Dygon as spade with 'dyg' and scrollwork letters 'on'. The British Library.

Peter of Poitiers, like Nicholas of Lyra, made an explicit reference in his text to the need for explanatory diagrams and images. In one copy, Bodleian MS Barlow 53, a Middle English translation of the *Compendium*, the text preceding a diagram of the forty-two mansions of Israel informs the reader how 'the names of þe places byþ put in þis figure under' (see also Chapter 1, fig. 18). The familial relationships in genealogical chronicles were much more effectively taught when laid down in diagrammatic form; such diagrams were considered crucial to the reader's understanding and were used at a level of importance with language, consciously so by Lyra and Poitiers.

Finally, I will suggest a provenance for this innovative manuscript. In general terms, the contents of Royal MS 1.B.x would point to ownership by a religious house or by a religious individual. The texts[369] added in the first part of the fifteenth century to the thirteenth-century Bible read as if they were a reference collection for an institution or for a person who needed detailed access to the Bible, possibly as if his livelihood depended on it.

The most important evidence, however, to the origin of Royal MS 1.B.x is the group of puzzling images in the miniature on the lower half of fol. 25v (fig. 93): a contorted blank scroll, two figure letters of scrollwork, **O** and **N**, and a metal-edged spade inscribed by the scribe with the word, *dyg*.[370] This apparent conundrum was identified by Pamela Robinson as a rebus for the name 'Dygon',[371] who was a known scribe. Dygon not only wrote books but also annotated prolifically; in fact, there are some nineteen manuscripts in Magdalen College alone with evidence of his hand.[372] Ian Doyle, Malcolm Parkes, Andrew Watson and Ralph Hanna have all been aware of this man and his work, whether as scribe, annotator, tabulator or donor.[373] Dygon was born in 1384, received an Oxford degree in 1406, and between 1406 and 1429 he was rector or vicar of various parish churches, until finally he served at St Andrew's, Holborn, from 1433 to 1435. He was admitted as a recluse in Sheen Priory, Surrey, in 1435, and was still living in 1449,[374] when he copied part of Magdalen College, Oxford, MS 150.[375] The annotations in Royal MS 1.B.x appeared to Pamela and me to be the hand of Dygon,[376] and this attribution was confirmed by Ian Doyle and Ralph Hanna.[377] The Poitiers *Compendium* – and, by association, the four other articles in the same hand – must certainly have been made for him on the evidence of the rebus.[378] It verges almost on the unbelievable to find a book that was commissioned by a scribe (if not the only hat he wore), and of such quality. The virtue of this recognition is that the production of the Royal manuscript can be located either in London or at Sheen Priory; Dygon's earlier rural livings were not likely to have supported this kind of artistic production. The production of Royal MS 1.B.x can also be limited with reasonable certainty to the latter part of Dygon's life, i.e. to 1433–49, and whether vicar or recluse, he was apparently able to underwrite this expensive copy of Poitiers' *Compendium*.

It is also of some interest in considering Dygon's taste in books that Hanna assigns BL Harley MS 612, Saint Bridget, Revelation, etc., as 'presumably' an order by Dygon 'for his personal use'.[379] If Dygon had this book made or even if he acquired it ready made, the extensive added decorations, mainly around corrections to the apparently frightful text, would have been to his taste. The hand of the corrector is not the hand of the text, which was signed by 'Colyngburn' on fol. 107v in the left margin; and Collingburn was connected to Dygan by several other books in the 'Dygon corpus'. The correcting hand called attention to omitted text by finely drawn and shaded images, mainly by lapped and twisted scrolls, sometimes inserted in an illusionistic fashion into the parchment or attached to the parchment by pins and nails or emanating from a nebuly, hung from a hook or cord, or held by the index finger of a hand or by a hand on a rod. The correcting scribe/artist was also capable of much more elaborate images, sometimes taking suggestions for the subjects of his drawings from the inserted text; a few examples of such images are an angel with shield (fol. 30), a dead man in a shroud (fol. 78v), a purse hanging from a pole in a window (fol. 80), open books (fols 82v, 218v), profile heads (fols 117, 118, 138v), a heart pierced by a lance (fol. 141v), an altar with host and paten (fol. 165), bust of the Virgin Mary (fol. 207v), a cardinal's hat (fol. 208v), and a full-scale tree bearing a scroll, barbed roses and other flowers (fol. 141).[380] Even without the connection to John Dygon, the decorative work in Harley MS 612 is impressive and important as an understanding of the attention that might paid to the secondary embellishment of books in the fifteenth century.[381]

In speaking of the Royal manuscript I have used the words 'unusual', 'rare' and 'unique' often enough with respect to its pictorial contents that it should have become clear just how 'innovative' this version of the *Compendium* is. I might also have used the word 'rogue' to describe the manuscript. Although unfinished, it contains so many miniatures either not found in other Poitiers chronicles (see Appendix E) or not found anywhere else – that it would seem to indicate a certain personal pressure by Dygon to expand traditional illustration with more extensive visual material than usual and with more meticulous detail, either through instructions to the artist or through an exemplar. One need only examine the particulars of Noah's Ark (fig. 75) or the Temple of Solomon (fig. 79), with every stone and crocket in place, to see the energy of the illustrative programme in Royal MS 1.B.x. In assessing the manuscript, we should also take into account the twenty large images that are not in any other Poitiers manuscript, not to speak of the numerous smaller images in roundels.

Even in an unfinished state, without an extant model for the sequence of images, and with no knowledge of the artist's hand elsewhere, Royal MS 1.B.x can be considered among the finest products of fifteenth-century book illustration in England.

CHAPTER V

A Gothish Episode in the Renaissance: BL Additional MS 21974, Longland's Pontifical Book of Benedictions

THE early sixteenth-century manuscript, BL Additional MS 21974,[382] with a Pontifical Benedictional, embodies one part of the split – one might even say chasm – that had begun to form in English book production in the fifteenth century around the time of Humphrey, duke of Gloucester (d. 1447). A division in style had evolved between the Gothic and humanistic modes of writing and illuminating manuscripts or, more accurately, a second mode of decorating had been introduced from Italy that occasioned a contrariety of styles within the same decorative environment. In Additional MS 21974 the decoration and script belong to the Gothic past, and the miniatures to the Renaissance interest in portraiture (figs 94, 99). The Additional manuscript is also of considerable interest as an instance of a certain kind of preservation of books that can be found from time to time in the fifteenth century. The Benedictional is essentially a recycled book in that the script, the two-line blue and gold flourished initials (fig. 96), and the shaded catchwords were produced in the third quarter of the fifteenth century, whereas the miniatures and borders (figs 95, 100) were made near the end of the first quarter of the sixteenth century, that is, they were added to blank leaves and spaces left in an apparently unfinished text. Given the prominent ownership of the benedictional, one must ask what bishop would be satisfied to take up a used and incompletely made codex, and on what occasion he might do so? In terms of the general issues of the Lyell talks, should the manuscript be considered a 'traditional' or an 'innovative' book? And, finally, are there other books illustrated by the Additional artist and, if so, who were the patrons?

The Additional manuscript is made up of eighty-nine parchment folios, of which the first three and last six were originally blanks. It measures 258 × *c.* 180 mm at fol. 3; the text space is 169 × 102 mm. Text has been added on fols 81v and 82r–v, as well as the prayer, 'Benediccio pro defunctis' on fols 82v–83. No signatures survive, but catchwords are present at fols 9v (in scroll), 17v (scroll), 25v (scroll), 33v, 41v, 49v, 57v (scroll), 65v, and 73v. Minor decoration includes rubrication, one-line blue capitals, cadels (fig. 96), two-line blue letters with red flourishing, gold letters with brown flourishing on fols 8–9v, and a parted blue and red letter with red flourishing on fol. 49v. Folios 82–89 were originally blank end leaves; only fol. 82 is ruled. There is a bookplate of Phillip Carteret Webb, who has been described as 'a notable antiquary and collector of manuscripts, coins and antique sculpture'.[383] A note at the front, from information given by the Reverend R.M. Woolley, Rector of Minting and Prebendary of Lincoln, 26 July 1922, states: 'In the will of John Longland, Bp. of

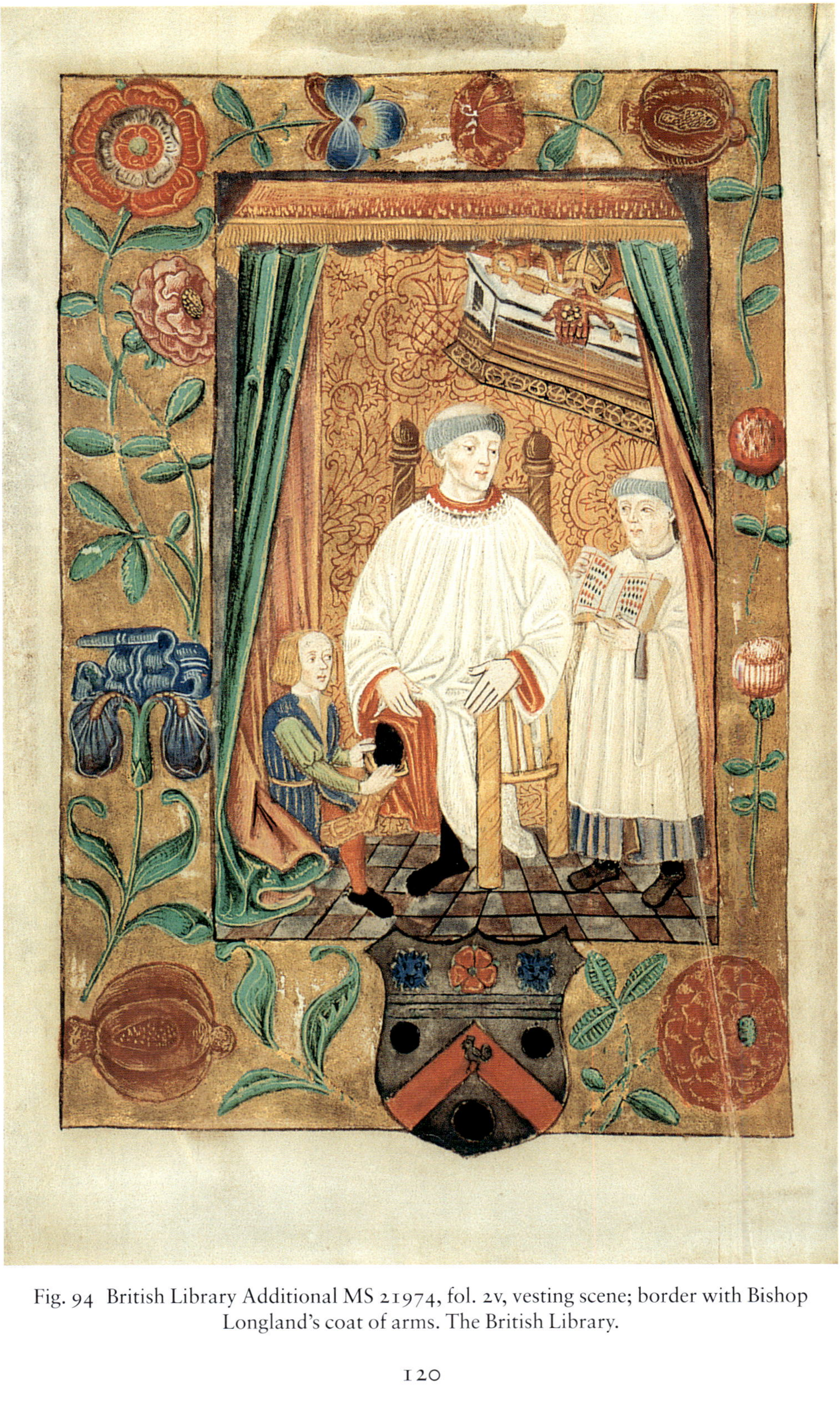

Fig. 94 British Library Additional MS 21974, fol. 2v, vesting scene; border with Bishop Longland's coat of arms. The British Library.

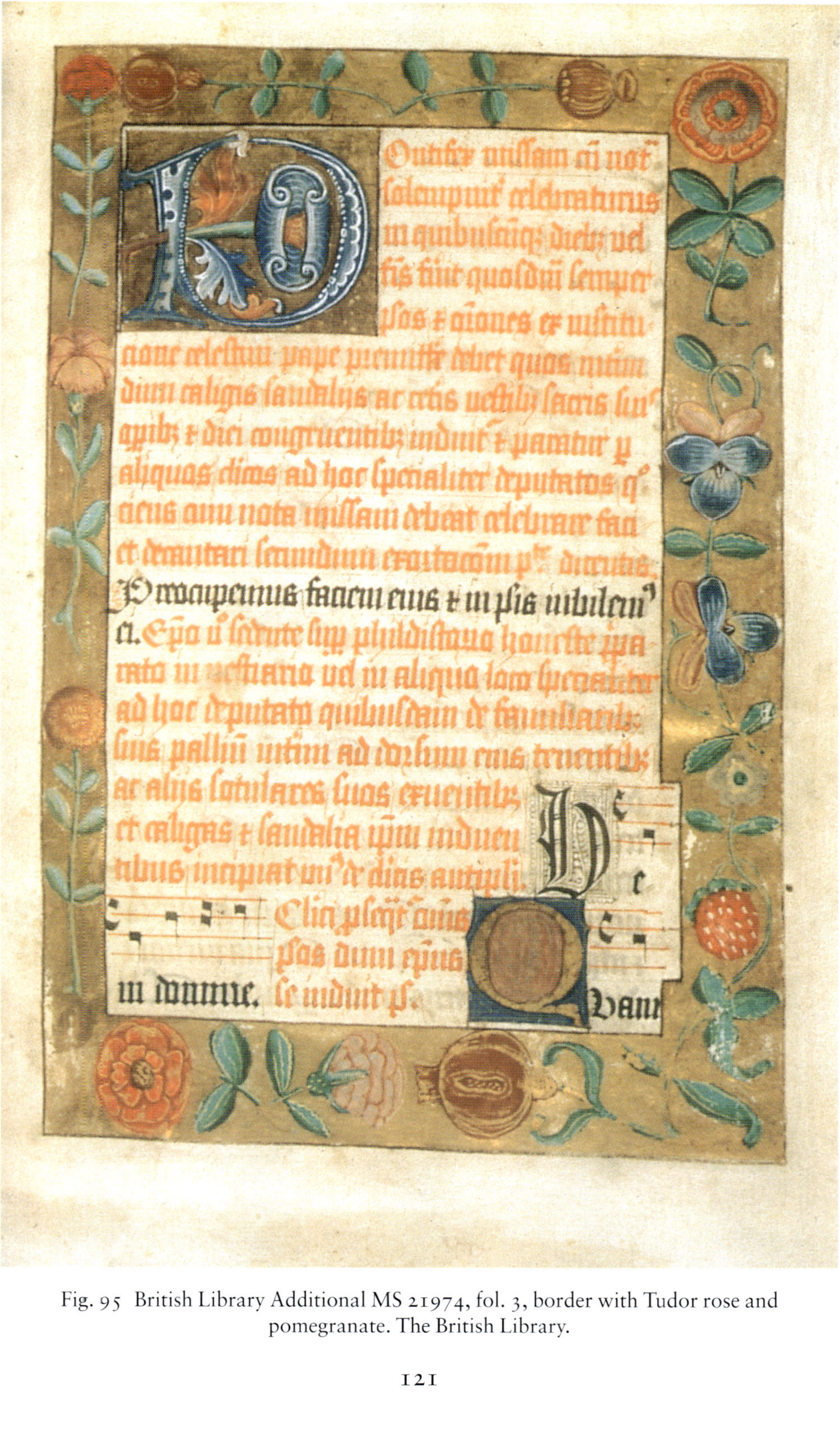

Fig. 95 British Library Additional MS 21974, fol. 3, border with Tudor rose and pomegranate. The British Library.

Lincoln 1521–47, among other things left to the use of the Bps. of Lincoln in the Cathedral only, are mentioned "twoo bokes, one for the gevying of ordres and consecracion of bissops, thother of benedictions, covered wt cloth of gold." The latter is evidently Add. MS. 21974.' The cloth of gold does not survive.

A benedictional is, of course, a book containing blessings and brief services that are the provenance of a bishop. It was seasonal in composition, following church offices from advent in the Temporale of the Missal through saints' days in the Sanctorale. The benedictional was a book, and I quote here Wordsworth and Littlehales, 'not likely to have been common at any time' because its contents were outside the range of daily services and would not normally have belonged to a parish church.[384] The script in the present benedictional is not identifiable to any particular locale, and there is no English in the Latin text, as sometimes happens, as a clue to the origin through dialect. The Additional manuscript, which was produced with musical notation (figs 96, 100), contains approximately 150 benedictions noted by title, as well as others not separately noted, and, in the main, they are associated with the standard Sarum offices and feasts. The first part of the Additional manuscript, fols 3–21, has, however, an unusual text, the *Praeparatio ad missam pontificalem*, the preparation or vesting of the bishop for Mass, as well as directions for singing of the pontifical high mass. The second part, fols 22–81v, contains episcopal benedictions that are ascribed to Archbishop John Peckham, even if they do not agree with all other collections said to be by him.[385] It is likely, on the evidence of a few of the blessings, that the Additional manuscript was originally made for Lincoln, if with personal interventions by the unknown bishop for whom the original part was made, and that some benedictions were composed expressly for it.

The bulk of the manuscript, the original eighty-nine folios, had seemingly been lying around in an unillustrated state, until the quires came into the possession of John Longland, Bishop of Lincoln from 1521–47, whose coat of arms appears in the borders on fols 2v and 21v (figs 94, 99).[386] A few words about Longland are necessary. He was born in 1473 at Henley-on-Thames, possibly went to Eton College, attended Magdalen College, Oxford, and in 1506/7 was principal of Magdalen Hall. In 1511 he was made doctor of divinity, in 1514 he became dean of Salisbury and canon of St Stephen's Chapel, Westminster, in 1519 canon at St George's Chapel, Windsor, and in 1521 he was consecrated Bishop of Lincoln, in which see he remained until his death in 1547. In 1524, as 'an influential preacher', he gained the notice of Henry VIII and was made confessor to the king. In 1532 he was selected by the king to be Chancellor of Oxford, where he tried to stop the distribution of heretical books. He laboured to restore standards of behavior in the monasteries in his diocese, if apparently without much success, and he was particularly active in condemning Martin Luther. At the same time as he was fiercely anti-heretical, Longland supported Henry VIII in the matter of Henry's divorce.[387] A number of Longland's works were printed,[388] and Longland is said to have enjoyed a 'warm friendship' with Erasmus,[389] who bequeathed him copies of his works. He was a protégé and friend of Thomas Cardinal Wolsey, Lord Chancellor, he was in correspondence with Juan Luis Vives,[390] and he was praised by no less than Sir Thomas More. So, like his manuscript, Longland was a man of two eras.

However Longland acquired the eighty-nine folios, he must have been – in addition

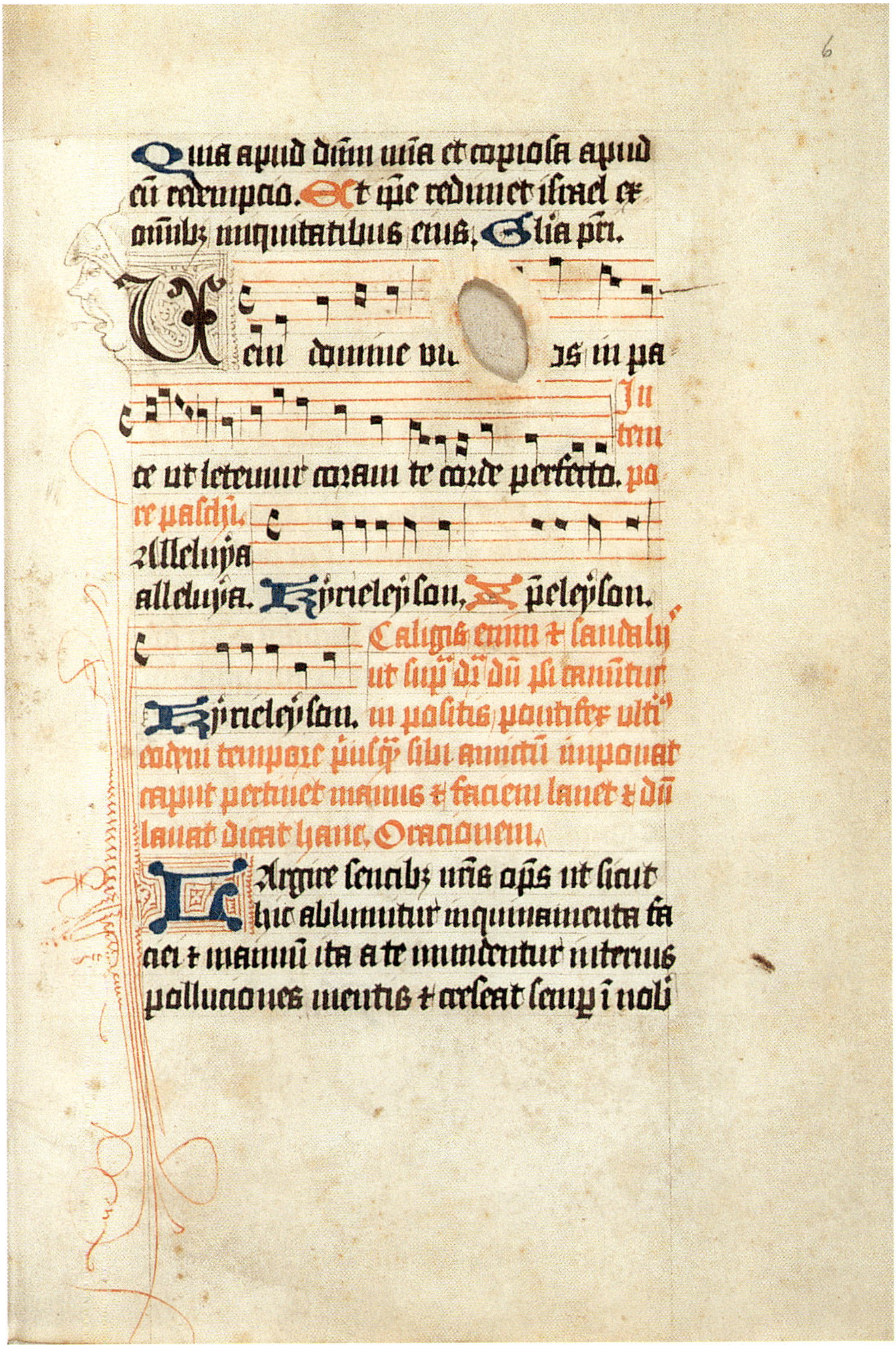

Fig. 96 British Library Additional MS 21974, fol. 6, text page with cadel on initial **u**. The British Library.

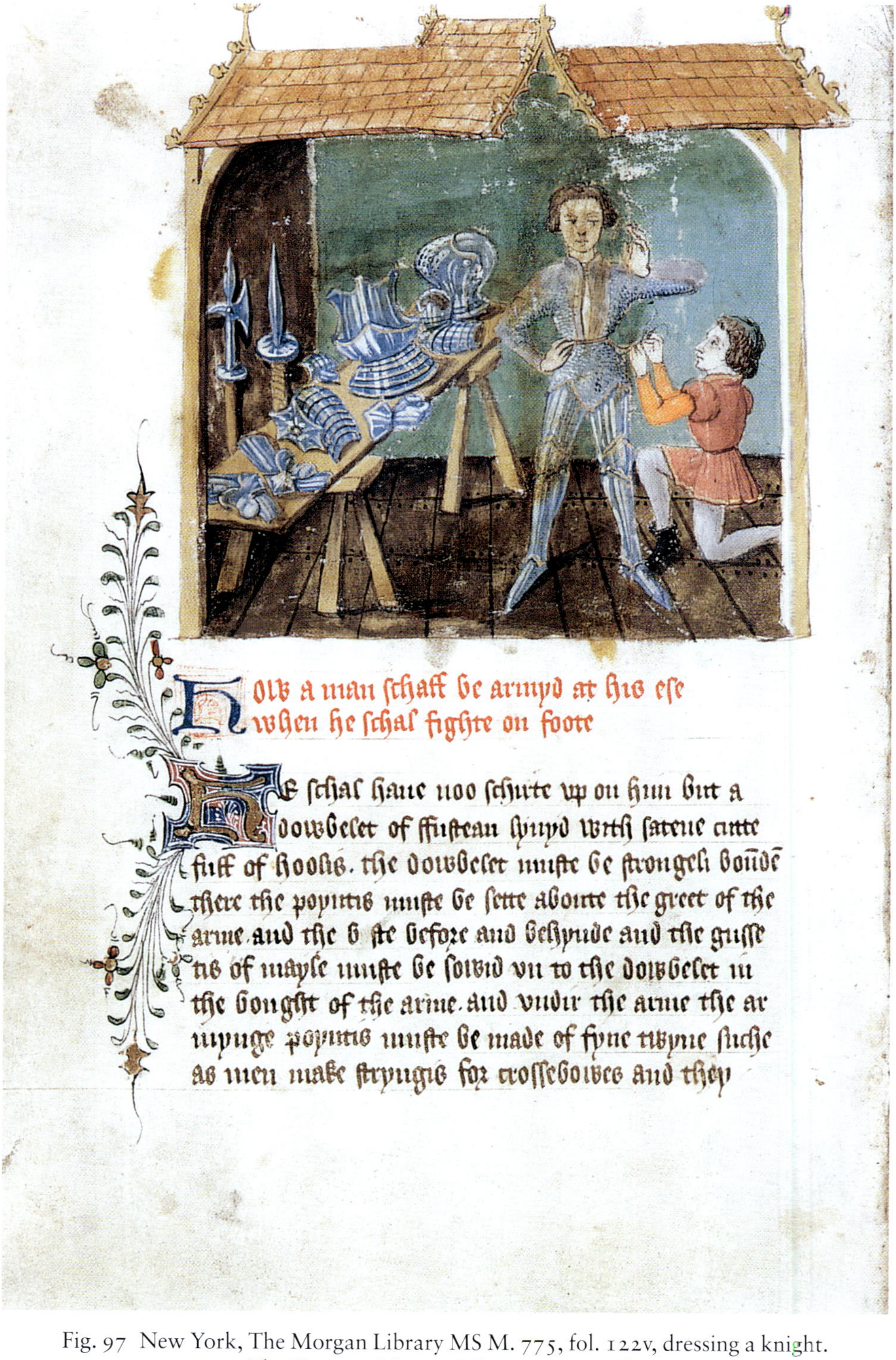
How a man schall be armyd at his ese
when he schal fighte on foote

He schal haue noo schirte up on him but a
dowbelet of ffustean lynyd with satene cutte
full of hoolis. the dowbelet muste be strongeli boundē
there the poyntis muste be sette aboute the greet of the
arme. and the b ste before and behynde and the gusse
tis of mayle muste be sowid un to the dowbelet in
the bought of the arme. and undir the arme the ar
mynge poyntis muste be made of fyne twyne suche
as men make strynges for crossebowes and they

Fig. 97 New York, The Morgan Library MS M. 775, fol. 122v, dressing a knight.
The Pierpont Morgan Library, New York.

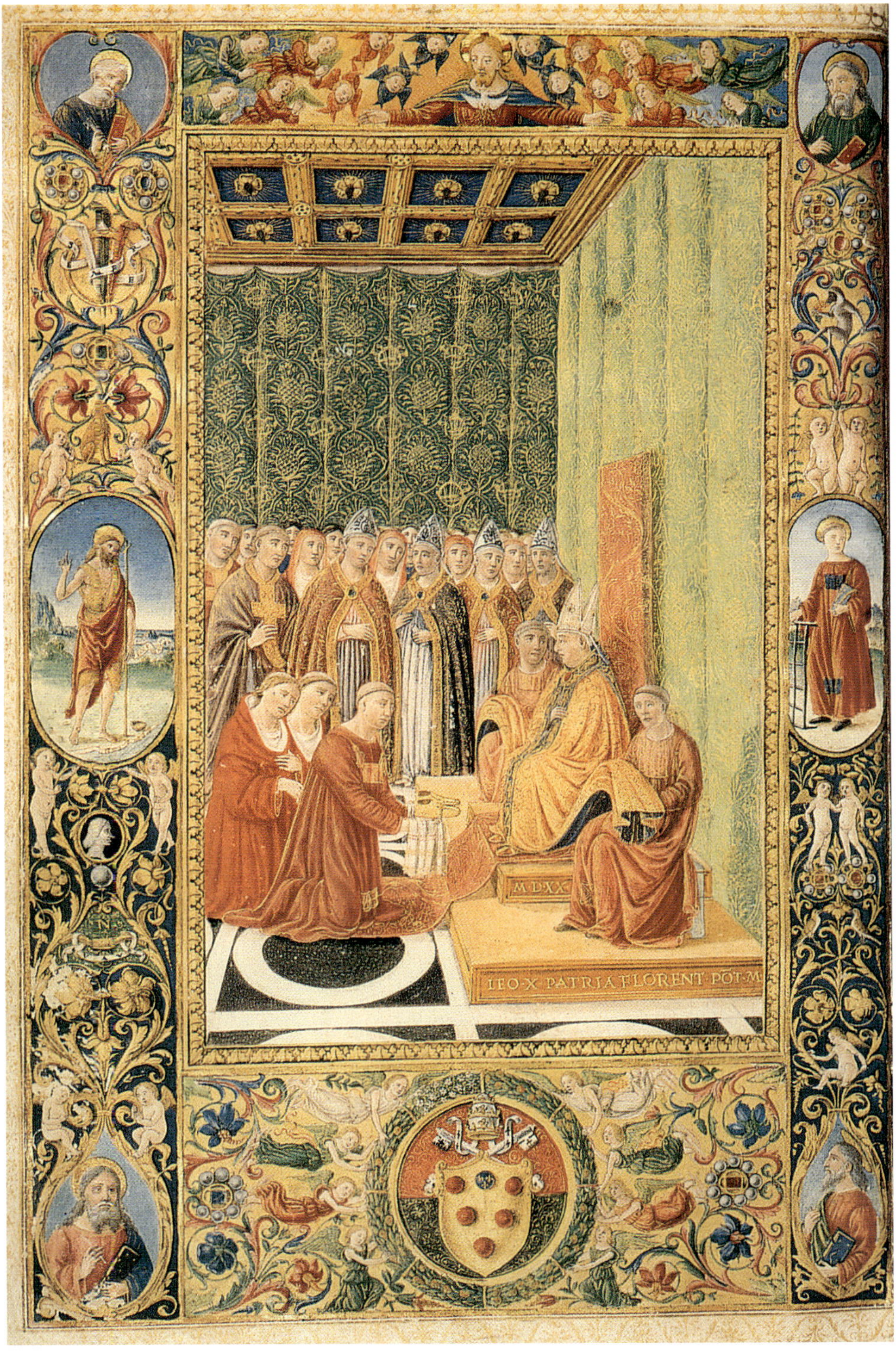

Fig. 98 New York, The Morgan Library MS H.6, fol. 1v, vesting of Pope Leo X. The Pierpont Morgan Library, New York.

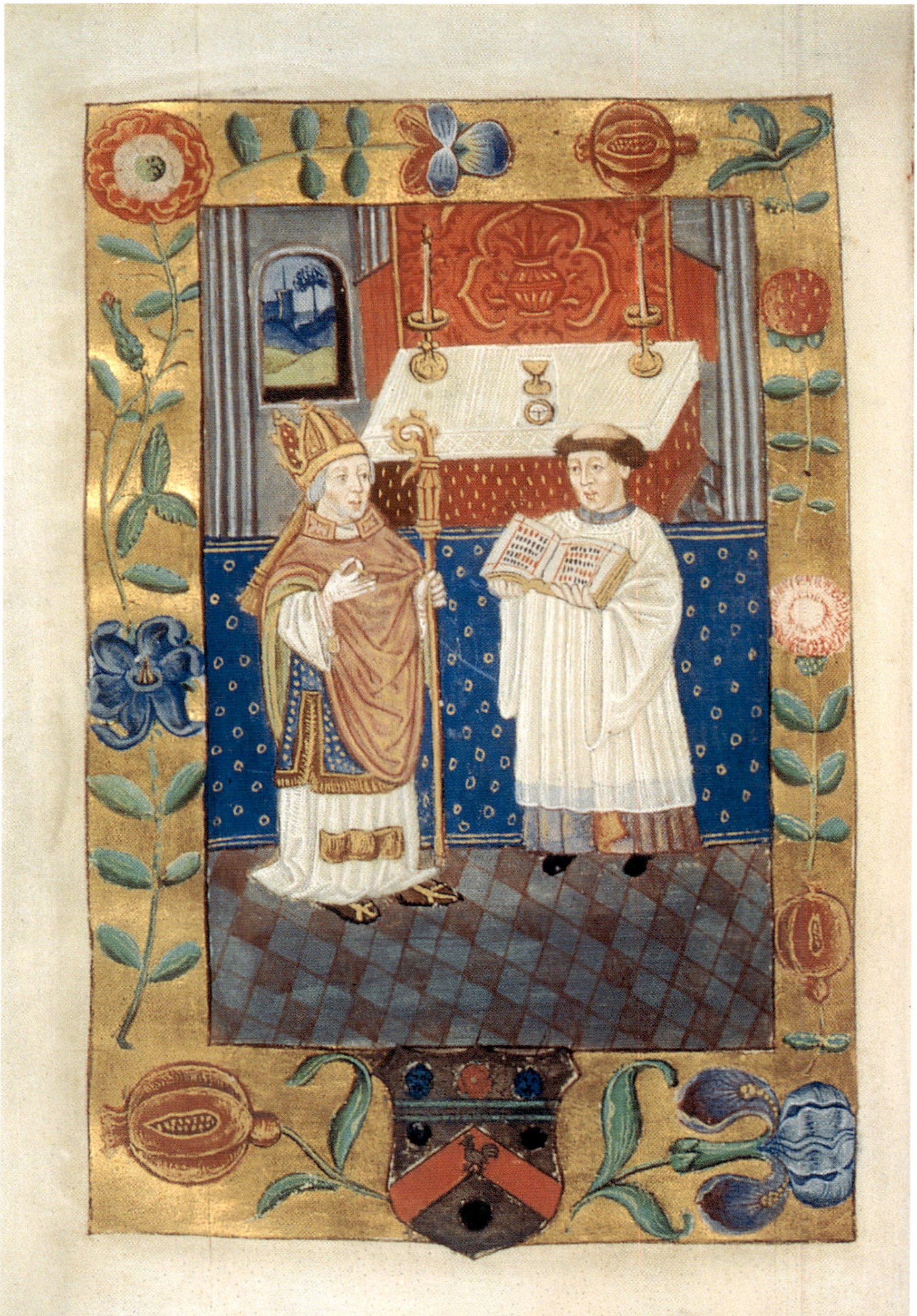

Fig. 99 British Library Additional MS 21974, fol. 21v, Mass scene; border with Bishop Longland's coat of arms. The British Library.

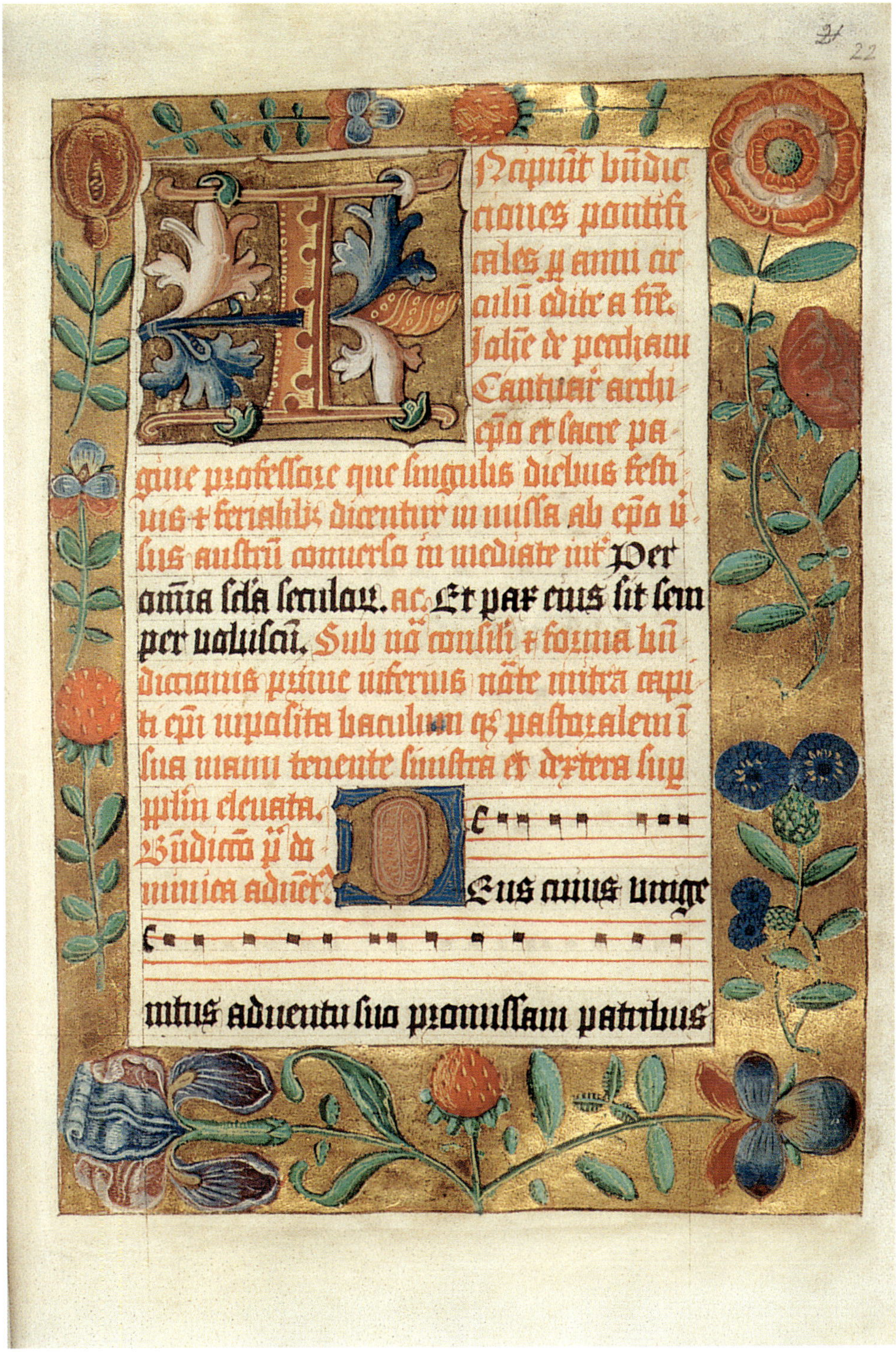

Fig. 100 British Library Additional MS 21974, fol. 22, border page with Tudor rose and pomegranate. The British Library.

to parsimonious – satisfied that the original unillustrated quires were of a good enough quality to upgrade, even though they are described by Wooley as 'carelessly written' and 'full of errors'.[391] Longland had two full-page miniatures, two large initials and four borders added to the existing blanks in the manuscript – the folios with miniatures are not insertions[392] – and his arms, as I say, were painted into two of the four borders. To judge from the selection of naturalistic motifs in the borders and the wash gold background, the Bishop knew enough about book decoration to require the most fashionable style available – that of strewn flower borders in the Flemish manner, almost certainly in direct imitation of Bruges manuscripts.[393] And he was also politically astute enough to make certain that one red-and-white Tudor rose of Henry VIII was included in each of the four borders (figs 94, 95, 99, 100), here certainly as the badge of a follower, not an owner.

It should be asked, however, why Bishop Longland was so enthusiastic about these forsaken folios that he would hire an artist who worked in a continental style, probably expensive at that, to upgrade the existing manuscript. The answer may be transparent: Longland's installation as Bishop of Lincoln in 1521. It seems quite likely that his rehabilitation of this book was meant to serve as a celebration of his ascension or, possibly, it was made for him as a gift on this occasion. If this suggestion is correct in one manner or another, it would place the addition of miniatures between 1521 and 1547; but because the installation at Lincoln was the high point of his ecclesiastical career, a date around 1521 would be the most probable time when the decorative additions were made.

Another recycled pontifical survives in CUL MS Mm.3.21 with the added arms of a different bishop of Lincoln, John Russell, bishop from 1480–94.[394] The book is finely made, if unillustrated, with calligraphic initials and borders and is probably from the illuminating shop of Hermann Scheerre, therefore made in the first decade or so of the fifteenth century.[395] Like Additional MS 21974, it cannot have been made for the bishop whose arms were added in the third quarter of the century. These two Lincoln instances of re-using liturgical books are not isolated: there is even a case of a thirteenth-century pontifical being used by an Archbishop of York between 1508 and 1514.[396]

The only other *illustrated* English Benedictional known to survive from England in the fifteenth century is in Keble College, Oxford, MS Roll 1, of the mid-century, with one damaged historiated initial at the head of the text on the face.[397] The scene shows, in so far as one can tell, a mitred bishop, with another cleric beside, blessing a kneeling group of people. Nothing is known of the bishop for whom the roll was made, but, because of the format, he presumably wished the Benedictional to be functional for travel.[398]

There are only two miniatures in the Additional Benedictional in contrast to the much longer pictorial cycles in other liturgical books used by bishops, in particular missals and pontificals. This small number might have been due to Longland's parsimony but it was more likely to the fact the book as received by Longland would have lent itself to the insertion of only two miniatures. Certainly no historiated initials or half-page miniatures could have been added without major recopying of the text. In the first miniature (fig. 94), which precedes the *Praeparatio ad missam*, the tonsured bishop is shown seated in a high-backed, wooden chair made with spindles and oval

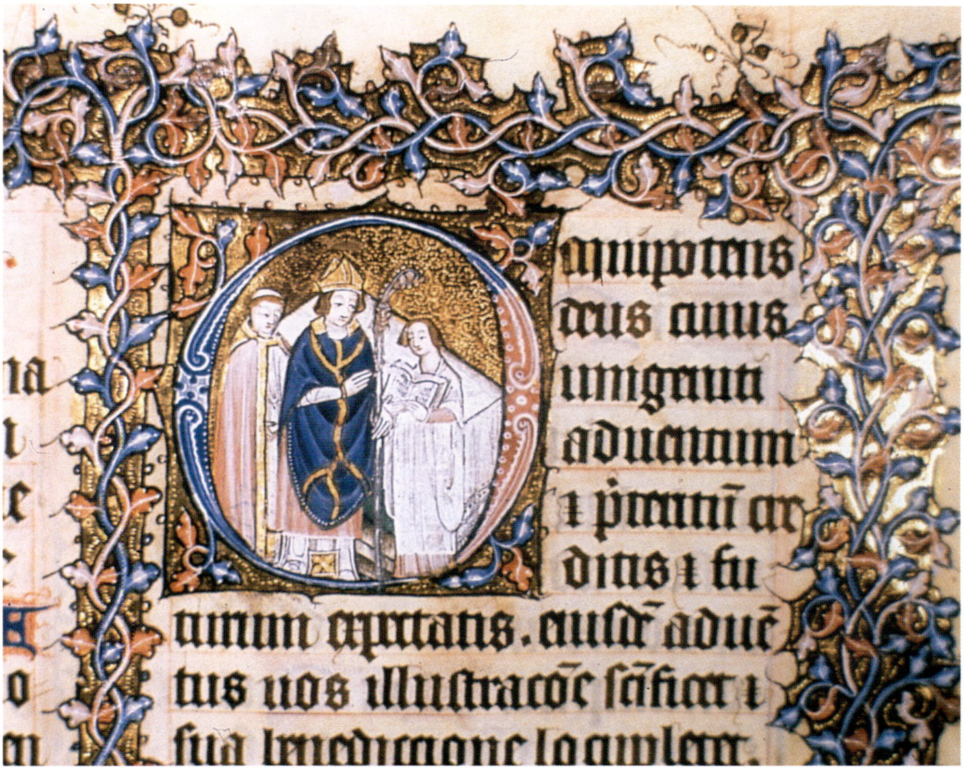

Fig. 101 Westminster Abbey, Chapter Library MS 37, fol. 164 (detail), bishop saying Mass, with acolyte holding open book. By courtesy of the Dean and Chapter of Westminster.

finials on a turned post. He wears a red undergarment which it does not seem possible to construe as an alb, black stockings, and a full, white surplice with gathered and cross-stitched embroidery at the neck. A young boy – I hesitate to call him a squire, though he is dressed like one and has the high, exposed aristocratic forehead – forces a leather buskin on the bishop's right foot. A third figure, a tonsured cleric, stands at right, holding an open book with text in red and black and with red framing lines. These are the 'familiars' serving the bishop, as mentioned on the page opposite (fig. 95).[399] The cleric wears a lavender tunicle, plain shoes and a less decorated surplice.[400] The triangular shape, bland colouring and pursed sweetness of the faces are characteristic of this artist. All three figures are placed below a fringed canopy that spans the upper width of the miniature and that supports full-length green curtains lined in a rose colour; the curtains are pulled back as if revealing a private scene. This bit of pictorial business also picks up on the text opposite (fig. 95): 'in vestiario vel in aliquo loco specialiter'. What looks like a floating chest is probably meant to represent a decorated shelf that had to be put in the scene by hook or by crook, as it were, in order to indicate that the bishop's 'parimenta' had been blessed. The shelf holds a mitre with infulae and a crosier lying across a decorated glove with tassel, in short, the most recognizable attributes of a bishop. The background of the scene is a golden

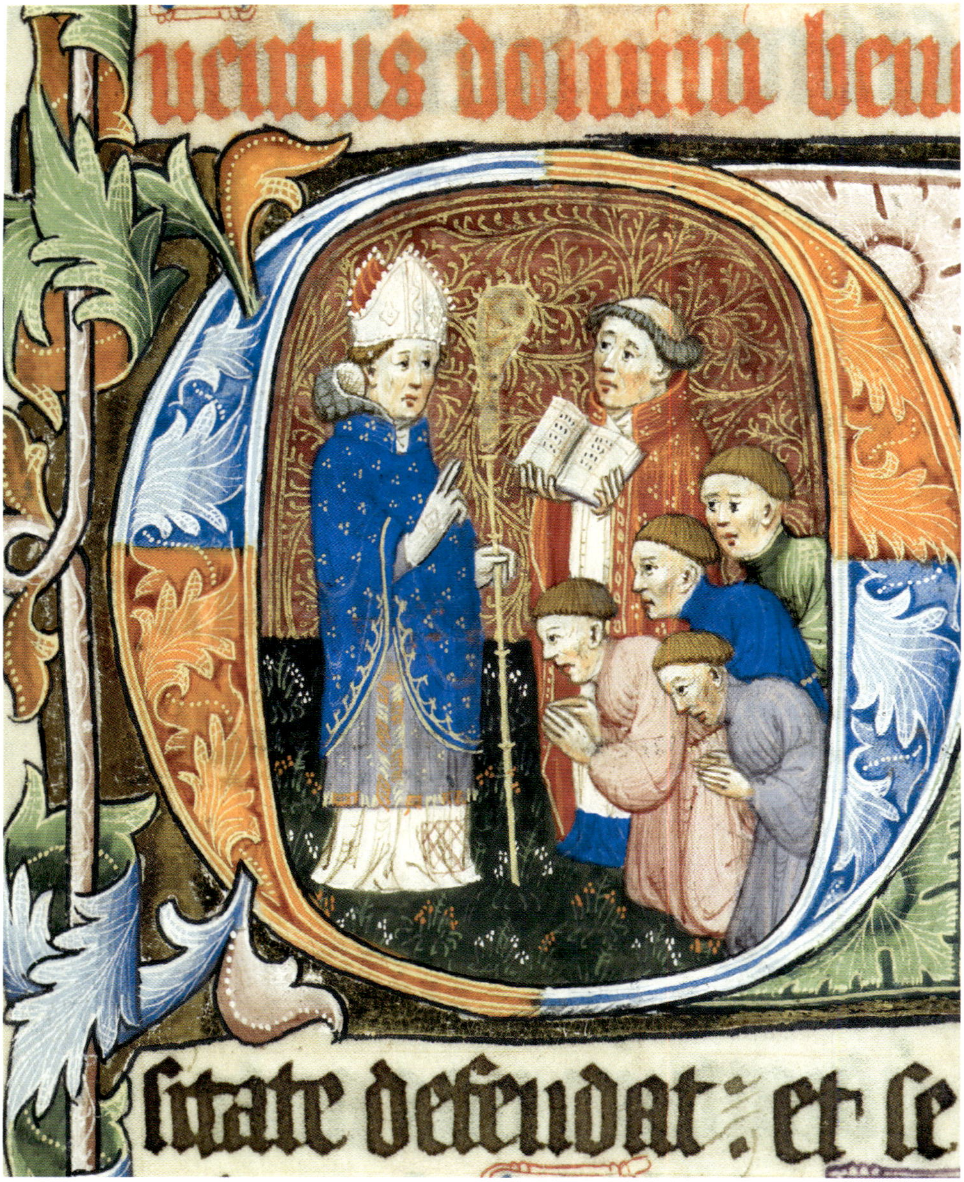

Fig. 102 British Library Lansdowne MS 451, fol. 198 (detail), bishop with cleric holding an open book. The British Library.

tapestry bearing pineapple and pomegranate designs in deep rose, and the floor is of rose and grey tiles, with some indication of perspective.

As far as I have been able to discover, the Additional scene of the vesting of the bishop is unique in English book art. The two closest comparable themes, which do not, however, involve a religious person, are, first, the miniature of 'How a man shull be armed … to fight on foot' – a different tradition entirely from Pierpont Morgan Library M. 775 (fig. 97), Ordinances of Chivalry,[401] after *c.* 1449-before 1461; and,

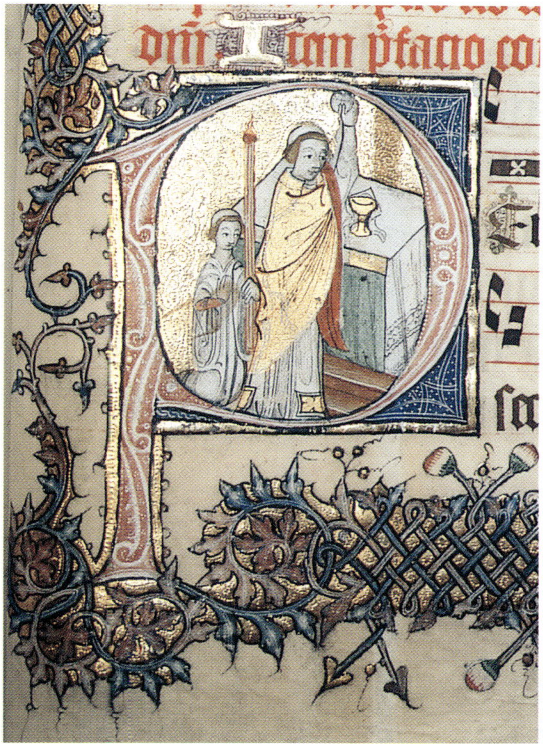

Fig. 103 Westminster Abbey, Chapter Library MS 37, fol. 156 (detail), Elevation of the Host. By courtesy of the Dean and Chapter of Westminster.

second, a similar scene from the Beauchamp Pageants (BL Cotton Julius E.iv, art. 6, after 1480–?before 1493, of the Earl of Warwick being dressed in armour by two familiars.[402] But if we turn to the Continent, there is a *Praeparatio ad missam pontificalem* in another Morgan Library manuscript (Heineman 6), an Italian book made for Pope Leo X and signed and dated in Rome, 1520, just at what I take to be the approximate time of the Longland miniature. This manuscript has as frontispiece a depiction of Leo X during his vesting, also at the moment when he is receiving his boots (fig. 98).[403] It would be perverse to try to demonstrate that the Italian miniature was a direct influence on the English scene in Additional 21974, especially in view of its sumptuousness, but we should at least be aware of its existence. It is conceivable that Longland had heard of Pope Leo's manuscript and decided to emulate it.

In the second Additional miniature (fig. 99), which introduces the Peckham benedictions, the bishop is dressed in full regalia: in a white alb with apparel, a blue gold-dotted tunicle with gold fringe, a wash-gold chasuble shaded in rose, an amice, gloves with tassel and ring, a gold mitre with infulae, and boots with crossed decoration in gold. The assisting cleric holds an open book – this book? – apparently for the bishop to begin the benediction for advent, as the text opposite states (fig. 100): 'Sub nota consimili et forma benediccionis prime inferius notate mitra capiti episcopi inposita baculumque pastoralem in sua manu tenente sinistra et dextera super populum eleuata. Benediccio pro dominica aduentus.' Although details concerning mitre and staff are pictured, the bishop's hand is not shown as raised in benediction,

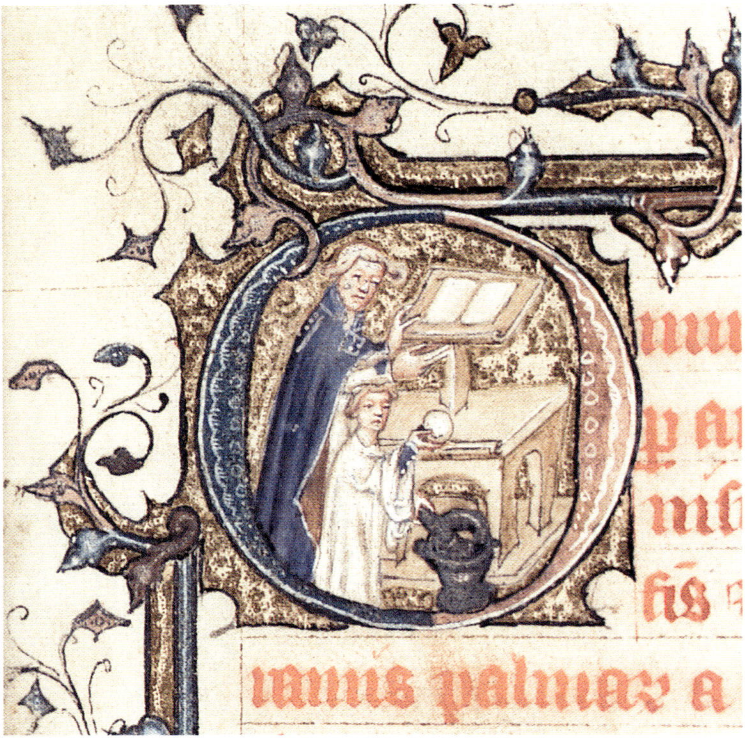

Fig. 104 Oxford, Trinity College MS 8, fol. 9 (detail), Blessing of the Salt. The President and Fellows of Trinity College, Oxford

nor is the populace. A curtain is stretched between the celebrants and the altar, which is dressed with a white cloth and fringed fontal and furnished with two lighted candlesticks, a chalice covered with pall, a paten with the Host, and a tapestry backpiece. The landscape view from the unglazed window is not typically English, but by this time this kind of rendering may have come into an English illuminator's vocabulary.

This scene is again especially rare, and one feature of it is not known at all elsewhere. The best I can do is to report on similar iconographies in two other manuscripts: the Litlyngton Missal, of 1383–84, Westminster Abbey Chapter Library, MS 38,[404] and the pontifical in BL Lansdowne MS 451, of *c.* 1400 and 1420–30. The Litlyngton manuscript has, at Advent, an historiated initial in which the two central figures are similarly placed and in a similar posture (fig. 101), if with different gestures. Lansdowne 451 (fol. 198) also shows at Advent the figure of a priest holding an open book for the bishop, as he blesses a group of laymen, also at Advent (fig. 102). This type of scene, as in the Lansdowne manuscript, may possibly have been a intermediary (although depicting the populace) between the Litlington Missal and the much later Additional 21974 miniature. In any case, all three pontifical manuscripts show a similar illustration at the feast of Advent, and it is unlikely that this is a coincidence, even if the artists had simply seen the scene *in vivo*.[405] The iconographies of a priest with acolyte or other assisting cleric that were actually conventional in fifteenth-century missals are those of the Elevation of the Host as, for instance, in San Marino,

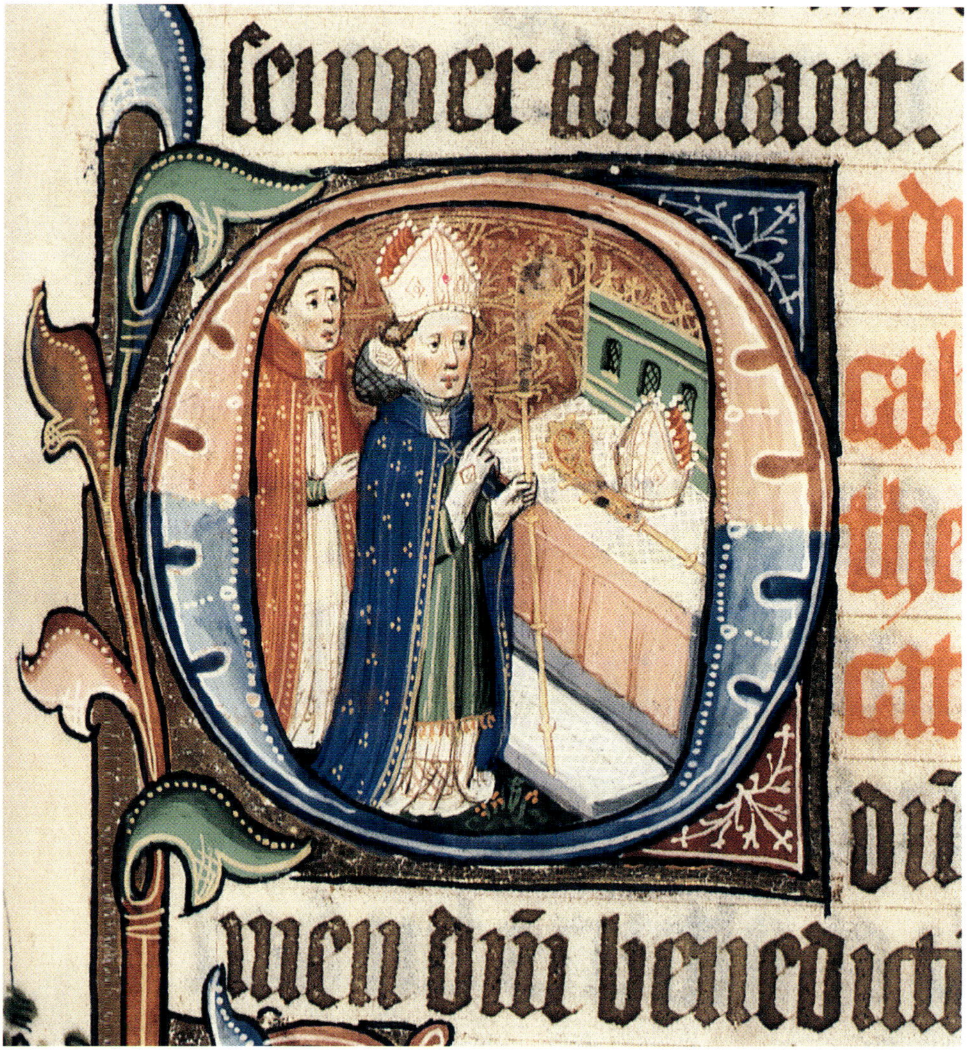

Fig. 105 British Library Lansdowne MS 451, fol. 176 (detail), bishop blessing apparel. The British Library.

Huntington Library HM 1067 (fol. 149) and in the Litlington Missal (fig. 103), and of the Blessing of the Salt, as in Oxford, Trinity College MS 8 (fig. 104). The Additional miniature for Advent might be described in Jonathan Alexander's phrase as 'expectation modified', which is to say that it was a known and previously used subject but one refashioned on a particular occasion;[406] in the present manuscript the scene was modified to suit a full-page format and the iconography altered to suit Longland's purposes.

One also has to ask why the figures of the bishop and cleric are separated from the altar by a piece of waist-high cloth strung behind them like a curtain? Was this an

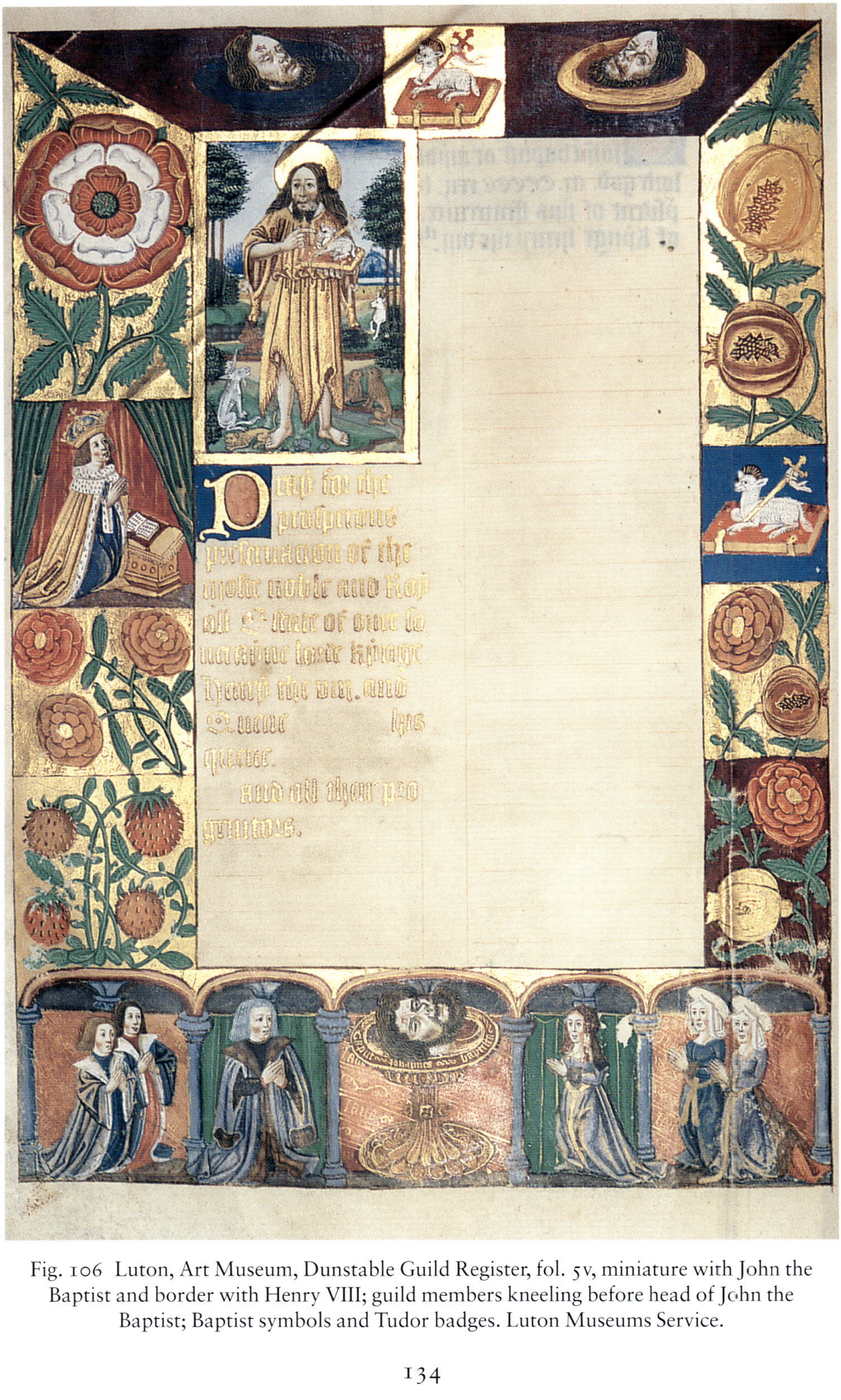

Fig. 106 Luton, Art Museum, Dunstable Guild Register, fol. 5v, miniature with John the Baptist and border with Henry VIII; guild members kneeling before head of John the Baptist; Baptist symbols and Tudor badges. Luton Museums Service.

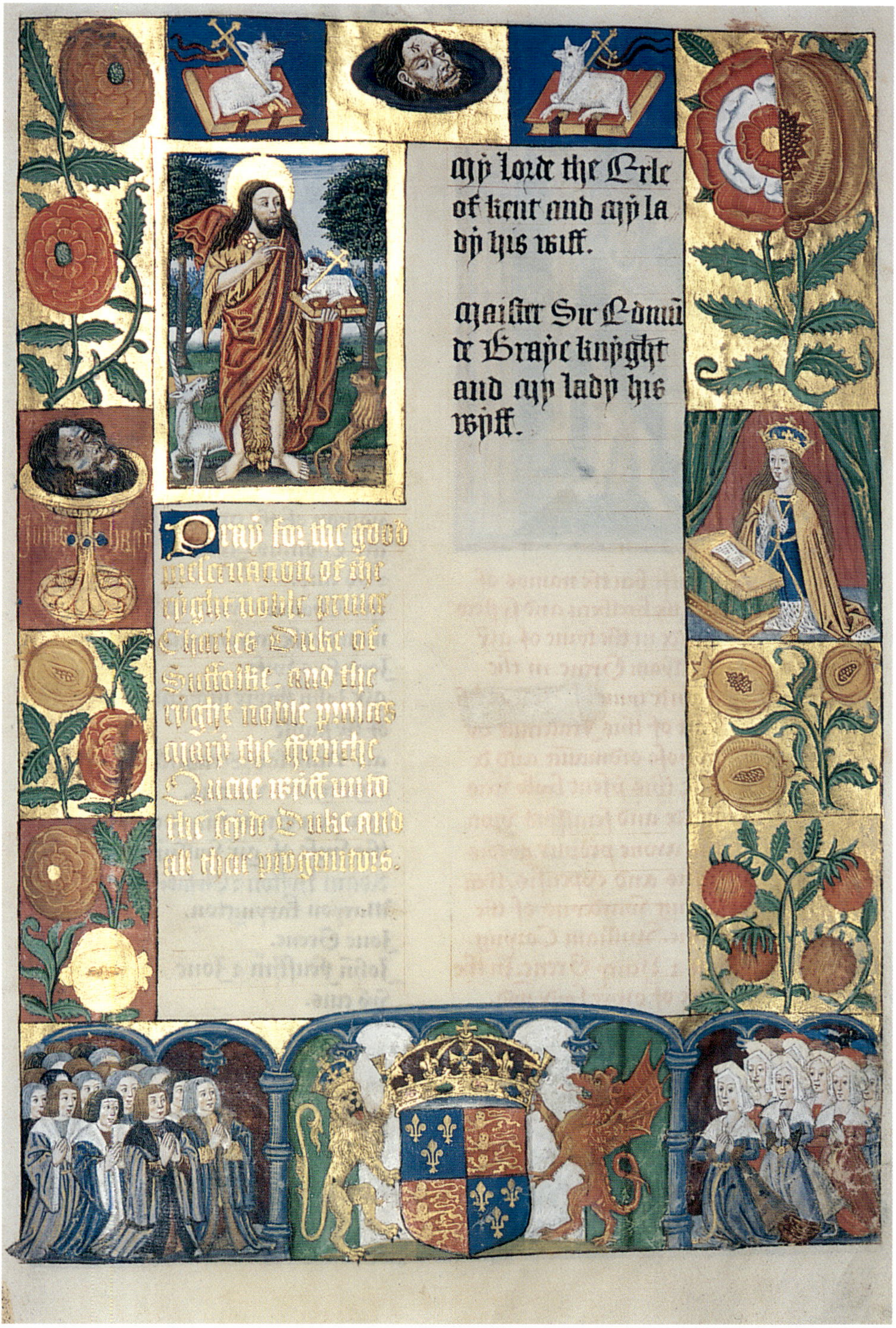

Fig. 107 Luton, Art Museum, Dunstable Guild Register, fol. 6, miniature with John the Baptist and border with Catherine of Aragon; guild members kneeling before crowned and supported royal arms; Baptist symbols and Tudor badges. Luton Museums Service.

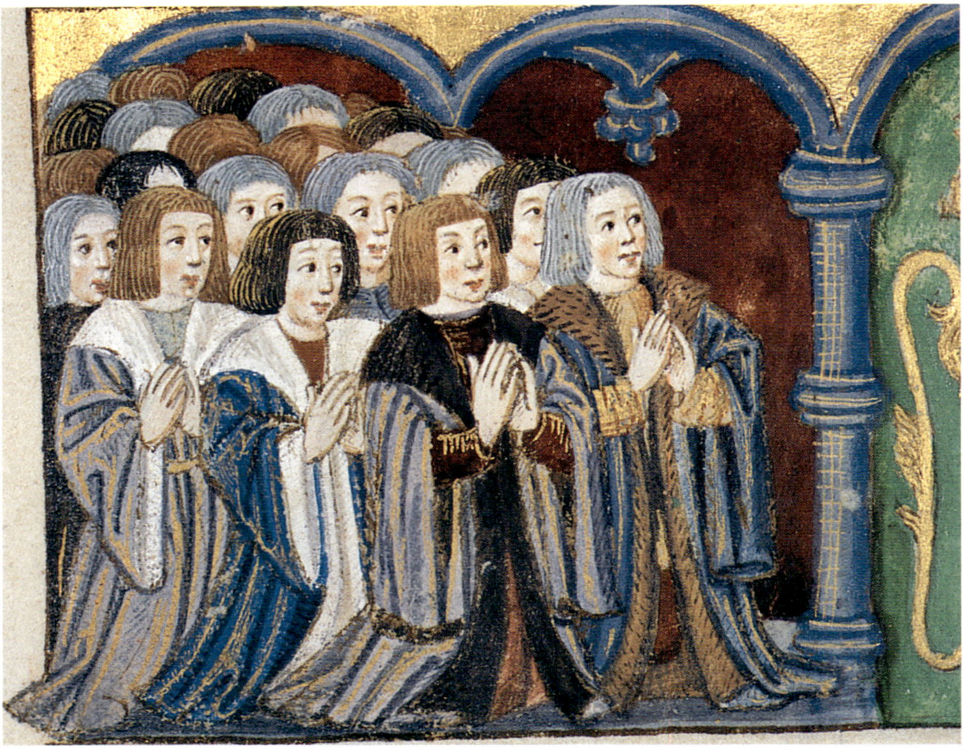

Fig. 108 Luton, Art Museum, Dunstable Guild Register, fol. 6 (detail), kneeling guildsmen. Luton Museums Service.

ignorant invention by the artist, or was there a *bona fide* liturgical reason for its presence? We may be witnessing a blessing 'super populum' and the curtain might be acting as a symbolic screen, separating the populace from the altar;[407] and we may be grateful to the artist for his rendering of the subject, which is probably unique and pictorially an otherwise undocumented realistic detail with respect to the celebration of the mass at this season.[408]

Perhaps it was something to do with the mentality of bishops, but two further important illustrated episcopal texts, full pontificals, are also made up of an unfinished portion and a later continuation in the manner of Additional MS 21974. These two are Cambridge, Corpus Christi MS 79,[409] early fifteenth century and second quarter of the fifteenth century, and BL Lansdowne MS 451,[410] *c.* 1400 and 1420–30. The first part of Corpus 79, which has seventy-five miniatures, was begun for Guy de Mona, Bishop of St Davids in 1397 and was completed after his death in 1407 for Richard Clifford, Bishop of Worcester and then of London; Clifford used it until his death in 1421, when it passed to Philip Morgan, Bishop of Worcester from 1419 to 1426, and of Ely from 1426 to 1435. As Frere says, Corpus 79 'throws interesting light on the habits of bishops with regard to their pontificals and is the best extant illustration of the fact that pontificals do not belong to any diocesan use, but represent the personal use of the bishop to whom they may happen to belong.'[411] Not exactly: if

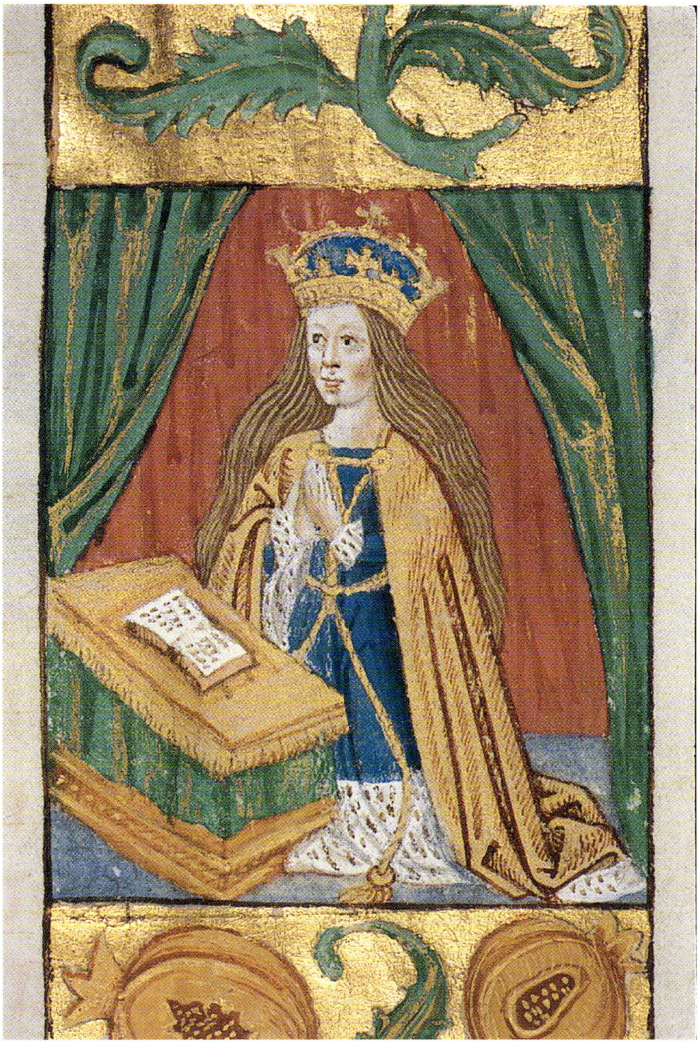

Fig. 109 Luton, Art Museum, Dunstable Guild Register, fol. 6 (detail), Catherine of Aragon kneeling. Luton Museums Service.

the bishop takes up a book made for someone else's use, he has to use what that person decided upon and is constrained by the pre-existing contents. The newer parts of Corpus MS 79, of *c.* 1421–35, are at the front of the book on fols 13–20v, and their decoration makes a distinct contrast with the older work on fols 21–286. In spite of a considerable number of miniatures in this manuscript, none is relevant to those in Additional MS 21974.

The other recycled pontifical, BL Lansdowne MS 451, which I have mentioned, has forty-six historiated initials and marginal scenes and is again of two distinct artistic periods, *c.* 1400 and 1420–30.[412] The text itself was written at one time from fols 5 to 249, but fols 5 to 131v were decorated in an earlier provincial but charming style, of around 1400, presumably about the time of the writing of the book. The completion of the decoration, from fol. 131 to fol. 249, did not take place until the 1430s, when line endings matching in colour the earlier ones, two-line coloured initials, nine historiated initials[413] and an astounding 187 borders were added to the manuscript. The style of the second artist is more sophisticated than that of the first, and probably from a London shop. The subjects of the historiated initials here are unusual and of some interest, e.g. those of placing relics in the altar (fol. 136v) and blessing of pontifical apparel (fig. 105), but only the single instance mentioned above of a bishop blessing the populace at Advent (fig. 102) has any clear relationship to a scene in the Additional manuscript.

What we have in the two Additional miniatures, then, is a wholly unique English iconography in the first miniature, and a second miniature whose primary elements were known and used a century before. Longland chose, it is clear, to focus the only two illustrations in his book on a large-scale image of a bishop rather than on a sequence of the bishop's possible interactions with penitents, acolytes, hermits, etc., even to omitting the populace in the second miniature. The Additional images strike me as a personal rather than pious statement, and, given the prominent coats of arms below each miniature, can we doubt but that the focus is on Longland himself as bishop, a self-reflecting image on each occasion that he opened the book. Full-scale miniatures of patrons were not part of the usual design of a liturgical book at this period,[414] and in spite of the Gothic rendering, we are here truly in the Renaissance.

I should like now to consider further the artist of Additional MS 21974. As I stated in the Introduction, my working principle is that in the study of illustrated manuscripts it is of utmost importance to locate the work of an artist in as many manuscripts as possible. Such associations give us some knowledge of the geographic range of an artist's professional activity in his society, of his status as judged by the status of his patrons, and, through his collaboration with another artist or artists, of the possible location of the centre of book illustration in England, with which he can be associated. In the case of Additional MS 21974, the book was upgraded with miniatures by a bishop who was established at the court of Henry VIII and who was also apparently accepted in the highest intellectual circles. But was this a typical patron for the Additional artist? Or was Longland a patron of an unusually high status for this artist?

We can obtain some further sense of the artist's connections by examining another manuscript whose illustration I attribute to him, a book that enlarges the scope of his patronage beyond a personalized book for an ecclesiastic to the sphere of wealthy confraternities and guilds. This manuscript, in the collection of the Luton Art Museum, Bedfordshire, contains a register of the membership of the Fraternity of St John the Baptist, a religious guild that had been founded in Dunstable, South Bedfordshire, in the 1440s.[415] The register survives with only eighty-three leaves, for the years 1506–1508, 1522, and 1525–41. It is, of course, the folios written, decorated and dated in 1522 that are of concern here, and in particular the two folios that depict miniatures of John the Baptist, with border panels showing Henry VIII (fig. 106) and Catherine of Aragon (fig. 107), both kneeling at a prie-Dieu. The lower borders have arched architectural spaces with kneeling male and female members of the Fraternity and, on fol. 6, the crowned royal arms of Henry VIII with the supporters of a gold lion and the red dragon of Wales. The Tudor badges of a red-and-white rose and a pomegranate are prominent but, in contrast to the design of the Additional borders, the naturalistic motifs, the emblems of John the Baptist, and the pictorial scenes are divided from each other into differently coloured compartments. Although there are other borders and miniatures in the Register in the years 1522 and 1525–41, these are the only two pages that that I attribute wholly to the Additional artist; a third illustrated and illuminated page (on fol. 6v) was probably designed by the Additional artist but executed by an assistant. There are some differences in the painterly rendering between the Luton Register and that of Additional MS 21974, notably, a heavier application of facial colouring on the cheeks of figures and, generally, a slightly rougher execution of faces, perhaps due to the much smaller size of figures in the Luton borders (fig. 108). The detail of Catherine of Aragon (fig. 109) shows, however, the triangular facial type, prominent neck, the use of pale skin colouring, and the handling of drapery, especially of the curtains, which are green with a rose background, another characteristic of the Additional artist. The very similar floral and plant motifs in the borders were certainly done by him or by the same assistant in both manuscripts.

The patron of this part of the Dunstable Register was William Grene, President of the Fraternity in 1522, who, as we know from an inscription on fol. 6v, had by his own ordinance and out of his own pocket had the Register made and paid for.[416] The Additional artist, who almost certainly had his business in London, was likely to have been obtained through one of the grander Fraternity members, and the relevant leaves taken to London for writing and illumination, or at least for the latter.[417] The general membership of the Fraternity comprised a few arms-bearing presidents,[418] wardens, and members with their wives who were largely townspeople of Dunstable. Their occupations included sheep-farming, malting, butchery, wine-making, and inn-keeping.[419] A few gentry and nobility such as the Dukes of Suffolk and Kent, perhaps pictured in the arched niches on fols 5v and 6, also belonged in 1522. We are safe in assuming, however, that Henry VIII and Catherine of Aragon were not in regular attendance at meetings and that their portraits were of an honorary and complimentary nature: not only a compliment to the sovereign, but the Fraternity complimenting itself on the high rank of its membership. So, although the Fraternity was nearly a microcosm of contemporary society, in its higher ranges it could be well considered as equal in patronage, from the artist's point of view, to the bishop-patron of Additional MS 21974.

CHAPTER VI
Conclusions

In the Introduction, I raised issues to which I should now like to return. I want first to revisit my question, which is probably the most fundamental, concerning the function of illustrations in late medieval books.[420] Why were illustrations there at all? No single response will do. Different types of texts had different reasons for incorporating miniatures or diagrams and, leaving aside pictures included apparently only for entertainment value, I see four other objectives for their appearance, in spite of the awkwardness their inclusion must have caused scribe and entrepreneurs. First, there is what I would name authorial mandate: by which I mean that the author himself expressly states that a miniature or diagram should be present at a particular place in the text in order to explicate it; such representations are implicitly a kind of exegesis without which the text cannot be correctly understood. This requirement occurred on numerous occasions in Nicholas of Lyra's *Postilla super totam bibliam*, and in the first chapter of this study I noted other instances of the imperative by other authors. Peter of Poitiers, a second of my authors, also insisted that his *Compendium* text be clarified by 'figures'. One unambiguous example is a quotation that I have illustrated from BL Additional MS 30509 (fig. 110) following a diagram of the Disposition of the Twelve Tribes of Israel around the Tabernacle of the Ark, 'This figure is put here to understande the processe that is put in the book of numeris ...' (a Middle English translation of fig. 18). I have not tried to compile an all-inclusive list of such authorial precepts, but I am certain that this was a more common occurence than we may now realize. The instructions of Geoffrey Chaucer, John Gower and John Lydgate, all of whose texts have recurrent and similar pictorial subjects, may not survive, but, as Stephen Jay Goulding has said, 'absence of evidence is not evidence of absence'. We simply do not know how many other illustrated books were derived from an authorial mandate.

The teaching imperative is another cause of illustration in manuscripts. Poitiers' reduction of the Bible with its miniatures and diagrams would also fit into this classification and, of the other manuscripts discussed here, Stowe MS 39, *The Abbey of the Holy Ghost*, contains an illustrated opening at the end of the text that I understand to be a teaching tool composed, as it is, of individually readable scenes in a non-sequential reconstruction of the text. Furthermore, the opening would seem to have been placed in this abnormal position relative to the text so as to act as a summarizing review of the *Abbey*. Various non-literary texts, such as medical and alchemical tracts, mathematical and astronomical treatises, herbals and agricultural almanacs, had a much more obvious need to emphasize and teach by image: illustrations that fall into this class would be Visceral and Skeletal Men, drawings of plants and medical instruments and procedures, maps, urine charts and eclipses, geometric demonstrations, etc., and saint's days and signs of the zodiac. And they may not have been ineffective as teaching tools.

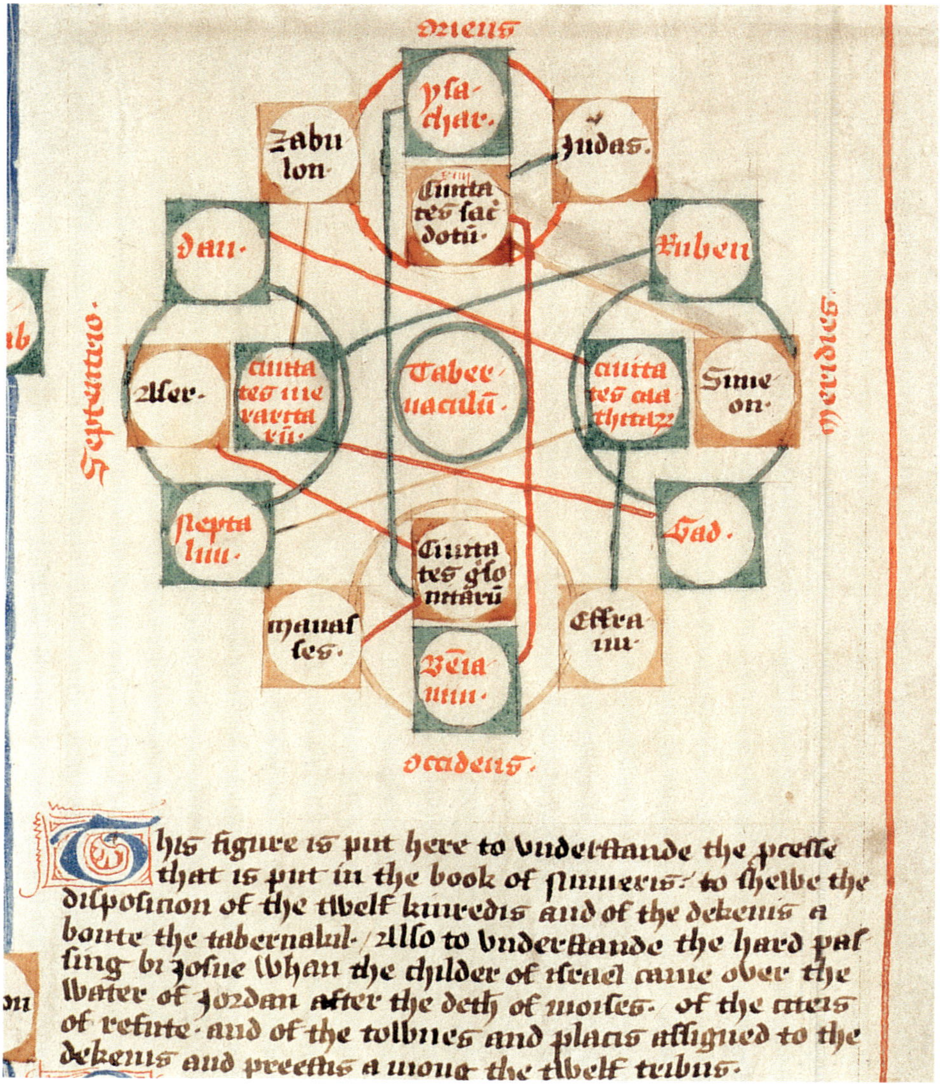

Fig. 110 British Library Additional MS 30509, membrane 2 (detail), diagram of the Levite camps around the Ark of the Covenant. The British Library.

A third reason for the implementation of miniatures is what can be called the authoritative principle. In this case, the entrepreneur producing a book, probably with the approval of the patron, decided to illustrate the opening of the text with a miniature of the author or presumed author of the text. The entrepreneur may simply have been following on from an exemplar in his possession or he may have made an independent decision, but in either case the main motive for rendering an author-figure was to give authority to that particular issue of the text. I have discussed this elsewhere[421] and here will mention it only with regard to All Souls MS 10, the subject of the second chapter. This principle behind the selection of a pictorial subject may have been particularly effective when the authors were Apostles or saints.

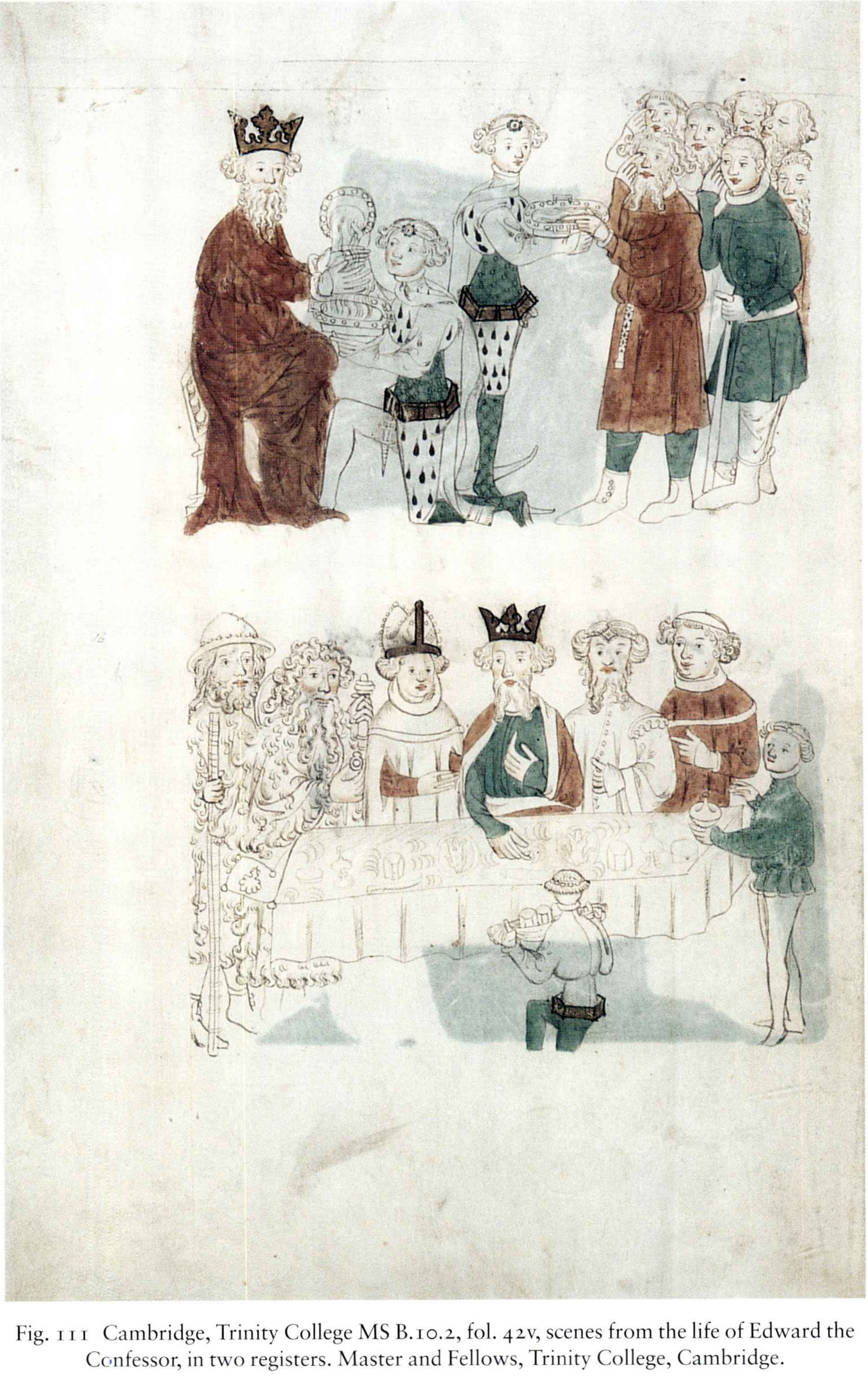

Fig. 111 Cambridge, Trinity College MS B.10.2, fol. 42v, scenes from the life of Edward the Confessor, in two registers. Master and Fellows, Trinity College, Cambridge.

The last and perhaps most obvious reason for the presence of miniatures in a manuscript would have been the fact of a patron willing to pay for them. But patronal fiat might have been responsible for change in a standard pictorial sequence and of course also for the existence of a patronal portrait in one form or another. As we have seen in Bishop Longland's Benedictional, the two added miniatures bear certain characteristics that, taken together, would suggest patronal interference: 1) they are full-page in size, a format which to my mind is not likely to be found in books made on speculation and certainly not in fifteenth-century liturgical books (apart from the usual Crucifixion page in Missals); 2) in one scene there is a centering and magnification of the pontifical figure; 3) coats of arms are present; and 4) one of the miniatures is highly unusual, if not unique in later English manuscripts in its subject matter, the scene of vesting the bishop. Commissioning owners were quite capable of making their presence known by intruding on borders and by pushing their way into a miniature, even into such unlikely books as missals and Books of Hours.

Now, by putting forward these reasons for the presence of illustrations in books, I do not intend to deny that they might also serve more commonly recognized functions such as calling attention to chapter or book divisions in texts or as providing a source of visual delectation. Miniatures could clarify or teach and still perform these last mentioned functions.

Even in the few manuscripts examined in the Lyell lectures, it is noticeable that English book illustration presents itself in a variety of formats and techniques. This is the second issue that I raised in the Introduction. The English miniatures that we have seen came lined up more or less in rows in a modelbook; enclosed within an introductory initial; arranged in registers in a full-page picture space; unframed and, in various sizes and shapes, worked in and around a text (figs 76, 84); and, finally, spread over a full-page format in the manuscript just discussed, Additional MS 21974. Two of these formats, the historiated initial and the full-page miniature are conventional, with the historiated initial being the most widely used format in English manuscripts. Scenes arranged in registers, as in Stowe MS 39, were not common, but do emerge from time to time in the fifteenth century (fig. 111).

The other non-standard format that we have seen is a grouping of figures, scenes, or diagrams, without an accompanying text, in a manner clearly indicating that they had no textual referent *in situ* but that they were meant by the artist to be used in some other manner. This arrangement of scenes and figures is rare: I know of the phenomenon in England only in two modelbooks,[422] and on a leaf in a thirteenth-century manuscript, BL Cotton MS Faustina B.vii (fig. 112) with images and diagrams of Noah's Ark stored for use with Peter of Poitiers' *Compendium*.[423] The leaves with stored images in the Laud modelbook (figs 1, 4, 11, 13, 20, 21, 22) and in Yale University MS Beinecke 640 (figs 12, 14, 19) have opened up our understanding to an entirely unsuspected mode of preserving and transmitting illustrations, a mode unlike the known artists' personal sketchbooks whose images have not yet been found as illustrations in surviving illustrated English manuscripts.

Lastly, it is clear that manuscripts with illustrations woven in and between the text, pressuring it, and breaking it up into non-standard chunks are also very rare, and particularly rare, I might add, in a costly manuscript like Royal MS 1.B.x (figs 76, 78, 83). All in all, I would go so far as to say that miniatures act according to the theory of

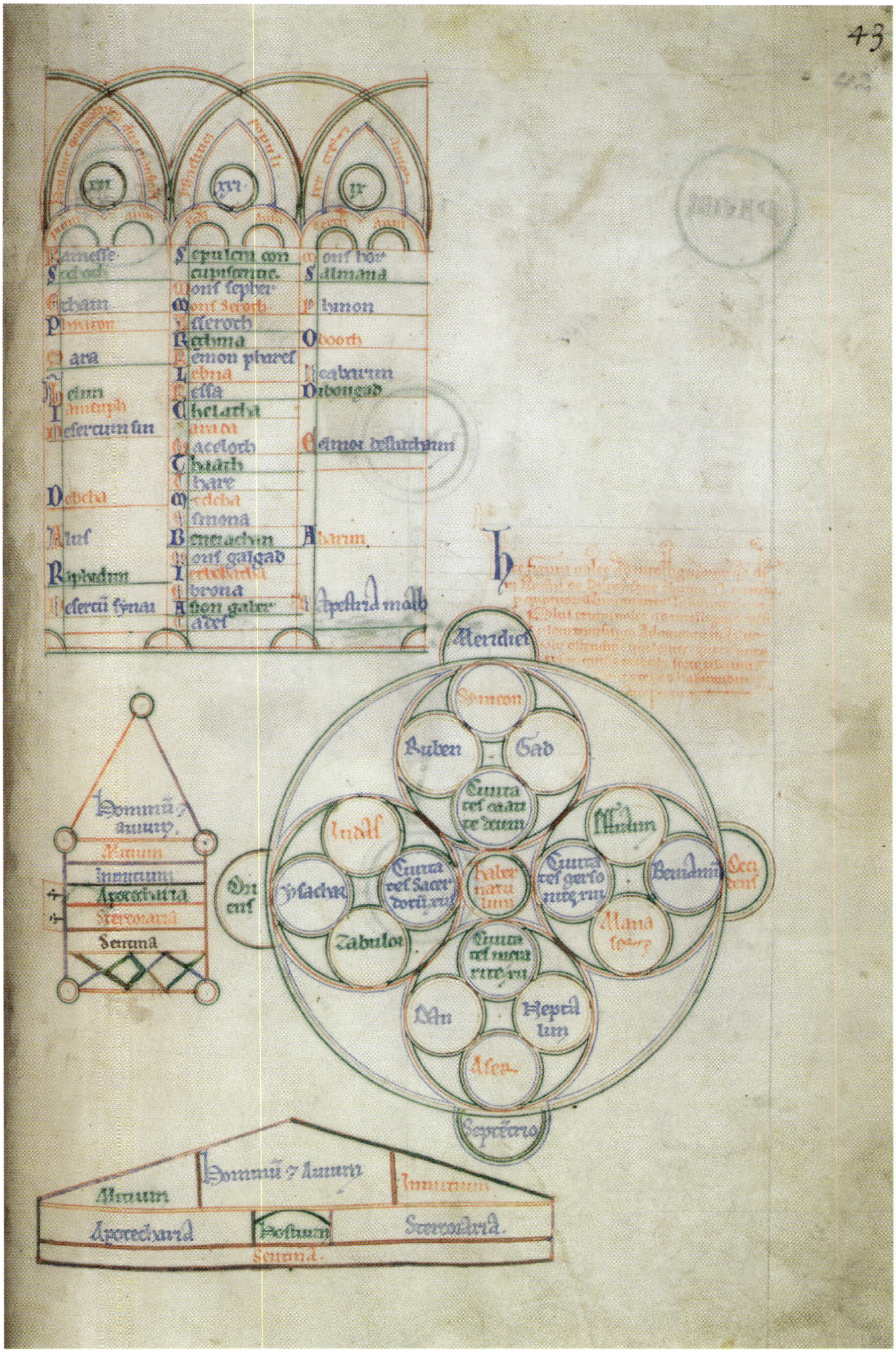

Fig. 112 British Library Cotton MS Faustina B.vii, fol. 42, thirteenth-century model page for Peter of Poitiers' *Compendium historie in genealogia Christi*. The British Library.

fractals, that, whatever the format of a miniature, there is still a basic, underlying identity that, like clouds, allows us to recognize them when we see them.

As for the artistic techniques that were employed to produce miniatures in the five manuscripts of the Lyell lectures, they, too, have a surprising aspect. Three of the five manuscripts have illustration rendered either only in penwork or in penwork and colouring to some degree. Royal MS 1.B.x is particularly interesting for its highly skilled use of pen and ink to sustain elaborate genealogical descents and detailed miniatures. The manuscript, datable between 1433 and 1449, precedes the flare-up of high-end books illustrated in the second half of the century in England, books such as the Beauchamp Pageants, the Rous Roll (BL Additional MS 48976), and the Guildbook of the York Barber Surgeons (BL Egerton MS 2572).[424] The artist of Stowe MS 39, who also apparently worked in the second quarter of the fifteenth century, took a different approach to the use of the pen for illustration. He handled the quill with a lighter touch but brought 'up' his characters and their structure through the restrained application of tint, usually rose or blue, and applied the tint in an outlining manner; the rose-coloured robe of the nuns, for example, both outlined and emphasized their shape, while the inner gown, faces and hands were left open to the parchment. This technique created a light, insubstantial effect for the Stowe miniatures in spite of the repeated architectural frameworks.

The third pen artist in the Lyell group was at the opposite end of the colourist range. His basic work in the Laud modelbook made use of a pen line but here the line was filled with heavy blocks of colour in dark blue, red and green, as if to emphasize the weighty import of the images, both in themselves and as objects for copying. All three of these manuscripts reinforce our previous impression that penwork illustration was considered desirable to the makers of books and appealing to their patrons. The remaining two manuscripts in this study were illustrated with pigments, using the full palette available to the late medieval English artist. The balance of techniques as used in the present five manuscripts, three to two in favour of penwork, may be skewed relative to overall surviving production in England in the century: it is likely that more manuscripts, when illustrated, were on the whole produced using pigments rather than with pen or pen and tint.[425]

The third question that I raised in the Introduction concerning English illustration was the nature of the iconography that we saw in the five manuscripts. Was it traditional and static, or expansive and forward-looking? On the whole I would, with some reluctance, have to say that it was largely traditional, if at the same time showing a few skimpy signs of change. Implicit in every one of the fifteenth-century and early sixteenth-century books that I have discussed is either the explicit or the ghostly presence like a fossil in stone of past production of the same text; a particularly late example is the sixteenth-century depiction of Noah's Ark in BL Kings MS 395. Although the author's earliest version does not survive, we know that the Nicholas of Lyra illustrations had a very long life and that they were probably author-original to the text. All Souls MS 10 with its initials of New Testament writers still fits fairly closely into a fifty- to 150-year history of illustrating French Bibles, and, if not using precisely the same iconography, Stowe MS 39, with its scenes from the *Abbey of the Holy Ghost*, has been found to retain the faint presence of one comparable full-page miniature in a thirteenth-century French copy. The Stowe sequence was, however, revised for contemporary purposes and placed, abnormally, at the end of the text. The two remaining manuscripts have illustration that shows awareness of earlier cycles but that either expanded or contracted them considerably. Royal MS 1.B.x took extensive liberties in adding a substantial number of scenes to the thirteenth-century sequences of Poitiers' *Compendium historie in genealogia Christi* as well as in elaborating the decoration of the genealogical lineages. Additional MS 21974, in contrast, substantially abbreviated the number of illustrations that usually occurred in pontifical manuscripts and changed the focus by including a personal vesting scene. So, to a greater or lesser degree, all five of the pictorial sequences were based on traditional iconography: four had some adaptation to suit contemporary circumstances or requirements, and only one, the Laud modelbook, persisted in recording verbatim, as it were, traditional illustration.

As far as ownership of the five unrelated manuscripts in this study is concerned, they are all variations on the not-surprising theme 'religious'. MS Laud Misc. 156, the modelbook, was owned and possibly commissioned by the Hospital of Saint John the Baptist, Exeter, that is, for a religious house. All Souls MS 10, the Bible in French, was probably made for a private lay person who wished to have use of the Bible in the vernacular for his own devout purposes. Stowe MS 39, the *Abbey of the Holy Ghost*, was certainly made for a nunnery, probably Benedictine and in the north of England. Royal MS 1.B.x was certainly made for a scribe, John Dygon, who was a secular priest and perhaps even a recluse at the time the book was compiled. The last manuscript, Additional MS 21974, a benedictional, was adapted for a bishop, John Longland, of Lincoln. This is an interesting range of owners from such a small selection of manuscripts, and it would be cheering to think that the selection mirrored in part the prevailing contemporary ownership by persons able to purchase books. Nobility and merchants, both important classes of book-owners in the fifteenth century, are missing – though represented in the Luton Fraternity Register by association with Additional MS 21974.

To conclude, I was recently struck by John Lowden's observations on luxury books and, in particular, by his thought that 'we need to try to tease out the complex particularities of each story' (i.e. of each manuscript).[426] The Lyell lectures have given me the opportunity to do just that, and a more diverse set of stories and of English manuscripts would be hard to imagine. I would take an oath that the five manuscripts were not pre-selected for any predetermined results. They were truly books that I liked and that had not been discussed before. From this selection we can see that the presence of art, in the form of illustration and decoration was, where affordable, both coveted and felt to be appropriate in English books of the later period; and that this book art, in all its Englishness, and, I feel, in its own peculiar glory, was important to English book production. Here I think it is best to accept English book art for what it was: both pen-drawn and painterly, accomplished and rough-hewn, an artistic system at rest, stable and focussed, not based in the environment (apart from a chair or room or fish), an antitype to naturalism, derivative yet individual, model-following, charming, and an art content with itself. And so should we be.

NOTES

INTRODUCTION

1 As in *The Cloister and the Hearth* by Charles Reade.

2 See L. Lawton, 'The Illustration of Late Medieval Secular Texts, with Special Reference to Lydgate's "Troy Book"', in *Manuscripts and Readers in Fifteenth-Century England: The Literary Implications of Manuscript Study*, ed. D. Pearsall (Cambridge, 1983), 43, 44, 45.

3 A theme of Margaret Rickert's *Painting in Britain: The Middle Ages* (Harmondsworth, 2nd ed., 1965), e.g. 208.

4 Others are described in my *Later Gothic Manuscripts*; to mention a few: nos 7, 12, 31, 41, 58, 62, 103, 112, etc.

CHAPTER I

5 A biography and comments on the early success of Lyra's work are available in H. Hailperin, *Rashi and the Christian Scholars* (Pittsburgh, 1963), 137-38. For further detail, see P. D. W. Krey and L. Smith, *Nicholas of Lyra: The Senses of Scripture* (Leiden, 2000), 1–6; as a recent, authoritative work, I follow Krey and Smith's version of the author's name.

6 A. J. Minnis, *Medieval Theory of Authorship: Scholastic Literary Attitudes in the Later Middle Ages*, 2nd ed. (Philadelphia, 1988), 86.

7 B. M. Kaczynski, 'Illustrations of Tabernacle and Temple Implements in the *Postilla in Testmentum Vetus* of Nicolaus de Lyra', *Yale University Library Gazette* 48 (1973), 3.

8 M. T. Gibson, *The Bible in the Latin West* (Notre Dame and London, 1993), 10.

9 Early printers also left spaces blank for biblical images which were never filled in (J. Strachan, *Early Bible Illustrations: A Short Study based on some Fifteenth and Early Sixteenth Century Printed Texts*, Cambridge, 1957, 17, and L. A. Armstrong, 'The Hand Illumination of Venetian Bibles in the Incunable Period', in *Incunabla and their Readers: Printing, Selling and Using books in the Fifteenth Century*, ed. K. Jensen, London, 2003, 107, 113).

10 For the Wycliffite translators see Anne Hudson, *The Premature Reformation: Wycliffite Texts and Lollard History* (Oxford, 1988), 236, 243 n. 83, 246, 271, 396. In Bodl. Lib. MS Bodley 554, a commentary probably by John Purvey (d. *c.* 1428) the scribe actually names the author of the glosses in red, e.g. fols 4, 16v, 'lire here'. For Luther see Peter Bloch, 'Nachwirkungen des Alten Bundes in der christlichen Kunst', *Monumenta Judaica*, 3rd ed. (Cologne, 1964), 756.

11 C. H. Krinsky, 'Representations of the Temple of Jerusalem before 1500', *JWCI* 33 (1970), 3–4.

12 B. Smalley, *The Study of the Bible in the Middle Ages* (Oxford, 1952; repr. Notre Dame, IN, 1970), 355. See also Hailprin, *Rashi and the Christian Scholars*, 142.

13 Hailprin, *Rashi and the Christian Scholars*, 144.

14 C.-O. Nordström, 'Some Miniatures in Hebrew Bibles', *Synthronon: Art et Archéologie de la fin de l'Antiquité et du Moyen Age* (Paris, 1968), 89–105 (89).

15 Nordström, 'Miniatures in Hebrew Bibles', 94.

16 Kaczynski, 'Illustrations of the Tabernacle', 4. It is possible that Kaczynski was too eager to demonstrate that Lyra's illustrations were 'independently contrived by him' (5).

17 C. Roth, 'Jewish Antecedents of Christian Art', *JWCI* 16 (1953), 44.

18 H. Rosenau, 'The Architecture of Nicolaus de Lyra's Temple Illustrations and the Jewish Tradition', *Journal of Jewish Studies* 15 (1974), 300, 303, 304.

19 Roth, 'Jewish Antecedents', 25.

20 For reproductions of Hebrew manuscripts with Temple illustrations, see Roth, 'Jewish Antecedents of Christian Art', pls. 6, 7, 9a (but Roth does not see in Lyra's *Postilla* 'any immediate affinities with the Jewish tradition' in his drawing of, specifically, the Sanctuary or any 'analogies in manuscripts of the Hebrew commentaries which he [Lyra] so prolifically used', 38 and n. 4); Nortström, 'Miniatures in Hebrew Bibles', figs 1–22; T. Metzger, 'Les objets du culte, le sanctuaire du désert et le temple de Jérusalem, dans les bibles hébraiques médiévales enluminées, en orient et en espagne', *Bulletin of the John Rylands Library* 52 (1970), 397–436, esp. pls II, III, IV; and Sotheby's, *Important Hebrew Manuscripts from the Montefiore Endowment*, 27 and 28 October 2004, lot 120 and col. pl. of a plan of the Temple with implements (this manuscript is fifteenth century).

21 Hailperin (*Rashi and the Christian Scholars*, 138) mentions the first estimate; Krey and Smith (*Nicholas of Lyra*, 16) refer to the 800 number of surviving manuscripts; and Kaczynski suggests the number of over 1,200 ('Illustrations of Tabernacle and Temple', 1–2). No source or method of counting is given by any of these three authors.

22 My count of eighteen *Postilla* manuscripts does not include manuscripts with extracts.

23 A. I. Doyle has, however, stated that 'only a few sets of the Lyra survive in manuscripts from England in the fourteenth and fifteenth centuries ...' ('Stephen Dodesham of Witham and Sheen', in *Of the Making of Books: Medieval Manuscripts, Their Scribes and Readers: Essays Presented to M. B. Parkes*, ed. P. R. Robinson and R. Zim (Aldershot, 1997), 101 n. 27).

24 Notably the two scripts differ in the **g**, final **s**, and medial **r**.

25 The Index is written in two columns of sixty-two lines and decorated with one-line red and blue letters (without flourishing) at each indexed item and four- or five-line blue or red and blue parted letters with red flourishing at the head of each new alphabet letter.

26 These hands differ in their renderings of **d**, **g**, **s**, and **r**, and the scribe of the model book shows more broken letter strokes than is characteristic of 'T.B'. Folios 60 and 65 are signed by 'T.B'.

27 Manuscripts with the scribal signature 'T.B' – but not to my eyes by the Laud Misc. 'T.B.' – are BL Additional MS 31970, Lansdowne MS 416, Cotton MS Claudius A.x.ii, fols 84–199v, and Harley MS 27. Manuscripts with scribal names beginning with monogram 'T.B.' are Bodl. Lib. MS Douce 147, probably written by Thomas Beaulieu, *c.* 1400; CUL Additional MS 7912, written by Thomas Banyard; BL Royal MS 8.F.vi, fols 31–44, written by Thomas Brewse; Arundel MS 327, written by Thomas Burgh, Cambridge, 1447; and Additional MS 10099, fols 205–212v, Thomas Burton or Buxton, XV^{3}. None of these appear to me to be the hand of 'T.B.' in MS Laud Misc. 156, nor are they signed 'frater'. I also checked all of the copies of William Norton's Index to Lyra's *Postilla litteralis* and found no evidence of 'T.B.''s hand. Malcolm Parkes stated to me that he had not seen 'T.B.''s hand before and that he had searched the *BRUO* and *BRUC* and supplements for names beginning with 'T.B.'; there were several from Exeter diocese but with no indication that they had returned to Exeter after attending the universities. I am grateful to Malcolm Parkes for his kind and extensive help in tracing this scribe.

28 CUL MS Dd.2.6, fol. 1.

29 Sharpe, *Handlist*, 795. In addition to MS Laud Misc. 156, the other manuscripts with copies of William Norton's *Tabula super doctorem de Lyra* are CUL MS Ff.4.38, book of Indexes; Eton College MS 108, composite miscellany (reproduced in K.L. Scott, *Dated and Datable English Manuscript Borders c. 1395–1499*, The Bibliographical Society (London, 2002), 32–33, pl. IV); Bodl. Lib. MS Bodley 42, composite miscellany; Oxford, Exeter College MS 15, composite miscellany; Lincoln College MS lat. 69, book of Indexes; and Merton College MS 12, miscellany.

30 One of the medieval references to a *Postilla* does, however, mention both texts or, at least, Lyra

and a 'tabula'; see Appendix B, Pt. II, B, 3.

31 Two of these, the Trees of Virtues and Vices, are reproduced in *Bodl. Index*, II: fig. 15 (fols 62v–63).

32 This group of diagrams was mentioned, but not by this name, by F. Saxl, 'A Spiritual Encyclopaedia of the Latin Middle Ages', *JWCI* 5 (1942), 110 n. 5; for much more extensive discussion, see Sandler, *De Lisle Psalter*, and for Laud Misc. 156, 110–11: no. 16.

33 This text is examined more completely in Chapter 4; the *Speculum* also occurs in BL Royal MS 1.B.x, the subject of that chapter.

34 The hand shows a characteristic **d** and **g** in both texts.

35 The parchment used for the Lyra miniatures and for the Index is similar and may have come from the same source.

36 J. Backhouse, 'An Illuminator's Sketchbook', *The British Library Journal* 1 (1975), 3–14; Scott, *Later Gothic Manuscripts*, no. 90, with further literature.

37 For example, BL Harley MS 641, fol. 118; Oxford, Queens College MS 304, fol. 1; New York, The Morgan Library M.126, fol. 54v; San Marino, CA, Huntington Library HM 268, fol. 79v.

38 Folio 11 is reproduced in *Bodl. Index*, II: fig. 14.

39 Genesis 6:14–16.

40 Also called the 'Mercy Seat'; Exodus 25: 21.

41 Exodus 25: 23–30.

42 The last two examples are reproduced in Scott, *Later Gothic Manuscripts*, I: ills 33 and 369. A diagrammatic Ark is illustrated above in chapter I, fig. 2; below in chapter IV, ill. 74 (BL Harley Rolls C.9); and in P. J. Lucas, 'John Capgrave, O.S.A. (1393–1464), Scribe and "Publisher"', *Transactions of the Cambridge Bibliographical Society* 5 (1969), pl. VII (Oxford, Oriel College MS 32, fol. 37).

43 Exodus 25: 31–40.

44 Exodus 26: 1–13.

45 Exodus 26: 15–29.

46 Exodus 27: 1–8.

47 Exodus 30: 18.

48 Exodus 28: 2–39. Apart from the robe of blue and the blue mitre, the colours of Aaron's costume in the miniature are, however, not biblical.

49 Exodus 28: 8, 27, 28.

50 Exodus 31: 18.

51 Numbers 3: 23–38; verse 6 reads: 'Bring the tribe of Levi near, and present them before Aaron the priest that they may minister unto him.'

52 1 Kings 6.

53 1 Kings 6: 31.

54 1 Kings 6: 36.

55 1 Kings 7: 2–12.

56 1 Kings 7: 16–22.

57 1 Kings 27–37.

58 2 Kings 20: 11; Isaiah 38: 8.

59 Ezekiel 1: 5–12.

60 Ezekiel 1: 15–21.

61 Folio 11 is reproduced in *Bodl. Index*, II: fig. 14. E. W. Goldman mentions the ground plans and illustrations in the commentaries of Lyra but seems to refer to only three manuscripts

('Maimonides' Illustration of the Temple in Jerusalem as a Model for later Copies', in *Manuscripts in Transition: Recycling Manuscripts, Texts and Images*, ed. B. Dekeyzer and J. Van der Stock, Paris, Leuven, Dudley, MA, 2005, 93 and n. 3).

62 For a discussion of these aspects of the Temple in Lyra's *Postilla*, see Rosenau, 'The Architecture of Nicolaus de Lyra's Temple Illustrations, 296–97. Her study is however based on only three manuscripts and the early illustrated printed edition by Anton Koberger (Nuernberg, 1481).

63 Ezekiel 43: 15–18.

64 Ezekiel 45.

65 I owe this suggestion to Malcolm Parkes.

66 This count does not include extracts or fragments; see Appendix B. I have not tried to match fragments with existing volumes or volumes separated from sets with each other.

67 These copies are e.g. Australia, New South Wales, University of Sydney, Fisher Library, MS Nicholson 1, New Testament only, ?XV^2; Durham, Cathedral Library, MS A.I.3, dated 1386, written by William du Stiphel of Durham Priory, Le Borwby, together with another scribe of Durham Priory, with one historiated initial, and MS. A.I.5, XV^1, written by John Wykingeston (J. B. Friedman, *Northern English Books, Owners, and Makers in the Late Middle Ages*, Syracuse, 1995, 241; L. Dennison, 'Monastic or Secular? The Artist of the Ramsey Psalter, now at Holkham Hall, Norfolk', in *Monasteries and Society: Proceedings of the Harlaxton Symposium of 1994*, ed. B. Thompson (1999), 257; and Oxford, Balliol College, MSS 166B and 171, *Postilla litteralis*: Genesis–Ecclesiatices, donated to Balliol before 1438, with blanks for miniatures (and possibly a lost third volume).

68 See Appendix B. Some copies have an outright statement that a miniature is lacking, 'hic deficit figura' (Cambridge, Peterhouse MS 85, fols 163, 164, 165; and Peterhouse MS 19, fol. 162), and some copies show little sense of the amount of space necessary for an image (e.g. BL Royal MS 4.A.xv, fol. 97v, written by Richard of London; and Oxford, Balliol College MS 166B) and yet at the same time mark spaces for a 'figura' (Balliol MS 166B). Others show precisely shaped spaces left by the scribe as if he were working from an illustrated examplar (Worcester, Cathedral Library MS F.26, e.g. fol. 179v); and still others may indicate the pictorial subject to be placed in the space (e.g. Cambridge, Pembroke College MS 11, 'Figura maris enei' (not foliated) or Pembroke MS 19, fols 162, 162v, 163), may even indicate where the picture is to be found (CUL MS Dd.2.6, fol. 161/281, 'figura in pagina sequenti'), or they may make certain that two versions of the image would be placed in the space (Cambridge, Peterhouse MS 85, fol. 45, blank space marked 'prima figura' and 'Secunda figura').

69 For more discussion of the New College set, see Krey and Smith, *Nicholas of Lyra*, 9–10. See also Oxford, Merton College, MS 163, *Postilla*, Genesis–Psalter (Krey and Smith, *Nicholas of Lyra*, 9).

70 Durham Cathedral Library, MSS A.I.3–5.

71 CUL MS Dd.2.6, London, Lambeth Palace MS 9, and Oxford, Oriel College MS 40.

72 Attribution by Doyle, 'Stephen Dodesham', 99–101.

73 P. R. Robinson, *Catalogue of Dated and Datable Manuscripts c. 737–1600 in Cambridge Libraries*, 2 vols (Cambridge, 1988), I: no. 9, II: pl. 265; Doyle, 'Book Production by the Monastic Orders in England (*c.* 1375–1530): Assessing the Evidence', in *Medieval Book Production: Assessing the Evidence*, ed. L. L. Brownrigg (Los Altos Hills, CA, 1990), 5. Only the first and third volumes of MSS Dd.7. 7–10 have miniatures; the fourth has several small historiated initials.

74 For Henry Mere, see C. E. Woodruff, 'Notes on the Inner Life and Domestic Economy of the Priory of Christ Church Canterbury in the Fifteenth Century', *Archaeologia Cantiana* 53 (1941), 14; M. B. Parkes, 'A Fifteenth-Century Scribe: Henry Mere', *Bodleian Library Record* 6 (1957–61), 654–59; Pächt and Alexander, 3, nos 987, 1067; Bodl. Lib., *Duke Humfrey's Library & the Divinity School 1488–1988* (Oxford, 1988), 99, nos 78, 101; N. R. Ker and

A. J. Piper, *Medieval Manuscripts in British Libraries*, IV: Paisley–York (Oxford, 1992), 706 (York Minster Library MS XVI.G.23).

For John Blacman, see M. R. James, *Henry the Sixth: A Reprint of John Blacman's Memoir* (Cambridge, 1919); E. M. Thompson, *The Carthusian Order in England* (London, 1930), 316–21; Ker, *MMGB*, 204–5; A. Gray, 'A Carthusian *Carta visitationis* of the Fifteenth Century', *Bulletin of the Institute of Historical Research* 40 (1967), 191–101; Pächt and Alexander, 3, nos 994, 1067; Ker, *MMBL*, II, 783–84 (Eton MS 213); R. W. Lovatt, 'John Blacman: Biographer of Henry VI', in *The Writing of History in the Middle Ages: Essays Presented to Richard William Southern*, ed. R. H. C. Davis and J. M. Wallace-Hadrill (Oxford, 1981), 415–44 (417–29); Lovatt, 'A Collector of Apocryphal Anecdotes: John Blacman Revisited', in *Property and Politics: Essays in Later Medieval English History*, ed. A.J. Pollard (Gloucester and New York, 1984), 172–97; Lovatt, 'The Library of John Blacman and Contemporary Carthusian Spirituality', *Journal of Ecclesiastical History* 43 (1992), 195–230; and A. S. G. Edwards, 'Geography and Illustration and Higden's *Polychronicon*', in *Art Into Life: Collected Papers from the Kresge Art Museum Medieval Symposia*, ed. C. G. Fisher and K. L. Scott (East Lansing, 1995), 102–3.

75 *A Catalogue of the Manuscripts Preserved in the Library of the University of Cambridge* I (London and Cambridge, 1856), 327–8; Strachan, *Early Bible Illustrations*, 17–19; Robinson, *Dated and Datable Manuscripts in Cambridge Libraries*, I; no. 9, II: pl. 265 (MS Dd.7.7, fol. 191); Doyle, 'Stephen Dodesham of Witham and Sheen', 99–101.

76 Three versions of the Brazen Sea occur on fol. 244.

77 H. O. Coxe, *Laudian Manuscripts*, Quarto Catalogues II (Oxford, repr. 1973), columns 144–45; Pächt and Alexander, 3, no. 1067, pl. XCIX; *Bodl. Index*, II: nos 645, 646.

78 This page is also reproduced in *Bodl. Index*, II, fig. 13.

79 Also reproduced in *Bodl. Index*, II, fig. 13.

80 The manuscript is of parchment with 272 folios (505 × 360 mm); the text is written in two columns of sixty-nine lines and finished with red and blue paraphs, catchwords in a red box, and four-line blue and gold letters with red and lavender flourishing. The copy was acquired by Yale University around 1983. For previous comment on the manuscript, see Sotheby, Wilkinson & Hodge, *Catalogue of Very Important Illuminated and other Manuscripts: The Property of Lord Mostyn*, 13 July 1920, no. 79: 19–20; Christie, Manson and Woods Ltd., *The Mostyn Hall Library: Printed Books and Manuscripts*, Part III: P to Z (24 October 1974), no. 1482; Laurence Witten Rare Books, *A Mirror of Manuscripts: Speculum Manuscriptorum* (Southport, Conn., *c.* 1983), no. 20; B. A. Shailor, 'A New Manuscript of Nicolaus de Lyra', *Yale University Library Gazette* 58 (1983), 8–16.

81 The book opens with a full trellis border and large initial on fol. 1 and has full bar borders on fols 14, 22, 31, 39v (partly reproduced by Shailor, 'A New Manuscript', fig. 3a), 51v, 62v, 71v, at standard divisions in the Psalter, as well as on fols 97 (partly reproduced by Shailor, 'A New Manuscript', fig. 3b), 143v, and 174, and partial borders on fols 243, 245v, 249v, 250v, 251v, 254v, 256, 257v, 259, 260v, 267, and 268v. Illustrations in the original two parts of MS Beinecke 640 are as follows: fol. 175v, col. A, leafy sprig (endpiece to column), col. B: full tree with leaves and stylised flowers; fol. 176, col. A: Vision of Ezechiel, with leafy shrubs on a mound in panels above and below (partly reproduced by Shailor, 'A new Manuscript', frontispiece); fol. 179v, col. A: diagram of the Temple with Sanctum Sanctorum; margin, cross-sections of walls; fol. 196, cols A and B: diagram of the Temple; fol. 196v, col. A: facade of tower; col. B: full leafy tree on mound; fol. 198v, col. A: panel with rose and leafy vines; col. B: half of a plan of the Temple area, with branches bearing daisy buds above and below; fol. 199, col. A: diagram of three areas of the Temple, with leaf and vine panels above and below; fol. 199v, col. B: diagram of the Temple; fol. 200, col. B: second half of a plan of the Temple; fol. 204, col. A: Altar of the Holocaust; fol. 205, col. B: plan of the city of Jerusalem, with portals; fol. 205v, col. A: plan of the Temple and environs; fol. 206, col. B: two panels, each with a leafy

tree; fol. 207v, col. B: plan; fol. 230, col. B: genealogical descent of 'Alexander magnus'.

82 It would be worthwhile if someone (else) were to undertake a study of the illustrated Continental copies of Nicholas of Lyra's *Postilla super totam bibliam* with a view to locating the source of the cycle in Bodl. Lib. MS Laud Misc. 156.

83 Shailor, 'A New Manuscript', 12.

84 Pächt and Alexander, 3, no. 902: pl. LXXXVI (Ark of the Covenant and Cherubim) and literature; in addition, see Lucas, 'John Capgrave, O.S.A.' 4, 29, 31 n.1, etc. as MS [9]; Lucas, 'A Bequest to the Austin Friars in the Will of John Spycer 1439–40', *Norfolk Archaeology* 43 (1993), 482–89.

85 Lucas, 'A Bequest to the Austin Friars', 484.

86 Lucas, 'A Bequest to the Austin Friars', 485.

87 Lucas, 'A Bequest to the Austin Friars', 485.

88 Fol. 114, two scenes of the Ark with propiciatory and cherubim; fol. 118v, two tables with Shewbread (in same miniature space); fol. 122, one Candelabrum; fol. 125, boards of the Ark; fol. 126, boards of the Ark; fol. 127v, joined boards; fol. 130, boards with carrying staves; fol. 133v, Altar of the Holocaust; and fol. 186v, (damaged) ?plan of the Temple.

89 The painting in gold is true of the Ark with propitiatory and Cherubim in CUL MS Dd.7.7, fol. 78v, but the iconography is not similar. The CUL scenes of the Altar of the Holocaust are also in gold.

90 For discussion, see Sandler, *De Lisle Psalter*, 62 (pl. 14, fig. 48), Appendix: nos 5, 7, 8, 9, 11, 15, 16, 17, 18, 20, 21, 23, 25, 26, 28, 29, 32, and Addendum: nos 1, 2, 4, and two unnumbered MSS.

91 His monogram also occurs within the *Speculum theologie* on fol. 65.

92 A further inscription in the manuscript concerning provenance is 'Liber Guilielmi Laud Archiepi Cant. Et Cancellarij Vniversitatis Oxon/1635' (fol. 5). Folio ii has the note upside-down, 'Rate the Raty'. Folio 16 bears a red cross form in the upper margin at the head of the Index.

93 Ker (*MMBL*, 86) includes both the modelbook and the Index to the *Postilla litteralis* in this ownership. Another hospital is known to have owned a Lyra commentary: the Hospital of St Alphage, Cripplegate within, has a surviving list of books from its library, including 'Lira super Novum Testament' (J. P. Malcolm, *Londinium Rediviuum: or, An Ancient History and Modern Description of London*, London, 1802, 29). I am indebted to Pamela Robinson for this reference.

94 Ralph Hanna first suggested to me that this might be a monastic shelfmark.

95 Ker, *MMBL*, 86. The inscription in the upper margin of Harley MS 3671 reads 'liber hospitalis sci johis Exon', with 'F.2' in large capitals in the lower margin. The inscription in Additional MS 38129, fol. 1, is very damaged, only the word 'liber' being legible without special means, and the pressmark 'F.7' is barely visible at the bottom of the page.

96 N. Orme and M. Webster, *The English Hospital 1070–1570* (New Haven and London, 1995), 65. It was apparently not unusual for a medieval hospital to possess a considerable library; see P. R. Robinson, *Catalogue of Dated and Datable Manuscripts c. 888–1600 in London Libraries*, 2 vols (London, 2003), I: Text, 5: Elsyng's Spital, Cripplegate, in an inventory of 1448, listed sixty-three books 'in libraria' and forty-three service books in the sacristy.

97 Orme and Webster, *The English Hospital*, 179.

98 N. Orme, *Education in the West of England 1066–1548* (Exeter, 1976), 15, 48–49; Orme and Webster, *The English Hospital*, 235–6.

99 Durham, Cathedral Library MSS A.I.3–5.

100 BL Royal MS 4.A.xv.

101 CUL MSS Dd.7.7–10.

102 Bodl. Lib., MSS Laud Misc. 152, 154.

103 Cambridge, Pembroke College MS 11.

104 Hereford, Cathedral Library MS P.IV.2 and Worcester, Cathedral Library MSS F.25–27.

105 Durham, Cathedral Library MS A.I.5, bears the inscription of his gift.

106 Oxford, Balliol College MSS 162, 172.

107 He owned a late fourteenth-century French copy of Part I, i.e. Bodl. Lib. MS Bodley 251 (2332), *Postilla litteralis* (Genesis to Ecclesiasticus).

108 K. V. Sinclair, *Descriptive Catalogue of Medieval and Renaissance Western Manuscripts in Australia* (Sydney, 1969), 171–74; M. M. Manion and V. F. Vines, *Medieval and Renaissance Illuminated Manuscripts in Australian Collections* (Melbourne, London, New York, 1984), no. 52, fig. 110.

109 'Miscellaneity and Vernacularity: Conditions of Literary Production in Late Medieval England', in *The Whole Book: Cultural Perspectives on the Medieval Miscellany*, ed. S. G. Nichols and S. Wenzel (Ann Arbor, 1996), 47.

110 Examples of these scenes are in Arundel Castle, Duke of Norfolk, s.n., John Lydgate, *Lives of Saints Edmund and Fremund*, fol. 48v; and BL Harley MS 1766, John Lydgate, *Fall of Princes*, fol. 141v. This point was made with respect to text decoration by L. L. Brownrigg, 'Ornament: Purpose and Play in Medieval Manuscripts', *Fine Print* 8 (1982), 64–67, 70–71, 73, with earlier literature.

111 J. J. G. Alexander, 'Art History, Literary History, and the Study of Medieval Illuminated Manuscripts', *Studies in Iconography* 18 (1997), 56. See also M. Hilmo, *Medieval Images, Icons, and Illustrated English Literary Texts from the Ruthwell Cross to the Ellesmere Chaucer* (Aldershot, 2004), xv, 'Images also serve to reshape a text and change its thrust by enhancing it, adding to it, and recasting it to suit an intended audience or the predilections of the designers'.

112 Alexander, 'Art History, Literary History', 57; P. M. Jones, 'Staying with the Programme: Illustrated Manuscripts of John of Arderne, *c.* 1380–*c.* 1550', *EMS* 10 (2002), 204.

113 In one case, at least, the medieval author may have 'copied a difficult piece such as a diagram, even when the main body of the text was copied by a proficient scribe'; see Lucas, 'John Capgrave, O.S.A.', 27.

114 See the instances in Bodl. Lib. MS Rolls 6, membr. 3, MS Bodley 302, fol. 59; and Oxford, St John's College MS 58, fol. 4v (fig. 18).

115 BL Additional MS 29969, fol. 15, and in his *Apologeticae defensiones Astronomice veritates*, see 'Hec figura docet domos exaltacionis et dignitates planetarum insignies' (same MS, fol. 70).

116 Bodl. Lib. MS Bodley 515, fol. 10.

117 Bodl. Lib. MS Laud Misc. 619, fol. 57.

118 Article 3 of the manuscript, fols 63v, 77v, *Breuiarum regulare musicae*.

119 Jones, 'Staying with the Programme', 205, 207–8, 211. The phrase commonly used by Arderne to indicate an illustration is 'sicut hic depingitur' (207). Jones has already recognized that illustration in the Arderne texts has 'a functional use in supplying information that the text cannot' (212) and that illustration serves 'an explanatory purpose that words cannot supply as effectively' (213).

120 From BL Egerton MS 1982, Mandeville's Travels.

121 Peter Murray Jones is an exception to this generalization; see note 115 above.

122 In MS Laud Misc. 156 these statements are on fols 7v, 8 (three times), 9v, and 12v.

123 For example, 'in situatum ymaginare' (MS Laud Misc. 156, fol. 12v); or 'defacili ymaginare per figuram frontis depicta in pagina precendenti'(fol. 7v).

Notes

CHAPTER II

124 Using an anglicana formata; so described by C. R. Sneddon (in *A Critical Edition of the Four Gospels in the Thirteenth-Century Old French Translation of the Bible*, 2 vols, D.Phil. Thesis, Oxford, 1979, I: no. 164, 434). Sneddon differentiates the two scribal hands as: Hand 1, 'probably as English scribe but imitating a French cursive script of s. XVin' = in quire 1; and Hand 2, signed by Doal (at fol. 204v) in quires 2–28; both scribes used the same exemplar (Sneddon, thesis, I: 436). Sneddon's thesis (I: 435) contains a collation of the manuscript with a notation of the contents missing from each book of the Bible; and he explains the abnormal order of the Gospels (Mark, Matthew, Luke and John) as a confusion between the two scribes (I: 436). He further states that certain characteristics of BL Royal MS 19.D.iii, 1411–12, 'suggest a connection with the source of All Souls 10' (I: no. 166, 437). For a more recent catalogue description, see A. G. Watson (*A Descriptive Catalogue of the Medieval Manuscripts of All Souls College Oxford*, Oxford, 1997, no. 10, 22–23), who describes the scribal hands as 'several' and as a 'careful continental hybrida'.

125 S. Berger, *La Bible française au moyen âge: Étude sur les plus anciennes versions de la Bible écrites en prose de langue d'oïl* (Paris, 1884); C. R. Sneddon, 'The "Bible du XIIIe siècle": its Medieval Public in the Light of its Manuscript Tradition', *The Bible and Medieval Culture*, ed. W. Lourdaux and D. Verhelst (Leuven, 1979), 130–31; Sneddon, 'A Neglected Medieval Bible Translation', *Romance Languages Annual* 5 (1993), 111, 113, 114. Sneddon describes the motivation for the joining of the two texts as for 'historical information' and 'the strong desire for a complete version of the Bible which had sufficient but not excessive commentary' ('A Neglected Bible Translation', 114). The *Bible historiale complétée* was probably compiled by 1314 (Sneddon, thesis, I: 20). See also P.-M. Bogaert, *Les bibles en français: Histoire illustrée du moyen âge à nos jours* (Brepols, 1991), 25–26.

126 *La bible française*, 187–99, 210–20; see also Sneddon, 'A Neglected Bible Translation', 113, 114; and Bogaert, *Les bibles en français*, 30–33.

127 Sneddon, 'A Neglected Bible Translation', 113; and Sneddon, thesis, I: 1. A fifteenth-century Old Testament (Genesis–Job) in French survives in CUL MS Ee.3.52; it was, however, made in France, not in England. It was given in 1442 to the Augustinian nuns of the priory of Flixton, Suffolk, by Thomas Croftys: (inscription on front endleaf) 'qui ... donavit Testamentam in duobus voluminibus Gallici ydyomatic ad singulare solacium priorisse sororumque suarum presencium et futurarum'. See M. Oliva, *The Convent and the Community in Late Medieval England: Female Monasteries in the Diocese of Norwich, 1350–1540* (Woodbridge, 1998), 66.

128 At fols 1v, 20v, 47 (2x), 48, 80v, 103v (4x), 114, 130 (2x), 131, 133v (2x), 140v (2x), 147, 155 (2x), 184, 186v, 188v and 192v.

129 At fols 2, 2v, 114v, 130v, 134, 140v, 145v, 148, 156, 184, 186v, 188v, 191v and 193.

130 A. Hudson, *The Premature Reformation: Wycliffite Texts and Lollard History* (Oxford, 1988), 231, notes the survival of Wycliffite translations of the Bible as 'over two hundred and fifty manuscripts'. C. de Hamel, *The Book: A History of the Bible* (London and New York, 2001), 168, repeats this number and states that it is 'far more than any other text in the Middle English language'. Another prominent scholar has deemed the Lollard Bible 'a huge success' and 'a movement toward ... a central English literary tradition' (R. Hanna, 'English Biblical Texts before Lollardy and their Fate', in *Lollards and their Influence in late Medieval England*, ed. F. Somerset, J. C. Havens, and D. G. Pitard, Woodbridge, 2003, 151, 153). But Bibles in French were not unknown in England, it should be noted. There is a record of two chained in the church of St James Garlickhithe, London, in 1449; see C. Burgess and A. Wathey, 'Mapping the Soundscape: Church Music in English towns, 1450–1550', *Early Music History* 19 (Cambridge, 2000), 46, nos 32 and 33. I am grateful to P.R. Robinson for this reference. H. S. Bennett, *The Pastons and their England* (Cambridge, 1932), 11, records a Bible among the

Pastons' French books; Sneddon ('The "Bible du XIIIe siècle"', 132 n. 18) quotes an inscription in BnF MS fr. 156, fol. 3v, which states that John Cheyne left his son John 'this Bible in French in .ii. volumes'; and Oliva notices that Flixton Priory was given a French copy of the Old Testament in 1442 (*Convent and Community*, 66). These Bibles may of course have been made before the fifteenth century.

131 Sneddon, thesis, I: 434.

132 Sneddon, private communication, 5 September 2003.

133 Warner and Gilson, II: 330; Watson, *Dated and Datable MSS British Library*, II: 402 (right column).

134 Parkes further notes that other letter shapes also appear in both manuscripts: tall ascenders in relation to the minim height; **f** and long **s** with long, tapering descenders with a slope that is only slightly out of the vertical, the secretary **s** slightly taller than minim height, which often tilts backward, and the variant of **v**.

135 The differences that I note are two types of **a** (two-compartment in the Royal manuscript and single in All Souls 10); different types of letter **v**: looped stroke over the top in Royal and a upward beginning stroke in All Souls; a distinct foot on the letter **l** in All Souls; and a less rounded **S** with distinct finishing strokes in All Souls. Doal's script in All Souls MS 10 shows a crisper presence on the page than that of the scribe of Royal MS 19.B.xvi, fols 33–164v. Letters that are similar to each other in the two manuscripts are **g**, **d**, and the long-tailed forms of **s** and **r**, as well as the rendering of **est**.

136 *La bible française*, 218–19, 412–13, with earlier literature.

137 Berger, *La bible française*, 219, 326. A brief description is available in Berger, *La bible française*, 356–57. Sneddon, on the other hand, saw BnF MSS fr. 15393, *Bible historiale*, as closer to the text in All Souls MS 10.

138 Scott, *Later Gothic Manuscripts*, no. 26, and for literature.

139 I have not yet been able to examine this manuscript, apart from the use of reproductions. In two of the Wolfenbüttel miniatures (fols 367v, 396) Paul is shown with an upturned sword, unlike his representations in All Souls 10. Mention of the manuscript is in C. Lindberg, 'The Manuscripts and Versions of the Wycliffite Bible', *Studia Neophilologica* 42 (1970), 333–47, no. 153: 336, early version; A. Hudson, *Lollards and Their Books* (London, 1985), 7 n. 34; Hudson, *The Premature Revolution*, 233 n. 33; and de Hamel, *The Book*, 173–74 and col. pl.

140 Lindberg, 'Manuscripts and Versions, no. 106: 335, early and later versions mixed; and Scott, *Later Gothic Manuscripts*, I: 70 n. 12, II: 105. Another series of Creation scenes can be found in the non-biblical text in Trinity College, Cambridge, MS R.4.12, *Scala mundi*, fol. 1v.

141 Warner and Gilson, I: 15.

142 M. Munsterbery, 'A Norman Manuscript of the Old Testament', *More Books* 14 (1939), 21. See also C.U. Faye and W.H. Bond, *Supplement to the Census of Medieval and Renaissance Manuscripts in the United States and Canada* (New York, 1962), no. 76: 207.

143 The subjects of historiated initials are: fol. 13v, (Genesis: Creation) half-figure of God the Father, gesturing; fol. 44v, (Exodus) half-figure of Pharoah; fol. 48, ('le premier liure de moysen') bust of ?Pharoah as king; fol. 52, ('le second liure de moysen') head of Moses with horns; fol. 64, ('le tiers liure de moysen') half-figures of four men (=?Hebrews); fol. 70v, ('le quart liure de moysen') bust of Moses with horns; fol. 73v, ('le quinte liure de moysen') bust of King Balak; fol. 81v, (Joshua) bust of Joshua, in hat; fol. 92, (Judges) bust of Phinehas, son of Eleazar, as young man; fol. 114v, (Ruth) bust of ?Ely; fol. 119, (I Kings) head of a lion; fol. 139v, (I Kings) bust of a king; fol. 234, (II Kings) bust of a king; fol. 251, (III Kings) bust of King Solomon; fol. 263, (III Kings) bust of a king; fol. 334, (Jonah) bust of man in hat; fol. 337, (Jeremiah), bust of King Josiah. The text of the manuscript does not follow the Bible closely. For information concerning the history of the text, see Munsterberg, 'A Norman Manuscript', 22 (but lacks precise references). MS 1482 bears the bookplate of Lord Aldenham (Henry Hucks Gibbs,

d. 1907), for whom see S. de Ricci, *English Collectors of Books & Manuscripts (1530–1930) and their Marks of Ownership* (New York, 1930), 166 and n. 3. The manuscript was acquired for the Boston Public Library in 1938 from E.P. Goldschmidt.

144 Scott, *Later Gothic Manuscripts*, I: ills 220–24, II: no. 55; M. T. Orr, 'The Hours of Elizabeth the Queen: Evidence for Collaboration between English Illuminators and an Artist from the Gold Scrolls Group', *Flanders in European Perspective: Manuscript Illumination around 1400 in Flanders and Abroad* (Leuven, 1995), 619–33.

145 Other writers working on a board are, for example, in San Marino, Huntington Library HM 268, fol. 79v; Philadelphia, Rosenbach Foundation 439/16, fol. 74; Oxford, Queen's College MS 304, fols 1 (fig. 26), 151v; BL Harley MS 2278, fol. 74; Royal MS 1.B.x, fol. 27; and New York, The Morgan Library M. 893, fol. 97.

146 Reproduced in Pächt and Alexander, 3, no. 841: pl. XCV.

147 A full list is in my article concerning scribal portraits edited by M. Gullick, *Pen in Hand: Medieval Scribal Portraits, Colophons and Tools* (Walkern, Herts, 2006), 145–49.

148 *The Mirroure of the Worlde: MS Bodley 283 (England c. 1470–1480) The Physical Composition Decoration and Illustration*, intro. by K. L. Scott, Roxburghe Club (Oxford, 1980), Chapter VIII.

149 See A.G. Watson, *The Library of Sir Simonds D'Ewes* (London, 1966), 113; Watson, *Dated and Datable Manuscripts Oxford*, I: no. 581, II: pl. 254a, b; and Sharpe, *Handlist*, no. 804: 283.

150 Reproduced in Warner and Gilson, IV: pl. 15.

151 See fols 98v (reading), 100v (writing), 103v (reading), 105 (possibly reading), 107 (reading), 108 (reading or writing), 113v (reading), and 135 (reading).

152 Reproduced in Scott, *Later Gothic Manuscripts*, I: ill. 199.

153 Hanna, *St John's Catalogue*, 21–23. A similar scene, with a bishop and a kneeling cleric holding an open book together is in Bodl. Lib. MS Wood empt. 23, Constitutions of Benedict XII, fol. 1.

154 Reproduced in Scott, *Later Gothic Manuscripts*, I: col. pl. 5.

155 Two further miniatures are of the same genre but less straightforward: in Bodl. Lib. MS Laud Misc. 165, fol. 5, William of Nottingham may be reading aloud at the same time as he receives both a book from a kneeling Benedictine and a comment from a second black monk (reproduced in Pächt and Alexander, 3, no. 739, pl. LXXIII); and in the Carmelite Missal, BL Additional MS 29704/5, fol. 100v, two religious, possibly a Dominican and an acolyte, seem to be following, each in his own book, a reading by a bishop (reproduced by Rickert, *Carmelite Missal*, pl. XIb, Saint Ambrose).

156 E.g. Berkeley Castle, Gloucestershire, Trustees of the Earl of Berkeley, Neville Hours, fol. 23v; Cambridge, Trinity College, MS B.11.11, Missal, fol. 187v; and Nottingham, University Library MS 250, Wollaton Antiphonal, fol. 160v; all are reproduced in Scott, *Later Gothic Manuscripts*, respectively, I: ills 97, 245, and 278.

157 E.g. BnF MS fr. 157, fol. 240; MS fr. 15394, fol. 508; MS fr. 20088, fol. 559v. See also *infra*, ill. 41 of MS fr. 10.

158 E.g. Karlsruhe, Badischen Landesbibliothek, MS St Georgen 12, *Santilogium salvatoris*, fol. 86.

159 *Catalogue de manuscrits français*, I: Ancien fonds (Paris, 1868), 1. A Pentecost scene with Saint Peter lying on the floor and reading from an open book, can be found in Sotheby's *A Second Selection of Illuminated Manuscripts from c. 1000 to c. 1522: The Property of Mr. J. R. Ritman*, 19 June 2001, lot 15, Book of Hours, French, use of Paris, *c.* 1420 (colour plate p. 89).

160 See also Bodl. Lib. MS Douce 104, fol. 47 (reproduced in K.L. Scott, 'The Illustrations of *Piers Plowman* in Bodleian Library MS. Douce 104', *Yearbook of Langland Studies* 4 (1990), 50, fig. 20; D. Pearsall and K. L. Scott, *Piers Plowman: A Facsimile of Bodleian Library, Oxford, MS Douce 104*, Cambridge, 1992, fol. 47; and K. Kerby-Fulton and D. L. Despres, *Iconography and the Professional Reader: The Politics of Book Production in the Douce Piers*

Plowman, Minneapolis and London, 1999, fig. 21); MS Rawl. poet. 223, fol. 142; Vatican, Biblioteca Apostolica Vaticana MS Ottob. Lat. 216, fol. 1 (Dominican).

161 Reproduced in Scott, *Later Gothic Manuscripts*, I: ill. 243.

162 Reproduced in Rickert, *Carmelite Missal*, pl. XVIb.

163 Twice Paul is also shown kneeling in a pulpit in this manuscript (fols 482v, 496v). For the transfer of such 'religious iconography to secular contexts', see E. Salter and D. Pearsall, 'Pictorial Illustration of late medieval poetic Texts: The Role of the Frontispiece or Prefatory Picture', in *Medieval Iconography and Narrative: a Symposium* (Odense, 1980), 100–123 (111), with illustrations of various pulpit scenes; and for an earlier discussion by Pearsall, 'The *Troilus* Frontispiece and Chaucer's Audience', *Yearbook of English Studies* 7 (1977), 68–74.

164 See also Karlsruhe, Badische Landesbibliothek, MS St Georgen 12, fol. 115; BL Cotton MS Tiberius A.vii, fol. 68, altar with saints; Harley MS 210, fol. 31; Harley MS 2887, fol. 3v, niche with Paul.

165 See Cambridge, Fitzwilliam Museum, MS 55, Hours and Prayers, fol. 128; BL Additional MS 22720, Perrot Book of Prayers, fols 46v and 67v; Cotton MS Tiberius A.viii, John Lydgate, Pilgrimage of the Life of Man, fol. 68, on altar; Harley MS 2887, Hours, fol. 3v, in niche; MS Lansdowne 451, Pontifical, fol. 219; Oxford, St.John's College, MS 94, Hours, fol. 3, with church; Aberyswyth, National Library of Wales MS 17520, Hours, fol. 2v; and York, Minster Library MS XVI.K.6, Hours, fol. 77.

166 BL Additional MS 29704–5, fol. 160 (reproduced in Rickert, *Carmelite Missal*, pl. XXIIb).

167 Cambridge, St John's College MS G.14, fol. 96v.

168 Reproduced in Pächt and Alexander, 3, no. 1000: pl. XCIII; and see fig. 48.

169 Reproduced in Alexander and Temple, no. 549: pl. XXXII.

170 See S. N. Stewart, *The Enclosed Garden: The Tradition and the Image in Seventeenth-century Poetry* (Madison, 1966); and D. Pearsall and E. Salter, *Landscapes and Seasons of the Medieval World* (Toronto, 1973), chapter 4.

171 The Sherborne Missal is BL Additional MS 74236; the Apocalypse scene is reproduced in J. Backhouse, *The Sherborne Missal* (London, 1999), p. 26 (p. 260 of the Missal). The only other scattered scenes from Revelation in later English manuscripts are a few images of the Beast from the Sea and of the Anti-Christ. The Beast is in Bodl. Lib. MS Bodley 283, *Mirroure of the Worlde*, fols 16, 137 (reproduced in Scott, *Mirroure of the Worlde*, pls X, XXI); MS e Musaeo 23, *Aventure and Grace*, p. 4 (reproduced in Pächt and Alexander, 3: no. 1051, pl. XCVII); and MS e Musaeo 16, fol. 165v (on an ascender). A drawing of the Anti-Christ is in Bodl. Lib. MS Douce 104, *Piers Plowman*, fol. 107 (reproduced in Pearsall and Scott, *Piers Plowman: A Facsimile*); Lincoln, Cathedral Library, MS 218, Richard Rolle, fol. 33; and BL Additional MS 37049, Carthusian Miscellany, fols 16, 16v (as a king; reproduced in Hogg, *Carthusian Miscellany*, 17, 18).

172 See R. K. Emmerson and S. Lewis, 'Census and Bibliography of Medieval Manuscripts Containing Apocalypse Illustrations, ca. 800–1550', *Traditio* 41 (1985), II: 367–409; 42 (1986), III: 337–79.

173 See, for instance, BR MS II.282, fol. 5 (371); Cambridge, Corpus Christi College MS 394, fol. 1 (373); CUL MS Gg.1.1, fol. 407 (377); BL Royal MS 15.D.ii, fol. 104 (388); Royal MS 19.B.xv, fol. 1 (389); Yates Thompson MS 10, fol. 1 (389); Lambeth Palace MS 75, fol. 1 (390) Bodl. Lib. MS Selden supra 38, fol. 37 (402); New College MS D. 65, fol. 1 (403); BnF MS fr. 9574, fol. 2 (406). The numbers in parenthesis refer to page numbers in Emmerson and Lewis, 'Census and Bibliography', II (1985).

174 See, for example, Cambridge, Trinity College MS B.10.2, fols 1–2v (375), R.16.2, fols 1–2, 28–31 (376); Eton, College Library MS 177, pp. 1–7 (387); BL Additional MS 35166, fols 1–2v, 31–38v (385), Additional MS 42555, fols 83, 84v (387); London, Lambeth Palace MS 434, fols

1–2v (391). The numbers in parenthesis refer to a page number in Emmerson and Lewis, 'Census and Bibliography', II (1985).

175 E.g. BL Arundel MS 302, fol. 152, Virgin and Child, within a hedge; BR MS IV.1095, fol. 9v, St Anthony, within a hedge, and fol. 14v, Anne teaching the young Virgin to read; Cologne, Kolumba, Diözesan Museum, Collection of Renate König, Hours of the Duchess of Clarence, fol. 22v, Garden of Gethesmane, with a hedge around the Tree of Life.

176 BL Arundel MS 302, fol. 152.

177 E.g. Oxford, Corpus Christi College MS 161, p. 11. See also Bodl. Lib. MS Bodley 283, fol. 99v, Garden of Virtues, with wall around Christ binding Tree and allegorical Virtues; Tokyo, Collection of T. Takamiya MS 43, *Polychronicon*, fol. 3, Paradise, with wall around tree.

178 See Scott, *Later Gothic Manuscripts*, under catalogue no. 47. The fragment was sold at Sotheby's (*Western Manuscripts and Miniatures*, London, 19 June 1990, lot 53, col. pl. and was subsequently identified by Nicholas Rogers ('The Artist of B.11.7 and his Patrons', in *England in the Fifteenth Century: Proceedings of the 1992 Harlaxton Symposium*, ed. N. Rogers (Stamford, 1994), 180–81) as an Old Testament type of the Betrayal, i.e. Joab's murder of Abner, apparently from a 'grand' book of Hours. Rogers and I do not agree on our attributions to the Master of B.11.7 (his 'Cornwall Master').

179 Discussed by Rogers, 'The Artist of B.11.7', 170–86, pls 24–27, 29–36; Scott, *Later Gothic Manuscripts*, no. 47: ills 194–96, colour pl. 9, with further literature; M.T. Orr, 'Illustration as Preface and Postscript in the Hours of the Virgin of Trinity College MS. B.11.7', *Gesta*, XXXIV (1995), 162–76.

180 See *Boutell's Heraldry*, revised by J.P. Brooke-Little (London and New York, 1973), 186, fig. 353.

181 Rogers, 'The Artist of B.11.7', 174. For further brief discussion of Cornwall with respect to All Souls MS 10, see below pp. 58, 60.

182 M. Meiss, *French Painting in the Time of Jean de Berry: The Boucicaut Master* (New York, 1968), 113–14; Scott, *Later Gothic Manuscripts*, II: under no. 47.

183 E. J. Beer, *Initial und Miniatur: Buchmalerei aus neun Jahrhunderten in Handschriften der Badischen Landesbibliothek*, 2nd ed. (Karlsruhe, 1965), no. 54: 51, pl. 87; A. I. Doyle, 'Book Production by the Monastic Orders in England (*c.* 1375–1530): Assessing the Evidence', *Medieval Book Production: Assessing the Evidence*, ed. L. L. Brownrigg (Los Altos Hills, CA, 1990), 14.

184 Doyle, 'Book Production by Monastic Orders', 14.

185 The borderwork in this manuscript is not by the limner of All Souls 10; nor does the more 'modern' border work in Trinity College, Cambridge, MS B.11.7 appear to be by him.

186 J. H. Wylie, *The Reign of Henry the Fifth*, 2 vols, Vol. I: 1413–1415 (New York, 1968), 220–1; D. Knowles and R. N. Hadcock, *Medieval Religious Houses: England and Wales* (New York, 1971), 202.

187 G. R. Keiser, 'Patronage and Piety in Fifteenth-Century England: Margaret, duchess of Clarence, Symon Wynter and Beinecke 317', *Yale University Library Gazette* 60 (1985), 45.

188 Keiser, 'Patronage and Piety', 37; and see A. M. Hutchison, 'Devotional Reading in the Monastery and in the Late Medieval Household', in *De Cella in Seculum: Religious and Secular Life and Devotion in Late Medieval England*, ed. M. G. Sargent (Cambridge, 1989), 226.

189 Preserved in Cambridge, Corpus Christi College, MS 141. Her gifts are listed in M. Bateson, ed., *Catalogue of the Library of Syon Monastery Isleworth* (Cambridge, 1898), 43: E1 (Bible), 91: L15 (Nicolas de Byard, *Distincciones*), 96: M1 (*Sanctilogium Salvatoris*), Pt. I), M2 (*Santilogium*, Pt. II), 21: Q11 (Guydo de Mesnilio, *Sermones dominicles*), and 181: S17 (*Sermones dominicales et festivales*). See also the revised version of the Syon catalogue by V. Gillespie, ed., *Syon Abbey*, with *The Libraries of the Carthusians*, ed. A. I. Doyle, Corpus of

British Medieval Library Catalogues 9 (London, 2001), 572 and nos 307, 690, 734, 735, 1043, 1124, and 1284.

190 It is so identified by A. G. Watson, ed., *Supplement to the Second Edition*, Royal Historical Society 15 (London, 1987), 64, of Ker, *MMBL*, where the manuscript is not noted.

191 I am endebted to Hans-Joerg Modlmayr for information concerning the whereabouts of the Clarence Hours. See Watson, *All Souls Catalogue*, 23; my *Later Gothic Manuscripts*, II: no. 56, for literature to 1990; and J. M. Plotzek, *Das Stundenbuch der Margarete Duchess of Clarence: Sammlung Renate König*, vol. 18 (Cologne, 2005).

192 Keiser, 'Patronage and Piety', 41–43.

193 See Keiser, 'Patronage and Piety', 38; de Hamel, *The Book*, 139, as well as for five further documented examples of thirteenth-century Bibles in use in England in the fifteenth century. See also Gillespie, *Syon Abbey*, xli, 99 (no. 307: E1).

194 It is however said that 'by 1400 most of the English of all classes preferred books in their native language' (A. Taylor, 'Into his secret chamber: reading and privacy in late medieval England', in *The Practice and Representation of Reading in England*, ed. J. Raven, H. Small and N. Tadmor, Cambridge, 1996, 48).

195 M. K. Jones, '"Gardez mon corps, sauvez ma terre" – Immunity from War and the Lands of a Captive Knight: The Siege of Orléans (1428–29) Revisited', in *Charles d'Orléans in England (1415–1440)*, ed. M. Arn (Cambridge, 2000), 15.

196 BnF, *Catalogue général des manuscrits latins*, ed. P. Lauer (Paris, 1939), I: 440–41; G. Ouy, 'Recherches sur la librairie de Charles d'Orléans et de Jean d'Angoulême pendant leur captivité en Angleterre', *Compte Rendu de l'Academie des Inscriptions et Belles-Lettres* (1955), 275–77, 278; F Avril and P.D. Stirnemann, *Manuscrits enluminés d'origine insulaire VIIe–XXe siècle* (Paris, 1987), no. 220: pls **P**, XCVII; Scott, *Later Gothic Manuscripts*, II: no. 57, I: ills. 227, 228, 232–5, 237, 238; G. Ouy, 'Charles d'Orléans and his Brother Jean d'Angoulême: What Their Manuscripts Have to Tell', in *Charles d'Orléans*, ed. M. Arn, 52–3 and n. 9.

197 Le comte de Laborde, *Les Ducs de Bourgogne: Études sur les lettres, les arts et l'industrie pendant le XVe siècle*, III: Preuves (Paris, 1852), 317–28; P. Champion, *La Librairie de Charles d'Orléans* (Paris, 1910), xxiv–xxv; E. McLeod, *Charles of Orleans: Prince and Poet* (London, 1969) 136, 144, 159.

198 Champion, *La Librarie*, xiv.

199 Champion, *La Librairie*, xxi.

200 For the history of this eleven-volume Bible, see J. Stratford, 'The Manuscripts of John, Duke of Bedford: Library and Chapel', in *England in the Fifteenth Century: Proceedings of the 1986 Harlaxton Symposium*, ed. D. Williams (Woodbridge, 1987), 332–36; Stratford, *The Bedford Inventories: The Worldly Goods of John, Duke of Bedford, Regent of France (1389–1435)* (London, 1993), 91–93; and see also Bogaert, *Les bibles en français*, 33–34.

201 The phrase is that of Pierre Campion (*La Librairie*, xxii).

202 De Laborde, *Les ducs de Bourgogne*, III: 317–28; I have omitted from this count two books crossed out because given away by Charles (Laborde, nos 6549 and 6574) and items that are not books (nos 6558, 6566, 6567, 6568, 6570, and 6571); Champion, *La librairie*, xxv–xxix. See also W. Askins, 'The Brothers Orléans and their Keepers', in *Charles d'Orléans*, ed. M. Arn, 28–30, 33, 34, for an appreciation of his library; McLeod, *Charles of Orléans*, 357; and Ouy, 'Recherches sur la librairie', 271. Seventy-four books were identified by Campion as brought back to France by Charles (*La Librairie*, 7, 10, 12, 17, 19(2), 21, 22(2), 28(3), 30(2), 33, 34, 36, 38, 39(4), 40(2), 41, 42–43, 47, 48, 49, 50, 53(2), 56, 60, 61, 65, 67, 68(3), 69, 72(2), 74(3), 75, 76(4), 77, 78, 79, 82(3), 83(2), 84, 88, 90, 92(3), 93, 95, 100(2), 104, 108, 109, 110). For further information concerning books made for or bought by the brothers while in England, see Avril and Stirnemann, *Manuscrits enluminés*, nos 162, 187, 195, 197, 209, 213, 214, 220–23, 224–28.

203 De Laborde, *Les Ducs de Bourgogne*, nos 6505 (in French), 6517 (in French), 6526 (in Latin), and 6586 (no language noted).

204 Champion, *La Librairie*, xlv, but on 15–19 Champion lists five Bibles in French (including the 'Grande Bible' that had belonged to Charles V), two in Latin, and one with no language noted.

205 If All Souls 10 did belong to Charles d'Orléans, it was not the only book that he left behind in England. BL Harley MS 682, an important book of his English poetry, also remained; see M. Arn, 'Two Manuscripts, One Mind: Charles d'Orléans and the Production of Manuscripts in Two Languages (Paris BnF MS fr. 25458 and London BL Harley MS 682)', in *Charles d'Orléans*, ed. M. Arn, 78.

206 The dates of his captivity are noted in Champion, *La Librarie*, 119. For his copyists, see Avril and Stirnemann, *Manuscrits enlumines*, no. 224.

207 Stratford, 'The Manuscripts of John, Duke of Bedford' 340, and further literature.

208 McLeod, *Charles of Orleans*, 163.

209 G. Dupont-Ferrier, 'La captivite de Jean d'Orléans, comte d'Angoulême (1412–1445)', *Revue historique* 62 (1896),74. But Askins ('The Brothers Orléans', 40) seems to suggest that Charles and Jean might have 'shared their manuscripts with their keepers.'

210 Ouy, 'Charles d'Orléans and his Brother', 50.

211 Champion, *La Librairie*, Appendix II, 119–24, esp. 120.

212 Paris, Bibliothèque Nationale, MS fr. 157. This manuscript was not the pictorial exemplar for All Souls MS 10, even though there are a few subjects (not iconography) in common; for these, see e.g. fols 169, 179, 198, 211v, 229, and 236v.

213 But on his return to France eight years after Charles, Jean also established a library (McLeod, *Charles of Orleans*, 295).

214 Rogers, 'The Artist of Trinity B.11.7', 176–77; Scott, *Later Gothic Manuscripts*, II: no. 47.

215 Sneddon (thesis, I: 130–36) lists the ninety-eight most commonly occurring miniatures, twenty-four of which illustrate the New Testament, in manuscripts of the *Bible historiale complétée*. The eight pictorial subjects in All Souls 10 that agree with those mentioned by Sneddon are on fols 2 (Mark with lion), 49 (Luke with winged ox), 130v (Paul with downturned sword), 134 (Paul with seated young man), 145v (Paul seated with open book), 156 (Pentecost), 184 (St Peter) and 188v (John with eagle). On the other hand, the two All Souls miniatures with Revelation disagree considerably with the usual *BHC* illustrations.

216 A. M. Dutton, 'Passing the Book: Testamentary Transmission of Religious Literature to and by Women in England 1350–1500', in *Women, The Book and the Godly: Selected Proceedings of the St Hilda's Conference, 1993*, ed. L. Smith and J. H. M. Taylor (Cambridge, 1995), 51 and n. 24.

217 Sneddon describes the thirteenth-century French Bible as 'perfectly orthodox' and as having 'nothing to do with heresy' ("Bible du XIIIe siecle", 139).

218 Sneddon, "Bible du XIIIe siècle", 136, 137.

219 Sneddon in fact remarks in his thesis that the known ownership of the *Bible historiale complétée* was 'overwhelmingly lay' (45) and that the introduction of this form of the text was the point at which the 'laity become the principal owners' (46).

220 Watson, *All Souls Catalogue*, 23.

221 M. Arn, however, sees Charles as a man 'more pleased by clarity than pomp', not interested in 'luxury' in his books ('Two Manuscripts, One Mind', 76).

222 Avril and Stirnemann, *Manuscrit enluminés*, no. 221, pl. XCVIII, and further bibliography. The border (fol. 1) in MS lat. 1201 differs from the borders in All Souls 10 mainly in having green-tinted lobes in the feathering rather than squiggles (although fol. 191v of MS 10 has only squiggles). The border on fol. 1 of BL Royal MS 20.B.iii may also be by this artist.

223 Arn ('Two Manuscripts, One Mind', 78) made a similar suggestion concerning BL Harley MS 682, a book of Charles's English poems. Arn suggested a further possibility, Sir Thomas Cumberworth, another of Charles' keepers who may have benefited from his generosity (her note 31). Janet Backhouse made a similar suggestion concerning BL Royal MS 16.F.ii, the famous collection of Charles's poems ('Charles of Orléans Illuminated', in *Charles d'Orléans*, ed. M. Arn, 162).

224 D. Pearsall, 'The Literary Milieu of Charles of Orléans and the Duke of Suffolk, and the Authorship of the Fairfax Sequence', in *Charles d'Orléans*, ed. M. Arn, 148.

225 McLeod, *Charles of Orléans*, 186–87. J. P. M. Jansen, *The 'Suffolk' Poems: An Edition of the Love Lyrics in Fairfax 16 attributed to William de la Pole* (Groningen, 1989), states that Suffolk 'probably wrote poetry' and that he was beyond doubt 'interested in poetry' (14–15), but that his career as a poet 'lacks convincing evidence'(20). I am most grateful to Mary-Jo Arn for this reference – as well as for a copy of it.

226 Askins, 'The Brothers Orléans', 27, 42; Pearsall, 'The Literary Milieu of Charles', 146, 148; and R. A. Griffiths, *The Reign of Henry VI: The Exercise of Royal Authority, 1422–1461* (Berkeley and Los Angeles, 1981), 484.

227 M. Jones, 'Henry VII, Lady Margaret Beaufort and the Orléans Ransom', in *Kings and Nobles in the Later Middle Ages: A Tribute to Charles Ross*, ed. R. A. Griffith and J. Sherborne (Gloucester and New York, 1986), 256.

228 Jansen, *The 'Suffolk' Poems*, 19.

229 Mcleod, *Charles of Orleans*, 243 n.*.

230 Askins, 'The Brothers Orleans', 41.

231 Ouy, 'Charles d'Orléans and his Brother', 50.

232 This connection might serve as one of the common elements that Askins hoped to find between manuscripts owned by Charles and his keepers ('The Brothers Orleans', 41–42).

CHAPTER III

233 This version of the *Abbey* in BL Stowe MS 39 seems not to have been known until listed by P. S. Jolliffe, *A Check-List of Middle English Prose Writings of Spiritual Guidance* (Toronto, 1974), 98. Editions are as follows: G. G. Perry, *Religious Pieces in Prose and Verse edited from Robert Thornton's Manuscript*, EETS, OS 26 (London and Oxford, 1867, 1914), 48–58 (from Lincoln, Cathedral Library 91 (A.5.2), fol. 271 (R. M. Thomson, *Catalogue of the Manuscripts of Lincoln Cathedral Chapter Library*, Cambridge, 1989, 65–69, and for further literature); C. Horstman, *Yorkshire Writers: Richard Rolle of Hampole and his Followers*, I (London, 1895), 321–37; D. P. Consacro, *A Critical Edition of The Abbey of the Holy Ghost from all known extant English Manuscripts with Introduction, Notes and Glossary*, Ph.D. thesis, Fordham University, 1971 (from Bodl. Lib. MS Eng.poet.a.1); and N. F. Blake, *Middle English Religious Prose* (London and Evanston, 1972), 88–102 (from Bodl. Lib. MS Laud Misc. 210). A translation into modern English from Horstman (*Yorkshire Writers*, 321–37) was made by R. Boenig, 'The Abbey of the Holy Ghost and the Charter of the Abbey of the Holy Ghost', *Studia Mystica* I (1995), 133–63. Recent literature with earlier references concerning the text follows: D. P. Consacro, 'The Author of the Abbey of the Holy Ghost: A Popularizer of the Mixed Life', *Fourteenth-Century Mystics Newsletter* (December, 1976), 15–20; G. R. Keiser, '"To Knawe God Almyghtyn": Robert Thornton's Devotional Book', *Analecta Carthusiana* 106, in *Spätmittelalterliche Geistliche Literatur in der Nationalsprache*, II (Salzburg, 1984), 107, 111–12, 114–18; J. B. Friedman, *Northern English Books, Owners, and Makers in the Late Middle Ages* (Syracuse, N.Y., 1995), 195, 196, 197, 199; J. W. Conlee, 'The *Abbey of the Holy Ghost* and the *Eight Ghostly Dwelling Places* of Huntington Library HM 744', *Medium Aevum* 44 (1975), 137–44; L. Carruthers, 'In Pursuit of Holiness outside the Cloister: Religion

of the Heart in *The Abbey of the Holy Ghost*', in *Models of Holiness in Medieval Sermons*, ed. B. M. Kienzle (Louvain-la-Neuve, 1996), 211–27; C. Whitehead, 'Making a Cloister of the Soul in Medieval Religious Treatises', *Medium Aevum* 67 (1998), 14–18, 23; N. R. Rice, 'Spiritual Ambition and the Translation of the Cloister: The *Abbey* and *Charter of the Holy Ghost*', *Viator* 33 (2002), 222–60; J. Boffey, 'The *Charter of the Abbey of the Holy Ghost* and Its Role in Manuscript Anthologies', *Yearbook of English Studies* 33 (2003), 120–30; Boffey, 'Conflations of the *Abbey of the Holy Ghost* and the *Charter of the Abbey of the Holy Ghost* in Manuscript and Print' in *The Medieval Book and a Modern Collector: Essays in Honour of Toshiyuki Takamiya*, ed. T. Matsuda, R. A. Linenthal, and J. Scahill (Cambridge, 2004), 245–54.

234 R. Hanna, 'Miscellaneity and Vernacularity: Conditions of Literary Production in Late Medieval England', *The Whole Book: Cultural Perspectives on the Medieval Miscellany*, ed. S. G. Nichols and S. Wenzel (Ann Arbor, 1996), 37–51 (48–49).

235 *L'Abbaye du Saint Éspirit*; possibly from BL Royal MS 16.E.xii (H. E. Allen, *Writings Ascribed to Richard Rolle, Hermit of Hampole and Materials for his Biography*, Oxford, 1927, 338). Consacro believes that, on the basis of the earliest French manuscripts, the *Abbey* was 'first composed as a sermon' ('Author of the Abbey', 16).

236 See Allen, *Writings Ascribed to Rolle*, 337; J. A. Alford, 'Richard Rolle and Related Works', in *Middle English Prose: A Critical Guide to Major Authors and Genres*, ed. A. S. G. Edwards (New Brunswick, N.J., 1984), 46; J. Hughes, *Pastors and Visionaries: Religion and Secular Life in Late Medieval Yorkshire* (Woodbridge, 1988), 227.

237 Carruthers, 'In Pursuit of Holiness', 211, 212, 222–24. Jeffrey Hamburger uses the phrase 'figures of interiority' for the literary representation of the heart as a house, the most frequently employed metaphor; see *Nuns as Artists: The Visual Culture of a Medieval Convent* (Berkeley, 1997), 151–58 (152). Hamburger further notes that 'elaborated in monastic meditational literature, the conceit of the soul as an architectural structure had become, by the end of the Middle Ages, one of the most useful and hence most familiar of devotional devices' (156). See also Whitehead, 'Making a Cloister of the Soul', 1–24.

238 The former text is edited in W. Hübner, 'The desert of religion. Mit dem des Richard Rolle of Hampole. Nach drei Handschriften zum erstenmal herausgegeben', *Archiv für das Studium der neueren Sprachen und Literaturen*, CXXVI, 1911, 58–74.

239 See Boffey ('*The Charter of the Abbey of the Holy Ghost*', 120–30) for a consideration of manuscript and literary forms of connection between the *Abbey* and the *Charter*; also Boffey, 'Conflations', 247 n. 9.

240 See below n. 244.

241 C. F. Bühler, 'The First Edition of *The Abbey of the Holy Ghost*', *Studies in Bibliography*, 6 (1954), 101–6; H. S. Bennett, 'Notes on Two Incunables: *The Abbey of the Holy Ghost* and *A Ryght Profytable Treatise*', *The Library*, 5th Series, 10 (1955), 120; R. R. Raymo, 'Works of Religious and Philosophical Instruction', *A Manual of Writings in Middle English 1050–1500*, 7, ed. A. E. Hartung (Hamden, Conn., 1986), [184], 2545; Boffey, '*The Charter of the Abbey*', 125–26; Boffey, 'Conflations', 252–54. The Morgan Library copy (PML 43328 [ChL 1816A]; STC 13608.7) has two woodcut illustrations (fols a1 recto and a1 verso) that bear no relationship to the Stowe 39 miniatures.

242 Friedman (*Northern English Books*, 195), quoting A. I. Doyle, who specified the North Riding of Yorkshire, but Friedman otherwise stating merely 'Yorkshire' (246).

243 The arms have been identified by Papworth and Morant as belonging to a considerable number of persons, including Adam, county Lincoln; Hartelow (or Hertlaw), Northumberland; Fitzgerald, Naseby, co. Northants; Fitz-Gerald, co. Kildare, Ireland; Fitz-Thomas, Ireland; Nevill, Hornby Castle, co. Lancaster; and the Rochester Benedictine Monastery and Cathedral, Kent (J.W. Papworth, *An Alphabetical Dictionary of Coats of Arms belonging to Families in*

Great Britain and Ireland, with A. W. W. Morant, 1874, repr. Baltimore, 1965, 1057). William O'Sullivan, in a note to me dated 12 July 2000, stated that the arms were 'Kildare but I expect other men's, too'. A. I. Doyle, in conversation 31 May 2000, related that Francis Wormald had tried to identify the arms and was 'defeated' by them; Wormald thought that both the arms and the nun's habit on fol. 10 (ill. 55) were 'imaginary'.

244 Other manuscript copies of the *Abbey of the Holy Ghost* are (Joliffe, *Check-List*, 98–99): Aberystwyth, National Library of Wales, MS Peniarth 334A; Cambridge, Jesus College MS Q.D.4; Trinity College MS O.1.29; CUL MS Dd.11.89; MS Ii.4.9; MS Ll.5.18; Lincoln, Cathedral Library MS 91 (Thornton); Warminster, Longleat House MS 4; BL Additional MS 22283 (Simeon), Additional MS 36983; Egerton MS 3245; Harley MSS 1704, 2406, 5272; former MS Bradford-Lawrence 8, now in the collection of T. Takamiya, Tokyo, MS 65; London, Lambeth Palace MS 432; Maidstone, Corporation Museum MS 6, fol. 14; Bodl. Lib. MSS Douce 141, 323, MS Eng. poet.a. 1 (Vernon), and MS Laud Misc. 210; Oxford, Corpus Christi College MS E.155 + BL Cotton MS Vespasian D. xiii, fol. 181; Stonyhurst, College Library MS B. xxiii; Winchester, College Library MS 33 (see Hanna, 'Miscellaneity and Vernacularity', passim). The Hopton Hall manuscript listed by Jolliffe (99; sold Sotheby's, *Western Manuscripts and Miniatures*, London, 5 December 1989, lot 89, with two colour plates) has been identified as a *Charter of the Abbey of the Holy Ghost*, now in Tokyo, Keio University MS 9; see T. Matsuda, ed., *Mostly British: Manuscripts and Early Printed Materials from Classical Rome to Renaissance England in the Collection of Keio University Library*, Tokyo, 2001, 56–63; I am indebted to A. S. G. Edwards for this reference and for my knowledge of the Maidstone MS 6 leaf. See also Edwards, 'The Hopton Hall Manuscript at Keio University', in *Codices Keionenses: Essays on Western Manuscripts and Early Printed Books in Keio University Library*, ed. T. Matsuda (Keio, 2005), 69–86. Julia Boffey corrected the Jolliffe list with respect to Bodl. Lib. MS Douce 323, Bradfer-Lawrence MS 8, the Hopton Hall manuscript, and Corpus Christi MS E. 155, now identified with a leaf in BL Cotton MS Vespasian D. xiii ('*The Charter of the Abbey of the Holy Ghost*', 120 n. 3).

245 *The Chicago Manual of Style*, 14th ed., Chicago and London, 1993, 35.

246 BL Egerton MS 847 may, according to a note at the front of the manuscript, have been originally part of Cambridge, Trinity College MS o.8.16; and parts may also be in Egerton MS 824.

247 The first border in BL Harley MS 2838 bears crowned royal arms enclosed in a garter, indicating ownership by Henry VII. The manuscript is illustrated by one of the Dutch artists called the 'Masters of the Dark Eyes' and decorated with partial borders by an English artist; see J. Marrow, H. Defoer, A. Korteweg and W. Wüstefeld, *The Golden Age of Dutch Manuscript Painting* (New York, 1990, section xii, 285–88; Korteweg, *Illuminated Manuscripts in Dutch Collections*, Koniklijke Bibliotheek, The Hague, 1993, 52; J. Backhouse, 'Illuminated Manuscripts Associated with Henry VII and Members of his Immediate Family', in *The Reign of Henry VII: Proceedings of the 1993 Harlaxton Symposium*, ed. B. Thompson (Stamford 1995), 177; and mentioned by Scott, *Later Gothic Manuscripts*, I: 30, 63, II: 301, 366.

248 For a definition more specifically related to printed books, see G. A. Glaiser, *Encyclopedia of the Book*, 2nd ed., with a new introduction by D. Farren (New Castle, Delaware, and London, 1960, 1996), 188.

249 Reproduced by Boffey, 'Conflations', 248, pl. 21–1.

250 I am grateful to Kate Harris, Librarian of Longleat House, for information concerning MS 4. Another well produced copy of the *Abbey* is in Columbia University, New York, Plimpton MS 263.

251 For example, as in Oxford, New College MS 288, fol. 3 (reproduced in Scott, *Later Gothic Manuscripts*, I: ill. 426); Bodl. Lib. MS Douce 323, fol. 159 (fig. 59); and BL Cotton MS Nero D.ii, fol. 314 (a pastedown).

252 Examples of this phenomenon are easily at hand in my *Later Gothic Manuscripts*, I: ills 307,

363, 377, 392, 417, 470, 494, etc. See also *infra*, fig. 97.

253 Cambridge, Trinity College MS R.14.5, fols 2v, 3, 3v (reproduced in D. E. Shoukri, ed., *Liber Apologeticus de omni Statu Humanae Naturae: A Defence of Human Nature in Every State (c. 1460) A Moral Play by Thomas Chaundler* (London and New York, 1974), pls 2, 3, 4).

254 BL Cotton MS Tiberius A.vii, fols 39–106v, with Charity (fol. 90), Reason (fol. 90v), Obedience and Discipline (fol. 97), Abstinence and five other women (fol. 97v), and Chastity (fol. 101v), all as nuns.

255 E.g. Cambridge, Trinity College MS B.11.20, fol. 16v.

256 E.g. BL Cotton MS Faustina B.vi, fol. 17v; Esholt Priory Charter (reproduced in Sotheby's, *Western Manuscripts and Miniatures*, 19 June 1990, lot 70, now in West Yorkshire Archives); Washington, D.C, Library of Congress MS 4, Benedictine Rule for Nuns, fol. 37v (half-figure of Benedictine nun; see J. Krochalis, 'The Benedictine Rule for Nuns: Library of Congress, MS. 4', *Manuscripta* 30, 1986, 23).

257 See BL Additional MS 74236, Sherborne Missal, p. 381 (upper right roundel: Wulfhilda); Cotton MS Claudius B.1, fol. 269 (Bridget); Cotton MS Faustina B. vi, fol. 21v (Hilda); Berkeley, University of California MS 150, fol. 241v (Scolastica); Bodl. Lib. MS Douce 25, fol. vii^{v} (added: Clare); and Cambridge, Fitzwilliam Museum MS 48, Carew-Pointz Hours, fol. 85v (Catherine of Siena).

258 See, for instance, Bodl. Lib. MS Rawl.C.446, fol. 115 (Pächt and Alexander, 3, no. 943; Scott, *Bodl. Index*, III: no. 892); Cambridge, Corpus Christi College MS 79, Pontifical, fol. 92 (profession of a nun); BL Additional MS 37049, Carthusian Miscellany, fol. 59v (reproduced in Hogg, *Carthusian Miscellany*, 91); Cotton MS Faustina B.vi, fols 17, 20v; and Melbourne, Australia, State Library of Victoria, MS *096/G 94, *Pilgrimage of the Life of Man*, fol. 88v (nun as one of eight monastic virtues; M. M. Manion and V. F. Vines, *Medieval and Renaissance Illuminated Manuscripts in Australian Collections* (Melbourne, 1984), 110–12.

259 San Marino, Huntington Library MS EL 26 C 9, Chaucer, *Canterbury Tales*, fol. 187, Second Nun, and fol. 148v, The Prioress (reproduced by T. Stemmler, *The Ellesmere Miniatures of the Canterbury Pilgrims*, 2nd ed., Mannheim, 1977, opposite 6 and 44).

260 Stephanie Gibbs reminded me of analogous scenes in Christine de Pizan's *Cité des dames*, which sometimes contains a frontispiece of women labouring in constructing, e.g. Paris, BnF MS fr. 607. I am grateful to her for the following reference: L. De Girolami Cheney, 'Christine de Pizan's Collection of Art and Knowledge', in *Contexts and Continuities*, I: 265, figs 2, 3.

261 BL Cotton MS Faustina B.vi, fols 1v–2 (reproduced in Scott, *Later Gothic Manuscripts*, I: ills. 249–250).

262 Cambridge, Fitzwilliam Museum MS 34, fols 2v–3 (reproduced in K.L. Scott, '*Caveat Lector*: Ownership and Standardization in the Illustration of Fifteenth-Century English Manuscripts', *EMS* I, pl. 10).

263 Five full-page preliminary illustrations (fols 1v–3v) and one full-page coat of arms (fol. 1) are in Bodl. Lib. MS Bodley 546, Master of Game; and twelve in the Chaundler manuscript, Cambridge, Trinity College MS R.14.5.

264 For author scenes, see my *Later Gothic Manuscripts*, I: figs 15, 30; ills 84, 150, 193, 243, 267, 287, 363, 367, 377, 391, 392, 428, 440; and my article concerning portraits of scribes, edited by M. Gullick (n. 147 above).

265 See e.g. BL Royal MS 2.A.xviii, fol. 23v, and MS 19.B.xvi, fol. 1v; New Haven, Yale University, MS Beinecke 281, fol. 5v.

266 Especially in Higden's *Polychronicon*, e.g. BL Royal MS 14.C.ix, fols 1v–2; Cambridge, Corpus Christi College MS 21, fol. 9; Oxford, Magdalen College MS Lat. 190, fol. iiiv; San Marino, Huntington Library HM 132, fol. 4v; Warminster, Longleat House, MS 50, fol. 7v. Maps also precede other texts such as Bristol, Record Office, MS 04720(1), plan of Bristol before *Maire of*

Bristowe is Calendar; Aylesbury, Buckinghamshire Record Office, Boarstall Cartulary, fol. 1; BL Royal MS 12.B.xvii, *Liber de optimo fato*, fol. 1; Chaworth Roll, beginning with map of Roman roads in Britain (Sam Fogg Rare Books, Catalogue 12, *Medieval Manuscripts*, London, 1989, lot 10).

267 BL Royal MS 17.B.xxxiv, fol. 132v.

268 BL Cotton MS Faustina B.vii, fol. 72v.

269 E.g. CUL MS Ii.6.7, fol. 7v.

270 Folio 14v; reproduced in Pächt and Alexander, 3, no. 974: pl. XCI.

271 Page 7; reproduced in Pächt and Alexander, 3, no. 892: pl. LXXXV.

272 Reproduced in Scott, *Later Gothic Manuscripts*, I: ill. 62, and catalogue 13 with further literature.

273 See also the full-page, non-frontispiece in Cambridge, Trinity College MS O.9.1, fol. 102.

274 Consacro, 'Author of the Abbey', 20; K. Chesney, 'Notes on some Treatises of Devotion intended for Margaret of York (MS. Douce 365)', *Medium Aevum* 20 (1951), 13. For two recently discovered French manuscripts, see K. Hall, '*The Abbey of the Holy Ghost, the Cité des dames*', Marine and Euphrosine: The Mixed Life and Female Authority, *Contexts and Continuities*, ed. A. J. Kennedy (Glasgow, 2002), II: 410 n. 4.

275 Consacro, thesis, cxxiv; and Chesney, 'Treatises of Devotion', 14–15.

276 Pächt and Alexander, 1, no. 352: pl. XXVII, and for further literature.

277 M. R. James, *A Descriptive Catalogue of Fifty Manuscripts from the Collection of Henry Yates Thompson* (Cambridge, 1898), 225–32 (MS 40); F. Wormald, 'The Yates Thompson Manuscripts', *The British Museum Quarterly* 16 (1951–52), 5. This manuscript is thought to be the oldest of the French versions (Hall, '*Abbey of the Holy Ghost, Cité des dames*', 410). R. H. and M. A. Rouse, *Illiterati et uxorati: Manuscripts and their Makers: Commercial Book Producers in Medieval Paris 1200–1500*, 2 vols (Turnhout, 2000), reproduce the first miniature in this manuscript (II: ill. 85).

278 The Holy Spirit as dove is in a connected roundel above, and a lamb with flag, bleeding into a chalice, is below.

279 Most copies have a phrase of address such as 'der brothir and sustern' (CUL MS Ii.4.9), 'My fulle cere and weell loued brethir and sisters' (Cambridge, Trinity College MS O.1.29) or 'My dere broder and suster' (CUL MS Ll.5.18), and others address only men, e.g. the Stonyhurst College copy HMC 26, 'I see þt many men wolde be in religion' (Ker, *MMBL*, no. 23: 393). See also fig. 68.

280 Middle English, 'Buxomness'.

281 M.E, 'Sufferance'.

282 M.E, 'Orison'.

283 M.E. 'Drede' (Carruthers, 'In pursuit of Holiness', 215 n. 12).

284 M.E., 'Honesty' (Carruthers, 'In pursuit of Holiness', 215 n. 13).

285 M.E., 'Lewte'.

286 It consumes about a quarter of the text or ninety-one lines of 396 (Carruthers, 'In Pursuit of Holiness', 216).

287 M.E., 'Orloge'.

288 M.E., 'Gelosye' (Carruthers, 'In pursuit of Holiness', 217 n. 19).

289 The phrase was used by S. G. Nichols (in *The New Philology*, 'Introduction: Philology in a Manuscript Culture', *Speculum* 65, 1990, 7): 'The manuscript folio contains different systems of representation: poetic or narrative text, the highly individual and distinctive scribal hand(s) that inscribe that text, illuminated images, colored rubrications, and not infrequently glosses or

commentaries in the margins or interpolated in the text. Each system is a unit independent of the others and yet calls attention to them; each tries to convey something about the other while to some extent substituting for it. Sometimes we see graphic examples of the systemic rivalry, as, for example, in the case of decorated or historiated initials at the beginning of passages …'

290 I am grateful to Kelvin W. M. Scott for implementing this design for me.

291 William Wordsworth, 'The Old Cumberland Beggar', lines 169–70.

292 Vincent Gillespie has previously recognized a similar kind of non-sequential ability with respect to Corpus Christi College, Oxford, MS 132; see his 'Medieval Hypertext: Image and Text from York Minster', in *Of the Making of Books: Medieval Manuscripts, Their Scribes and Readers: Essays Presented to M. B. Parkes* (Aldershot, 1997), 208 n. 10, 215, 224, 227.

293 Pächt and Alexander, 3, no. 923: pl. LXXXVIII; *Bodl.Index*, 1: no. 245.

294 A. M. Hutchison, 'Devotional Reading in the Monastery and in the Late Medieval Household', in *De Cella in Seculum: Religious and Secular Life and Devotion in Late Medieval England*, ed. M. G. Sargent (Cambridge, 1989), 217, 223; M. Oliva, *The Convent and the Community in Late Medieval England: Female Monasteries in the Diocese of Norwich, 1350–1540* (Woodbridge, 1998), 61–62. L. Carruthers ('In pursuit of Holiness', 211, 218–20, 224) sees the text of the *Abbey* as a 'form of preaching', if not precisely a sermon. For nuns' books and libraries, see M. C. Erler, *Women, Reading, and Piety in Late Medieval England* (Cambridge, 2002), 27–47.

295 N. Orme (*From Childhood to Chivalry: The Education of the English Kings and Aristocrary 1066–1530*, London and New York, 1984, 64) states that 'teaching was almost the only pastoral role allowed to nuns' and that 'income from boarding children and teaching them must also have been an attraction …'. See also E. Power, *Medieval English Nunneries c. 1275 to 1535* (New York, 1964), 261, 264.

296 W. W. Skeat, *The Vision of William concerning Piers the Plowman in three parallel texts … by William Langland (about 1362–1399 A.D.)*, 2 vols (Oxford, 1886, repr. 1954), I: 245.

297 As quoted by V. Gillespie, 'Vernacular Books of Religion', in *Book Production and Publishing in Britain 1375–1475*, ed. J. Griffiths and D. Pearsall (Cambridge, 1989), 326.

CHAPTER IV

298 P. S. Moore, *The Works of Peter of Poitiers, Master in Theology and Chancellor of Paris (1193–1205)* (Catholic University of America, 1936), 99.

299 Moore, *Works of Peter of Poitiers*, 100. The opening of this genealogical chronicle is, as Richard Sharpe has pointed out, easily confused with the opening of Roger Alban's *Progenies regum Angliae*, a genealogical chronicle of the kings of England (*Handlist*, under 'Roger Alban', 580). The opening in Royal I.B.x is as follows: '[C]onsiderans historie prolixitatem necnon et difficultatem scolarium quoque circa studium sacre lectionis …'. The opening of Alban's chronicle reads: 'Considerans cronicorum prolixitatem necnon et difficultatem scolariumque circa studium nobilis progeniei regum Anglie …'. Because the Poitiers text was frequently produced in an English translation, it is worth noting that incipit as well, 'Consideryng the lenght and the hardnesse of holy scripture and nameli of the ground of the lettir historial …' (Bodl. Lib. MS Lyell 33). For further English-made copies of Poitiers' chronicle in various Latin and English versions, see A. C. de la Mare, *Catalogue of the Collection of Medieval Manuscripts Bequeathed to the Bodleian Library Oxford by James P. R. Lyell* (Oxford, 1971), 80–85. See also E. D. Kennedy, *Chronicles and Other Historical Writing*, vol. 8 of *A Manual of the Writings in Middle English 1050–1500*, gen. ed. A. E. Hartung (Hamden, Conn., 1989), 2674–75, 2676–77, 2888–89.

300 L. F. Sandler, *Gothic Manuscripts 1285–1385*, A Survey of Manuscripts Illuminated in the British Isles, 5, ed. J. J. G. Alexander (Oxford, 1986), II: no. 22, concerning BL Additional MS 14819.

301 A few other fifteenth-century copies of Poitiers' work were also produced in roll-codex form, as we know from de la Mare, *Lyell Catalogue*, no. 33.

302 Literature: Warner and Gilson, I: 11–12; M. Evans, 'The Geometry of the Mind', *Architectural Association Quarterly* 12 (1980), 31–55, figs 5, 7, 8, 10 with two reproductions from the *Speculum* in the three last figures (I am endebted to Lucy F. Sandler for this reference); H. F. Hilpert, 'Geistliche Bildung und Laienbildung: Zur Überlieferung der Schulschrift *Compendium historiae in genealogia Christi (Campendium veteris testamenti)* des Petrus von Poitiers (+1205) in England', *Journal of Medical History* 11 (1985), 315–31.

303 *Nota bene* signs by this fifteenth-century hand are on fols 9, 15, and 32 of the Poitiers *Compendium* and fols 23, 73, 117v, and 230v of the Bible. The *nota bene* hands on fol. 8 may not be by the same annotator.

304 The final words on fol. 33v are: column A, 'de functa est salome soror herodis ascalonite'; and column B, 'passus est exhiberi tristem mortis nuncium bubonem vidit', that is to say that the text ends at the Crucifixion and before the Anna and Emeria passage, which concludes with roundels naming or illustrating the Apostles.

305 The Bible has a drawing, added by a different fifteenth-century hand, of a hooded monk on a horse or ass with bridle and reins, beating it with a branch; a scroll in the animal's mouth is inscribed in red, 'Cur percuus me'. There are also preparatory sketches for scrolls on fol. 3v (bottom left) and fol. 7 (top right).

306 I am grateful to A. S. G. Edwards for the approximate date of the notes on fol. 1 and for corrections to my transcription of the inscription on fol. 3v.

307 The scene is in two other English copies of the *Speculum humanae salvationis*: New Haven, Yale University, Beinecke MS 27, fol. 10, and Chicago, Art Institute, MS 23.420, fol. 12. It is also in Bodl. Lib. MS Rawlinson D.939, section 4, Agricultural Almanac. Only the figure of Eve with spindle is in the Pepys Sketchbook, Cambridge, Magdalene College, Pepys MS 1916, fol. 16v.

308 Scott *Later Gothic Manuscripts*, I: ills 172–74, II: no. 40.

309 Manchester, John Rylands University Library MS Chronicle Roll 2 (formerly Bromley-Davenport roll). Sharpe (*Handlist*, 580) lists other manuscripts of Roger Alban, if not this one; Warminster, Longleat House MS 348 and BnF MS lat. 6055 would also seem to contain Alban's version.

310 The subjects are: Noah loading animals onto the Ark, the Sacrifice of Isaac, Moses and the Israelites at the Red Sea, and the Anointing of David by Samuel, with a figure holding a crown beside.

311 BL Cotton MS Faustina B.vii, fol. 45; Royal MS 14 B.ix, membr. 1, at the Poitiers incipit but following introductory text and the illustration of a Christ in Majesty.

312 The visual proverb occurs on at least one other occasion in English illustration: in Bodl. Lib. MS Don.d.85, Psalter, added drawing on fol. 1v, in waters below St Christopher (reproduced in Pächt and Alexander, 3, no. 803, pl. LXXVI).

313 Fig. 2 shows the diagrammatic version of the Ark in Dublin, Trinity College MS 486, fol. 39.

314 E.g. London, Society of Antiquaries MS 501, membr. 3, Noah's Ark (reproduced in Scott, *Later Gothic Manuscripts*, I: ill. 369); and Cambridge, Corpus Christi College MS 116, membr. 1.

315 See, for example, BL Additional MS 14819, membr. 1; Additional MS 24025, membr. 1; Royal MS 4 B.vii, fol. 194; Royal MS 8.C.ix, fol. 3v; Bodl. Lib. MS Laud Misc. 151, fol. 1; MS Laud Misc. 270, fol. 1; or the modelbook page in BL Cotton MS Faust.B. vii, fol. 42 (fig. 112).

316 The scene is on membr. 2; see N. Morgan, *Early Gothic Manuscripts [II] 1250–1285*, ed. J. J. G. Alexander, A Survey of Manuscripts Illuminated in the British Isles, 4 and ills 377–80 (London, 1988), no. 177. See also Bodl. Lib. MS Lat. theol.b.1, membr. 2, but together with two small diagrammatic arks.

317 It is at least worth mentioning, at least, BL Cotton MS Titus D.iii, a Poitiers manuscript, with on fols 3–4v an interesting and possibly unique series of various images and diagrams of two sets of the Ark (according to such authors as Moses, Josephus, and Augustine) as frontispieces and of a further three diagrams on fol. 7v.

318 Reproduced by Veronica Sekules (*Medieval Art*, Oxford, 2001, 130, ill. 88), where the provenance and dating of the manuscript are erroneously noted as 'French, fourteenth century'.

319 Reproduced by Hogg, *Carthusian Miscellany*, 7.

320 On fols 11v (twice), 12, 14r–v, 15v and 16.

321 See, for example, BL Additional MSS 14819 (*c.* 1300) and 24025 (?early thirteenth century). For a fifteenth-century scene of the Sacrifice, see London, Society of Antiquaries MS 501 (after 1447 and ?before 1455), membr. 4.

322 The only illustrated manuscript that I know with more than one pen artist on the job is Tokyo, Collection of T. Takamiya MS 43, Ranulf Higden, *Polychronicon*; the illustrations are discussed by A. S. G Edwards, 'Geography and Illustration and Higden's *Polychronicon*', in *Art Into Life: Collected Papers from the Kresge Art Museum Medieval Symposia*, ed. C. G. Fisher and K. L. Scott (East Lansing, 1995), 103–6, figs 2–13; and Scott, 'The Illustrations of the Takamiya *Polychronicon*', in *The Medieval Book and a Modern Collector: Essays in Honour of Toshiyuki Takamiya*, ed. T. Matsuda, R. A. Linenthal and J. Scahill (Cambridge and Tokyo, 2004), 161–78.

323 E.g. York, Minster Library MS Add. 256, membr. 1; London, Society of Antiquaries MS 501, membr. 6 (with harp, but not harping).

324 See, e.g. Bury St Edmunds, Grammar School, s.n., fol. 1; Cambridge, Fitzwilliam Museum MS McClean 46, fol. 1; Trinity College MS B.11.6, fol. 1; CUL MS Dd.12.67, fol. 7; MS Ff.4.5, fol. 1; Cape Town, South African Library MS Grey 4.c.5, fol. 12; Edinburgh, National Library of Scotland MS Advocates 18.8.11, fol. 7; London, Victoria and Albert Museum MS Reid 41, fol. 9; Reid 42, fol. 114; Stockholm, Kunglige Bibliotheket MS A.182, fol. 7; and Turin, Biblioteca Nazionale MS I.I.9, fol. 23v.

325 For instance, CUL. MS Dd.7.7, fol. 115; Dd.7.9, fols 150v and 162; New Haven, Yale University Beinecke MS 640, fols 40v: fig. 14, 179v, 198v, 200, 205v; Bodl. Lib. MS Laud Misc. 152, fol. 225v; and Laud Misc. 156, fols 6v, 7, 11, 12, 13: fig. 4: copies of Nicholas of Lyra, *Postilla litteralis* (see Chapter I).

326 See, for instance, CUL MS Dd.7.9, fol. 153; New Haven, Yale University Beinecke MS 640, fol. 96; and Bodl. Lib. MS Laud Misc. 156, fol. 7: fig. 20: copies of Nicholas of Lyra, *Postilla litteralis* (see Chapter I).

327 The psalms are nos 120–134.

328 For instance, see the scenes of Winchester College in Oxford, New College MS 288, fol. 3, and of Westminster Abbey in Cambridge, Trinity College MS B.10.2, fol. 44.

329 Oxford, Corpus Christi College MS 161, *Speculum humanae salvationis*, p. 127; London, Victoria and Albert MS Reid 42, Psalter, fol. 77; Canterbury, Cathedral Library MS H.H.L.3.4, book of prayers, fol. 78v.

330 See Hogg, *Carthusian Miscellany* for a world map with Rome (5) and for a drawing of 'roma caput mundi' (7). The *Polychronicon* is in the Collection of T. Takamiya, Tokyo, MS 43, fol. 9 (reproduced by Edwards, 'Geography and Illustration', fig. 8).

331 The Esdras drawing is reproduced in my study on portraits of scribes, edited by M. Gullick in *Pen in Hand*, fig. 31 (n. 147 above).

332 The headdress is described by F. M Kelly and R. Schwabe (*A Short History of Costume & Armour chiefly in England*, I: 1066–1485, London, 1931, 1968, 43); and C. W. and P. Cunnington (*Handbook of English Mediaeval Costume*, London, 1952, 128), where the date is suggested. Kelly and Schwabe reproduce a heart-shaped version dated 1427, whereas

M. Scott (*A Visual History of Costume: The Fourteenth & Fifteenth Centuries*, London, 1986, 71) shows one of *c.* 1427. Apart from the round neckline, Judith's gown most closely resembles a dress reproduced by Scott (*Visual History*, 71). The headdress in Royal MS 1.B.x does not have the customary veil.

333 New Haven, Yale University, MS Beinecke 27, fol. 55v, and Oxford, Corpus Christi College MS 161, p. 118.

334 See also BL Additional MS 11758, membr. 3; Harley Rolls C, membr. 16; Lansdowne MS 456, fol. 15; Kings MS 395, fol. 17: CUL MS Dd.3.56, membr. 2.

335 BL Additional MS 37049, fol. 3 (reproduced in Hogg, *Carthusian Miscellany*, 6).

336 See also e.g. BL Additional MS 24025, membr. 4; Cotton MS Faustina B.vii, fols 42, 50; London, Lambeth Palace MS 499, fol. 10v; Bodl. Lib. MS Fairfax 13, fol. 5; MS Lat.theol.b.1, fol. 7; and MS Laud Misc. 151, fol. 5.

337 Two drawings of Diogenes can, however, be found in Tokyo, Collection of T. Takamiya MS 43, Ranulf Higden, *Polychronicon*, fol. 68, Diogenes in a barrel, speaking with Alexander of Macedonia and fol. 68v, Diogenes spitting at a man; in both drawings the figures are busts.

338 The thirteenth-century Poitiers codex, BL Cotton MS Faustina B.vii, contains a roundel of the Nativity of Christ rendered as the infant Christ in a manger with a star and the heads of an ox and ass (fol. 51v), and BL Additional MS 14819, membr. 5, Additional MS 24025, membr. 5, and Royal MS 14.B.ix, all three have a Nativity of Christ, the first two with a Virgin *lactans*.

339 See, for instance, Cambridge, Corpus Christi College MS 29, fol. viii; CUL MS Ff.3.7, fol. 11v; BL Cotton MS Faustina B.vii, fol. 52; Cotton MS Vitellius C.iii, fol. 10; Royal MS 4.B.vii, fol. 199; MS 8.C.ix, fol. 13; Bodl. Lib. MS Laud Misc. 151, fol. 6v; MS Laud Misc. 270, fol. 6v, and MS Lat.theol.b.1, membr. 10.

340 E.g. BL Royal MS 14.B.ix, membr. 8 (partially reproduced by Morgan, *Early Gothic Manuscripts [II]*, ill. 379). The amount of missing text may be judged by comparison with the last membranes of BL Additional MSS 14819 and 24025 or with Bodl. Lib. MS Auct.D.4.10, fol. 5?3.

341 MS Lyell 33 is reproduced in de la Mare, *Lyell Catalogue*, pl. VI. See also Oxford, Corpus Christi College MS 207, fol. 3v (reproduced in Scott, *Later Gothic Manuscripts*, I: fig. 427). In a few instances the Poitiers chronicles are ilustrated with pen drawings, i.e. Bodl. Lib. MS Bodley Rolls 5 and BL Additional MS 21219; and they may also have tinted drawings as in London, Society of Antiquaries MS 501 (Scott, *Later Gothic Manuscripts*, I: ill. 370).

342 Furthermore, the Royal *Compendium* has, as I have said, little correspondence to the sequences of illustrations in thirteenth- and fourteenth-century copies. The early copies may begin with a miniature of the Fall (see, for instance, BL Cotton MS Faustina B.vii, fol. 45; Royal MS 14.B.ix, membr. 1; Bodl. Lib. MS Lat.theol.b.1, membr 1; MS Laud Misc. 151, fol. 1; MS Rawl.C.563, fol. 1; and BnF MS lat. 15254, fol. 4v); and they may also show Noah's Ark (for example, BL Additional MS 24025, membr. 1; Royal MS 4.B.vii, fol. 194; MS 8.C.ix, fol. 3v; MS 14.B.ix, membr. 2; and Bodl. Lib. MSS Lat. theol.b.1, membr. 1; MS Laud Misc. 151, fol. 1). The finer early copies they may then go on to a pictorial sequence including, variously, the Nativity of Christ (BL Additional MS 14819, membr. 5; Cotton MS Faustina B. vii, fol. 51v; Royal MS 14.B.ix, membr. 7; BnF MS lat. 15254, fol. 9; Bodl. Lib. MS Lat.theol.b.1, membr. 12; Philadelphia, Free Library, MS Lewis E.249a (reproduced in *Leaves of Gold: Manuscript Illumination from Philadelphia Collctions*, ed. J. R. Tanis and J. A. Thompson, Philadelphia, 2001, no. 68); Christ as a Child (BL Cotton MS Faustina B.vii, fol. 51v), the Sacrifice of Isaac (e.g. BL Additional MS 14819, membr. 1; MS 24025, membr. 1; Royal MS 14.B.ix, membr. 2; Bodl. Lib. MS Rawl.C.563, fol. 3v; BnF MS lat. 15254, fol. 5), the Dream of Nebuchadnezzar (BL Royal MS 14.B.ix, membr. 5; Bodl. Lib. MS Lat.theol.b.1, membr. 5), Sedechias enthroned (BL Royal MS 14.B.ix, membr. 5; BnF MS lat. 15254, fol. 7v), Moses crossing the Red Sea (BL Additional MS 14819, membr. 1; Additional MS 24025, membr. 1), a Crucifixion (BL Royal

MS 14.B.ix, membr. 8; Bodl. Lib. MS Lat.theol.b.1, membr. 13; Philadelphia, Free Library MS Lewis E. 249a), a Resurrection (BL Additional MS 14819, membr. 5; Royal MS 14.B.ix, membr. 8; Philadelphia, Free Library MS Lewis E. 249a, or even a Virgin and Child (Bodl. Lib. MS Rawl.C.563, fol. 24v, XIV).

343 Folios 1–7v. Folio 7v is a ruled blank, and the stub is not foliated.

344 For an exposition of this text, see Sandler, *De Lisle Psalter*, 23.

345 Sandler, *De Lisle Psalter*, 23; the group of drawings in Royal MS 1.B.x was noticed earlier (but not by the *Speculum* title) by F. Saxl, 'A Spiritual Enclyclopaedia of the Later Middle Ages', *JWCI* 5 (1942), 110 n. 5.

346 M. J. Carruthers, *The Book of Memory: A Study of Memory in Medieval Culture* (Cambridge, 1990), 253, 256.

347 See Morgan, *Early Gothic Manuscripts [II]*, no. 177. Otherwise, most of the miniatures in Royal MS 14.B.ix (Sacrifice of Isaac, Solomon and ?Ecclesia, the Dream of Nebuchadnezzar, Sedechias, Nativity of Christ, the Crucifixion, Resurrection, and row of seated Apostles) are not in Royal MS 1.B.x.

348 Folios 1, 2v, 3, 4v, and 5.

349 In conjunction with her fine study of the early fourteenth-century Psalter of Robert de Lisle, Lucy F. Sandler compiled a register of thirty-eight manuscripts, both English and Continental, that contain the *Speculum theologie*, from the thirteenth to the fifteenth centuries (*De Lisle Psalter*, 107–115). Sandler's compilation demonstrated that the number of diagrams in the *Speculum* can vary between three and nineteen in any given manuscript and that the collection was clearly not a stable entity, whatever the provenance. Since writing this study of Royal MS.1.B.x, I have located a fifth fifteenth-century English *Compendium* manuscript with four drawings from the *Speculum*, BL Additional 17358 (Tree of Vices, Tree of Virtues, Ten Commandments, Seven Petitions). It is not possible to discuss this copy here.

350 There is also one fourteenth-century English manuscript, CUL MS Gg.4.32, a miscellany, containing three of the *Speculum* diagrams in Royal MS 1.B.x; these diagrams were, however, not made for the book in which they are now found..

351 For this manuscript, see Sandler, *De Lisle Psalter*, Appendix, 114, Add. 4.

352 There is a rough drawing of the Tree of Knowledge, *Sciencia*, divided into two branches *Philosophia* and *Eloquentia*, added on fol. 52r of Cambridge, MA, Harvard University, Houghton Library MS Lat. 127, Boethius, *Philosophiae consolatio*, England, XIIe; see L. Light, *Catalogue of Medieval and Renaissance Manuscripts in the Houghton Library Harvard University*, I: MSS Lat. 3–179, Medieval and Renaissance Texts & Studies 145 (Binghamton, NY, 1995), 165–67. The *Sciencia* diagram is mentioned by M. Evans, 'The *Ysagoge in Theologiam* and the Commentaries attributed to Bernard Silvestris', *JWCI* 54 (1991), 23 n. 102.

353 N. Rogers, 'The Artist of B.11.7 and his Patrons', in *England in the Fifteenth Century: Proceedings of the 1992 Harlaxton Symposium*, ed. N. Rogers (Stamford, 1994), 172. M. V. Ronan states that there were 'more chantries in her honour' in the Herefordshire diocese than in any other in England (*Saint Anne: Her Cult and her Shrines* (London and Edinburgh, 1927), 87–88.

354 P. Sheingorn, 'Appropriating the Holy Kinship: *Gender and Family History*', *Interpreting Cultural Symbols: Saint Anne in Late Medieval Society*, ed. K. Ashley and P. Sheingorn (Athens, GA, and London, 1990), 169–98 (170–71).

355 Hanna, *St John's Catalogue*, 77–79, pl. 4.

356 The intervening tabular diagrams are on fol. 3, Table of the Seven Acts of the Passion; fol. 3v, the Table of the Seven Works of Mercy, Seven Degrees of Wisdom, Seven Curialitates and Seven Sacraments; fol. 4, Table of the Seven Requests of the Lord's Prayer, Seven Gifts of the Holy

Spirit, Seven Virtues, Seven Vices; fol. 4v, Table of the Seven Bodily Blessings, Seven Bodily Ills, Seven Blessings of the Soul, Seven Ills of the Soul; and fol. 5, Table of the Seven Degrees of the Church, Seven Blessings, Seven Internal Joys and Seven External Joys. Three of these tables, those on fols 3v, 4v, and 5, are on no other list of contents of the *Speculum theologie* (Sandler, *De Lisle Psalter*, Appendix, 108–15).

357 The full text of the jingle is 'Humilitas exornat virtutibus/Prudencia exornatum decorat/Fortitudo decoratum colorat/Iusticia coloratum leticat/Temporancia letificatum conducit/Fides conductum erigit/Spes erectum dirigit/Caritas directum coronat' (reproduced in Hanna, *St. John's Catalogue*, pl. 4).

358 These are subdivided into thirty further increments of virtue (Sandler, *De Lisle Psalter*, 82).

359 See, e.g. Sandler, *De Lisle Psalter*, 82, pl. 24.

360 One of these rare instances is in New York, The Morgan Library, MS M. 46, book of Hours, *c.* 1430, fol. 37v, showing the Cherub standing on a wheel, but without inscriptions of any kind; a small male figure in a radiance stands beside.

361 The Cherub can also be found in a thirteenth-century English copy of the *Compendium* in Cambridge, Corpus Christi College MS 29; appended to a fourteenth-century copy in CUL MS Gg.4.32, fol. 11; and without other *Speculum theologie* diagrams in a fourteenth-century miscellany in Cambridge, St John's College MS E.24, Clement Llantony, *Declarationes alarum et pennarum cherubin et seraphin*, fol. 59, all again apparently from exemplars different from Royal MS 1.B.x.

362 The fifteenth-century version of the Tree of Virtues in Bodl. Lib. MS Laud Misc. 156 is also imitative of the thirteenth-century mode of presenting the image.

363 The jingle is: 'Superbia spoliat virum iustum/Avarcia spoliatum dedecorat/Invidia dedecoratum debilitat/Ira debilitatem exsecat/Ceuedoxia exsecata seducit/Gula seducta inficit/Accida infecita deicit/Luxuria deictum interficit.' One of the other English fifteenth-century copies of Poitiers with the *Speculum theologie* (CUL MS Dd.3.56) also contains a Tree of Vices.

364 This Tree is reproduced in *Bodl. Index*, II: fig. 15. One of the other English fifteenth-century copies of Poitiers with the *Speculum theologie* (CUL MS Dd.3.56) also contains a Tree of Vices. The Tree of Vices in BL Cotton MS Faustina B.vi, fol. 6, is reproduced as the frontispiece of Scott, *Later Gothic Manuscripts*, II, opposite Catalogue no. 1.

365 Cambridge, Jesus College MS 24 (Q.B.7), fols 51–58v (Sandler, *De Lisle Psalter*, Appendix, no. 1); CUL MS Gg.4 32, fols 10v–15v (Sandler, Appendix, no. 2); BL Arundel MS 83I, fols 2v–5v, 12–13 (Sandler, Appendix, no. 7); Arundel MS 83II, fols 123v–135 (Sandler, Appendix, no. 8); and Arundel MS 507, fols 16v–21 (Sandler, Appendix, no. 9).

366 Scott, *Later Gothic Manuscripts*, II: no. 63, and for further literature.

367 Carruthers, *The Book of Memory*, 250.

368 The *Speculum* diagrams occur in other textual settings as well, in Psalters (Sandler, *De Lisle Psalter*, Appendix nos 7, 8), theological and religious tracts by various authors (Sandler, Appendix, nos 9, 13, 18, 22, 25, 29), texts for preachers (Sandler, Appendix, nos 17, 24), and in miscellanies (Sandler, Appendix, nos 1, 2, 5, 6, 12, 14, 19, 23, 26, 27, 31, 32, etc.), where the brevity and flexible selection of contents would have been a virtue.

369 These are tables of the Epistles and Gospels for the whole year, fols 34–39; a table with the first words of each Psalm, fols 40, 41; and a concordance of the Gospels, fols 41v–43.

370 The text at this point, which has no connection with the illustration, begins: *[p]ost mortem porredis incepit Britannia habere quincque reges .... Hic construxit intrinonanto templum concordie ad confirmacionem legum suarum & cum quadraginta annis reguasset iuxta idem templum ut ipse idem ordinauerat sepelitur.*

371 A. S. G. Edwards also identified the images as a rebus.

372 Information courtesy of Ralph Hanna.

373 A. I. Doyle, in his Lyell lectures, Oxford, for 1967 (unpublished); M. B. Parkes, *English Cursive Book Hands 1250–1500* (Oxford, 1969), no. 24; Watson, *Dated and Datable Manuscripts Oxford*, I: nos 827, 831, II: pls 386, 468; Hanna, *St John's Catalogue*, no. 77. Dygon is also mentioned in L. R. Mooney's review of Hanna's catalogue in *Speculum* 79, 2004, 499); and Hanna, 'Producing Magdalen College MS lat. 93', *Yearbook of English Studies* 33 (2003), 142–55. In a communication to me of 26.XI.2003, Doyle stated that 'the annotations by a current anglicana (with final 6-like s), slanting, look very like John Dygon of Sheen reclusory (but not the notes on fols 54–55)'. Seven books were donated by Dygon to Magdalen College, Oxford (Emden, *BRUO*), a number that has been much augmented by R. Hanna: see his forthcoming study, 'John Dygon, Fifth Recluse of Sheen: His Career, Books, and Acquaintance', in *Imagining the Book*, ed. J. Thompson, Belfast conference proceedings. I am grateful to Ralph Hanna for allowing me to read his study in advance of publication.

374 For his life see, Emden, *BRUO*, 6151; and Hanna, 'John Dygon, Fifth Recluse', forthcoming. A discussion of scribes working at the Sheen house in the fifteenth century is available by A. I. Doyle, 'Book Production by the Monastic Orders in England (*c.* 1375–1530): Assessing the Evidence', in *Medieval Book Production: Assessing the Evidence*, ed. L. L. Brownrigg (Los Altos Hills, CA, 1990), 13–15.

375 Watson, *Dated and Datable Manuscripts Oxford*, I: no. 831, II: pl. 468.

376 This attribution was confirmed by Ian Doyle and Ralph Hanna. Dygon's notes, corrections, and signs are on fols 8r–v, 9r–v, 15r–v, 17v, 19v, 21v, 23v, 25v, 27, 28r–v, 29v, and 30r–v.

377 Hanna usurped my announcement of the discovery in 'Two British Library Biblical MSS: Some Observations; A New John Dygon Manuscript', *Journal of the Early Book Society*, 8 (2005), 189–92.

378 By coincidence, there is a fifteenth-century rebus, not a common an occurrence, in another copy of Peter of Poitiers' *Compendium*, i.e. in Bodl. Lib. MS Laud Misc. 270, fol. 1, a codex of the second quarter of the thirteenth century. The rebus is a coloured drawing of a tun inscribed with the letter 'mor' for Cardinal John Morton (d. 1500), together with his arms.

379 Hanna, 'John Dygon, Fifth Recluse', forthcoming.

380 There is a gap in the shaded decoration between fol. 251v and fol. 257. One of the shaded images is reproduced in my *Later Gothic Manuscripts*, I: 13, of fol. 218v, an open book in cloth cover with tassels. Neither Collingburn nor the hand of the corrector in Harley 612 appears to have written Royal MS 1.B.x. The correcting scribe/artist did not render the occasional drawings on the Harley catchwords (e.g. fols 25v, 137, 193v), which are usually in scrolls. There are fine seven-line and other initials, much coloured with purple and green but without gold, in a foreign style; these are sometimes historiated as on fols 66v, 73v, 160v, 168v, and 208, or illusionistically pinned to the parchment (e.g. fol. 2) or in a frame (fol. 104).

381 Another example of exceptional secondary decoration is the late fourteenth-century elaboration of catchwords in Manchester, Chetham's Library MS 6713; see my 'The Remains of a Missal: Chetham's Library MS 6713', in *Studies in Manuscript Illumination: A Tribute to Lucy Freeman Sandler*, ed. K. A. Smith and C. H. Krinsky, forthcoming, 2007.

CHAPTER V

382 Literature: *Catalogue of Additions to the Manuscripts in the British Museum in the Years MDCCCLIV–MDCCCLX* (Norwich, 1875, repr. 1965), 566; W. H. Frere, *Pontifical Services. Illustrated from Miniatures of the XVth and XVIth Centuries*, Alcuin Club Collections 3, 2 vols (London, 1901), I: 104, II: pl. II; C. Wordsworth and H. Littlehales, *The Old Service-Books of the English Church* (London, 1904), 227; R. M. Wooley, *The Benedictional of John Longlonde Bishop of Lincoln*, Henry Bradshaw Society 64 (London, 1927); J. Brückmann, 'Latin Manuscript Pontificals and Benedictionals in England and Wales', *Traditio* 29 (1973), 425.

383 Sotheby's, *Catalogue of Western Manuscripts and Miniatures*, 24 June 1980, lot 60. Three inscriptions survive on fol. 1, the first medieval leaf: 1) 'A° Dni 1613 Maij 5to/Cura St Viuas Stanton'; 2) 'M._ _ 9.'; and 3) 'Purchased at Sotheby's/24th April 1857/Lot 552/'.

384 *The Old Service-Books*, 225–26.

385 Wooley, *Benedictional of John Longlonde*, xiii. Two blessings in the manuscript, those for St Anne and St Peter Martyr, do not occur elsewhere (Woolley, xiii–xiv), and the feast of St Peter Martyr was not observed at all in Lincoln (Woolley, xiv). The benediction for St Hugh of Lincoln is part of Peckham's collections of blessings, but is nonetheless not found outside of the Additional manuscript (Woolley, xiv).

386 *Argent* two bars gemelles: (above) a barbed cinguefoil *gules* between two lion faces affronté *azure*, (below) a chevron *gules* with a cock combed *argent* between three bezants *sable*.

387 I owe the information concerning Longland's life to the article by M. Bowker in the *ODNB*, 34: 395–98.

388 Wooley, *Benedictional of John Longlonde*, xi. For his publications, see A. W. Pollard and G. R. Redgrave, *A Short-Title Catalogue of Books Printed in England, Scotland, and Ireland... 1475–1640*, 2nd ed., vol. 2: I–Z (London, 1976), 117, nos 16790–97. These comprise mainly sermons and expositions on psalms, printed by R. Pynson, R. Redman, and T. Petyt. It is also possible that Longland compiled an important list of manuscripts found in Lincolnshire religious houses in the period leading up to Henry VIII's divorce of Catherine of Aragon (J. P. Carley, *The Libraries of King Henry VIII*, Corpus of British Medieval Library Catalogues 7 (London, 2000), xxxiii).

389 F. L. Cross, ed., *The Oxford Dictionary of the Christian Church* (London, 1963), 820. See also Wesley, *Benedictional of John Longlonde*, xi.

390 *ODNB*, 34: 395.

391 Wooley, *Benedictional of John Longlonde*, xv.

392 This is shown by the collation, which is as follows: Quire **1**: fols 2–9v; **2**: 10–17v; **3**: 18–25v; **4**: 26–33v; **5**: 34–41v; **6**: 42–49v; **7**: 50–57v; **8**: 58–65v; **9**: 66–73v; **10**: 74–81v, with strings visible between fols 5–6, 13–14, 21–22, 29v–30, 37v–38, 45v–46, 53v–54, 61v–62, 69v–70, and 77v–78.

393 Some manuscripts with border components similar to those in Additional MS 21974 are reproduced in A. Arnould and J. M. Massing, *Splendours of Flanders* (Cambridge, 1993), no. 24: 83, 100; no. 43: 137; and no. 52: 157.

394 Argent on a chevron fleury sable. The arms are added on fols 5v, 91v, and 142. For descriptions of the contents, see Frere, *Pontifical Services*, 91, 103–4; and Brückmann, 'Latin Manuscript Pontificals', 414–16 and literature.

395 For discussion and further literature concerning Hermann Scheerre, see Scott, *Later Gothic Manuscripts*, II: nos 21, 29, 30.

396 CUL MS Ff.6.1, the Bainbridge Pontifical; printed by the Surtees Society 61, *Liber Pontificalis Chr. Bainbridge, Archiepiscopi Eboracensis* (Durham, 1875). See also Frere, *Pontifical Services*, 104.

397 M. B. Parkes, *The Medieval Manuscripts of Keble College Oxford: A descriptive catalogue with summary desriptions of the Greek and Oriental Manuscripts* (London, 1979), 332.

398 Brückman, 'Latin Manuscript Pontificals', 456; Parkes, *Medieval Manuscripts of Keble College*, 332.

399 The full passage is: (in red) 'Episcopo uero sedente super phildistorio honeste preparato in uestiario uel in aliquo loco specialiter ad hoc deputato quibusdam de familiaribus suis pallium interim ad dorsum eius tenentibus ac aliis sotulares suos exuentibus et caliges & sandalia ipsum induentibus incipiat unus de clericis antiphonam. ...' In other words, the miniature is more or

less a version of the text opposite.

400 He is not wearing a halo; the apparent rays are from the design of the tapestry behind.

401 Scott, *Later Gothic Manuscripts*, II: no. 105, and literature.

402 William, earl of Carysfort, *The Pageants of Richard Beauchamp Earl of Warwick*, Roxburghe Club (Oxford, 1908), Pageant XXIV, fol. 12v; Scott, *Later Gothic Manuscripts*, II: no. 137, and literature.

403 J. Plummer, *Liturgical Manuscripts for the Mass and the Divine Office*, Pierpont Morgan Library, exhibition catalogue (New York, 1964), 30–31, no. 35; J. J. G. Alexander, ed., *The Painted Page: Italian Renaissance Book Illumination 1450–1550*, exhibition catalogue (Munich and New York, 1994), 59–60, no. 4 (by R. S. Wieck), pl.

404 See L. F. Sandler, *Gothic Manuscripts 1285–1385*, A Survey of Manuscripts Illuminated in the British Isles, 5, ed. J. J. G. Alexander, 2 vols (Oxford, 1986), I: ills. 393, 402–405, II: no. 150.

405 A suggestion made by A. I. Doyle.

406 J. J. G. Alexander, *Medieval Illuminators and Their Methods of Work* (New Haven and London, 1992), 141.

407 I am grateful to Ann Eljinholm Nichols for offering a solution to this mystery (personal communication).

408 The only remotely analogous use of a curtain that I have found is in two English copies of Guillaume Deguileville's *Pilgrimage of the Soul*, at the scene in which souls stand before the Court of Heaven but are separated from the divine figure by a curtain; see New York, Public Library MS Spencer 19, fol. 12, and Hatfield House, Cecil Papers MS 270, fol. 4v (both reproduced in Scott, *Later Gothic Manuscripts*, I: ills 292, 295).

409 Brückmann, 'Latin Manuscript Pontificals', 404–5; Scott, *Later Gothic Manuscripts*, II: no. 18 and literature; and J. Lowden, 'Illuminated Books and the Liturgy: Some Observations', in *Objects, Images, and the Word: Art in the Service of the Liturgy*, ed. C. Hourikane (Princeton, 2003), 40–43, figs 11–12.

410 Brückmann, 'Latin Manuscript Pontificals', 442; Scott, *Later Gothic Manuscripts*, no. 71, and literature; Lowden, 'Iluminated Books and the Liturgy', 43–44, figs 13–14.

411 Frere, *Pontifical Services*, 89.

412 The contents are said to be 'identical' with those of Corpus 79, though the wording may vary (Frere, *Pontifical Services*, 90; Brückmann, 'Latin Manuscript Pontificals', 443).

413 The historiated initials are at fol. 136v (Order for enclosing relics), fol. 169 (Reconciliation of a church), fol. 176 (Order for blessing of apparel ['parimenta']), fol. 198, (Benediction for the First Sunday of Advent), fol. 219 (fig. 105), (Benediction of Common of Saints), fol. 224v, (Order for Baptism; by priest not by a bishop), fol. 230 (Order for marriage ceremony), and fol. 234 (Order for visitation of the sick).

414 The frontispiece with two kneeling patrons in Cambridge, Fitzwilliam Museum MS 34, Missal, is the only exception known to me.

415 A. Buck, 'The Register of the Fraternity of St John the Baptist, Dunstable, 1506–8, 1522–41', *Bedfordshire Historical Record Society* 25 (1947), 10–14; anon., 'The Dunstable Fraternity', *Bedfordshire Magazine* 1 (1947–49), 132–3; F. Hackett, 'The Register of the Fraternity of St John the Baptist', *Bedfordshire Magazine* 18 (1981–83), 74–75; R. Marks, 'Two Illuminated Guild Registers from Bedfordshire', *Illuminating the Book: Makers and Interpreters: Essays in Honour of Janet Backhouse*, ed. M. P. Brown and S. McKendrick (London and Toronto, 1998), 123–36; K. L. Scott, 'The Illustration and Decoration of the Register of the Fraternity of the Holy Trinity at Luton Church, 1475–1546', in *The English Medieval Book: Studies in Memory of Jeremy Griffiths*, ed. A. S. G. Edwards, V. Gillespie and R. Hanna (London, 2002), 173.

416 Marks, 'Two Illuminated Guild Registers', 124.

417 At the end of the Fraternity's year, as Richard Marks suggests.

418 Marks, 'Two Illuminated Guild Registers', 124.

419 Marks, 'Two Illumiated Guild Registers', 131.

CHAPTER VI

420 This question has of course been asked on more than one occasion; see, for instance, L. Lawton 'The Illustration of Late Medieval Secular Texts, with Special Reference to Lydgate's *Troy Book*', in *Manuscripts and Readers in Fifteenth-Century England: The Literary Implications of Manuscript Study (Essays from the 1981 Conference at the University of York)*, ed. D. Pearsall (Woodbridge, 1983), 41, where the conclusions were that in Lydgate's *Troy Book* the purpose of illustration was 'by and large, to stress the formal division of the text' and that generally they possibly served to offer a reading of the text (46, 69).

421 K. L. Scott, 'Design, Decoration and Illustration', in *Book Production and Publishing in Britain 1375–1475*, ed. J. Griffiths and D. Pearsall (Cambridge, 1989), 47.

422 Bl Sloane MS 1448A; Cambridge, Magdalene College Pepys MS 1916 (see fig. 3).

423 The model sheet is on fol. 42. Although these coloured drawings are on a leaf preceding the Poitiers chronicle, which begins on fol. 45, they are, obviously, not incorporated in the text.

424 Scott, *Later Gothic Manuscripts*, I: 51, II: nos 137 (ills 495–99), 138 (ills 500–501), and 139 (ills 502–3).

425 This impression is not based on a full-fledged count of surviving illustrated English manuscripts.

426 See 'Illuminated Books and the Liturgy', 48.

APPENDIX A

The Contents of Bodleian MS Laud Misc. 156 (*c.* 1430–40)

Fols i recto–ii verso, 1–v: blanks

Fols 2–3: *Tituli quaestionum N. de lira super Bibliam* (? added)

Fol. 3v: blank

Fol. 4: pen drawings of two meditation hands (added; not inscribed)

Fol. 4v: blank

Fols 5–15: modelbook for Nicholas of Lyra's *Postilla litteralis super totam bibliam* (Old Testament only)

Fol. 15v: blank

Fols 16–60: *Tabula super doctorem de Lyra* (Index to N. of Lyra's *Postilla*), compiled by William Norton in 1403; copied in this manuscript by '*frater* T.B.'

Fol. 60v: blank

Fols 61–66v: *Speculum theologie*

Fols 67–v: blank (+ stub)

The manuscript, of parchment, measures *c.* 421 × *c.* 230 mm.

APPENDIX B

PART I Surviving Fourteenth- and Fifteenth-Century English Manuscripts and Fragments of Nicholas of Lyra's *Postilla litteralis* on the Old Testament

The manuscripts are grouped according to the presence of illustration, the intended provision of illustration, and manuscripts without provision for illustration. The modelbook in MS Laud Misc. 156 is the anomaly. Copies that do not survive with the early books of the Old Testament are listed as 'irrelevant'; surviving New Testament copies are not listed, although they may suggest the former presence of Old Testament volumes.

Manuscripts with miniatures

1. Cambridge, University Library MSS Dd.7.7, Genesis-Nehemiah; Dd.7.8, Hesther-Ecclesiasticus; Dd.7.9, Isaiah–Macabees II. XV$^{1-2}$
2. New Haven, Yale University, Beinecke Library MS 640, Psalms-Baruch (+ two added leaves). XV^{2}
3. Oxford, Bodleian Library MSS Laud Misc. 152, Psalms–Macabees; 154, Genesis–Job. Dated 1463

Manuscripts with blank spaces and/or rough sketches

4. Cambridge, Gonville and Caius College MSS 476, Genesis–Job; 477, Wisdom–Baruch. XIV^{4}–XV^{1}
5. Cambridge, Pembroke College MS 11, Genesis–Kings. XIV^{4}
6. Cambridge, Peterhouse MS 19, Genesis–II Chronicles. XIV^{4}–XV^{1} (1 space, fol. 10v)
7. Cambridge, Peterhouse MS 85, Genesis–Maccabees. XIV^{4}
8. Hereford, Cathedral Library MS P.IV.2, Genesis–Deuteronomy. XIV^{2} (1 drawing, fol. 35v, and spaces)
9. Lincoln, Cathedral Library MS 19, Genesis–Job. Mid-XIV
10. London, British Library Royal MS 4.A.xv, Genesis–Job. XIV^{4} (drawings, probably scribal, and spaces)
11. Oxford, Balliol College MSS 166B, Genesis–Ecclesiasticus; 171, Psalms–Maccabees. *c.* 1400 (before 1438) (spaces marked 'figura')
12. Oxford, Merton College MS 163, Genesis–Psalms. ?XIV^{4} (rough drawings in margins and spaces)
13. Oxford, New College, MSS 8–12, Genesis–Malachi. XV$^{3-4}$ (sketches and spaces)
14. Worcester, Cathedral Library MSS F.25, Genesis–Esther; F.26, Isaiah–Malachi; F.27, Psalms–II Esdras. Late XIV^{4}

Manuscript with no miniatures or spaces

15. Durham, Cathedral Library MSS A.I.3, Genesis–Judith; A.I.4, Job–Apocalypse. 1386–XIV^{4}

Irrelevant copies

16. Cambridge, University Library MS Dd.2.6, Proverbs–Maccabees. ?XV^{2}
17. London, Lambeth Palace MS 9, Psalms–Apocalypse. XIV^{4}–XV^{1}
18. Oxford, Oriel College MS 40, Proverbs–Maccabees (miniatures and initials cut). XIV$^{3-4}$

Modelbook

Oxford, Bodleian Library MS Laud Misc. 156, fols 5–15 (no text). XV^{2}

Fragments

Cambridge, Pembroke College No. 313/E, Exodus 15:1 (one-half leaf). XIV
Eton, College Library MS 221, no. 20, Psalms 23–24 (one leaf). XV^{2}
New Haven, Yale University, Beinecke Library MS 22, Psalms 4–8 (3 folios). Mid-XIV

(The Pembroke College and Eton College fragments were located through Ker, *MMBL*, II: 247, 788.)

Continental Manuscripts of English Ownership

London, British Library Royal MS 3.D.vii, Genesis–Chronicles. XIV. fol. 1, unidentified English arms (?Fitz-Alan) (drawings)

Oxford, Bodleian Library MS Bodley 251, Genesis-Ecclesiasticus. French, XIV^{4}. Owned by William Courtenay, Archbishop of Canterbury (d. 1396) (fine drawings)

PART II Medieval References to Copies of Nicholas of Lyra's *Postilla litteralis* on the Old Testament

It should be noted that, although once located in English libraries, the manuscripts may not have been produced in England. Mention of Lyra copies in two or more volumes are assumed to include the Old Testament. Some of the items below may refer either to Lyra's *Postilla litteralis* or the *Postilla moralis*; they were worth recording in spite of the ambiguity. The survival of a copy of Lyra's *Postilla litteralis* on the New Testament is not taken as a certain indication of a non-surviving Old Testament. The following list is unlikely to be complete.

A. Nicholas of Lyra manuscripts mentioned in medieval library catalogues.

1. K. W. Humphreys, ed., *The Friars' Libraries*, Corpus of British Medieval Library Catalogues (London, 1990), 85, no. 353, Austin Friars, York: 'Item Lyra super pentateucum. ...'
2. Humphreys, *Friars' Libraries*, 223, no. 47, Franciscans, London: 'Item pro scripto Doctoris de Lyra in duobus voluminibus jacente iam in cathenis c. marcas. ...'
3. R. Sharpe, J. P. Carley, R. M. Thomson, A. E. Watson, eds, *English Benedictine Libraries: The Shorter Catalogues*, Corpus of British Medieval Library Catalogues 4 (London, 1996), no. B55.32, Monk Bretton, 'In primis Nicolaus de Lyra super totum vetus testatum in quatuor libros'; no. B64.18, Norwich-Yarmouth, [one volume only] 'Postilla doctoris de Lira'; no. B87.24, St Albans, 'Item primam partem Lire'; no. B105.49, Westminster, 'Item primum uolumen de Lira'.
4. T. Webber and A. G. Watson, eds, *The Libraries of the Augustinian Canons*, Corpus of

British Medieval Library Catalogues 6 (London, 1998), 140, no. 144, Leicester abbey: 'Doctor de Lira in sex volumninibus super vtroque testamento'.

5. Webber and Watson, *Augustinian Canons*, 140, no. 145: 'Idem super vtroque testamento in tribus voluminibus'.
6. J. P. Carley, *The Libraries of King Henry VIII*, Corpus of British Medieval Library Catalogues 7 (London, 2000), 145, no. 758, 'Lyra super Pentateuchum, Psalterium, et Iob' = BL Royal MS 4 A.xv; 204, no. 1197, 'Lyra' = BL Royal MS 3.D.vii [see above for both of these manuscripts].
7. V. Gillespie, ed., *Syon Abbey*, with *The Libraries of the Carthusians*, ed. A.I. Doyle, Corpus of British Medieval Library Catalogues 9 (London, 2001), 756: 'Postilla litteralis in uetus et nouum testamentum'.
8. P. D. Clarke, *The University and College Libraries of Cambridge*, Corpus of British Medieval Library Catalogues 10 (London, 2002), 850: about forty-five copies in whole or in part of Lyra's commentary on the Old and New Testament.
9. D. N. Bell, *What Nuns Read: Books and Libraries in Medieval English Nunneries*, Cistercian Publications (Kalamazoo, 1995), 119: William Pownsett, steward of Barking Abbey, d. 1554, inventory, 'Certayne bookes yn the Abbey of Barkynge', 9, 'Item a booke de epistola Nicholai lier ... viij d'.

B. Nicholas of Lyra manuscripts mentioned as gifts or in medieval wills. Some of the items below may represent either the *Postilla litteralis* or the *Postilla moralis*.

1. M. R. James, *A Descriptive Catalogue of the Manuscripts in the Library of Pembroke College, Cambridge* (Cambridge, 1905), xiv, no. 58: 'Ex dono Mag. Sudbury (ob. 1434)'; 'In primis dedit Liram in iiii voll'.
2. M. R. James, *A Descriptive Catalogue of the Manuscripts in the Library of St Catharine's College, Cambridge* (Cambridge, 1925), 4: 'Lira super vetus testamentum'; 'Libri ex dono Roberti Wodlarke primarii fundatoris eujus collegii cathenati in libraria'.
3. H. R. Plomer, 'Books Mentioned in Wills', *Transactions of the Bibliographical Society* 7 (1902–4), 108: John Moeer, vicar of Tenterden, Kent, left a 'Doctorem de Lira cum sua tabula' to St Augustine's church, Canterbury; 116: in 1448 William Byconyll bequeathed a four-volume de Lyra with prologue, to All Souls, Oxford; see also below under Cavanaugh, a).
4. J. B. Friedman recorded thirteen copies of Nicholas of Lyra 'on the whole Bible' from 'published and unpublished wills 1369–1497 proved in the Province of York, by published wills of the dioceses of Beverley, Durham, Ripon and Carlisle and by the inventories of Auckland College and Jesus College, Rotherham' (*Northern English Books, Owners, and Makers in the Late Middle Ages*, Syracuse, NY, 1995, 255, 264). [More precise references are not available.]
5. F. M. Powicke, *The Medieval Books of Merton College* (Oxford, 1931), 91: 'Item Nicholaus de Lira super pentatheuchum et spalterium', given by William Rede to New College, Oxford. See also 218 (no. 1087) and 239 (1228).
6. All of the following references to Nicholas of Lyra and/or references in some form to his *Postilla litteralis* are drawn from S. H. Cavanaugh, *A Study of Books Privately Owned in England 1300–1450*, D.Phil., English, University of Pennsylvania, 1980. Each of the entries is preceded by the page number of the reference in the thesis and followed by the name of the testator and the approximate date of the will or other document. Ambiguous references, which may be either to the *Postilla litteralis* or to the *Postilla moralis*, are included. The

sources of Cavanaugh's references are not repeated here, nor are references to Lyra's *Postilla super novum testamentum*. There is usually more information concerning the testators in Cavanaugh's thesis.

a) (pp. 94–95:) William Byconnel, Canon of Bath, Chancellor of Wells, d. 1448: Nicholas of Lyra 'in quatuor voluminibus cum prohemie'.
b) (p. 136) Geoffrey Bryce, Warden of St Gregory's College, Sudbury, will 1446: 'Lira super spalterium & xij prophetas in alio volumine.' 'Lira super 8–6 libros Moysi'.
c) (p. 178) Lewis de Charlton, Bishop of Hereford, d. 1369: (p. 178) Nicholas of Lyra on the Pentateuch (willed to Hereford).
d) (p. 203) Richard Colling, fellow of Balliol, d. 1438: Nicholas of Lyra, *Postilla litteralis*: Genesis–Eccleisasticus [=MS 166B]; Psalms–Maccabees [=MS 171]; and a third volume (willed to Balliol).
e) (p. 214) William Courtenay, Archbishop of Canterbury, d. 1396: Nicholas of Lyra, *Postilla super Bibliam* [=Bodl. Lib. MS Bodley 251].
f) (p. 215) Richard Courtenay, Bishop of Norwich, d. 1415: bought a de Lira for 80 francs.
g) (p. 227) Robert Cuttyng, chaplain, will 1382: 'unam liram'.
h) (pp. 371–72) John de Grandison, Bishop of Exeter, d. 1369: 'Ita tamen quod Scripta Nicholai de Lira ...'
i) (p. 437) Richard Holme, Warden of King's Hall, Cambridge, d. 1424: 'Doctor de lira in tribus voluminibus ...' [See Cavanaugh for contents of each.]
j) (p. 495) Simon de Langham, d. 1376: (p. 498) 'Item lira moralizans totam bibliam' (willed to Westminster Abbey).
k) (pp. 499–502) Thomas Langley, Bishop of Durham, will 1436: (p. 501), 'Lectura integra Nicholai de Lira in tribus voluminibus ...'; (p. 502) 'Lectura Nicholai de Lira super quinque libros Moisi'.
l) (p. 563) Thomas Markaunt, fellow of Corpus Christi College, Cambridge, d. 1439: (p. 566) [de Lira] 'Postille super Genesin, Exodum ... Esdram et Machab'.
m) (p. 578) Walter Medford, Dean of Wells, will 1421: (p. 580) 'Item lego ... Henrico (Beaufort) Wintoniensi episcopo librum meum de Lyra ...'
n) (p. 626) William de Odyham, monk of St Augustine's, Canterbury, fl. 1327: 'Postille Nicholai de Lyra super pentateucum super Josue Judicum Ruth et super 4 libros Regum ...'; 'Postille [idem]super librum paralipomenon super Esdram Neemiam Hoster [sic] Job. Ysaiam Jeremiam Trenos Jeremie. Baruch. Susannam Ezecheilem et danielem', etc.
o) (p. 674) Robert Ragenhill, Advocate of the Court of York, will 1430: '... duos libros compilatos per Nicholaum de Lira ... videlicet unum super certis libris Veteres Testamenti quem de novo scribi feci ... quem emi de executoribus magistri Willelmi Dorem, quondam rectoris de Betham.'
p) (p. 704) William Rede, Bishop of Chichester, will 1382: 'Item Nicholaus de Lira super pentateuchum et spalterium ...'; etc.
q) (p. 786) John Shirforde, Canon of Wells Cathedral, will 1417: 'Item I will that my book called Lira which I have caused to be written in part here in Constance, shall be completed and given to the Cath. Church of Welles, there to remain forever'.
r) (p. 788) Ralph of Shrewsbury, Bishop of Bath and Wells, d. 1363: 'Item lego schloribus in aule que vocatur Oreole Oxon' studentibus in theologia i postill compilat' per nicholaum de Lira super vetus testamentum' (= ?Oriel College MS 40).
s) (p. 790) Walter de Skirlaw, Bishop of Durham, will 1404: 'Item Lira in tribus voluminibus ...'
t) (p. 888) John Turk, Chancellor of Oxford, Canon of Salisbury, fellow of Merton College, Oxford, will 1395, d. 1397: gave biblical commentary to Merton.

u) (p. 905) William Walleworth, Lord Mayor of London, will 1385: 'Item lego priori et conuentui fratrum augustinorum London' librum vocatum Lira in duobus voluminibus ...'

v) (p. 924) John de Whitfield, monk of Rochester Cathedral Priory, fl. 1330: Gave *Postilla* (= BL Royal MS 4.A.xv) to Rochester Cathedral Priory.

w) (p. 935) William Wymble de Hokyton, fellow of Clare College, Cambridge, d. by 1445: 'Doctorem de Lyra super prophetas' (given to Clare Hall).

[A copy of Lyra's *Postilla* in four volumes with provenance not known and the volumes not found is noted by E. Leedham-Green and D. McKitterick in *Books and Collectors 1200–1700: Essays Presented to Andrew Watson*, ed. J. P. Carley and C. G. C. Tite (London, 1997), 228.]

APPENDIX C

The Contents of Yale MS Beinecke 640, Nicholas of Lyra's *Postilla litteralis*

Part I of MS Beinecke 640

Fols 1–39v: Psalms 1–68

Scribe A
Border Artist A

[Inserted leaf:

Fol. 40: end of text and images from Exodus
Fol. 40v: full page with images from Exodus

Scribe C
Artist A
end insert]

Fols 41–95: Psalms 68–150

Scribe A
Border Artist A

Fol. 95v: Blank

Part II of MS Beinecke 640

[Inserted leaf:

Fol. 96: images from 1 Kings
Fol. 96v: full page of images from Isaiah and four astrological diagrams

Scribe C
Artist A
end insert]

Fols 97–272: Isaiah–Baruch

Scribe B
Artist B
Border Artist B

Fol. 272v: blank

APPENDIX D

The subjects of the historiated initials in Oxford, All Souls MS 10, a New Testament in French, are as follows:

Folio 2: (Tabula) St Mark, tonsured, seated in a wooden chair with dowled arms and back, at a writing board, apparently writing on a scroll that laps over the top of the board. (fig. 32)

Folio 2v: (Gospel) St Mark seated in a cathedral chair, with an open book on his knees, with a winged lion beside with raised paw.

Folio 49: (Gospel) St Luke seated on the ground, using an open book that rests on a winged ox. (fig. 33)

Folio 114v: (1 Corinthians) St Paul standing, with book, speaking to four men seated on the ground. (fig. 49)

Folio 130v: (Galatians) St Paul seated on a cloth-covered bench, holding a down-turned sword by the blade.

Folio 134: (Ephesians) St Paul seated on a bench, with open book and with a young man seated on the ground before him. (fig. 39)

Folio 140v: (1 Thessalonians) St Paul seated on an elaborate stone bench, holding a sword downwards by the blade. (fig. 27)

Folio 145v: (2 Timothy) St Paul seated on a stone bench, with open book, reading. (fig. 34)

Folio 147v: (Hebrews) St Paul in pulpit, with hands crossed on chest, addressing three seated men. (fig. 42)

Folio 155: (Acts) Pentecost, with Virgin and eight Apostles, one seated on the ground, reading from an open book. (fig. 40)

Folio 181v: (Epistle) St James in grey habit with cowl, in pulpit, with two young men on the ground before him. (fig. 29)

Folio 184: (1 Peter) St Peter dressed as pope, holding cross-staff, with man seated on either side. (fig. 46)

Folio 186v: (2 Peter) Simon Peter seated on a stone bench, with open book on lap. (fig. 35)

Folio 188v: (1 John) St John the Evangelist seated on stone bench, gesturing with pointed finger towards the text; an eagle with raised wings beside. (fig. 44)

Folio 191v: (Prologue to Revelation) St John holding a scroll on Patmos depicted as an island with trees; a bird with raised wings beside. (fig. 45)

Folio 193: (Revelation) Apocalyptic Christ standing in radiance with hands raised, within a *hortus conclusus*; five candlesticks before him and two at each end of the garden. (fig. 50)

APPENDIX E

The following list records the drawings in Peter of Poitiers' *Compendium historie in genealogia Christi* in BL Royal MS 1.B.x, fols 8–33v. The list does not take note of scrolls, roundels, or lines of descent drawn as columns. All the drawings are in brown ink, sometimes touched with red. The *nota bene* hands are drawn in sleeves or cuffs. The drawings or blank spaces for miniatures marked with an asterisk are of, or for, pictorial subjects not found in other illustrated copies of Poitiers *Compendium*.

Folio 8:	Fall of Man (unfinished) (fig. 71) Adam delving and Eve spinning (unfinished) (fig. 71) [three *nota bene* hands]
Folio 8v:	Walled city with towered gate, enclosing church and houses with chimney pots* [five *nota bene* hands]
Folio 9:	[two *nota bene* hands]
Folio 9v:	Noah's Ark (fig. 75) blank space for miniature, inscr. 'Puarphara'* [*nota bene* hand]
Folio 10v:	Tower of Babel (fig. 76)*
Folio 11v:	Blank space for miniature, inscr. 'Melchisedech' Blank space for miniature, inscr. 'Dixit angelus ad abraham. ...'
Folio 12:	Blank space for miniature, inscr. 'De submersione sodomorum & gomorre & aliis civitatibus. ...'
Folio 13v:	Mitre with infulae, inscr. '[]ic oritur linea pontificale'
Folio 14:	Mitre with infulae
Folio 14v:	Blank space for miniature, inscr. 'De dacione legis in monte synai'* [one *nota bene* hand]
Folio 15:	[one *nota bene* hand with ?sprig]
Folio 15v:	Blank space for miniature, inscr. 'De serpente eneo'* [hand holding scroll] Blank space for miniature [no title, but perhaps for Mount Abarim*] [hand holding scroll, inscr. 'Quomodo ostendit dominus Moysy terram promissiam',* probably for untitled blank on opposite page, fol. 16]
Folio 16:	One-third page blank for miniature, not inscr. [see previous folio]
Folio 16v:	Death of Moses,* as draped bier with mourners (fig. 77) Globular flask [symbolizing Apollo*] Four cinquefoils [on roundel]
Folio 17:	Mitre with infulae (fig. 78) Four cinquefoils [on roundel] (fig. 78)

Hurdygurdy* (fig. 78)
Harp* (fig. 78)

Folio 17v: Six mitres with infulae
Four cinquefoils [on five roundels]
Bust of woman praying,* inscr. ‘conniges’
Bust of angel with palm,* inscr. ‘Angelus’
Sampson slaying the lion* [in roundel with cinquefoils]

Folio 18: Mitre
Head of Anna, in headdress*

Folio 18v: Mitre
[*nota bene* hand]

Folio 19: Mitre
David with harp
Two crowns [surmounting roundels]

Folio 19v: Three mitres
Crown

Folio 20: Temple of Solomon as church with fifteen steps leading up to entrance, inscribed with first verses of fifteen gradual psalms* (fig. 79)

Folio 20v: Mitre
Nine crowns

Folio 21: Nine crowns

Folio 21v: Mitre
Helyas (Elijah) ascending to heavens in fiery cart, handing down cloak to Helyseus (Elisha)*
Head of woman in headdress
Four crowns

Folio 22: Mitre
Nine crowns
Jonah in mouth of the whale*; ship

Folio 22v: Mitre
Isaiah holding scroll*
Seven crowns

Folio 23: City of Rome,* with wall enclosing an octagonal building and houses with chimney pots
Two mitres
Eight crowns
One falling crown

Folio 23v: Five crowns
Two mitres
Head of Ezechiel,* crowned, with scroll

Folio 24: Two mitres
Seven crowns
Head of Jeremiah,* in ziggurat hat, with hand raised

Head of woman, in veil

Folio 24v: Three crowns
Two mitres
Head of Ezechiel,* with book, gesturing
Hat [on roundel, for Sedechias]
Head of Daniel*
Misach, Sidrach and Abdenago kneeling in fiery furnace*

Folio 25: Two crowns

Folio 25v: Crown
[Rebus:] scroll + scrollwork letters **O** and **N** + spade inscr. 'dyg' (fig. 93)

Folio 26: Crown
Two mitres
Head of Joachim,* in hat
Head of Susannah,* in headdress
Head of Habakkuk,* in hat, with scroll

Folio 26v: Six crowns
Judith with raised sword and head of Holofernes* (fig. 80), in cut-away chamber

Folio 27: Mitre
Three crowns
Ezra (the scribe),* with open book on writing board

Folio 27v: Disposition of the city of Jerusalem (fig. 81)
Two mitres
Three crowns
[Blank roundel, for ?Nemuel]

Folio 28: Mitre
Two crowns
Head of Hester,* in veil
Bust of Socrates,* in hat, drinking the hemlock
Bust of Diogenes,* in pileus, with teaching gesture

Folio 28v: Mitre
Three crowns
Aristotle,* in pileus, at board desk, with Plato seated with open book
Bust of Hippocrates,* pointing
Bust of Demosthenes,* with raised hand
Bust of Aristotiles,* gesturing
Mount Garizim* as church with towers on hill (all above, fig. 83)

Folio 29: Six crowns
Alexander the Great,* with upright sword, drawn by two chained griffons

Folio 29v: Two mitres
Five rows of heads,* in black hats ('Septuaginta interpretes')
Five crowns

Folio 30: Three mitres
Five crowns
Front of a church made by a bishop near Ely*

Appendix E

Folio 30v: Five mitres
Seven crowns
Bust of bishop*

Folio 31: Two mitres
Four crowns

Folio 31v: Two crowns
Head of woman,* in headdress and necklace (= ?wife of Johannes Hircanus)

Folio 32: Imperial tiara
Five crowns
Head of woman,* in headdress and necklace (= ?wife of Aristobolus)
[*nota bene* hand]

Folio 32v: Imperial tiara
Four crowns
Half-figure of John the Baptist,* pointing to lamb with cross-staff

Folio 33: Six crowns
Nativity scene, inscr. 'Partita anne ex Ioachim' (fig. 84)

APPENDIX F

Late Fourteenth- and Fifteenth-Century English Manuscripts of the *Speculum theologie*

Cambridge, University Library, MS. Dd.3.56, dorse, with Peter of Poitiers, *Compendium historiae in genealogia Christi*, XV; five diagrams of the *Speculum theologie*.

London, British Library, Additional MS 17358, fols 15–16, with Poitiers, *Compendium*, *c.* 1431; four diagrams of the *Speculum theologie*.

London, British Library, Arundel MS 507, fols 16v–21, with theological tracts, before 1389; ten diagrams of the *Speculum theologie*.

London, British Library, Royal MS 1.B.x, fols 1–7, with Bible, XIII; thirteen diagrams of the *Speculum theologie*, XV^2. (figs 85, 86, 88, 90, 92)

London, Gray's Inn, MS 9, fols 150v–154v, with *Speculum humanae salvationis*, XIV^4; nine diagrams of the *Speculum theologie*, XV^1.

Oxford, Bodleian Library, MS Laud Misc. 156, fols 1v–7, with Nicholas of Lyra Modelbook, etc., XV^2; twelve diagrams of the *Speculum theologie*. (fig. 89)

Oxford, St John's College, MS 58, fols 1v–2, 10–11, with Poitiers, *Compendium*, XV^1; five diagrams of the *Speculum theologie*. (figs 87, 91)

For earlier English and continental manuscripts of the *Speculum theologie* and for a complete list of the diagrams in each manuscript, see Lucy Freeman Sandler, *The Psalter of Robert de Lisle in the British Library* (London, 1999), 107–15. To her list can be added London, British Library, Additional MS 17358 (see above); Paris, Bibliothéque Nationale, MS lat. 8564, Pierre des Vignes, Épitres, XIII, with eleven (?added) *Speculum* drawings; and Cambridge, MA, Harvard University, Houghton Library, MS Lat. 127, Boethius, *Philosophiae consolatio*, England, XII^4, fol. 52, with an added *Sciencia* drawing.

INDEX OF MANUSCRIPTS